RISK BEHAVIOUR AND RISK MANAGEMENT IN BUSINESS LIFE

Risk Behaviour and Risk Management in Business Life

Edited by

Bo Green
Interdisciplinary Risk Research Programme,
Stockholm University, Sweden

Co-editors

Robert Cressy
Frederic Delmar
Theodore Eisenberg
Barry Howcroft
Mervyn Lewis
Dirk Schoenmaker
James Shanteau
Robert Vivian

KLUWER ACADEMIC PUBLISHERS
DORDRECHT / BOSTON / LONDON

A C.I.P. Catalogue record for this book is available from the Library of Congress.

ISBN 0-7923-5868-6

Published by Kluwer Academic Publishers,
P.O. Box 17, 3300 AA Dordrecht, The Netherlands.

Sold and distributed in North, Central and South America
by Kluwer Academic Publishers,
101 Philip Drive, Norwell, MA 02061, U.S.A.

In all other countries, sold and distributed
by Kluwer Academic Publishers,
P.O. Box 322, 3300 AH Dordrecht, The Netherlands.

Printed on acid-free paper

Printed in the Netherlands.

Table of contents

Foreword

In 1985 I chaired "the bankruptcy investigation" in Sweden. The investigation in different ways showed that basic knowledge of risk assessment is important for the capacity of banks to organise and manage loan granting to small and newly started businesses and entrepreneurial ventures. The examination also showed that deficiencies in insolvency legislation had resulted in insufficient incentives for banks to invest in competence training in risk management.

In my report to the Swedish government I argued for a change in the insolvency law with the aim to encourage the banks to follow up loans to small firms and to create incentives for bank management to educate their loan officers in risk management and personal judgement.

In the debate at the bankruptcy seminars organised during the spring of 1986, I pointed out that a bank officer should know and understand more about entrepreneurship. In my speeches at the "anti bankruptcy seminars" organised during the autumn 1986, I strongly emphasised the need for knowledge in psychology. Many bank managers in Sweden did not agree with these conclusions and what they saw as implied criticisms.

During 1990-1994, I chaired a national research project on risk analysis, risk behaviour and risk management in which 25 researchers from different scientific disciplines at Swedish universities participated. A network of researchers and practitioners was created. During the spring of 1991, six seminars took place in which banks, accounting firms, credit managers in business and other investors in the Swedish business world participated.

The purpose of the Risk Research Project was to identify questions relating to risks in business as taught in higher education. The aim first of all was to make bank officers and credit managers in business aware of the need to gain knowledge in the field of risk management. The research programme sought to initiate a creative process in which researchers and people from business life participated.

At the beginning of the analysis it was assumed that the crises in the banking system in Sweden was largely the result of insufficient knowledge in the basics of risk assessment and credit management. In my report to the Swedish government in the autumn of 1993, I stressed that laws, rules and norms relating to business transactions determine the action of different parties and the risk distribution. I also suggested that the universities in Sweden should allocate more resources to business risk research. With the aim of forming interdisciplinary risk research projects, I strongly recommended that the government and the banks should create a joint risk research foundation.

In order to fulfil this "vision" in the spring of 1994 I decided to leave my job as project manager at the Swedish National Board for Industrial and Technical Development and formed a risk research group at Stockholm University.

Risk problems in business vary and should therefore be addressed in an interdisciplinary way. That was the reason why Stockholm University organised The First International Seminar on Risk Behaviour and Risk Management in June 1995. The purpose of the first seminar was to create a forum for an international exchange of know-how within the field of risk management. The seminar focused on banks and their role in business life. A total of 150 researchers and practitioners from 17 countries participated in the seminar.

In June 1997 Stockholm University organised The Second International Stockholm Seminar on Risk Behaviour and Risk Management. A total of 200 researchers and practitioners from 26 countries participated. The seminar was divided into four main topic areas: *Risk assessment and credit management, Psychology in business life, Risk management in small firms and Law and business risks.*

In conjunction with the second seminar (hereinafter called the Seminar) as chairman of the Programme Committee I invited eight researchers from four continents to assist me in writing a comprehensive book within the risk management field. The book is based on the best papers and the key-note speeches presented at the Seminar.

In assisting me in the editing of this book I told the invited professors that we should do our utmost to make the reader aware of why it is so important that researchers from different disciplines work closely together in concrete research projects and in co-operation with the industrial world in seeking out and solving risk research problems.

Chapter 1 titled *Cross the borders* contains my own and the invited co-editors experiences and thoughts on the need for interdisciplinary, multidisciplinary and cross-disciplinary research projects. One of the invited co-editors, Professor Barry Howcroft, Loughborough University, also presents his view on why it is so important to develop holistic methods in approaching risk problems in business. The chapter also includes a story about a communicative failure in a socio-technical system written by Professor David Weir, Newcastle Business School, and ends with a contribution written by myself on the analysis of complex systems related to business conditions.

In chapter 2, Professor Mervyn Lewis, University of South Australia, introduces the reader to *Risk assessment and credit management* The chapter contains six selected and re-written papers and three key-note speeches. The key-note speeches are written by Professor Mervyn Lewis, Per Lundberg, Director, SE-Banken and David Kresge, Director, Dun & Bradstreet.

In chapter 3 Professor James Shanteau, Kansas State University explains the importance of *Psychology in business life.* The chapter contains eight selected papers re-written for the volume.

In chapter 4, Assistant Professor Frederic Delmar, Entrepreneurship & Small Business Research Institute, introduces the reader to the field of *Innovation, growth and entrepreneurship.* The chapter contains four selected re-written papers.

In chapter 5, Professor Robert Cressy, Warwick Business School, provides an overview for the reader about the basic ideas of the *Loan guarantee scheme in risk management.* The chapter contains two selected papers and a key-note speech given by Professor Rudy Aernoudt, Hogeschool Gent.

In chapter 6, Professor Theodore Eisenberg, Cornell Law School, gives an introduction to *Insolvency risks and the role of insolvency law.* The chapter contains five selected papers and one of the contributor's comments on the co-editor's conclusions. The chapter ends with a contribution written by myself on how the bankruptcy system as a whole functions.

In chapter 7, Professor Robert Vivian, University of the Witwatersrand, introduces the reader to the field of *Insurable risks in business.* The chapter contains two selected papers and a key-note speech given by Wolf-Ingo Darius, Chief Executive Officer, Hermes Kreditversicherungs-AG.

In chapter 8, Economist Dirk Schoenmaker, Bank of England, outlines for the reader *The role of the supervisory authorities in the financial system.* The chapter consists of five selected and re-written papers. The chapter ends with a contribution written by myself on the role of the banks in the financial system.

I wish to thank Lars Silver, Hans Lind, Wayne Marano, Katarina Svensson, Nicholas Wilson, Hans Landström, Barbara Summers, Rob Ranyard, Leif Sanner, Fabian von Schéele, Anna Mette Fuglseth, Lisbeth Hedelin, Jan Warhuus, Istemi Demirag, Stefan Sundgren, Jocelyn Martel, Karin Thorburn, Esben Eckbo, Björn Palmgren, Charlotte Möller, Peter Wendt and Liisa Halme for their excellent work in presenting exclusive summaries and re-written papers. They have done their utmost in order to follow the editors and the co-editor's instructions and comments of the editor and the co-editors.

Many thanks are given to Nicholas Wilson, Poul Wolffsen, Lisbeth Hedelin and Hans Landström for acting as workshop organisers at the Seminar. Special thanks are due to Karin Thorburn who inspired me to enter the debate on the bankruptcy system and to Liisa Halme and Björn Palmgren who encouraged me to enter the discussion on how the financial system as a whole functions.

Per Lundberg, David Kresge and Wolf-Ingo Darius are thanked for their help in transferring excellent key-note speeches into relevant contributions to the understanding of the credit management field.

Many thanks are given to Mervyn Lewis, James Shanteau, Frédéric Delmar, Robert Cressy, Theodore Eisenberg, Robert Vivian, Dirk Schoenmaker and Barry Howcroft for their excellent work in introducing the reader to the complex risk behaviour and risk management field. Their willingness to co-operate with me in the development of this cross-disciplinary and comprehensive presentation of risk management problems is considerable and was greatly appreciated. Special thanks to Mervyn Lewis for his fruitful comments and for his helpful advises in the editing process.

I wish also to thank David Weir for his outstanding presentation of the Kegworth incident and for his introduction to the study of complex systems from an interdisciplinary approach. His way of lateral thinking gave me inspiration to present my own experiences in analysis of complex systems related to business condition.

My research colleagues at Stockholm University have supported me in my work as organiser of the Seminar. Many thanks are due to John Skår, Henry Montgomery, Claes Hägg and Bill Dufwa for their work as workshop organisers at the Seminar. Special thanks to Professor John Skår who during the last 20 years has given me eminent support on my way from executive officer to a successful researcher.

Agneta Delibaltas has personally assisted me as project secretary since 1991. She has worked hard on this book along with Anna Green, Christina Kanholt and Lena Porsander who assisted me in my last work with the manuscript.

Professor Gustaf Lindencrona, Vice Chancellor of Stockholm University has during the last five years given generous support to my vision to create interdisciplinary risk research projects in co-operation with universities around the world.

Finally we come to the sponsors of the Seminar; The Bank of Sweden Tercentenary Foundation, Marcus and Amalia Wallenbergs Foundation, Henrik Granholms Foundation, Hermes Kreditversicherungs-AG, Intrum Justitia and Skandia Insurance Company. Without their commitment, this volume would have remained a vision rather than reality. The same is true for the publisher.

Stockholm April 1999

Bo Green

CROSS THE BORDERS

1.1 Introduction

by Bo Green
Programme director, Stockholm University

Risk exists because there is incomplete information about the future. This can take a variety of forms – about the weather, about income, about tax receipts and payments, about interest rates or foreign exchange rates, or about the actions of others. The phenomenon of risk is thus as pervasive in economic life as it is in life in general. Just as we learn to deal with the risks of crossing a road or driving a car, we need to cope with risk in business and financial life.

Since risk refers to the possibility that events may turn out differently from those, which are expected, it is, for the most part, unavoidable. Nevertheless, the consequences of risk can be minimised, if appropriate action is taken. In this respect, risk exposure can be distinguished from the risk itself; exposure to the consequences of risk can be managed even if the risk cannot. Taking out standard fire insurance or accident insurance for these risks of damage are obvious examples. The use of credit insurance and credit risk hedging are examples in the context of credit management.

Risk behaviour and risk management in business life influence a wide range of fields in which only a very limited amount of research has been undertaken. These topics have often been treated as if they were theoretically and practically isolated from other fields, the so-called risk archipelago problem. What is actually needed is another focus, in which the problem of risk is treated as a central theme. The demand for interdisciplinary research means that there is a need for crossing scientific boundaries and the borders between different departments at a university. There is a need for co-operation between researchers from different countries in developing new methods and approaches for dealing with risk problems. There is also a need to standardise terminology.

The rapid development of information technology and the growth of global business activities make greater and greater demands upon managers and decision-makers operating in the complex business world. Bank officers and business managers require comprehensive knowledge about financial risks, credit risks, business risks, risks in product development, risks in the innovation process, organisational risks, project risks, political risks etc. There is no doubt that risk management in business life today constitutes an important part of a firm's strategic management. Also in day-to-day management there is a need for crossing the borders between different divisions of an individual company.

In approaching risk problems from a holistic perspective there is also a parallel need for linking the scientific and the business worlds. Researchers must work closely together in concrete multidisciplinary research projects and in co-operation with the industrial world in seeking out and solving research problems of importance.

The need for co-operation in business risk research is the reason why I as the editor of this book have invited eight professors from four continents to assist me in the editing process and to explain the need for interdisciplinary and multi-disciplinary research in a field of great interest to practitioners in the business world. In an attempt to explain the need for multidisciplinary research risk management one of the co-editors, for example, uses a metaphor.

In editing the book I have emphasised that the co-editors should select papers and exclusive summaries in each chapter with the above-mentioned need for developing new research methods in mind.

As a researcher, business manager and investigator for the Swedish government I have been very interested in methodological aspects in the process of analysis of complex systems related to business conditions. That is the reason why in the last part of this chapter I present my own experiences in *'joint problem solving'*. In my paper I also present a normative model for the analysis of complex systems in which several actors interplay and in which the basis for control of the system consist of laws, rules and norms in industrial settings. I also reflect on the need for crossing the borders between authorities, business organisations *and* the universities in managing government investigations.

Before I give the floor to my colleagues and co-editors, I would like to invite a professor from the United Kingdom to tell a story about a complex management situation. The Kegworth incident illuminates why it is important for a manager to search for information in crisis situations.

The related story inspired me to reflect on how to approach risk problems in business life.

My own experiences in analysis of complex systems was the reason why I as editor of this book invited the above mentioned professor from United Kingdom to answer the following question 'Why is it important for researchers to study complex systems in our world from an interdisciplinary approach?' In his answer, he tells the reader a story about himself as a researcher and why the problems of risk and risk management in complex systems are important to study with an interdisciplinary perspective.

The aim of this introduction to the complex area of risk in business is to attract senior researchers doctoral students and students across the world to cross the borders. It could, for example, be of great interest for a researcher in business administration to understand that the insolvency law affects the decision making of bank officers and credit managers in a number of different ways.

When searching for reality in the complex business world all persons involved need to *cross the borders*. The purpose of this book is to stimulate this on going process.

It is, for example, of value to people from the business world to know more about the entrepreneur's attitudes to risk, and behaviour in crises etc and the psychological factors, which influence decision-makers and the decision making process.

1.2 A case of communication failure in a socio-technical system – The Kegworth incident

by David T.H. Weir
Professor, Newcastle Business School

On 8 January 1989 at 20.25 hours a British Midland 737/400, number G-OBME, of recent manufacture, 1988, on a scheduled passenger flight between London Heathrow Airport and Belfast Airport crashed on the M1 motorway at Kegworth near East Midlands Airport in Leicestershire in the centre of England. Of the 8 crew 7 were seriously injured. Of the 117 passengers 47 were injured fatally and 67 seriously. The aircraft was destroyed.[1]

The information is taken from the AAIB inspector's investigation under the Civil Aviation Investigation of Accidents Regulations 1983. The analysis and the interpretations are my own. The final crash took place at relatively low speed and although it was a major disaster it could have been considerably worse had the M1 motorway not been surprisingly and unusually empty in relation to the normal traffic expectations of that time of night.

The aircraft had been engaged in a double shuttle between London and Belfast. Having landed at Heathrow Airport at 18.45 hours, after completing the first

---

[1] These details are taken from: *Report of the AAIB Inspector into the Kegworth crash*: Civil Aviation Authority, 1989.

shuttle flight, it took off again for Belfast at 19.52 hours with the first officer handling the aircraft. After take-off the aircraft climbed initially to flight level 60 where it levelled off above a layer of strata cumulus cloud for 2 minutes before receiving clearance to climb to flight level 120. Soon afterwards at 19.58 hours clearance was passed for the aircraft to continue its climb to its cruising flight level of 350 on a direct track to the Trent very high frequency omni range beacon where it would re-route for Belfast.

At 20.05 hours as the aircraft was climbing through flight level 290 the flight crew experienced moderate to severe vibration, a burning smell and smoke. At the same time the passengers in the passenger cabin and the cabin crew saw flame and heard an explosion in the left hand engine.

The Commander immediately took control of the aircraft disengaging the auto-pilot and the automatic throttle. Following a brief conversation on the flight deck the pilots diagnosed the symptoms of vibration and smoke as indicating a problem in the right engine. Twenty seconds after the onset of the vibration the Commander instructed the First Officer to throttle back the right engine. The Commander stated later that the action of closing the right throttle reduced the smell and signs of smoke and he was conscious of no continuation of the vibration after the right throttle was closed.

Immediately after throttling back the right engine the First Officer advised the London Air Traffic Control that the aircraft was at flight level 300 and they had an emergency situation. The indications were it was an engine fire. When this message had been passed the Commander ordered the First Officer to shut down the right hand engine which had been throttled back. The flight crew then decided to divert to East Midlands Airport at Castle Donnington.

In the passenger cabin, everyone had been conscious that the events had occurred in the left-hand engine. In the cabin the passengers and cabin attendants had heard an unusual noise accompanied by moderate to severe vibration. Some passengers had also been aware of, what they described as, 'smoke'. They described the smell of burning as rubber, oil, hot metal many had seen signs of fire from the left engine which they described variously as fire, torching, or sparks. Several of the cabin attendants described the noise as a low repetitive thudding. One described that the vibration had been severe enough to shake the walls of the forward galley. Soon after the right engine has been shut down and in response to a cabin chime from the Commander the flight service manager came to the flight deck. The Commander asked him if they had smoke in the cabin. He replied that they had.

After a statement from the flight service manager that the passengers were becoming concerned the Commander broadcast, on the cabin address system, that there was trouble with the right engine which produced some smoke in the cabin, that the engine was now shut down and that they could expect to land at East Midland Airport in about 10 minutes. The right engine was shut down 2 minutes and 7 seconds after the vibration began. By that time power had been reduced in the left engine which continued to operate in comparatively low power. After the accident the Commander stated that during the remainder of the descent the indications from the engine instruments were such as to confirm that the emergency had been successfully concluded and that the left engine was operating normally.

The right engine was shut down at approximately 5 nautical miles north west of East Midlands airport, London ATC cleared the aircraft to turn right and descend to flight level 100. Then London ATC passed the control to Manchester ATC who passed headings for the aircraft to descend to the north west of the East Midlands airport before vectoring it to the east of the airport to begin its approach to runway 27 that is the east to west runway. Control of the aircraft approach was then transferred to Castle Donnington.

The approach then continued until the aircraft was on the localiser of the instrument landing system for runway 27. The flaps were lowered to 5°. At 2,000 feet the landing gear was lowered and as the outer mark was passed at 4.3 nautical miles from touchdown 15% of flap was selected. One minute later at 20.23.50 hours when the aircraft was 2.4 nautical miles from touchdown and a height of only 900 feet above the ground the left engine lost power completely with compressor speed reducing rapidly. High vibration levels were also experienced. At this stage the Commander told the First Officer to re-start the right engine. Seventeen seconds after the power loss the fire warning system operated on the left engine. It was too late to re-start the right engine and no power was available from it before the aircraft struck the ground within a minute at 20.24.43 hours, 36 seconds after the fire warning. The initial ground impact was on level ground just to the east of the M1 motorway, the aircraft then passed through trees and suffered its second major impact on the western, north-bound carriageway of the M1 motorway and the lower part of the western embankment. This second impact occurred 70 metres after the initial impact and 10 metres lower the fuselage was extensively broken and the aircraft came to rest entirely on the wooded western embankment approximately 900 metres only from the threshold of runway 27, displaced 50 metres to the right of the centre line of the approach lights.

Witnesses on the ground who saw the final approach of the aircraft saw clear evidence of fire in the left engine. The intake area of the engine was filled with yellow/orange fire and flames were observed streaming aft of the engine nacelle pulsating in unison with thumping noises emanating from the left engine. Metallic rattling noises were also heard and flaming debris was seen falling from the region of the burning engine. Almost everyone in the aircraft will recall the pictures on television and in the press of this crash. The loss of life and injury was considerable and the aircraft was completely destroyed.

Let us now examine, in some detail, the sequence of events, trying to keep the technical and organisational factors equally in mind. The original cause of the events, which led to the failure of the left engine, has been thoroughly analysed. There are some specific recommendations in the accident inspectors' investigating report about the hardware and its operating characteristics. The engine was of a new design and had not been extensively proven at the high stress levels experienced in a prolonged, rapid climb-out. It may be that there are some ineradicable design features of this engine, which make these operating characteristics likely. Other operators have reported similar events short of catastrophic engine failure. In any event, the manufacturers subsequently issued instructions that the aircraft was not to be operated within its full power range. So a technical 'cause' for some of the events has been identified. But is this why the plane crashed? Why did the captain shut down the good engine, which was operating normally, and attempt to fly on the engine which had exploded? Why did the captain decide to make for East Midlands Airport instead of returning to Heathrow Airport, which they had just left, or seek to put down at, say, Luton, Coventry, or Birmingham, which were en route?

In subsequent analysis, attention was drawn to the instrumentation. Where a failure involving vibration occurs in one engine, there is a likely aftermath of surging in the other good engine as it takes up the additional strain. A quick glance at the instrumentation could have resulted in a genuine visual error.

But is even this the whole story? Further examination of the transcripts of the subsequent enquiry indicates some additional features. Firstly, it is likely from the taped discussions between the captain and the co-pilot on the flight deck that initially the co-pilot did believe the problem to be in the left engine. Indeed, on the tape he is heard forming the letter "l" before the captain interjects "*right engine*". Moreover, the passengers and cabin crew was all aware that the initial problem was in the left engine. Why was this perception not transmitted to the captain? Predictably, the inquiry concentrated on this point. But when the flight service manager was asked directly "Why did you not tell the captain that the problem was in the left engine?" he replied "I thought he knew because we could all see it".

Why did the plane crash where it did? Even flying on an almost totally destroyed engine, producing minimal power, the aircraft crashed only 900 yards short of safety. Another two minutes in the air would certainly have brought all of the passengers and crew down safely. Why did the crew choose to divert to East Midlands Airport when, from the time of the initial event at 20.05 hours, there were many other options including returning to Heathrow Airport. But the plane passed over half a dozen available landing fields, which could have been the object of the diversion. Why did they have to go to East Midlands?

It is, of course, quite easy to cut through these questions and say, in effect, that this is over-elaboration. The pilot made a mistake, it was his fault, he was subsequently disciplined and, incidentally, he was seriously injured. He and the co-pilot lost their jobs. Fate evens things up. The categorisation of pilot error seems never clearer than in this example.

Likewise, in the report of the 1980 crash of a New Zealand Air DC10 into Mount Erebus in Antarctica, the report concludes in paragraph 337 that "The probable cause of this accident was the decision of the captain to continue the flight at low level towards an area of poor surface and horizon definition when the crew was not certain of their position and the subsequent inability to detect the rising terrain which intercepted the aircraft's flight path." This pejorative rewording of the circumstances of the accident actually explains nothing about why this apparent act of folly took place and, indeed, a subsequent Royal Commission of Inquiry into the Mount Erebus disaster concluded that "In my opinion, therefore, the single dominant and effective cause of the disaster was the mistake by those airline officials who programmed the aircraft to fly directly at Mount Erebus and omitted to tell the air crew ... That mistake is attributable, not so much to the persons who made it, but to the incompetent administrative airline procedures which made the mistake possible (Mahon 1996). Neil Johnson (1996), from whom I have taken this extract, concludes that Justice Mahon's findings "gave an insight into the underlying systemic deficiencies that have to be addressed if similar accidents are to be prevented."

Let us now the review the Kegworth incident and see if we can find answers to some of these puzzles. In the first place, what happened on the flight deck? There is now abundant documentation of a particular type of communication problem on flight decks involving very experienced commanders and relatively inexperienced first officers. In the Kegworth case, the Commander's total flying experience was 13,180 hours of which 765 hours were on Boeing 737, 300 or 400 types. The co-pilot had less than 1,000 flying hours-flying experience no command experience and, of course, much less flying experience than the commander does on this type of aircraft. The captains of large jets are selected for, and programmed to live up to, the perception that they are capable of flying the aircraft single-handed, of taking control in emergency, and of handling potentially catastrophic situations. They are expected to be 'leaders' and in an emergency take control. They are not selected for, or trained to acquire, team playing abilities such as listening skills.

Clearly in situations as complex as these, where there is a multiplicity of information and a need to be entirely clear what the information all adds up to, there is equally a need to listen and to be prepared to accept information from all sources, including from passengers and less experienced colleagues. But, in principle, pilots have not been trained for these behaviours. (Weir 1996).

Following a damaging series of disasters in the early 1980's, United Airlines became so concerned at the way in which disaster scenarios involving poor flight deck communication unfolded, that they started a training and recruitment programme to "deselect for positive pilot quality".

"Deselecting for positive pilot quality" is a curious terminology. By it United Airlines meant that they would find it useful to discover which applicants for pilot positions in United Airlines would have the appropriate combination of physical fitness, motor skills, mental agility, self confidence and other characteristics that would make them intrinsically good pilots. Many of those so selected would, of course, include those who had had experience in a military flying context. But having identified those among this group who also had 'leadership qualities' they would carefully discard them and not permit them to go through the systems and become pilots of big passenger jets. The reason is that United Airlines had found that the 'right stuff' was bred into pilots who had come through that route. They had what we might call the 'Biggles factor'.[2] In a crisis they would try to fly the plane on their own. But their endeavours would very likely lead to catastrophic disaster if they discarded or failed to heed the first hand information of others. The fact is **no** one person can fly a plane. Team players and good listeners are safer personalities to have on the flight deck. The technology guided by the manual should keep the plane in the air long enough to permit team skills and contributive behaviours to bring the plane down safely.

A good example of these behaviours and actions is the Sioux City disaster of a couple of years ago. This was a plane, which had suffered a catastrophic explosion in the rear engine. This had destroyed all of the control surfaces and hydraulic and electronic linkages in the rudder area. The plane was technically unflyable. Once the flight crew had communicated the extent of the damage to the design engineers in Seattle the latter put their head in their hands and prayed. They **knew** that the plane could not possibly land safely. But the pilot and co-pilot tried things out and found that by altering the pitch of the engines they could exercise some degree of control over where and how the plane was flying. The nearest available airport with a runway that was at all appropriate was at Sioux City. All the emergency services were alerted. In order to keep airborne the plane had to attempt to land at more than twice the normal speed. In the event having touched down reasonably safely it slewed off the runway, fire broke out and several casualties ensued. But subsequent analysis concluded that this was a successful accident because the majority of passengers and crew did survive the technically unsurvivable.

One of the key factors in the Sioux City story was that the cabin staff had followed recently introduced procedures for disaster situations. They had quietly gone round the passengers and enquired what their jobs were. They had found a qualified and experienced pilot from the training department who had simulated disaster scenarios in a training situation. He came up to the flight deck and became an extra pair of hands. At times it was his physical presence holding down control levers which permitted the degree of stability that got the plane as far as Sioux City. His experience was also another qualified voice to add to the brainstorming that was going on, on the flight deck. Each new situation was a new experience. No previous training had in fact prepared any of the participants for the behaviours, which were necessary. A combination of considerable experi-

---

[2] After the heroic exploits of Major Bigglesworth: 'Biggles' in the boys' fiction novels of Captain W E Johns.

ence, basic listening skills and team playing brought the plane down to the ground.

1.3 Multidisciplinary research into risk and risk management

by Robert Cressy
Professor, Warwick Business School

Interdisciplinary research involves the coming together of two or more different academic disciplines for the purpose of understanding how the world works. In the case of the present volume, this means the coming together of two or more disciplines for the purpose of understanding the nature and management of risk in business. This coming together of course involves communication between people, the meshing of ideas and blending of methodologies. For research to be genuinely interdisciplinary, researchers from different disciplines need to approach a given topic and combine their skills to provide a perspective or a solution to a problem *that would not be provided if they were to have examined the problem independently.* There must be a genuine value-added to the joint work, and if this is not there, we have simply a set of researchers doing exactly what they would have done without each other's perspective on the subject to enhance their productivity: *they would have not learnt anything of use from each other.*

Different academic disciplines are generally recognised by their development of a *language* for describing reality, or a *map* of the world. Developing the second metaphor, we can say that the territories defined by these maps may well be, or seem (to the owners) to be, different. The methods of projection from the map to the territory may also be different. Even where territories described by the maps overlap there may be disputes over the nature and extent of the terrain described. Sometimes there may even be disputes between mapmakers (researchers) over who *owns* the terrain!

An important thing to recognise is that *the function of a map is its use.* A map is used to guide us through territory. So the question we must ask is: Is it a good guide? If it isn't, can we make it better? And how? Interdisciplinary research may help us to expand the terrain mapped, and to improve the qualities of any one map by combining mapping techniques.

There is clearly nothing singular about a mapping technique. Each may be useful for different people, and for different uses. For example, the general traveller will have a different interest and so use of a map from the traveller with an interest in geology, antiquities, walking routes, motoring routes etc. Colouring, design and metrics can differ, and also 'modes of projection'. For interdisciplinary research, the question we must ask is: Does the combining of two different maps or mapping techniques help us to see the lie of the land better and therefore to move through the landscape better? Does it help us better to find our destination? This presupposes we can define a common destination. It also presupposes we have some common standard of judgement in evaluating whether the combined mapping technique has greater utility than the individual techniques taken separately.

To make this concrete, some academic disciplines are closer to one another than others. For example, if we think of combining the languages of Economics and Finance, we are discussing maps that cover different but closely related territories, and whose methods of projection are very similar (they both use the optimisation calculus, and both cover different aspects of the economy and economic decisions). This suggests that there is great scope for complementarity and that the individuals using the map will agree on the outcome, or on the lie of the land. This prediction is needless to say well borne out in practice, with many journals dealing with both disciplines and academics from each contributing to the writing of joint papers.

Likewise, although the methodology of Economics and Law is rather different (the former being more theory-based, mathematical and statistical, the latter being more discursive, case study based, and 'logical'), there is again scope for defining different areas where two different mapping techniques are useful, and indeed, where the theory of economics can say something about the way the legal system develops, and vice versa. In the area of risk management for example, the development of the limited liability company in 18th England, was both an important legal and economic development, and significantly influenced the decisions of banks to lend to firms, and equity investors to offer equity. It redistributed risk between firm and bank and shareholder.

There are many examples of how academic disciplines have fed off each other to their mutual or single benefit. So interdisciplinary research can be successful and rewarding to the participants. However, a precondition of it working is that there should be a genuine desire to co-operate, to understand the perspective of the other's discipline, to treat its approach, axioms and hypotheses as useable tools rather than as gospel or heresy. This can be difficult if one has spent a large number of years in the confines of a single discipline, a way of life and a philosophy. Academics are no less capable of prejudice and close-mindedness than people from any other walk of life, though they are often less likely to admit it!

1.4 Interdisciplinary risk research in credit

by Mervyn K Lewis
National Australia Bank Professor, University of South Australia

The Stockholm Seminar took place in June 1997. While participants were enjoying the warm summer days and long tranquil evenings, a financial disaster was beginning to unfold on the other side of the globe which could well prove to be as defining an event for that region as the Great Depression of the 1930s was for the West – the so called 'Asian meltdown' or 'Asian currency crisis'.

No single set of explanations holds for all of the East Asian economies, but two factors are common to all of the countries concerned. Throughout the region a violent boom and bust cycle in asset prices (real estate and equities) preceded the currency declines. In addition, in each case, banks and other financial institutions lending recklessly on property and other development projects constitute the core of the problem. Fuelled by inflows of overseas private capital, and seemingly convinced that the demand for offices, luxury hotels and expensive shopping plazas would continue to expand, banks lent excessively against rising collateral values. When the bubble burst, a downward spiral of asset values and exchange rates began which fed on itself in a contagious and systemic fashion, producing a liquidity crisis which soon spilled over to corporate sector indebtedness and the real economy.

It has been suggested that such problems typify the adjustment to a more liberal and open economy environment (BIS, 1997). For example, banks previously operating under regulated and controlled regimes lacked the experience to evaluate credit risks in the less regulated environment. Or, it may be that prudential supervisory systems were not tightened sufficiently, or soon enough, to cope with the greater risks. Perhaps, in addition, there was the expectation of implicit government support for the banks should they run into difficulties, producing an over-guaranteed and under-regulated financial system (Krugman, 1998).

Yet, these arguments ignore that asset price cycles funded by easy bank credit were also a common feature of the financial crises, which occurred in the industrial countries in the earlier years of this decade. The same 'inexperience' arguments carry less force for these countries, especially since many banks (those in the UK and US, for example) had been severely blighted by the property boom and bust which took place less than twenty years earlier in the 1970s.

Then there is a further question. Why didn't the bankers and property developers of East Asia learn from the mistakes made in the industrial countries in the late 1980s and early 1990s? In China, for instance, as much office space was built in Shanghai in the space of three years as Hong Kong had taken thirty-three years to construct. Perhaps what we learn from history is that we don't learn from history!

The examination of such corporate amnesia and myopia would seem to call out for interdisciplinary research. Psychologists, in particular, have long studied collective behaviour and heard instincts of the type, which appear to characterise 'bubbles'. Recent property booms and asset price cycles look increasingly like once-in-a-lifetime periods when the endless growth and 'boom that will not end' psyche takes hold, and people temporarily suspend customary prudent standards and even common-sense. Bankers are presumably as prone to such 'bubbles' as are others.

Indeed, the possibility that bubbles might occur in banking poses special significance because of the extent to which bankers rely on group behaviour on both sides of the balance sheet. On the loan side, syndication of loans allows banks to commit funding in amounts that their own balance sheets could not support. Much loan participation is carried out under conditions of *uberrimae fidei* in which the many small banks needed for enhanced risk spreading have to trust the risk assessment and recommendation of the syndicate leaders. On the liabilities side, bankers rely on access to purchased funds through the interbank and other wholesale funding markets, thereby economising on cash reserves.

A group of banks prepared to support each other in these ways is stronger than any of its constituents, but the group identity may also encourage excessive risk-taking. There is an obvious sense in which this must be so; balance sheet growth rates for individual banks well in excess of the growth of GDP simply could not occur when banks had to grow 'organically' by collecting deposits from retail markets and their own corporate client base. Even so, a bank seeking to tap the interbank market will obtain funds only if the other banks are of a similar mind and do not view the activities of the borrowing bank as excessively risky. It is in this way that the collective mechanisms upon which bankers rely may facilitate risk-taking responses.

Psychologists studying decision-making in groups have found that group members are willing to make decisions involving greater risks than their individual preferences – behaviour, which they refer to as the 'risky-shift phenomenon'. In particular, group behaviour is marked by the suppression of private doubts, pressures towards uniformity, close-mindedness, the downplaying of warning signs, and the illusion of invulnerability (Buchanan and Huczynski, 1985; Arnold, Robertson and Cooper, 1992). While the parallel is not exact, it would seem that bankers do exhibit many of the features of what Janis (1968), after a study of 'disasters' in American foreign policy, called 'group think' - the psychological drive for consensus at any cost that suppresses dissent and the appraisal of alternatives in cohesive decision-making groups. (p8). This line of investigation would seem to be a useful avenue for further study when considering credit cycles and disasters in banking and financial markets.

1.5 Reflections on the multidisciplinary nature of research into risk in banking

by Barry Howcroft
Professor, Loughborough University

Almost by definition, any student of banking must take into account risk when undertaking a study of banking. Risk, without exaggeration, can be said to be the very 'essence of banking' and bank management is, therefore, primarily concerned with taking actions and implementing systems and controls to protect against material downside events and encourage material upside opportunities. By analysing present circumstances and ascertaining the probability of certain risks occurring in the future, a bank, like any other organisation, can reduce the possibility of incurring losses. Fundamental, however, to these processes for identifying, estimating and controlling bank risk is the provision and interpretation of information which will enable the bank to either avoid a high risk situation altogether or take some risk reduction strategy in the form of hedging, collateral or diversification, etc.

Over the last few decades, events have taken place throughout the World's financial markets that have served to increase the risks faced by banks. Possibly the most important of these 'events' has been the systematic deregulation of financial services markets throughout the World which has reduced entry barriers and increased competition to unprecedented levels. Not only have levels of competition increased, but also the patterns of competing have changed and, in this respect, technological innovations have had a significant impact. Like deregulation, technology has reduced entry barriers, but it has also globalised wholesale banking and made twenty-four hour banking a reality in the domestic retail markets. Increased customer sophistication has also increased the risks faced by banks by making customers increasingly demanding and this has forced banks to be aware of the importance of service quality and market share. Consequently, customer retention and cross selling strategies aimed at making the existing customer base more profitable have increased in importance.

This brief résumé of the main causes of risk is not meant to be exhaustive, but it does, nevertheless, make it clear that risk in banking is a diverse and complicated subject that reflects the multifaceted and multidisciplinary nature of modern day banking.

This multidisciplinary nature of risk emanates from the wide range of risks that impinge on banking. At the risk of over-simplification, all of these risks can be categorised under five broad headings: marketing risk, human resource risk, innovation risk, technology/operating risk and financial risk. Taking each of these in turn it becomes evident that risk permeates every facet of the business of banking and in so doing demands a detailed understanding of a wide range of related issues. For example, marketing risk typically relates to product pricing, distribution strategy, customer behaviour, market performance and legal or regulatory issues. Human resource risk is similarly concerned not just with headcount, but also with productivity and the structure and quality of management. Innovation risk impinges on new product development and obsolescence and technology/operating risk typically encompasses product-service quality, productive capacity and cost versus productivity. Finally, arguably the most important risk to affect banks, namely credit risk, is primarily concerned with how to price-to-risk and make correct lending decisions, but it is also concerned with how to maintain adequate levels of liquidity. In this respect, it introduced issues relating to funding risk, i.e. the availability of funds to meet current and future obligations and has direct implications for capital adequacy and, in some instances, foreign exchange risk and interest rate policy.

In seeking to understand and manage the problem of risk in banking more effectively, it is essential that research is interdisciplinary. The five broad categories of banking risk (identified above) necessarily involve a number of quite separate academic disciplines which need to be taken into account in order to fully understand the nature of risk and its ultimate control by management. For example, an effective approach to managing corporate credit risk involves an ability to interpret financial accounts and, therefore, draws upon the discipline of accountancy. Equally important, however, are the disciplines of psychology in order to assess management competencies; industrial economics in order to put business customers in an economic context; organisátional behaviour in order to understand the organisational structure of business customers and also to better organise credit decision making within the bank itself; and, finally, financial theory in order to manage credit risk from a loan portfolio perspective.

In conclusion, although the above example is not exhaustive, it does serve to illustrate that banking risks, in general, draw upon a potentially wide and diverse range of academic disciplines. Quality research is also dependent upon the accessibility of empirical data and in many instances the ability to develop models which simulate the real world by combinations of applied mathematics, econometrics and statistics. These sort of considerations help to explain why research into risk in banking is both exciting and challenging and, once again, service to illustrate why good quality research is best facilitated by teams of researchers with complimentary skills and different academic backgrounds.

1.6 Reflections on the need for an interdisciplinary approach to the study of insolvency risk

by Theodore Eisenberg
Henry Allen Mark Professor of Law, Cornell Law School

The area of insolvency risks is particularly suited to an interdisciplinary approach that exploits economic theory, accounting principles, and modern statistical techniques. Assessing the economic forces that help route firms towards insolvency requires knowledge of the field of finance. When an industry is distressed, it affects the prospects of all firms in that industry. Rescue of troubled firms is more difficult when the potential rescuers are themselves financially troubled. And the nature of a firm's assets may affect its viability as a going concern. Some assets can be more easily transferred to new uses than others. Knowledge of finance can help explore which economic effects and asset structures might be expected to correlate with insolvency risks and to what extent they may do so.

At the individual firm level, accounting concepts supplement knowledge of finance to help assess a firm's financial status. Concepts such as return on assets, leverage, interest coverage ratio, and liquidity can all provide ways to measure whether a firm is in financial distress. Some may prove to be better predictors of bankruptcy or the risk of loss than others.

Graduate students working in the insolvency area should be able to combine their knowledge of accounting and finance with sound econometric and statistical methodology. From early studies in the area of insolvency to the present, statistical modelling of firms and individuals plays an important role in helping to make an informed credit decision. Firms such as Dun & Bradstreet make substantial use of statistics and econometric modelling in assessing credit risks.

In analysing firms in financial distress, a researcher or doctoral student must understand the nature of proper sampling and the statistical biases often introduced by the absence of a random sample of firms. Bankruptcy of large firms, for which data are available, is a rare event. Unless the researcher makes a special effort to find bankrupt firms, studying them is not possible. But this special effort leads to oversampling of bankrupt firms compared to healthy firms. Many existing studies of bankruptcy fail to properly account for sample biases.

It is also important to understand the evolving statistical techniques available to researchers and analysts. Statistical analysis has progressed a long way since the early use of discriminant analysis to model bankruptcy. Modern tools include logistic regression analysis, probit analysis, cox regression models, multinomial logit models, and competing risk models. Generalised estimating equations, as implemented by statistical software packages, can be considered. When panel data are available, techniques that account for the existence of multiple observations per firm should be used.

1.7 Reflections on how to introduce doctoral students to the complex scientific field of risky business

by Robert W Vivian
IISA Professor of Insurance and Risk Management
University of the Witwatersrand

A feature of modern commercial society is the size and complexity of the modern firm. These complex firms operate in an equally complex and risky environment. The tradition in educational institutions has been to break a firm down into various business functions, such as accounting, finance, marketing, human resources, technical and so on and then to give academic instruction within these disciplines. Each of these is today highly specialised. With the increase in specialisation, very little space is left over in curriculum development for a more general education and hence the average graduate has had little time to study the changes in the environment, even in his own discipline. For example, a graduate may specialise in taxation and have taken virtually no courses in the history or impact of taxes on society. The practical effect of this concentration is that graduates and hence most managers, in practice, have a myopic view of business and life.

Risk is pervasive and permeates through all aspects of business and life. It is not confined to separate business disciplines but impact across them. This can be illustrated by the escalation of legal liability risks. The escalation in claims has been across all areas: professional liability, product liability, and environmental liability. The risk could not be confined to or managed within any single discipline or even sector of the industry. Thus manufacturers, mines, and insurers faced insolvency because of this risk. When the cause of the risk was investigated by a commission set-up by President Reagan the problem was found to be the American judicial system. The cause was within society and not the firm.

In order to manage risk effectively, it is necessary to appreciate its pervasiveness and that it is indeed multi-disciplinary. A complex system is needed to manage it and the educational approach must recognise this complexity. The first step in designing the educational response to this problem is to identify the core discipline involved. There may be a difference in opinion as to what this core discipline is, but to me its seems that it is one of management. Management by its very nature is non-specific and recognises the multi-disciplinary nature of the problem. Consider the general manager of a firm. He or she is concerned with maximising profits by co-ordinating all the activities of the firm. In the field of risk management the emphasis is on management and not risk. Accepting these two aspects become important, and involves identifying the general principles which are common to most individual risk areas and the generalised management principles which must be applied in each case. For example, it may be agreed that decision theory is fundamental to most areas of risk and, if so, decision theory should form the basis of undergraduate courses. But it is not possible to be an expert in all disciplines and at an undergraduate level a student should major in at least one facet, for example legal liability risks.

It is for this reason that risk management is ideal for postgraduate studies. The student already has an undergraduate education and is then in a better position to pursue a management solution to any number of complex issues involving risk.

This complex nature of risk and its management can be introduced to doctoral students in a number of ways, depending on whether or not the doctoral programme is by research or by research and course work.

First, the student should be referred to appropriate readings covering the conceptual nature and development of risk management. Second, a list of appropriate research topics, with supporting readings, can be compiled covering management aspects of risk, fundamental aspects and aspects applied to specific disciplines or risks. It would be desirable if a database of research topics, and course outlines could be available on the internet for this purpose. Third, a database of readings could be kept on the internet that could be added to by various people working in the field. Finally, a directory of persons working in the field could be com-piled. This would be useful so that students could obtain the benefit of synergy and the list could be used as a source from which external examiners for doctoral theses could be selected.

1.8 Psychological perspectives on risk management

by James Shanteau
Professor, Kansas State University

Several years ago after a particularly bad day on the stock market, I received a phone call from a reporter for the *Boston Globe*. He wanted to know if I could explain why investors would suddenly panic and try to sell all their holdings. Because I had studied decision making under risk, he felt that I might offer some explanation.

Since stock market behaviour was not my speciality, I responded by asking him why he did not talk to market economists or to finance researchers. He said that he had already talked to several experts on the stock market, but that they were unable to explain panic selling using economic principles. Instead, these specialists had recommended that the reporter "talk to a psychologist to explain the unexplainable." Hence, he called me.

Psychology is often seen as a 'court of last resort' when all other more rational grounds of explanation have been exhausted. If we can explain behaviour using purely economic or financial principles, then we do so. When those principles are no longer adequate, we turn to psychology. In my view, this is the wrong approach. Psychology should be considered jointly with other disciplines right from the start.

The Seminar provided an excellent opportunity to see the advantages of including psychological perspectives, along with those of other disciplines, from the beginning. As a fundamental building block of human behaviour, psychology is needed to help 'put the pieces together' for an understanding of risk behaviour and risk management. Indeed, it is hard to image how it could be otherwise.

A cursory examination of the other sections of this chapter reveals an emphasis on following issues: *team decision making, communication, risk misperception, cognitive maps, collective behaviour, group/mob psychology, extremity effects (in groups), management of technology, consumer behaviour, organisational (mis)-*

performance, and *goal setting.* Each topic (and many others) fundamentally involves psychology. Yet the other sections in this chapter are written by non-psychologists.

But perhaps most central to all the topics raised in the present volume is that of *risk taking and risk management.* This is an issue that has been studied for over 50 years by researchers within the field of *Judgement and Decision Making.* Although there are many questions yet to be answered, researchers have discovered many basic principles (see Shanteau, 1992). To make further progress, however, it will be necessary for decision researchers to work with scholars from other disciplines. By combining theories, methods, and results, new opportunities will emerge to advance understanding. That is the promise of the Seminar.

In the May 1998 *American Psychological Association Monitor*, a special section is devoted to the importance of *cross-disciplinary research.*[3] Numerous examples, primarily involving psychology and medicine, were cited to illustrate the advantages of co-operative efforts between disciplines. However, no mention was made of the potential for combining psychology and economics or related disciplines. This oversight reflects an important difficulty in such efforts – it is hard to see the benefits of an untested collaboration beforehand. As a result, there is a high-perceived risk to cross-disciplinary research.

What are the sources of this perceived risk? As identified in the special issue, three factors stand out. First, the needed level of interaction is expensive, time consuming, and labour intensive; co-ordination across disciplines requires a great deal of effort. Second, there is a constant danger that researchers will not fully engage with other disciplines, i.e. each investigator will pursue the same directions that she/he would have anyway. Third, there is a concern that the resulting research will be less rigorous than research in 'pure disciplines', cross-disciplinary research is seen as 'soft science' by many investigators.

So why would researchers want to take on the additional risk to work on cross-disciplinary teams? There are at least four major advantages. First, no single discipline possesses all the skills needed to conduct cutting-edge research these days. For instance, economists traditionally are stronger in theory whereas psychologists have great skill in methodology. It will take both fields working together to advance in both theory and methods of behavioural economics.

Second, researchers in one discipline often ignore data sources in another. The General Social Survey, for example, has been conducted since 1972 by sociologists. Yet it provides access to many issues that would be of central interest to

---

[3] The term *cross-disciplinary* has become common in the United States to avoid confusion and argumentation. There had been considerable debate on the relative advantages and disadvantages of the terms *inter-disciplinary* and *multi-disciplinary*. Some have argued for using one or the other of these labels. At the same time, others have used the two terms interchangeably. To avoid confusion, therefore, the *cross-disciplinary* label has been introduced and is used here as a neutral description.

psychologists and economists, e.g., women in the workplace. Only recently, have researchers outside of sociology started working with this database (available at http://www.icpsr.umich.edu/gss). It could be an invaluable source.

Third, many recent advances have come about only because of cross-disciplinary research teams. In a report just released by the National Heart Lung and Blood Institute in the United States, collaborative research teams were strongly encouraged. "The most effective research on the behavioural dimensions of disease comes from interdisciplinary teams," the report states. Presumably, the same conclusion applies to other collaborations involving psychologists, including business and finance.

Finally, cross-disciplinary research can extend understanding of a phenomenon beyond description to causation. Separately, intra-disciplinary studies have a strong record of describing and cataloging results. However, elucidating causal mechanisms has proved frustrating for all fields. By working together, cross-disciplinary teams have the potential to develop and confirm causal relationships, e.g., between individual risk attitudes and financial behaviour.

According to Bennett Bertenthal (1998), Director of the Social, Behavioural and Economic Sciences Directorate at the National Science Foundation, "cross-disciplinary projects represent a new way of conducting research that is somewhat foreign to the majority of scientists." Although he was sceptical initially, he "now counts himself as a true believer" in the feasibility of such efforts. Indeed, National Science Foundation now has a number of initiatives that target such research.

The two Stockholm Seminars on Risk Behaviour and Risk Management have begun an important series of interactions between researchers from different disciplines. The products of initial efforts were evident in the keynote addresses and the workshop papers presented at the seminars. In nearly every session, the value of combining psychological perspectives with those of other disciplines was evident. Some examples of collaboration discussed include combining *psychology* with one or more of the following fields: *economics, engineering, law, statistics, banking, sociology, accounting, education, finance,* and *marketing.*

The value of these interactions is also borne out in the chapters of the present book. In Chapter 3 (*Psychology in business life*), every contribution provides an example of cross-disciplinary efforts. Still, there is a great deal more to be done. Extended effort will be needed to achieve the full potential of teams made up of researchers from varied disciplines. That is the challenge for all of us.

1.9 Why is it important for researchers to study complex systems in our world from an interdisciplinary approach?

by David T. H. Weir
Professor, Newcastle Business School

In trying to answer this question I shall try to explain why the problems of risk, risk management and risk minimisation in complex systems seem to come to me to be the most significant area in which I could make a contribution, and why an interdisciplinary perspective has been fruitful.

For my bachelor degree I studied politics, philosophy and economics at Oxford University. This combination of disciplines is extraordinarily well balanced to produce the misleading comfort of apparently hard predictive theory in economics, the exposure to the real interpersonal dynamics of complex political systems in operation in a particular historical context, and the critical analytical tools of philosophy to guard against premature or, perhaps indeed, *any* generalisation until the conceptual framework of the study is well established. So I started out on a career in Social Research hoping for certainty, but becoming increasingly confident that it was not to be found in the operation of human systems.

At graduate school I concentrated in Sociology which seemed to have a body of relatively tough, but well-grounded theory. At the time there was an ongoing debate between the structural functionalism of such theorists as Parsons and the neo Marxist criticism of C Wright Mills. The latter was more appealing psychologically but increasingly I leant to the structured functionalistic approach, which seemed to have achieved such important advances in social anthropology, particularly in the study of primitive societies. In particular, the concept of emergent properties which seemed to identify what it was that was different about complex systems, compared to the properties of the individuals and simpler systems which constituted them. The historical evolutionary studies of Max Weber identified the crucial importance of the bureaucratic form of organisations as the most characteristic type of social structure in our advanced technologically based society. So for some time I concentrated my search for integrated theoretical frameworks on the emerging sub-discipline of Formal Organisations. By the time I became a lecturer in Sociology in the Department of Sociology and Social anthropology at Manchester University I had identified formal organisations as my special area. But almost accidentally, the previous ten years I had been increasingly intrigued by emerging theories of deviance which were becoming potent in the field of criminology.

I had taught criminology to policemen and prison staff both in the UK and the US. I found that these theories were also powerful and were rooted very often in quite precise anthropological observation of, for example, criminal gangs or in the subterranean world which seemed some how to escape the interest of social scientists engaged on behalf of official authority.

In 1970 I made a career move to the newly formed Manchester Business School. One evening, almost in despair, I sat by my fireside in my small house in Manchester realising that I had made a terrible blunder. It seemed to me then that I had nothing – I had no experience of management, no exposure to the real problems of managing, no knowledge of finance, marketing or the other specialists topics which made up the corpus or the typical MBA programme. What could I offer my new masters and new customers? Almost in desperation I started to piece together on a blank sheet of paper what I knew about how organisations worked. For simplicity I was using knowledge, theories, insights, and understandings from the two fields of complex organisations and studies of deviance. One thing became obvious, an emergent property of this new subject matter, if you like, on the whole things did not work.

Later I parlayed this common sense insight (well understood by the meanest labourer in the most hierarchical organisation) into the slightly more intelligent sounding 'all organisations operate in degraded mode'. There was something else borne of a willing exposure over the previous ten years to the low life aspects of complex society – that the accounts of lower participants in organisations contained a partial view of reality but nonetheless a critical and in, many ways, a more realistic view of how things were made to work than that offered by those who only saw the complex organisation from the top down. I did not at that time put all of this into a comprehensive theoretical framework. That did not seem to reflect the nature of subject matter, but I put all of the topics into a new programme, which was offered first on a short three-week programme for very senior executives at the Manchester Business School. I did so in some anxiety and trepidation.

I need not have worried. After the first session on Computer Fraud, which was then a quite new topic on which I had got hold of some American research, a group of the Executives came up to me after the class and said "thank you very much for this. In three weeks this is the first time we have come across a topic which reflects the real sense of what we have to do in our jobs, which is dealing with screw-ups, attacks on our systems, and the deliberate manipulation of information". My feelings that this had been a good topic to introduce to such a group were reinforced a few weeks later when I was invited to undertake a consultancy in a large engineering manufacturing company. The Chief Executive who had asked me "I had to have you come and see our problems, because it was obvious to me when I heard your presentation that you must have worked in our company or at least in one like it". To this day the delightful feedback of this kind has never ceased.

What is it about the subject matter, which appeals to Chief Executives? Firstly, it is that good explanatory theories in the social sciences need to be grounded in precise observations of specific historically situated social situations. And theory does not work in this field. The researcher must combine the open minded and often open eyed learning and listening abilities of the social-anthropologist, operating amongst a strange and to some extent terrifying tribe whose language and practices he is starting to learn. Secondly, and also in an anthropological and sociological sense, but echoing the poets Yeats and Eliot, the researcher must understand that 'all things connect'. That in Stafford Beers terminology we are dealing with a highly interconnected complex structure of a living organism. As Beer writes "it is now suspected that any other system, whether social, economic, industrial or purely managerial must reach a similarly high level of complexity if it is to attain viable characteristics". Complexity does not necessarily imply interconnectedness, but the interconnections may themselves be structured on a different level of complexity, producing what strategicians and taxonomic theorists identify as the problem of Local Order.

The researcher must understand some at least of the basic ideas of cybernetics and of information systems to identify the characteristic problems of most risky situations in this problem of Local Order, of highly complex interconnected segments of organisational structure which are densely interconnected, while the modes linking them to other parts of the structure may be quite loosely articulated.

Channel width, redundancy, and noise are important concepts in understanding why it is that messages, even of the utmost potential importance for managing risk, do not get through to those charged with risk management responsibilities. But the overarching set of concepts which I have applied to the understanding of risky situations still derive from those original interests in formal organisations, in the apparently ubiquitous manifestations of bureaucracy first noted by Weber, and in the phenomenological aspects of organisation, the relationship between inner and outer lives identified by Schutz, and in the historically specific operations of the class system which, (despite the fall of the Berlin Wall and the euphoria of Mrs Thatcher), has by no means been eliminated as a master analytical category. It is the role of communication, of barriers to information transmission in complex highly articulated systems, the displacement and the bifurcation of goals and the power and potential value of lower participants and their information which still intrigue me as much as they did in 1970. I cannot think that anything other than a multi-disciplinary approach can be illuminating in these complex matters.

1.10 Reflections on the need for a holistic view in research projects

by Barry Howcroft
Professor, Loughborough University

There are instances where a more focussed approach to a research problem is appropriate and the importance of this type of research must not be underestimated. There is no doubt, however, that with applied research, which is looking to solve problems, a broader or holistic perspective needs to be taken. Not only is it important to understand how specific research initiatives relate to each other, but the inherent quality of focussed research is invariably enhanced by placing it within a context and having an understanding of the broader issues.

The appropriateness of such an approach stems, to a large extent, from good research practice. In most instances, research craftsmanship demands, as an essential prerequisite for getting started, a comprehensive review of the available literature. This will inform the researcher about what other researchers think and what is already known conceptually about the subject area and its related problems. Specifically, the review process is, therefore, necessary in order to address the question of sufficiency of theory: how much is known about the subject in question, what entitles researchers to investigate particular subject areas and, finally, what are the appropriate methodologies or ways of resolving the research questions.

The research process will normally include a comparison with similar or 'classic' studies in the risk research area. This will enable the researcher to discuss the implications of the chosen research methodology, the results and also the conclusions in a more meaningful way. It often happens, however, that there are different and sometimes competing schools of thought on theoretical tradition. It is, therefore, important to establish what the state of knowledge is, the different views that prevail in the literature and explain how your research fits into the general picture. In this respect, research can be regarded as an iterative process, each discrete research project adding to and developing earlier works and adding to our understanding of particular problems.

Good research practice also demands that analysis and discussion are not confused. Analysis is primarily concerned with the significance of the research findings in terms of the research objectives, approaches and methodology. In this respect, it necessarily involves evaluation in terms of the research model; in essence seeing how well the model fits or reflects the real world situation. Discussion follows from analysis and is necessarily wider and more speculative as the research generalises the wider meanings and implications of the research findings.

In an ideal or perfect world, the researcher would follow a fairly logical process broadly in accord with what has been discussed above. In practice, however, these broad generalisations or rules of thumb relating to research methodology typically do not work and the researcher can make mistakes by trying too hard to be scientific or 'exact'. In many respects, the research must effectively make a trade-off between wanting to categorically prove things and analytical quality. This is particularly the case where the theoretical background is weak and is often the case with interdisciplinary projects where several disciplines need to be consulted to arrive at meaningful research objectives and testable hypotheses.

Experience suggests that in social sciences in general and in academic business research in particular it is difficult to prove or disprove hypotheses. The required level of theoretical abstraction is typically too high and the results are too specific to be meaningful for statements of theory which could have a general application. Academic business and social science research is less deterministic than pure science and is more investigative in nature. Consequently, it is generally concerned with solving practical and clearly defined problems. Solving problems or issues in one particular setting, however, does not imply that the researcher can extend the results in the form of a general theoretical law.

Banking research is a good example of the sort of research which is essentially investigative and which does not readily lend itself to general theories. To prove this point, we could ask the question: what is the general theory of banking? If we had an answer to this question, we could possibly explain and define exactly what constituted a bank and who could (and could not) be a bank. In resolving these fundamental questions, we could also perhaps gain additional insight into the likely future of banks and the markets in which they operate. In reality, of course, there is no general theory of banking and the theories, which do exist tend to be specific, typically relating to asset-liability or gap management. In order to address and resolve some of the issues raised by the above questions, academics have turned away from bank specific theories and looked at the theories of the firm (Llewellyn, 1994). This seems to illustrate that although applied business research does not normally result in a general theory, researchers must, nevertheless, take an essentially broad and interdisciplinary perspective in resolving some of these very real issues facing modern businesses.

So far the discussion has attempted to show that good research practice inherently demands a fairly broad approach which takes into account all of the relevant literature and related studies. In general, applied business research, and this includes banking, is essentially problem solving rather than theory generating. This is largely because industries such as banking are far too complicated to lend themselves to general theories. Banking by definition is a multidisciplinary industry involving a wide range of academic disciplines, i.e. marketing, human resource management, operations research, financial risk management, etc. Applied research must similarly be multidisciplinary in order to truly understand and resolve the issues facing the banking industry.

This inherent complexity, which is largely a reflection of the nature of banking, has encouraged a multidisciplinary approach to bank research. Different academic disciplines have been typically brought together under the one project to resolve fairly specific issues, but in order to implement the recommendations; a holistic approach needs to be taken. For example, most of the research into customer service has tended to focus on comparisons between customer expectations and actual service performance. The perception of service quality in a bank, however, is determined not only by the outcome but also by the process. A holistic approach would, therefore, appear to offer the most appropriate model of bank customer service (Le Blanc and Nguyen, 1988). This sort of approach puts emphasis on the ability of the organisation to satisfy customer expectations and by necessity looks at diverse issues relating to: the commitment of the organisation to quality service; the design and availability of services; external business issues relating to selling and promotion, delivery systems, customer support, image, etc. Apart from these external considerations, internal business issues such as culture, management quality, teamwork, training, etc, are also important in determining service quality. This holistic approach is normally very important if the research is to change bank practice and resolve specific issues.

The problems of risk in banking similarly necessitate the same holistic approach, but risk in banking can manifest itself in so many different ways, i.e. credit risk, funding risk, interest rate risk, regulatory risk, etc, and this makes the subject area more problematic. However, looking specifically at credit risk, the lending abilities of the individual branch managers are clearly important, but so too is the way the lending function is organised with the bank and the extent to which the process is computerised. Similarly, other issues relating to portfolio management and regulatory control will determine pricing policy and overall lending strategy.

In conclusion, in this paper I have argued for a broad based approach to specific research projects in banking. The complexity of banking has generally made it impossible, or at best, very difficult, to generate general theories in banking. Consequently, research has tended to be fairly specific and problem solving in its orientation. In order for research to be applicable and of real benefit to the banks, it must be holistic and concentrate not just on the outcome but also the process. Research seminars, which bring together academics from different disciplines looking at related problems (in this instance, risk in banking) but from essentially different perspectives are, therefore, an absolute necessity in understanding and resolving the problems facing banks.

1.11 Analysis of complex systems related to business conditions

by Bo Green
Programme Director, Stockholm University

During the last twenty years, I have studied five complex systems relating to business conditions. The methodological approach to analysing a complex system, both in regard to underlying conditions of the system as well as the analysis and interpretation of how the system as a whole functions are an important part of the study.

The investigation and research projects have revealed the main causes of the problems in the systems as well as the necessary conditions for systems to function effectively. An action-oriented investigation method has gradually been developed and is built upon the premise that an analysis of a system should incorporate a dialogue with the actors and interested parties. Feedback in the form of observations that illuminate and help the actors gain insight into how the system as a whole works have been an important part of the investigation process. In the 'developmental-projects' differences between different scientific disciplines and different interpretations of reality, eventually contributed to an increased understanding and an appreciation of the need for change. A number of methodological problems were noted. To a certain extent these problems are due to the present practice in the Swedish commission system. For example, the fact that government investigations are so strictly formulated, makes it difficult for an investigator to penetrate complicated social and business problems.

The methodological conclusions are presented in a normative model for analysing of complex systems related to business conditions. In the model the process is divided into two steps. In the first step the investigator [4] concentrates primarily upon viewing the problem from different perspectives in dialogue with the various parties involved and with the representatives of the organisations. In the second step negotiation enters the process and consensus is sought in regard to the definition of the problem and its solution.

The aim of the research project was to illuminate important relationships in complex systems in which several actors interplay and in which the basis for control consists of laws, rules and norms in industrial settings.

---

4 In the presentation of the research project and in the normative model for analysis of complex systems related to business conditions I use the concept investigator for the person (investigator, researcher etc) who is responsible for the analysis.

Methods

Several methods were used to analyse each of the different systems in specific companies and interpret different parts of the system functions. In the study of the complex systems, case studies, interviews with the actors and interested parties, discussions in reference groups as well as statistical analyses were used. In the analysis of the systems interpretations and reflections were also an important part of the search for dependencies and relationships within the system.

When I have been working on methodological aspects I have thought through and reflected upon the different steps in my work for each of the five systems. In my reflections I have taken into consideration the interpretations that were made in relation to the discussions in the reference groups and seminars. After I once again had acquainted myself with the considerations in the investigation process, new interpretations and reflections concerning the complex function of the system and its characteristics were made.

How the scientific and theoretical frame of reference developed

An analysis of a complex system relating to business conditions includes a study of what is happening in companies and other organisations that the system is set to serve as well as how the interaction in the system functions.

Feedback during the process of investigation is of central importance in an attempt to produce a multifaceted picture of 'reality', inasmuch as the conceptions that people have of reality are not consistent. An outsider might therefore find it difficult to interpret the presentation.

The need to provide feedback on the observation of a complex system should be made in terms that allow both the investigator and the actors involved to gain insights into the system as a whole. This is done to encourage the investigator to perceive a complex system as an 'organisation', and consider the conditions for the use of a hermeneutic perspective in the analysis of complex systems. I have, for example, emphasised that development of a deeper understanding of a specific phenomena should occur in dialogues with the actors and interested parties concerned.

The issue of change is another important part of my philosophy in regard to science and research. I consider it important to analyse reality critically, not just to portray it, in an attempt to improve it. I emphasise that an aspect of action research is inherent in analysis of complex systems, consequently knowledge that the actors and interested parties have is an important source of information in understanding how a system functions.

In order to understand what comprises a complex system and how it functions, it is important to observe that the boundaries of a system are not clear in the beginning. Insight regarding these boundaries develops gradually as the complexity, relationships and dependency in the system become evident.

A concept that I have increasingly found essential is that of *cross-view*. By this I mean that an investigator should strive to observe and penetrate different views of reality and different perspectives of the same system. If both the investigator and the actors involved relate to the system with a cross-view, it is possible that such a view can promote the development of a holistic view of the system. This method of viewing the problem can be applied both to the different parts of the system and to problems of differing complexity and magnitude.

I have noticed that when the individuals involved begin to understand new relationships, they strive to gain greater insight into the variety of boundaries that exist in complex systems. This observation illustrates the distinction I make between 'understanding' and 'insight'. I define understanding as an understanding of a specific phenomena and its part in a specific system. Insight, on the other hand, means a deeper understanding of the system as a whole.

The systems studied

The export system

In 1977 I co-conducted a study that dealt with Swedish exports to newly industrialised countries. The main purpose of the study was to investigate the long-term conditions for adaptability and the possibilities for improving the export system, from the perspective of Swedish export firms to be improved. An area that was focused upon was that of planning and strategy development, for which both companies and authorities lacked resources for long-term initiatives. The result of the study pointed at insufficient co-operation in regard to resources and lack of guidelines for the development of export promotion. Another area that was covered in the study was that dealing with the conditions for co-operation in export.

The existence of many units and many interested parties that are dependent upon one another under a loose structure are all characteristics of 'the export system'. The factors that contribute to the difficulty to organise and lead export-promotion are, respectively, an inadequate flow of information and unclear roles for the actors in the system.

The tourism-promotion system

In 1982 I conducted a study to investigate part of the transition and adaptation problems caused by the very rapid development of the regional tourist organisation in Sweden. The study strove to illuminate the conditions for co-operation between government-financed units in the tourist trade. In the analysis of the causes of the problem, it was emphasised that politicians had based their decision to build large-scale regional booking companies on an altogether too narrow definition of the problem. This definition was based on the assumption that the problem was primarily an information and marketing problem. Another factor was the exaggerated optimism of the plans to change the structure of the regional tourist organisation.

The existence of many interested parties with unclear goals and roles, indistinct, boundaries of the system and the need for co-operation in product development are all characteristics of the 'tourism-promotion system'. In the public arena, municipalities, development foundations, tourist organisations, regional booking companies, etc., are all engaged in tourism-promotion. In the business world, hotels and conference centres, travel agents, sales agencies, etc. are all engaged in the marketing of tourism.

The bankruptcy system
In 1985 I was involved in a study to investigate the causes of the dramatic increase in bankruptcies in Sweden during the first half of the 1980s. The study showed that there were many interested parties and that the system included many different areas of knowledge. In the overall description of the problem, it was stressed that insufficiencies in insolvency legislation had resulted in insufficient incentives for banks to control credit risk and invest in competence training in risk assessment and risk management.

Laws, rules and norms for business transactions determine the actions of different interested parties. This, and the fact that laws, rules and norms determine the manner in which the system functions, are characteristics of the bankruptcy system. The goals are unclear, and different actors and interested parties have different opinions about what influences what in the system. The boundaries in the system are also unclear, and different interested parties, such as business owners, accountants, bankers, bankruptcy liquidators, experts in government organisations and business organisations, etc., have different perspectives in regard to 'the bankruptcy system'. The system is determined to a large extent by political decision-making through changes in legislation. The system also lacks other forms of leadership.

The regional development grant system
In 1987-88 I studied a system that focused on providing economic aid for the establishment of firms and businesses in areas that had been chosen to receive financial support from the government. The purpose of the study was to analyse and evaluate how the regional development grant system functions and to investigate the need for improvements to stimulate the development of newly-started firms and businesses. In the analysis it was pointed out that the actors and the interested parties differ in regards to their understanding of the system as a whole. Furthermore, the analysis showed that the manner in which the rules for the allocations of grants and the manner in which the grant was distributed influenced the conditions and likely success for newly-started firms and businesses.

The regional development grant system is characterised by a need for co-operation between the actors and interested parties. This co-operation as well as the rules for loans and grants and the norms for depreciation of the government's claims on loans are the basis of 'the regional development grant system'. This is a system in which the goals are unclear and the different actors and interested parties interpret the goals in different ways. This makes co-operation between public organisations as well as between public organisations and business owners more difficult. The regional development grant system does not, however, have a formal leadership. Changes in rules, responsibility for decisions, etc., take place primarily when the government investigates regional politics.

The risk management system
During 1990-1994 I managed a development project that dealt with economic risks in business life. Twenty-five researchers at universities and institutes of higher education as well as bankers and auditors participated in the project. At the beginning of the analysis it was assumed that the crisis in the banking system in Sweden was largely the result of insufficient knowledge in the basics of risk management and risk assessment. This was the result of a lack of research and education in this area. The purpose of the project, therefore, was first of all to make bankers and other interested actors and parties in business aware of the need to gain knowledge in the field of risk management. An observation that was made was that one of the reasons why basic knowledge in risk was lacking had to do with the legislation that governs business and business practices.

One of the characteristics of 'the risk management system' is the fact that there is a need for knowledge on how risks are influenced by the norms for risk-taking and risk distribution established. If banks are familiar with the associated risks when granting credit to companies, this will influence the kind of knowledge that is necessary for a bank official to have when handling loans and loan applications. In other words, the complex risk management system deals with the *knowledge* of risk and risk management that is necessary to handle risks in business transactions. The boundaries in the risk management system are unclear, due to the multitude of rules and laws that affect business. When the risk management system is in balance, the roles that the public wishes the actors to have in a well-functioning business world are in harmony.

Analysis of the systems characteristics

In analysing these complex systems, some of the differences that can influence the magnitude and the strength of the characteristics have been discussed. Amongst others, the extent to which the systems are characterised by loose or rigid structures and the degree to which a system is controlled by laws, rules and norms or by an "organisation" are examined. As can be seen in Figure 1.1, the analysis has shown that the bankruptcy system has a loose structure but is also controlled primarily by laws, rules and norms. The regional grant system has a rigid structure and is controlled by laws, rules and norms. The tourism-promotion system has a rigid structure and is primarily controlled by an organisation, while the export system has a loose structure and is controlled primarily by an organisation.

It is important, therefore, that the responsible politicians and decision-makers should attempt to identify the structure and the means by which the system is best controlled. Such a classification of complex systems in relation to the 'controlling mechanisms' could, for example, be done in terms of government regulation and control, institutional control, co-operative directives and organisational control.

Such a classification could provide politicians with a basis for choosing the structure and for clarifying the need for leadership. Perrow's classification (1986) has provided decision-makers in the business world with a classification that takes into consideration the conditions for centralised and decentralised leadership.

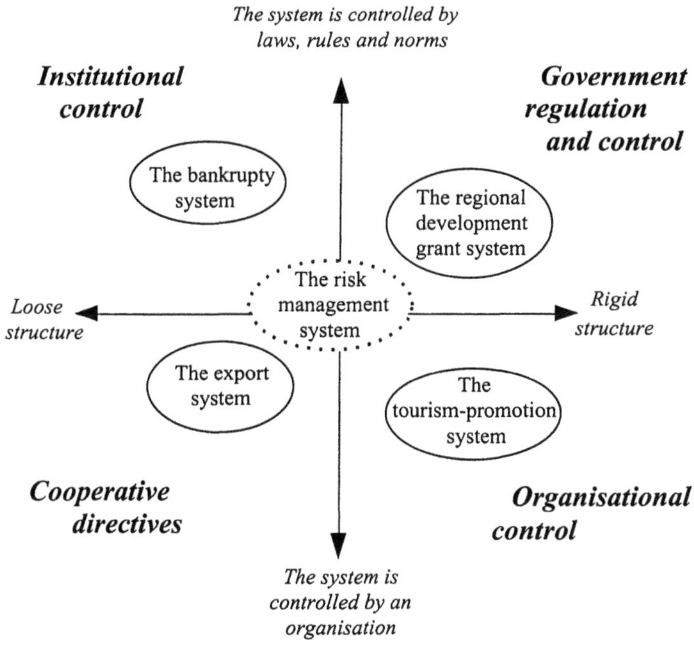

Figure 1.1 Analysis of the systems characteristics

Observations and conclusions

One of the observations that have been made concerns the participation of interested groups in the process of investigation. It is, for example, not unusual that the participation of interested parties in the evaluation process makes the organisational structure rigid.

Another problem is that certain fixed conceptions of reality exist among actors in official capacities and among experts in organisations, institutions and authorities. These conceptions have often been difficult, if not impossible, for parties to share. One of the conclusions I have made is that, if one or more dominant conception is diffused throughout the complex system it will make the search for solutions difficult.

In this context a special problem exists, namely the problem of polarisation. After some time the process of polarisation begins, in which groups of people develop different conceptions about what the causes of a problem in a specific system are and how they ought to be treated. One of the problems in regard to change is that the dominant actors over a long period of time become intransigent. This behaviour can be explained by the fact that the individual will strive to give the impression of being credible by consequently maintaining her or his initial decision. Thus I conclude that the investigator should be aware of which arguments organisations have used previously in regard to different issues. My observations support Cialdini's (1993) conclusions regarding the influence of political decision-makers.

Change in complex systems is seldom undertaken on the basis of a holistic perspective. Therefore, it is very difficult in practice to radically change the conditions for how the system functions. One of the reasons for this is that, due to the existing structure, we are forced to limit the 'problem' under investigation. Many phenomena interact in the functioning system. Thus a limited problem area will often not be large enough. The fact that an investigation has to study a limited part of a complex system results in the investigator not being given the opportunity to examine and evaluate the goals of the system. I find it important therefore for the investigator to search for the boundaries of the system. This search may provide information that otherwise might not be regarded as relevant in the analysis of a complex system.

When providing feedback to the involved actors and interested parties, I have observed that insight into the understanding of the complexity and boundaries of the system differ among politicians, civil servants, business owners, etc. The participants have different perceptions of reality. It is very difficult, therefore, for the individuals in a complex system to comprehend the relationship between laws, rules and roles.

It is also important for the investigator to realise that these decisions are often made in an early stage of the decision-making process, a fact that influences the conditions for an analysis of a complex system. A psychological explanation is that decision-makers tend to choose one alternative and seek information that supports that alternative at an early stage. My reflections are consistent with Montgomery's (1989) theory of dominance structures.

Normally, not enough importance, time or resource are devoted to developing an understanding of the problem and an analysis of the relationships in the complex system before 'solutions' (in the form of new aid forms, adaptations of rules, changes in legislation, etc.) are developed. Most often not enough time is allotted for sufficient insight to be gained in regard to the magnitude of the problem.

There are often insufficient resources available for the development of goals for the complex system, and this creates leadership problems in the system. As is apparent in several of the systems, the choice of boundaries influences the clearness of the goals. It seems feasible to hypothesise that, the wider the boundaries are and the greater the number of units that are forced to co-operate, the more difficult it will be for the actors involved to agree on the goals. It is difficult to develop goals and policies from the 'top down'. One of the consequences of this is that unrealistic demands have been placed on politicians to first set goals. Therefore, it is important to observe that those who work with the development of goals and guidelines in a complex system related to business conditions should have certain special personal characteristics.

A relevant observation in this context is that complex systems often lack good leadership. A lack of clarity in regard to what is to be done and how it is to be accomplished relates to, the fact that society has not clarified what kind of leadership is necessary in a complex system. I have concluded therefore that the government organisation with responsibility for a specific system should not have responsibility for the evaluation of the system.

A normative model for analysis of complex system is developed

In the model for the analysis of complex systems related to business conditions, which has been developed, the formulation of the problem is central. As can be seen in Figure 1.2, the examination begins with an overall *problem analysis* in which the investigator sets herself/himself into the problem, interprets and analyses the different conceptions of what constitutes the system and how it functions. The observations will constitute the subject matter in a dialogue about conceptions of reality. After the first *dialogue* has taken place, the investigator reflects on the different descriptions, roles, interactions between laws and rules as well as the manner in which the system functions and what constitutes the system (arrow 1 in the model). These reflections provide material for a number of analyses that are conducted with the purpose of studying the complex system from different perspectives. If possible, studies and investigations should be interdisciplinary. Such studies and analyses, however, do not necessarily have to be thorough in order to provide a holistic picture of the complex system.

The purpose of the next phase of the analysis, the *cross analysis* is primarily to provide the investigator with a view of the system' s boundaries. In this phase the investigator interprets analyses and reflects upon the cross analyses that have been made. The cross analysis and the conclusions that the investigator has drawn in the problem analysis are provided as feedback to the actors and interested parties, and constitute the source of material for a second dialogue on alternative solutions to the problem.

In the next phase of the analysis, the investigator interprets and analyses the opinions and reactions of those involved which were expressed in the second dialogue that took place on the cross analysis (arrow 2 in the model).

I tend to stress the importance of including reflection in the process of investigation. In the model I have incorporated this by marking the phase of the process that should be used in the process for *reflection*. I emphasise that it is appropriate for only a few of the interested parties to participate in this third dialogue phase.

The work with cross analysis is a process that involves interaction between the different phases in the investigation. For example, the reflections may give rise to a need for the investigator to review the different perceptions that the involved persons have (arrow 3 in the model). In conjunction with the third problem solving dialogue it may also be of interest for the investigator to go back to the square cross analysis with the aim of penetrating the complex system's characteristics and boundaries. It may also be appropriate to conduct a new problem analysis(and a second turn in the model).

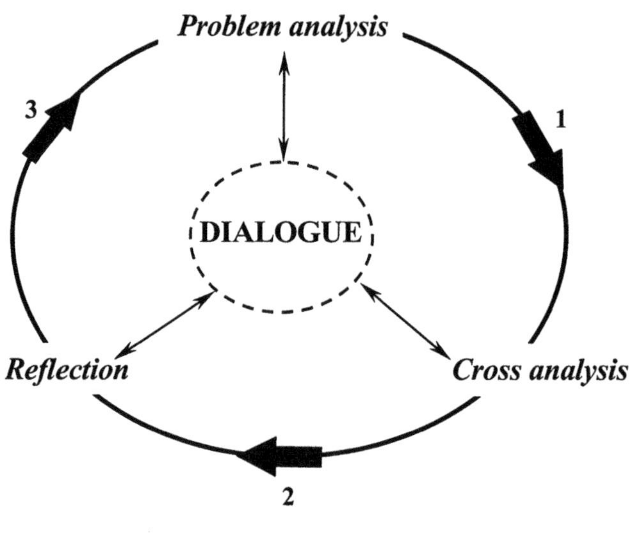

Figure 1.2 A normative model for analysis of complex systems

In an attempt to develop new working methods for public investigation, I have suggested that it is possible to divide the process into steps. Essentially *the first step* deals with the collection of information and knowledge as well as providing the investigator with the opportunity to set herself/himself into the views that interested parties have regarding the problem under consideration. In this first step the interested parties should be given the opportunity to reflect upon and comment on the information from the interview material, in the cross analysis and in reflection phase. This will create the conditions for the first step of the process and concentrate primarily upon viewing the problem from different perspectives in light of this knowledge. In a *second step* an aspect of negotiation may enter the process, if consensus is to be reached in regard to the definition of the problem and suggestions for solutions. In this step a dialogue with the parties involved and representatives of the organisations takes place. Different interpretations of reality, in-depth studies, alternative solutions, etc. are discussed; the purpose of which is to keep the decision-making process 'neutral'.

It is important that the investigator in the initial phase does not think in terms of solutions, but rather concentrates primarily on the task of clarifying the complex problem. If the investigator and the interested parties who participate in initial phase of the investigation are open enough to present their different interpretations of reality based on different perspectives, then they create conditions for reaching a consensus in regard to the problem.

Should a new code be established, knowledge from research and the exchange of experience provide us with the basis for the work that politicians do in regard to writing and composing the directives that guide the problem-solving process. The research will also emphasise the importance of creating incentives to stimulate organisations to actively participate in reflecting on the descriptions of 'reality' that have been elucidated both in the investigator's dialogue with the interested parties as well as those who conduct the cross analysis.

According to the normative model for the analysis of complex systems, the first step in the analysis ought to be aimed at knowledge in order that the dialogue receives a central position in the model. This position gives the investigator the opportunity to have a dialogue with the interested parties during different phases of the process. The construction of the normative model allows the investigator to have a clearly defined leadership role.

The fact that dialogue is placed in the centre of the model provides the conditions for different people to participate in the dialogue during different phases of the process. In the initial problem analysis phase, a large number of representatives of the interested parties, such as business owners, banks, etc., can participate via seminars, etc. In conjunction with the execution of the cross analysis (analysis of research results, new research, etc.), a limited number of representatives of the interested parties can be gathered in reference groups, for example, to work with analysis. In the phase that deals with reflection, it would be appropriate that a more limited group, such as a group composed of experts in the interest group, participate in the analysis.

Reflections

One aspect that I have reflected upon is power in the investigative process. In my model for the analysis of complex systems I have pointed out that it is important for an investigator to have sufficient influence on the process of investigation, in order to facilitate a dialogue from a holistic perspective with the actors involved and with the other interested parties. I have observed that in the initial phase of an investigation it is possible for the investigator to have greater potential to acquire information in regard to 'reality' than it is in subsequent stages of the investigation. In the initial phase, those who are to be interviewed are more open and have greater interest in making their standpoint clear. Information is more difficult to acquire in the later stages of the investigation, when interested parties expect information about the analyses and the conclusions the investigator has made.

The norms and practice that guide how an investigation should be conducted and formed by the 'investigative system', provide a form of power over the process, which is a type of 'organisation culture'. This limits, the possibilities to conduct an unconditional dialogue with the actors and interested parties.

In the normative model for the analysis of complex systems two levels of feed back are specified. The *first level* is the stage in which feedback promotes a well-defined picture of the problem and the conditions to develop a specific system related to business condition. The *second level* influences the possibilities to reach an understanding of the reflections the investigator has made and influences the causes of the problems that occur with the analysis.

The normative approach I have developed in my studies of complex systems relating to business conditions constitutes a *third level* of feedback, in the hope that this will illuminate a central social problem and facilitate change in the way planning is organised.

RISK ASSESSMENT AND CREDIT MANAGEMENT

2.1 Introduction

by Mervyn K Lewis, FASSA
National Australia Bank Professor, University of South Australia

Some years ago the derivatives group Refco advertised its financial risk management services under the slogan 'Risk is everywhere'. There is, of course, an important truth here. The phenomenon of risk is pervasive in economic life as it is in life in general. Just as we learn to deal with the risks of crossing a road or driving a car (Graham 1988), we need to cope with risk in business life.

Risk refers to the possibility that events may turn out differently from those which are expected and risk is, for the most part, unavoidable. Nevertheless, the consequences of risk can be avoided, if appropriate action is taken. In this respect, risk exposure can be distinguished from the risk itself; exposure to the consequences of risk can be managed even if the risk cannot. Taking out standard fire insurance or accident insurance for these risks of damage are obvious examples. Loan workout arrangements or the use of credit insurance, credit derivatives, and credit risk hedging are examples in the context of credit management.

Coping with risk incorporates two main elements: risk analysis and risk management. One involves characterising and measuring risk exposures, the other involves developing systematic responses to them. Risk analysis specifies the relevant attributes and exposures, and measures and estimates the likely outcomes associated with the attributes, so facilitating choices between the various outcomes. Risk management develops a strategy to ensure that the risk exposures are consistent with the objectives of the enterprise, with unwanted exposures removed or offset (Lewis and Morton, 1996).

For example, in the case of an insurance company, risk analysis (or risk assessment) requires estimates to be made of the distribution of payouts (or losses) both for each type of policy and for a portfolio (or pool) of policies. Risk management endeavours to reduce the payouts (or loss ratio) and also the variance of the payouts. Essentially the same 'insurance' type principles operate for credit risk (Lewis, 1990). Sometimes, a further distinction is made between risk management and risk control (Gumerlock, 1996). Risk management may be left to the operating division concerned. Risk control is responsible for ensuring that the risk position which then results is consistent with the limits and authority delegated to the operating centre.

This chapter brings together a selection of papers and summaries of papers analysing the assessment and the management of credit risk. A number of factors have combined to increase the importance of credit management, for both financial and non-financial enterprises. One factor has been the structural increase in bankruptcies and insolvencies. Declining values of real assets (property and real estate) and thus collateral have in many cases accentuated this trend. Conditions in most loan markets remain strongly competitive, and margins have remained under pressure. Disintermediation, trade credit, and 'cherry picking' by non-traditional lenders in the markets for mortgage loans, automobile lending, personal finance, leasing and other areas have probably lowered the average quality of bank loans. Derivative instruments such as futures, forwards, options and swaps and trading activities in securities markets highlight the need for an integrated approach to risk management.

Firms are responding to these challenges in a variety of ways, and the seminar brought together evaluations by academics and practitioners on how well the enterprises are doing this and how they should proceed in the future. In all, there were 30 presentations at the Seminar dealing with these issues, approaching the topics from four different perspectives. One group of papers selected by Barry Howcroft focused on bank management of credit risk. Another group chaired by Nicholas Wilson examined trade credit and credit management in business enterprises. A third group under John Skår considered the risks of venture capital. Because of the mixture of debt and equity usually incorporated into financing packages, and thus the need for financiers to either participate in, or closely monitor, the venture projects, special risks are involved. These risks are examined in chapter 4, and two of the papers of this third group and included there. Finally, the fourth group of papers, chaired by Claes Hägg and Mervyn Lewis, analysed issues from the viewpoint of real estate and property markets.

It is perhaps worth emphasising from the outset that, despite the diversity of the papers presented in the four groupings, there was strong agreement on two points. The first was a recognition that risks need to be made more visible and thus more manageable. Systems and models must be designed to facilitate better management by identifying and quantifying risk. Examples are credit scoring systems, rating systems, early warning systems, risk concentration measures, and risk pricing models. A variety of techniques such as neural networks, logit models and decision trees were explored. The second recommendation and area of agreement concerned the need to reorganise and restructure the credit process in order both to increase efficiency and reduce costs. To this end, decision making may need to be changed and emphasis placed on procedures, which introduce uniformity into decisions and allow risks to be assessed and monitored centrally. Various decision-making criteria, expert systems and management control systems can assist, but the greatest requirement is to develop an integrated credit risk management process, in which all areas of the credit risk function are consistent with each other and the organisation's goals.

Turning now to be four individual areas studied, we may note that risk management has always been central to the operation of banks dating back to their origins as moneychangers and goldsmiths (de Roover, 1954). Funds accepted in exchange or lodged for safekeeping had to be protected from theft and embezzlement. Of course, banks must still devote considerable resources to security matters, but the risks have also changed. When banks evolved into financial intermediaries and began transforming funds on deposit or in float into finance for borrowers, they were exposed to credit risk on their loans and investments – the risk that borrowers may be tardy in repaying funds or may go into default. Management of this risk is still fundamental to banking. Nowadays, as well, it is fashionable to view banks as risk managers and providers of risk management services (Sandford, 1994). This role is the result of a risk transfer process which operates in financial markets whereby financial risks are routinely transferred to banks and other specialist risk managers. Banks accommodate to customers' demands for assets, liabilities and derivatives that establish different maturities, different currencies and different degrees of interest rate flexibility, thereby taking upon themselves the management of those risks. In some cases, the risk transfer process results in banks acquiring a balance sheet position; in other instances, banks acquire off-the-balance-sheet exposures from derivatives. Either way, this has become a major growth area for banks and other financial institutions, and banks must manage the inherent credit risks, market risks and operational risks.

The first workshop of the Seminar was devoted to the design of systems and organisational models to facilitate risk analysis in banking, and demonstrated how academics and practitioners need to work in close co-operation in resolving some of the challenges currently facing banking. Three of the papers in this section reflect this interaction. A paper presented by Katarina Svensson Kling focuses upon credit intelligence system, i.e. the organisational support and monitoring systems for credit managers. A second paper presented by Lars Silver, examined the decentralised loan organisation model used in Swedish banks for analysing small and medium sized enterprises, and a summary is provided here. The third presentation is a keynote speech by Mr Per Lundberg, Head of Risk Control and Credits, Skandinaviska Enskilda Banken, focuses upon implementing quantitative models assessing capital at risk in a traditional banking environment. The paper reflects the important advances in recent years in terms of the measurement and assessment of risk using 'value at risk' methodology.

Trade credit is widely used in business and, in fact, constitutes the largest single source of short-term financing for enterprises in market economies. A feature of trade credit is that it arises as a consequence of ordinary business transactions between firms, but in comparison with payment of goods on cash terms, use of trade credit separates the payment date from the date of delivery and often means that the buyer forgoes a discount for early payment. Since the implicit interest charge is frequently much higher than funds obtained elsewhere, one must ask why trade credit is preferred to substitutes such as bank financing and factoring, and why sellers are willing to offer trade credit and manage the associated collection costs and credit risks. Extension of trade credit must therefore be examined in a broader context of payment behaviour and inter-firm relationships. The same is true when considering the analysis and management of the risks. These issues were explored in keynote speeches given by David Kresge of Dun and Bradstreet and Katarina Svensson Kling of Lund University, and in the paper by Barbara Summers and Nicholas Wilson, presented in the second workshop of the Seminar.

Experience suggests that economic conditions and macroeconomic cycles exert a significant influence on credits risks. Property markets in particular are very sensitive to the economic cycle and changing financial conditions. The use of property as collateral for borrowing provides a direct link between property risk and credit management. Lending by banks to finance enterprises engaged in property development provides another link. In the most recent property cycle, of the late 1980s and early 1990s, commercial property values fell by as much as 50% in some countries, eroding the value of real assets and the collateral base for loans forcing many borrowers (and lenders) into difficulties. The general lesson is that risks cannot be considered in isolation and that those managing credit risks have a direct incentive to familiarise themselves with the vagaries of the property market. This interrelationship, and the nature of property cycles, forms the basis of the keynote speech given by Mervyn Lewis.

The potential for commercial property to create special risks for those borrowing against it or financing or investing in property has its origins in a number of peculiarities of the property market. Whereas the prices of shares can be measured and the changes in prices compared through time, this is more difficult to do in the case of property, because of the uniqueness of each property site. Valuation of property is an arcane art, yet with banks adopting various rules of thumb for lending such as loan-to-valuation ratios of 70-80%, the value placed on real estate clearly matters. This is the topic of the paper by Erik Persson, Hans Lind, Stellan Lundström and Mats Ekelid given in the fourth workshop of the Seminar. Another feature of property is that those involved in the property market are dealing not so much in the physical land and buildings but the legal rights associated with them, and the nature of those legal rights seems likely to influence the decision. The length of the lease, rent review provisions, rent adjustment or indexation formulae, obligation to make repairs, expenditure on maintenance, usage of space, zoning restrictions, and the right to assign the lease are factors additional to the type of property itself affecting values. Wayne Marano and Mervyn Lewis summarise how the lease agreement governs the risk sharing division between landlord and tenant, and thus the nature of the risks to those providing credit.

One other feature of the link between property and credit deserves to be noted. Lending on commercial property was so central to banking difficulties in the early 1990s (and the same sorry saga has been repeated in the Asian financial crisis of the late 1990s), that one must ask why banks moved so strongly into commercial property lending in so many countries. Various standard economic explanations such as loose monetary policy, deregulation and the competition for market shares have been cited as contributory factors (Schinasi and Hargraves, 1993), but these seem insufficient (Lewis, 1994). Once again the 'herd instinct' seems to have taken hold amongst bankers, and the forces driving such collective behaviour may be susceptible to psychological, as well as economic, analysis – a point that was argued in Chapter 1. Such an observation suggests the value of approaching credit management and risk problems from an interdisciplinary perspective.

2.2 Risk measurement and management – implementing quantitative models assessing capital at risk in a traditional banking environment

by Mr Per Lundberg
Risk Control Manager, Skandinaviska Enskilda Banken

All financial institutions are involved in developing and improving existing procedures regarding risk management and risk control. The ambitions may differ somewhat between banks, often related to the actual business situation and chosen strategy, but the importance of understanding risk (the backbone of all banking activities) and utilising this knowledge from a risk – reward point of view, is indeed obvious. Regulators all over the globe are closely following and involving themselves in this development.

The work within institutions normally addresses a broad scope of activities; from practical procedures, e.g. independence of risk control and segregation of duties between front office and back office, to implementations of sophisticated mathematical and statistically based models for assessing risk. The combination of these very different procedures into an overall framework including financial and strategic planning and control, should give us a better overall understanding of business opportunities and provide a basis for good risk policies throughout the organisation, from the Board downwards. This is paramount in developing long term values for our shareholders.

I would like to share with you some rather practical issues in the implementation of a new approach to risk measurement and management in a traditional banking environment. The Bank to which I am referring is Skandinaviska Enskilda Banken, whose history goes back to 1856. Both investment and commercial banking activities are included in the scope of activities. The Bank seeks to be the leading international bank for corporations and institutions in Sweden, Finland, Norway and Denmark. We have a strongly expressed ambition to fulfil our traditional support to these clients internationally. High competence within the private individual market is also a cornerstone. At the end of the financial year 1996 total assets of the Bank amounted to 100 billion USD. Notional value of derivatives was around 530 billion USD, where the sum of positive values amounts to 1.5% of the notional value and is in balance with the negative ones. Total number of employees is around 10.000. Market capitalisation value at the year-end 1996 was close to 5 bn USD.

The Bank began a systematic program to improve risk measurement and risk management throughout the whole organisation in 1994. Although the Bank, as all banks in Sweden (and many other countries), had been hit by the severe financial crisis of 1991/92, this fact was not the main reason for the new programme. The start up was dictated by a future oriented vision to safeguard the competitiveness of the Bank. This is not a new way of doing business. It is to provide the Bank with better tools to *understand, quantify* and *handle* risk. Not in the first instance to avoid losses but to improve all the Bank's key players' ability to structure deals in an improved way to decrease capital requirement and to increase risk/reward for the banking group.

At a very early stage we decided to try to handle the total balance sheet, on and off, and thereby the overall capital structure of the Bank. In other words, our methodology would capture total market risk, total counterparty risk and to some extent also operational risk, from a capital at risk perspective. Our ambitions were, however, somewhat lower regarding operational risk. From the start we planned to address operations risk once the overall methodology was in place, since the assessment of providing risk capital for operations risk is highly subjective. We utilised some external consultancy assistance to begin with but we were very determined to involve the Bank's 'own organisation' in the process from a very early stage. This meant also that the programme function was kept very small.

The following key factors were considered to be of major importance to be able to fulfil our ambitions:

- Strong support from top management and the Board of Directors.
- Involve the key business and support units from an early stage.
- Find pragmatic ways in building models. Do not build a Ferrari if a Saab or Volvo could be OK.
- Establish a common database for risk control and financial control. If base systems do not have relevant risk information, which is quite common, find practical solutions.
- Find reliable market reference data, which are stable and consistent over time.
- Be prepared to make organisational changes and to change rules regarding policy matters based upon a more risk oriented view of the Bank's different activities.

- Be aware of the importance of consistent education throughout the organisation.

- Keep an open attitude towards regulators. Inform them about models used and experiences. There should be a common understanding between banks and regulators to allow the utilisation of own (proved, documented, tested) models instead of standardised methodology.

- Lastly, let us not forget that sound judgement and common sense can never be replaced by computers.

I would now like to present an overview of our models. Models, which are used to measure and analyse the overall, risk level in the Bank Group with quantitative methods. We are interested to divide our activities into four different dimensions, a *product*, a *client*, an *organisational* and a *geographical* dimension. Actual risk levels in the various parts of the organisation are the basis for attribution of capital and will also assist in pricing calculations and structuring of deals, as a reference in pricing negotiations.

Before commenting on capital allocation *ex ante* and *ex post*, I would like to go through some parts of our models and how they are working. Let me start with the *credit risk.* Two models are being used. One is for calculating risk capital required for individual transactions (for counterparty) and the other for measurement of the risk capital usage for the whole Bank and for selected business units. The two models are based on what we call a *C-E-C* concept (Counterparty-Exposure- and Collection).

All corporations in our total portfolio are risk classified reflecting each counterpart's probability of default. We are talking of around 30.000 corporations. From research and educational point of view it has been a major task to create training throughout the organisation, meaning client executives and the independent members of the credit organisation. S-E-Banker's risk grading scale consists of 11 different risk classes ranging from 1 to 11 with four sub classes. Risk class 11 is stated as default within 24 months. The basis for the risk classes is Standard & Pool's 20-graded riskclass scale calibrated into ours. No risk class has a zero probability of default. Our riskgrading judgement is both quantitative and qualitative. The tools are two risk grading handbooks, one for corporates and one for banks. These are also the basis for education. Guidelines consist of financial analysis, comparisons to external risk grading, handling of companies belonging to the same group (depending on guarantees, risk transfers into better risk grades could be arranged) size and type of ownership. For banks, the standing of the financial system, and the different banks' importance in the system etc are considered. Most important are sets of verbal definitions guiding the analysts to conclusions on different degree of qualities. Experience has of course increased since the new system was launched during 1995. It is quite obvious that quality in risk - grading has improved.

Regarding small corporations, with credit exposures below 150 thousand USD, we have more standardised analysis methods, based on the rating from a domestic rating institute with our own 'add ons' related to actual knowledge of each company, to improve quality. A fairly basic portfolio view is used on private individuals and credit card customers.

The final rating decision of a corporation is taken by an appropriate credit committee after a recommendation from the client executive.

On the *Exposure* side, which is the second step in evaluating the counterparty risk, we are using our global administrative limit system in which we address the possible exposure towards a client including unutilised and committed lines in a from a risk point of view worst case scenario. For the time being we are in a process to improve our systems considerably to be able to more carefully follow actual exposures' real time, not only with financial institutions but also corporations. I am talking of gross as well as netted positions. I am also talking of how to find statistical patterns over time in exposures to different counterparts, time series that could be useful in tracing abnormal movements to prompt and incite timely reactions.

The last C stands for *Collection*, which is an estimation of present market value in a winding down of a bankruptcy situation. The analysis is concentrated on an evaluation of the effectiveness in financial covenants, actual guarantees, actual collateral etc. Our insights into the banking crisis have given us some experience in the often too optimistic *ex ante* views of collection values. We have hopefully now a fairly conservative attitude in our estimates.

In the described C-E-C concept, credit risk is defined as the volatility of the average expected credit loss and expresses the need for risk capital to be hold. Average expected credit loss should be considered as a budgeted cost that reduces the expected result and does not express risk, because a risk is something unexpected. The capital at risk to cover the unexpected loss is the *maximum* amount that the Bank stands to loose within a given confidence interval. We have chosen this probability level to be 97,5% of the cases, which corresponds to a 95% (two-sided) confidence level. The probability distribution of the value is *not* normal for credit risk. Because of this uncertainty concerning the distribution the Bank uses a worst case solution, the so called Tchebyshev's theorem, and the confidence interval used corresponds to around six standard deviations, which probably overestimates the credit risk.

The counterpart risk includes a valuation of credit risk in different kinds of derivative products, calculated as a loan equivalent factor. This is the close out value of transaction plus a factor for price volatility in these instruments, which together could be the credit loss if not settled in accordance with the underlying contracts.

From a theoretical aspect it is also of interest to discuss portfolio or diversification effects in a credit portfolio. We are taking into consideration these effects on a group level from an industry-, geographical- and size- (risk concentration) point of view. The question is how independently should we treat our different branch offices. Should they have an individual responsibility for the structure of their respective portfolio and thereby only get the effect from the diversification caused within such a portfolio? Or should they have the advantage of getting the overall group effect from the total credit portfolio, meaning that they will have the advantage of belonging to a large organisation? In the first case, local variations would influence the required capital at risk and ultimately the pricing and structuring of an individual deal. The branch office would be considered to be a kind of stand-alone bank in itself. The offered price to a client of a certain transaction would probably be very different if the branch office is in Gothenburg or in Stockholm. We have chosen to base the diversification effects on the *total credit portfolio of the group*, which means larger consistency in the treatment of clients. From a strategic point of view we are considering the branch offices as parts of a sales network and any local initiative to diversify the credit portfolio will have only an indirect influence on the total. On the market risk side, we have a totally opposite attitude.

Let me now address the *market risk*, where we have two models for quantification, one *tactical* and one *strategic*. The tactical model calculates the maximum capital that can be lost within a certain level of probability or confidence factor, value at risk, using a one-day holding period. The strategic market model shows the Bank's market risk level within a time horizon of one year and is being run once a month. Both models presently use JP Morgan's *RiskMetrics* time series services, pending our own development of comprehensive historical data.

The daily market risk model is executed on three organisational levels, nine trading centres, ten locations, over 15 different products and 18 currencies. It also covers equity indices, bond and swap yield curves (17 in all). To get net present values we are using 12 different time buckets. In total this leads to 485 different indices and close to 120.000 correlations. There is also a freedom to use variable time horizons and variable confidence intervals.

The implementation of value at risk models in a trading-oriented environment is normally very well received by the personnel. The traditional use of notional limits, delta 1% measurement, stop loss rules etc could in a productive way be combined with value at risk models in describing the risk situation. Within our value at risk procedures we are using a fairly simple variance/covariance model that attempts to quantify, within a specified confidence interval (or probability level) the maximum potential loss for a given trading position, a portfolio, trading units or the whole bank. This is the status presently. The next step would be to introduce on a limited scale, stochastic simulation models, such as the Monte Carlo simulation.

I mentioned earlier that in contrast to credit risk measurement we are in assessing market risks treating diversification effects to specific portfolios, individual group traders' etc. Within given risk limits for such an entity it is important to follow what could be achieved from a risk reward point of view for the small entity without influences of risk concentrations or diversification from other entities. Full portfolio effects will of course be dealt with on group level. This means that the purely accumulated values of capital at risk of different entities will be higher than the overall group requirement after reductions for diversification. The handling of this fact complicates the combination of financial control and risk control. But it is manageable.

During this year we have started a group wide project on improved treatment of operational risk. In the overall assessment of capital at risk the operational risk is 'manually' taken into consideration. We are using a wide definition:

The risk that environmental factors, operational problems, inadequate information systems, breaches in internal controls, fraud, legal problems, reputation problems or unforeseen catastrophes will result in unexpected losses for the Bank.

In the use of quantitative methods in assessing risk, there is one area for the *overall banking society* of paramount importance, and that relates to means of risk reduction in payments, clearance and settlement systems. The attention devoted to this area has for good reasons increased dramatically during recent years. It is certainly coupled with the increased complexity in interconnections in financial transactions and to the ongoing globalisation of financial markets. A failure in one system has the potential to cause considerable damage to financial markets. There is an overall need to gain better understanding of risk associated with payments, clearance and settlement or systemic risk as it is frequently described.

Due to the increase in international trade, deregulation of financial markets, the development of new financial instruments and new technology in a more general sense, global foreign exchange trading exceeds 1 trillion USD on a daily basis. Stock and bond markets together with markets for financial futures, options and swaps, create additional trading volumes in the range of 10-20 trillion US$ on a yearly basis.

In today's interconnected markets the critical systems for payments, clearance and settlements are only as strong as their weakest links. There is a need to strengthen the private sectors control through risk monitoring and risk management systems. An increased co-operation between financial institutions within countries and between countries will be necessary as co-operation with and between regulators.

"The group of 10" has taken the initiative in its "Orange book" issued in March 1996 to require private sector efforts to bring about a substantial and permanent reduction in foreign exchange settlement risk in the two years following the issuing of the book. Skandinaviska Enskilda Banken is now conducting an internal project to better handle these types of risk, which constitute to some extent a part of risk capital needed to carry on our business.

I mentioned earlier the importance of openness with regulators in the development of own models. First of all, the BIS risk based capital guidelines do not distinguish high quality and well diversified portfolios from the low quality and concentrated portfolios which have proved to be essential in risk management. We have been keen to share our views with our regulators to demonstrate the advantages and the potential disadvantages in using our own models in assessing risk. Therefore, we participated in the "Basle test" on market risk models in 1995 and had a follow-up in 1996 in co-operation with the International Institute of Finance. The result showed great differences between the traditional and market risk model's calculation of risk capital, and our impression is that the value at risk approach more effectively estimated the market risk. We hope that the BIS has drawn a similar conclusion. However, new guidelines from the BIS have not yet arrived. It would also be valuable if the EU would take advantage of the experience that the BIS has gained and promote capital requirement based upon 'real risk'.

Let me so end with a short discussion on other conclusions/actions taken within the Bank as a consequence from our work in risk measurement and risk management. During 1995 the role of the S-E-Banken was strengthened. Under the chairmanship of the chief executive officer a more strategic orientation has been implemented to handle business opportunities, risk aspects, allocation of capital etc. A specific new group staff, Group Risk Control, has been established provide a second opinion to the Groups Asset and Liability Committee on different kind of business and risk proposals from the Treasury and other business functions of the Bank. The Group Risk Control has also an overall Group responsibility on the development of methodology and models as well as a group wide functional responsibility for risk control. During 1996 we have integrated credit organisation into the Group Risk Control unit. This is a quite natural step as all kinds of risks should be understood and treated in a comprehensive way.

Next step on the agenda is to implement an overall management of the Bank based upon return on capital at risk. A couple of pilot studies are currently running to decide when and how (in a very detailed way) the total risk and financial management of the Bank according to our actual capital at risk should get started. In my book this is of great importance to obtain the ability to use consistent measurement, *ex ante* and *ex post*, on different levels – product, client, business unit and geographic unit – of the Bank. This is also the basis from which to create improved shareholder value.

I have in my overview tried to explain pragmatically ways of improving risk measurement and risk management by using a combination of different means, especially the implementation of quantitative models. Once again I would like to underline some of the key factors for success. These are:

Board and top management support; education; a pragmatic view finding risk data and methods as well as market reference data; necessary organisational changes; an open attitude toward regulators; and lastly, sound judgement and common sense.

2.3 The decentralised loan organisation

by M.Sc. Lars Silver
Uppsala University

In designing the loan organisation banks will have to take into account a number of potential problems arising from unpredictability in the lending process. The loan organisation must be able to protect the bank from potential losses, while not discouraging individual bank managers from taking risks. There is an inherent contradiction in banking practices. On one hand banks have to accept credit risks if they are to survive; on the other hand, banks may very well find themselves in danger by taking these risks. The lending process is characterised by a number of rules, procedures and policies. To an outside observer it seems improbable that all the rigorous systems created by the banks would fail at all, and yet the banking crisis in Sweden, as well as elsewhere, make it all too apparent that they occasionally do. In the extension of credits to firms, the rules, procedures and policies by themselves will not be a guarantee of safe lending.

The Swedish Model

Consider the Swedish banks loan organisations for corporate lending to Small and Medium Enterprises (SME's), and the currently dominating decentralised organisational model used for handling these credit risks. The focal relationship is that between the branch manager and the regional management, as this is where most of the difficulties within the loan organisation arises in this model. The fundamental question under review is whether the decentralised model has been superior due to successfully implemented control mechanisms, or whether a decentralised organisation is better equipped to make valid credit risk assessments. In order to analyse the impact of control mechanisms on lending behaviour the communication between regional management and branch manager was investigated, using a sample of 45 qualitative interviews with primarily branch managers in Svenska Handelsbanken, Nordbanken, Föreningsbanken, Skandinaviska Enskilda Banken, Sparbanken and Gotabanken. Thirty of these interviews followed a structured questionnaire focusing on communication within the loan organisation.

The decentralised loan organisation model is without doubt appreciated by the branch managers, since it gives them considerable autonomy in an otherwise heavily regulated and centralised industry. As most branch managers deal mainly with corporate customers, and have a considerable influence over the lending decisions, it is fair to assume that the branch manager requires a thorough knowledge about credit risk assessment. Unfortunately time is a scarce resource, and the danger of compromising the credit risk assessment procedures is constantly present. Generally the branch managers have great confidence in their own ability accurately to assess corporate customers' capabilities and willingness to repay any outstanding debts. They are also aware of the unforgiving environment surrounding them, and if anything goes wrong they will inevitably have to face the consequences. Out of 30 interviewed branch managers, nearly 50% (14) had predecessors who were forced to leave their positions due to bad loans. In such an environment it is obviously important for the individual branch managers to realise just what their organisation demands from them while the targets set by regional management are clear, there is just no indication given as to how they can be achieved.

The regional management for their part have a difficult task to accomplish. They have to convince the branch managers that it is possible to achieve greater profitability without compromising the standards required to maintain low credit losses. At the same time they need, along with central headquarters, to be able to balance the demands from stockholders to increase the profitability of the bank, the demands from society to provide risk capital, and the requirement not to repeat the bad practices reverted by the banking crisis. They have to ensure the public that they possess a safe system prohibiting extensive losses, though it is obvious that no such system exists. The contradiction situation is accentuated at the regional meetings where the regional management will have to perform a delicate balancing act. Basically, regional management focuses heavily on the C/I-ratio, while at the same time discouraging the branch managers from excessive lending. The C/I-ratio (Cost divided by Income) is a rather simplistic method of measuring performance. In order for a branch manager to improve the all-important C/I-ratio it is necessary to reduce costs by dismissals, which is a complicated and tedious task. The alternative is to extend more credits, which of course may increase the overall risk profile of the branch.

Conclusions

The conclusion seems to be that the formal systems of rules, procedures and policies apparently have a relatively minor influence on decisions reached in lending to SME's. Informal communication probably has a greater influence, but it is not a control system in itself. In arguing that the banks have implemented better policies in order to prevent a repeat of the banking crisis, the leadership in the banks appear more concerned with keeping state authorities at a distance than anything else. The decentralised loan organisation seems to be as decentralised as the name implies.

Almost every Swedish bank would today claim that they have a decentralised loan organisation. In the Swedish banking industry one bank in particular, Svenska Handelsbanken, has argued that it is more decentralised than the others.

The founder of Handelsbankens decentralised strategy, Jan Wallander, and his successor, the current CEO Arne Mårtensson, both strongly supports the old saying that "a banker should never extend credits beyond an area that can clearly be seen from the top of the church tower". Furthermore, it is said that the decentralised structure is the major reason why Handelsbanken emerged as something of a winner from the banking crisis, albeit having itself sustained heavy losses. It is further argued that most of the losses incurred during the banking crisis were due to loans processed through regional management, thereby implying the benefits of a decentralised system which shifts the decision-making process towards the branch level. The advantages of a decentralised loan organisation include reducing the workload for regional management and while achieving higher competence throughout the organisation. The disadvantages are mainly connected to the maintenance of a high and consistent standard in credit risk assessments.

Is the decentralised model more capable of assessing credit risks than a centralised model? It can be argued that decentralisation certainly has a positive effect in those areas where local informants can be used to further strengthen the assessment process. In metropolitan areas, however, the positive effects of decentralisation are probably wasted. Therefore it seems reasonable to argue that a bank's loan organisation in metropolitan areas should be divided into sections working toward specific industries, where the positive effects of joining the organisations may be regained. It appears as if the division of a metropolitan area into geographically oriented districts is relatively pointless, at least to the extent that it would facilitate lending toward SME's. In rural areas it is evidently still important to maintain a presence in the local marketplace. The market share of banks lacking branches in rural communities is virtually non-existent. Vital information may be retrieved locally, therefore the decentralised organisation may prove to be beneficial in rural communities. At the same time the close proximity to customers may in some cases prohibit bankers from fair assessments. Perhaps a slightly altered approach in the organisation of lending in rural communities could revitalise a rather dormant willingness to extend credits in these markets.

2.4 A credit intelligence approach to service design in banks

by Katarina Svensson Kling
Doctoral Student, Lund University

The numerous bank crises that have swept over large parts of the world have been explained by, for example, a lack of training, shortcomings in routines and procedures, and the pursuit of market share after deregulation. One explanation that seems to have been neglected is a failure of what can be called 'credit intelligence', that is, the organisational decision support and monitoring systems for credit management in banks.

In the ongoing search for competitive advantages in credit services, banks have traditionally opted for the customisation/differentiation strategy of frequent contacts with their corporate customers and being able to closely follow their activities. A bank official's knowledge and experience as well as the customer's participation and sharing of information have been of vital importance to successful lending. However, due to increasing price competition (e.g., Howcroft, 1988), the resources for managing each of the many loan accounts have had to be decreased (e.g., Riding & Summers, 1995), resulting in a more low cost/standardisation strategy for the credit services, especially towards the small companies.

While standardisation has reduced operating costs, it has also reduced the contact with and knowledge that the banks have on their corporate customers. Normally, the customers' willingness to pay a premium price determines whether customisation/differentiation is a worthwhile strategy or not. Following this logic, service standardisation makes sense given that customers are not likely to want to pay extra for giving more information to the banks.

However, to the extent that customer knowledge gained from service customisation can reduce credit losses (which in times of crises typically exceed the operating cost reduction gained through standardisation) credit service customisation can create substantial value for the banks even if it is not able to command a premium price. Consequently, customer interaction has a credit intelligence function. The bank's perceived value of customer knowledge to satisfy the internal needs of controlling the risk and having a good readiness for action in case of the customer getting problems in repaying the credit is an equally important issue in determining the strategy. The intelligence side of credit services therefore needs to be taken into account when designing the credit service.

Traditionally, the service design literature has mainly had a customer satisfaction/marketing orientation. This perspective seems to have been adopted by the banks where the discussion of cost reduction has been characterised by issues such as how to render a more cost-effective division of labour between the production of financial services and their distribution (OECD, 1992), the customer's participation or decoupling in the production and distribution of service (Larsson & Bowen, 1989) and about routinisation and automation (Eriksson, 1991; 1994). The focus of the discussion has mainly been on the marketing and organisation of credit services, without considering the resulting effects on credit intelligence. However, the intelligence side gives a new dimension in the production and delivery of credit services in that a large part of the cost for credit services derives from customer losses that better information might have prevented.

The purpose of this paper is to develop a conceptual framework for credit intelligence connected to service design, through a study of how banks work with credit intelligence. The paper begins with a framework for understanding credit intelligence as an integrated activity in the process of performing a credit service. This theoretical framework is further developed in an empirical study of some of the major European banks. Different identified patterns of credit intelligence are presented and discussed related to different credit situations as perceived by the interviewees.

The double-sided coin of credit service management

Credit is a major type of financial service and a service perspective on credit is relevant for understanding this particular business relationship. Customer contact within service creation is a crucial factor. At the same time, it is costly, uncertain and the single largest constraining factor for an improved service production efficiency. The input (person or good) is not owned, nor controlled by the organisation, which creates an increasing uncertainty (Argote, 1982), and operational disturbances (Chase, 1978) in service organisations as compared with the possibility of 'isolating the technical core' (Thompson, 1967) in the management of manufacturing and marketing of goods.

Much attention has been given in the service literature about how service operation management can be rendered more effective (Chase, 1981). This has resulted in a move from a differentiation/customisation approach to a production approach (low cost/standardisation) to services (Levitt, 1976), reducing the customer contact as far as possible and moving the production from front-to back-office. Maister & Lovelock (1982) have suggested a matrix with one axis representing the organisation's degree of customer contact (Chase and Tansik, 1983) and the other the amount of customisation. Focusing on a limited range of output means moving away from customisation and high client contact towards a more labour-intense 'service-factory' environment (Schemenner, 1986), where large parts can be isolated and run like a manufacturing plant.

Many service firms have adopted a production approach and view themselves from a manufacturing perspective, applying manufacturing efficiency models on their services. The negative consequences have been a perception of less quality in the service creation through a decreasing market orientation and an increasingly bureaucratic orientation (Schneider, 1980). Banks, as well as other organisations, have been criticised for bad service or no service at all.

Consequently, a major issue in the service literature has been how to integrate and manage the tension between operations and marketing. The operation function creates and assembles the service product – focusing on costs (e.g., Sasser, Olsen & Wyckoff, 1978). Marketing is concerned with identifying the true needs and trends within the marketplace, satisfying them (at the customers convenience) and developing a strategy for targeting specific market segments – focusing on the customer satisfaction. From a *marketing perspective* the customer's willingness to pay a premium price determines whether a customised service design is a worthwhile strategy or not.

However, credit is a special kind of service. A credit means that you borrow something which should be returned in a better condition than it was in the first place, which, in this particular case, means together with interest (Jungerhem, 1992). Furthermore, the sale and production of credit services differ from more traditional forms of service. In credit granting, the customer cannot be sure of being accepted (the credit application could be rejected). It is generally the seller, that is, the bank, which has the power to decide if there is going to be a deal or not. The credit assessment is aimed at assessing the trustworthiness of the borrower, that is, the intention and the ability of the borrower to repay the credit according to the credit agreement. Since a credit is extended over time trustworthiness must be continually evaluated. Interaction between the bank official and the credit customer is crucial for the bank to receive up-to-date information about the customer (Svensson & Ulvenblad, 1994; 1995). From a *credit intelligence perspective* the value of the customer's knowledge determines whether a customised service design is a worthwhile strategy or not.

Consequently, there are at least two sides to managing credit services – marketing and intelligence. In credit service design these two sides are integrated and the competitive advantage of the bank created. This feature is illustrated in Figure 2.1.

Figure 2.1 shows the two basic ways for an organisation to create a competitive advantage (differentiation or low cost) as well as the matching service designs (customisation or standardisation). From the marketing side the choice for the bank organisation between these two competitive advantages/strategies and service designs depends on if the customers will to pay a premium price for special service is high (differentiation/customisation) or low (low cost/standardisation).

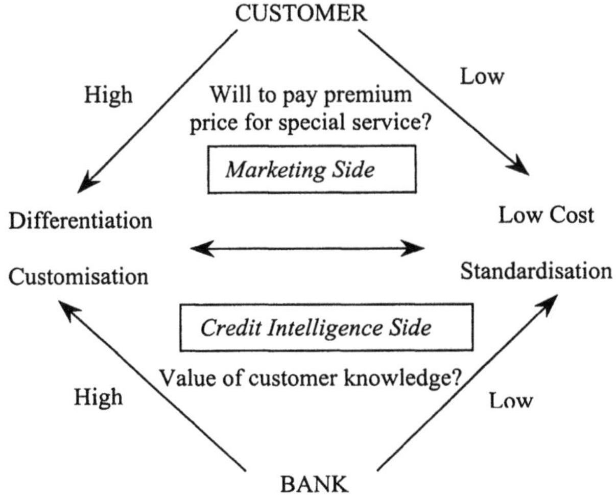

Figure 2.1 The double-sided coin of credit service management

However, information collection is only part. The processing and organisation of information into something that makes sense and that can be used in decision making is another aspect. The term 'intelligence' is used to capture this process. In its broadest sense intelligence means a system's *ability* to adapt itself to or master environmental changes (e.g., Porter, 1980; Quinn, 1992), and is the means, that is, *process, activity and organisation* of transforming signals into actionable decisions (e.g., Herring, 1996; Wilensky, 1964). Intelligence is also used for the results of the process – *the knowledge, insight, sense, meaning,* etc., that is used for decision making (e.g., Baumard, 1992; Gilad, 1994). Consequently, intelligence can be simultaneously seen as a product, a monitoring process, an activity or a type of knowledge, but is not synonymous with data or information.

The purpose of intelligence in credit management – credit intelligence – could be formulated as the ability to correctly select and monitor credit customers, that is, without credit losses and without rejections of customers that would be able to fulfil the obligations of a credit agreement. This usually includes at least the following; to evaluate new customers, to anticipate changes among and monitor existing customers and to provide early warning for threats or opportunities. Depending on the characteristics of the corporate credit customer (e.g., the risk involved) the need and value of customer input varies.

When integrating the two sides of credit service management – the marketing and intelligence sides, it might turn out that the bank's need and perceived value of customer knowledge matches the customer needs and willingness to pay a premium price in terms of customisation or standardisation. For example, when both are high the bank might decide that the customer should have a personal bank official that could attend to the specific needs of the company as well as exploit the opportunity to gain customer knowledge for the bank. Similarly, when both are low the bank might chose to let the customer get the same package of services that is given to the other customers without any specific adjustment to that customer and without any extraordinary attempt to gain customer knowledge. In these situations both the bank and the customer ought to be satisfied.

However, it might be the case that the two sides do not match. While the choice for the bank might be simple when the customer is willing to pay a premium price (customisation), it does not mean that the bank should merely choose to standardise when the customer is not willing to pay. The bank needs to consider the value of the customer knowledge. For example, when the customer is willing to pay for a personal bank official that attends to their specific needs the bank might chose to do so even if they do not perceive the value of customer knowledge from a credit intelligence perspective to be high. The most difficult situation is when the customer is not willing to pay for a customised attention and the bank perceives the value of customer knowledge as high (which could be the case for a rapidly expanding small company who is neither willing to nor able to pay a premium price). In these situations it becomes a trade-off for the banks between costs of customisation versus the benefit of customer knowledge. The dilemma is illustrated in Figure 2.2.

Figure 2.2 integrates the two sides of credit service management, that is, the marketing side (where the customers' will to pay a premium price determine the strategy of the bank organisation) and the credit intelligence side (where the value of customer knowledge determines the strategy of the bank organisation). When these match (see main diagonal) the choice is simple, but when they don't there is a dilemma for the bank. From a credit intelligence perspective this is especially the case when the value of customer knowledge is high (would be suitable with a customised approach) but when the customer is not willing to pay a premium price (which calls for a standardised approach).

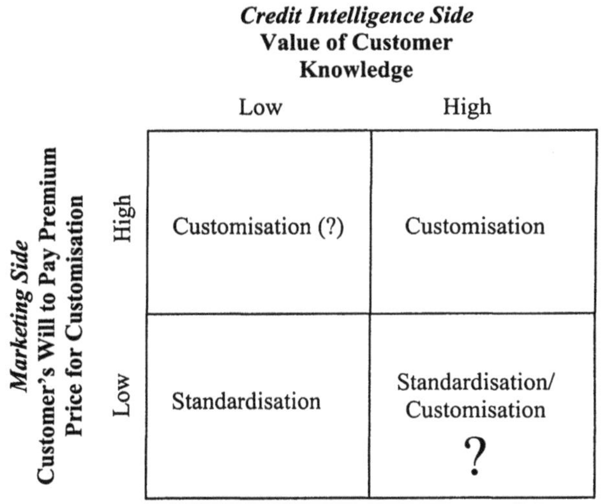

Figure 2.2 Integration of the marketing and credit intelligence sides of credit services

Consequently, an interesting question is how to determine the value of the customer knowledge and thereby decide in what situations the bank may standardise the credit service respectively when the benefits of customisation for the bank is higher than the operating costs and therefore is preferable.

Method

This paper is part of an ongoing research project aiming at generating a better understanding of the credit intelligence process in banks. Three rounds of data collection have been conducted during 1991 to 1996. The first round of data collection (1991) focused on the individual account manager's credit information management. Interviews with 55 account managers in the (at the time) seven largest banks in Sweden concerning their credit assessments were conducted. The second round of data collection built on the results from the first round and focused on the importance of the interaction between the account manager and the small firm to get relevant information in time. In-depth studies were conducted in two Swedish commercial banks where the interaction between one bank official in each bank and their corporate credit customers and others in their network was studied during one year (1993/1994). While the first two rounds of data collection had mainly been aimed at the individual account manager and his/her information management, the third round of data collection (1995/1996) focused on the overall organisational design of and its impact on credit management. Interviews were conducted with 31 senior bank officials in 15 major European universal banks in England, France, Germany, Holland and Italy concerning their credit intelligence and designs of credit services. In total, 86 bank officials in 22 banks in six European countries have been interviewed. In addition, the banks have also made available internal documents, annual reports, policies, risk rating documentation, education materials, etc. The banks offer a range of different financial services to many customer segments (and in different countries) and provide different forms of credit to companies of varying sizes and missions.

Results

When the banks were asked about how their credit intelligence systems were structured, their answers reflected different starting points. Some started from the organisational solution, that is, the allocation of work and decision making. Others started from how they had segmented their customers in terms of classifications of risk, profitability, etc. Yet others started from an explanation of their computerised solutions.

Nevertheless, there was a common base about credit intelligence. The bankers' reasoning centred on how information should be collected, how analysis should be performed and the situations in which various forms of information collection and analysis were appropriate. Some of the bank officials' reasoning regarding customer characteristics, intelligence requirements and credit intelligence system are selected as illustrations in Table 2.1. The citations in one row come from the same bank official's reasoning.

The citations should be read from left to right, where customer characteristics pose intelligence requirements that are solved with a credit intelligence system. The texts in *Italics* highlight the interpreted core messages. These are late summarised in Figure 2.3.

In the case of credit information collection, a distinction was made depending on whether the bank was required to update the information often or seldom (see first and second rows of citations in Table 2.1). The need for collecting information often or seldom was linked to how quickly a company changed versus its stability. Implicit in the bankers' answers was that when a company was changeable it could become bankrupt more quickly. Stable companies did not present such surprises and so did not need the same degree of attention.

Table 2.1. Six illustrative citations from the interviews

Customer Characteristics	Intelligence Requirements	Credit Intelligence System
High customer change: "...so much is happening in a company, especially if the company is small and active when it expands..."	***Often information collection:*** "...therefore, it is important that the communication is constantly ongoing so that the bank and the account manager understand what is going on..."	***Interactive Customer-specific or Back-office Support:*** "...you have to have a good relationship with the customer..."
Low customer change: "...if there are no surprises... the firm develops as planned... follows the budget..."	***Seldom information collection:*** "...I don't spend much time on him..."	***Specialist Support or Automated:*** "...we just collect the annual report once a year...no contact..."
High customer complexity: "...different industry sectors..."	***Specialised analysis:*** "...requires different competencies..."	***Interactive Customer-specific or Specialist Support:*** "...we have industry-specialist for our most important industries..."
Low customer complexity: "...the standard customer...we have many of them..."	***Generalised analysis:*** "...we do a basic credit assessment..."	***Back-office Support or Automated:*** "...we can handle most of them with our computerised system...but for more difficult customers you have to go deeper..."
High perceived risk: "...if there is a problem...the company appears on our signals list..."	***Often information collection and specialised analysis:*** "...takes a lot of the account managers time...follows the customer very closely...goes into details"	***Interactive Customer-specific:*** "...we have a work-out group for problems...but the account manager is still responsible..."
Low perceived risk: "smaller amounts...up to $65000..."	***Seldom information collection and Generalised analysis:*** "this kind of customer normally receives income each day so there are many transactions...the main focus of the scoring-system is the turnover...you can receive 1/5 of your turnover...if the turnover goes down or there is a problem we close the account and shut down the credit..."	***Automated:*** "we only use the phone and we have no offices...no cross-selling and no advise..."

Credit analysis was discussed in terms of whether it required specialist knowledge (e.g. industry knowledge or special knowledge about the corporate customer concerned) or whether it could be more generalised (see third and fourth rows of citations in Table 2.1). The need for specialised or generalised analysis was related to whether the customer was perceived as complex or simple. Often the question about complexity involved the number of customers in an area and hence the level of competence within the bank in the category of customers concerned. Complexity was further related to company size, credit volume and industry.

Except for complexity and change a third concept was used by the bank officials in classifying the credit customers', namely the perceived risk (see fifth and sixth rows of citations in Table 2.1). The perceived risk of a customer was expressed in terms of a function of volume and risk. Volume refers to the amount of credit outstanding to a company, while risk refers both to the *risk of* a company going into bankruptcy and the *risk in* a bankruptcy, that is, how protected the bank is by collateral. Also, the perceived risk was linked to whether a company was seen as complex or simple (large or small volume) and whether the company was classified as changeable or stable (small versus high risk of and in bankruptcy). The reason for linking the volume to the company's complexity seems to be connected with the fact that as a company becomes larger and more complicated, more complex financial solutions and larger amounts are required. A high-risk classification is often related to change that is already underway. The logic behind a negative change (e.g. reduced profitability, loss of an important customer) is perhaps easier to link to the risk of bankruptcy than a positive change. However, apparently positive changes (e.g. rapid expansion) have in some cases been shown to result in acute liquidity crises, and bankruptcy in the worst case, because the company is not prepared (e.g. in terms of staff, liquidity).

According to the interviews, the different characteristics of the customer/situation, that is, the complexity, change and perceived risk was said to pose certain requirements on their credit intelligence, that is, their collection and analysis of credit information about the customer. In the citations presented in Table 2.1 the characteristics of the customer/situation and the intelligence requirements are logically connected to and seem to having been used as a basis for how the banks have designed their credit services. Integrating the collection and analysis gives us four basic types credit intelligence systems; interactive and customer specific, specialist support, automated and back-office support. These systems are presented in the matrix in Figure 2.3 within the framework of the matching customer characteristics.

Figure 2.3 consists of two pair-wise matched dimensions. The first dimension – the credit customer characteristics and its situation – is illustrated in the outer framework (customer change, customer complexity and perceived risk). These characteristics pose intelligence requirements (on information collection and analysis) which are the second dimension. Customer change (and perceived risk) is matched with credit information collection and customer complexity (and perceived risk) is matched with the credit analysis. The resulting credit intelligence systems in the boxes are described below.

Interactive customer-specific: Close contact with the customer was necessary when the analysis required specific knowledge and when information collection had to be carried out often. It was then possible both to keep up to date on what was happening and to know about the customer so well that problems were spotted early. In these situations the account manager could not have too many customers.

Specialist support: When the analysis had to be specialised but information did not need to be collected often or be very detailed, the account manager could make use of support from industry specialists or risk specialists (analysis of financial data) who kept up to date on developments in the surrounding world or the company itself. Well-defined warning signals were needed to indicate when it was necessary to make contact with the customer and collect more (detailed) information.

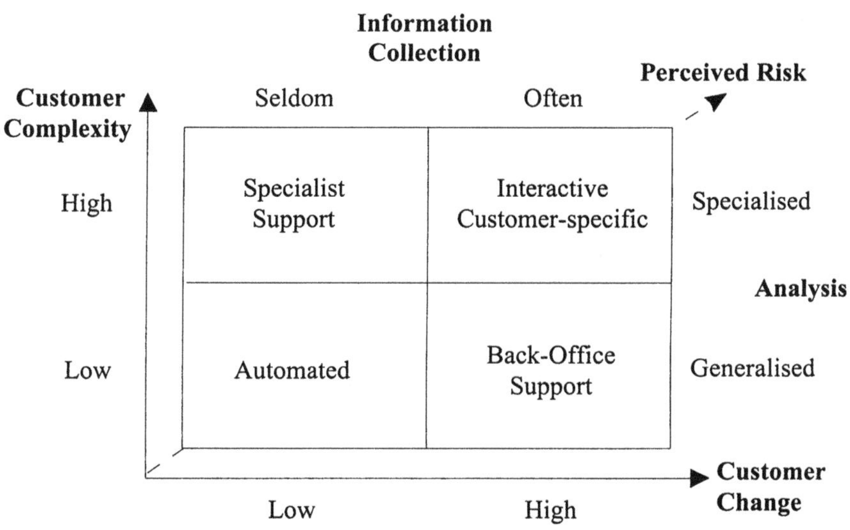

Figure 2.3 Credit intelligence requirements and systems

Automated: The management of the customer could be automated when the analysis did not need to be specialised, and when information collection did not need to be frequent/detailed. This often meant no contact generally. In the most extreme type of automated credit management the company was scored on material submitted, and followed-up via certain variables at specified intervals.

Back-office support: When the analysis could be simple and generalised, but when frequent follow-up of the customer was needed, support from the bank's back office could be appropriate. It often required less competence, and computer support could be used extensively. Then the account managers could delegate some contact with customers to their assistants rather than handling it all personally.

These results show that for highly complex and changing customers the value of customer knowledge is high. This is illustrated by the interactive customer specific intelligence system (high complexity and change). From an intelligence perspective these companies need a customised service design. The results also show the opposite, i.e., that for less complex and changing companies the value of customer knowledge is low. This is illustrated by the automated intelligence system. From an intelligence perspective these customers could be managed within a standardised service design. However, for companies that are either complex or changing but not both, illustrated by the specialist support and back-office support intelligence systems, there is some value of customer knowledge. From an intelligence perspective these companies need a semi-standardised/customised service design.

Conclusions

From a marketing perspective credit services tend not to be suitable for a customised service design since customers in general do not want to pay a premium price for giving more information to the bank. Nevertheless, from a credit intelligence perspective, the value of customisation might be high for the bank. The problem lies in determining when the value of customisation is higher for the bank than the operating costs (including credit losses).

The results from this study point to certain situations when the banks from an intelligence perspective found customer knowledge and thereby a customised approach to be of specific value. These situations where related to customer characteristics such as high complexity and change, and were considered to require a specialised analysis and a frequent information collection. These results indicate a promising way to segment customers based on what intelligence requirements they pose and for the bank to decide in what situations the value of customer knowledge is high.

The interviewees, however, indicated that the intelligence requirements were not always used as a basis to decide the intelligence system and service design, especially for small companies. A suggestion for future research is to focus on in what situations and why misfits/mismatches occur between intelligence requirements and intelligence system due to a specific credit service design.

Acknowledgement

The author wants to thank Rikard Larsson, Lund University and Mervyn Lewis, University of South Australia for helpful comments on this paper.

2.5 Knowledge-based decision systems for the management of small business risks

by David T Kresge
Director, Dun & Bradstreet, USA

Risk Management has never been an easy task but it can be particularly challenging when the portfolio of accounts being managed consists primarily of credit extensions to small businesses. Typically, there is limited information available concerning such firms and often, in addition to being small, the firms are very young as well and lack any established track record. In addition, the fortunes of the smaller firms are prone to change dramatically, with little advance warning.

Despite the difficulty in assessing the risks in small firms, market forces put on unrelenting pressure to deliver 'faster, better, cheaper' decisions. For small loans, with correspondingly small profit margins, there is an especially critical need to establish a decision process that controls risks effectively but at a cost that is low enough to still provide a reasonable return.

While the challenges confronting risk managers have undoubtedly intensified, the tools available to meet those challenges have also seen great improvement. Through modern information networks, a vast range of information is now available at very low cost. Advances in information technology make it feasible to compile, audit, and integrate quantities of information that were unthinkable just a few years ago. The advances in information technology also make it feasible to apply sophisticated analytical techniques to convert large quantities of raw data into reliable, actionable knowledge. This paper describes how the power of information technology can be utilised to build effective decision systems for the management of small business risks.

Availability of information

One of the keys to the successful implementation of a knowledge-based decision system is to incorporate and make effective use of the widest possible range of information. The data should be gathered from all available sources and it should be as wide-ranging and cover as many dimensions of the firms' operations as possible. Experience clearly demonstrates that good credit decisions cannot be based on just a small number of factors.

Financial statements
Historically, credit decisions have often relied heavily, if not solely, on the information obtained from the firms' financial statements. The types of financial data that are most commonly useful in making credit decisions are those that provide a good summary measure of some critical aspect of the firms' financial status. A sound estimate of the firms' net worth, for example, can be a valuable piece of information. Other types of financial data that have typically been used in credit decisions include items such as current assets, accounts receivable, working capital and profits.

When available, these same financial data elements should be evaluated for possible inclusion in credit scoring models. When dealing with small businesses, however, the financial data is notoriously unreliable and frequently is not available at all. Fortunately, as will be shown below, it is usually possible to build effective credit scoring models even when the financial data is not available.

Credit history
Some of the types of information that have proven to have the most predictive power come from the previously observed credit behaviour of the applicant. If, for example, a firm is not paying its bills on time, that is often an early indication of impending financial problems. Items drawn from the credit history of the firm that have proven useful in developing credit scoring models include such things as payment promptness, previous delinquency, previous history of bankruptcy, and suits/liens/judgements.

Business demographic information
Data elements pertaining to the business demographics or operating characteristics of the firm invariably play an important role in constructing credit-scoring models. These elements include such things as line of business, number of employees, sales, age of business, management history, location, and growth trends.

Information Warehousing

The various risk factors interact in complex ways to determine the overall level of risk associated with any particular firm. Analytical tools like credit-scoring models have to be employed because they are capable of pulling together and evaluating the implications of the full range of financial, credit, and demographic information. However, before the credit scoring models can be developed or applied, the information itself needs to be brought together and made available for use in the decision systems.

With data flowing in from an enormous variety of sources the challenge is not in simply obtaining the data but in converting the raw data into valid, useful information. As illustrated in Figure 2.4, the key to this process is data integration.

To begin, the compiled business information discussed in the previous section (financial statements, credit history and business demographic information) will play a central role in any effective risk management decision system. This data may be gathered directly or it may come from a variety of outside sources such as third party data the telephone yellow pages, court filings, or government agencies.

Another extremely valuable source of information is provided by the *internal customer files maintained by the company making the credit decisions.* When dealing with small businesses, it is frequently useful to supplement the various sources of business information with *information pertaining to the owners or principals of the firms.*

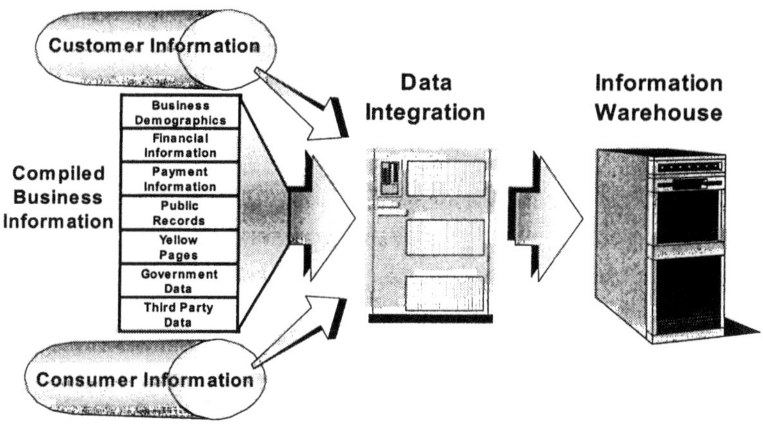

Figure 2.4 Information warehousing: Data compilation and integration

The data integration process is the key to extracting useful information from this vast body of raw data. The first step in the process is to tie each piece of data, no matter which source it comes from, to a uniquely identified business establishment. This unique identifier can then be used to pull together all of the individual data elements pertaining to any single establishment.

The next step is to audit and cleanse the data coming into the system. Invariably, some of the data will be invalid and will need to be purged. Very often the data from one source will prove to be inconsistent with the data from other sources. When this occurs, rules will have to be imposed either to combine the data or to specify which data source takes precedence over the other sources. Another function of the data integration process is to provide family tree linkage so that all of the operating units or subsidiaries of a given company can be tied together. At the conclusion of the process, the audited, cleansed, and linked data is fed into an information warehouse. Needless to say, the information in this warehouse needs to be refreshed on a regular basis since the timeliness of the information is as important as its accuracy.

Credit scoring

Once the information warehouse is built, the challenge for the risk manager is to use the information efficiently to make quick, accurate, and cost-effective credit decisions. Some type of formal analytical technique, such as credit scoring, will have to be applied to select, process, and evaluate the information. There are a variety of advanced analytical techniques (logistic regression, neural networks, etc.) that can be used to derive and validate the models. In general, the choice of technique is not critical to the success of the decision system. Each technique has certain strengths and weaknesses and, if properly applied, each can be expected to produce satisfactory results.

Commercial credit score
After a scoring model is derived, and it may actually consist of a family of related models, it is tested against an independent set of data. The test has two purposes: first, to validate the model's soundness, and second, to measure the performance that can be expected from the model when it is used to make the actual credit decision.

The results of validation testing on one particular type of credit score are reported in Figure 2.5. This test was performed on a model that was designed to predict severe delinquency and that utilised only the compiled business information. The test consisted of scoring a set of credit applications at a specified point in time and then tracking the accounts over the subsequent twelve months to see which accounts performed satisfactorily and which turned out 'bad'. In this context, a bad account was defined as one that paid its bills more than 90 days past due.

The bar furthest to the left in Figure 2.5 contains the 10% of the firms that had the worst credit scores. These are the firms that, on the basis of the credit scores at the start of the period, were judged as having the highest risks. Over the next twelve months, fully 28% of those low-scoring firms did in fact become significantly delinquent. In contrast, the 50% of accounts with the best credit scores (the five bars to the right in the figure) had delinquency rates of only about 2-3%. Clearly, the test results demonstrate that the credit score is doing a good job of distinguishing high-risk accounts from low risk accounts.

Financial stress score
A different type of credit scoring model is used to predict 'financial stress', where financial stress denotes the likelihood of the firm failing over the next 18 months. Failure is here defined not simply as bankruptcy but as any disconti-

nuance of operations with loss to creditors. All bankruptcies count as failures, but, a firm can also fail by shutting its doors and leaving unpaid bills behind, even though it may never go through formal bankruptcy proceedings.

Figure 2.6 reports the results of validation tests performed on the financial stress models and illustrates a different way of measuring the performance of credit scoring models. In this test, a set of accounts is scored and then rank-ordered along the horizontal axis from worst to best. Thus, the 20 on the horizontal axis represent the 20% of the firms that had the worst scores.

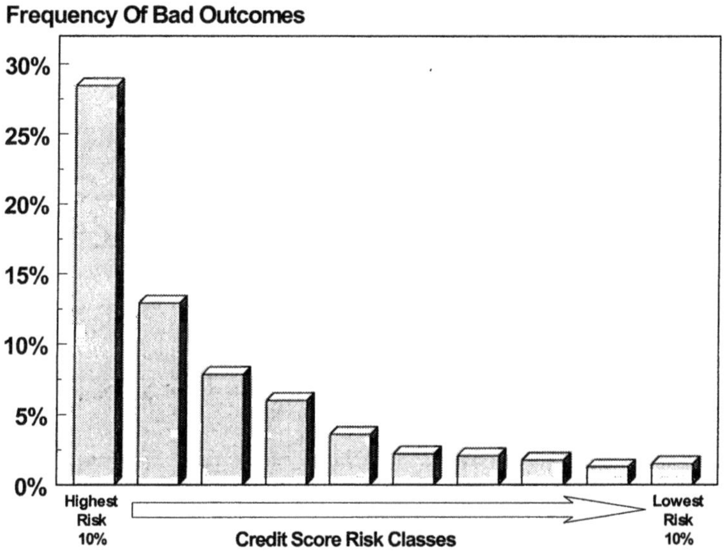

Figure 2.5 Unsatisfactory credit performance occurs much more frequently in the higher risk score classes

As would be expected, some of the firms in the test sample failed over the subsequent 18 months. The vertical height of the curve shown in Figure 2.6 measures the proportion of these failures that are contained within each of the credit score blocks. As shown by the solid line curve, the 10% of the firms with the worst scores contained 58% of the actual failures; and the 20% of the firms with the worst scores contained 74% of the failures.

A second test was run utilising a financial stress model that incorporated no financial data. That is, no data derived from the firms' financial statements was incorporated in the models used to predict the risk of failure. The results of this test are shown in the figure as a dotted line. Using the scores produced by that model, the 20% of the firms with the worst scores contained 67% of the actual failures.

There are two important observations to be made concerning these test results. First, the model utilising financial data does perform better than the model without that data. This confirms the fact that the availability of financial data does indeed improve our ability to predict the risk of failure. The second, and equally important, point is that even when no financial data are available, it is possible to construct scoring models that very effectively predict the risk of failure. The performance of the model that used no financial data is still quite acceptable.

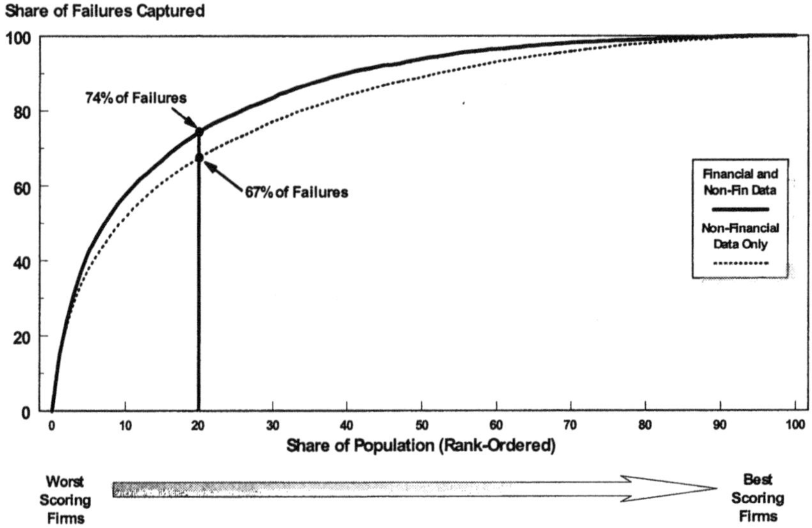

Figure 2.6 Financial information adds to power of scoring but non-financial data alone is also highly predictive

Blended commercial/consumer scores

It is often difficult to make sound credit decisions on small businesses because there is so little commercial information available on such firms. One way of dealing with this problem is to supplement the commercial information with information obtained from consumer credit bureaus pertaining to the principals of the firms. The credit history of the principal of the firm provides valuable information that can be used to predict the likely credit behaviour of the firm itself. By using a combination of commercial and consumer data, it is possible to design highly efficient credit decision systems for dealing with small businesses. Since consumer credit information is available on virtually every adult in the U.S., the system offers the important added advantage of providing 100% resolution; that is, the system will be able to deliver a valid score on close to 100% of the applications that are submitted.

Figure 2.7 presents the results of tests run on three different types of scoring models. The first set of scores comes from a blended model (shown by the dotted line) that uses all available information from both commercial and consumer sources. The second consumer data model (shown by the dotted and broken line) uses consumer data only and the third model (shown by the solid line curve) uses commercial data only. To test the applicability of these scores for small businesses, the sample of accounts used in the test was taken exclusively from *firms with five or fewer employees*. The first two models (blended and consumer data) were designed specifically to be applied to smaller firms. In contrast, the commercial score is a generic credit score designed to be used with firms of all sizes.

The test results are presented in the figure in the form of 'trade-off curves' show the combinations of delinquency rates and approval rates that are attainable using each of the three different credit scores. It is always possible to lower the delinquency rate by rejecting a larger proportion of the high-risk applications, and thus reducing the approval rate. The trade-off curve shows the best attainable combination of delinquency rates and approval rates. A score that provides superior performance will produce a higher trade-off curve.

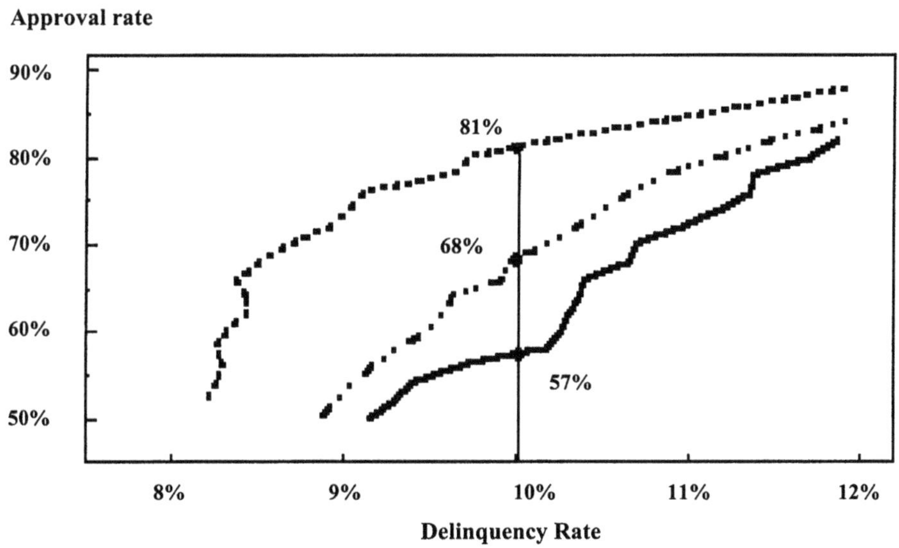

Figure 2.7 For smaller firms, blended scores produce substantial gains in performance (firms with five or fewer employees)

As shown in Figure 2.7, if it is acceptable and profitable to operate with a 10% delinquency rate, then the *blended score* makes it feasible to attain an approval rate of 81%. If higher delinquency rates are tolerable, the approval rate can be moved higher. If it is necessary to achieve lower delinquency rates, then the approval rate will have to be lower than 81%. When commercial data are unavailable and the score has to be based on consumer data only, the predictive performance is reduced and the attainable trade-off is lowered, dropping to the middle of the three curves shown in Figure 2.7. At a delinquency rate of 10% the maximum approval rate that can be achieved with this score is 68%. If the generic score based on commercial data only is utilised, the available trade-offs are reduced still further, dropping to the lowest of the three curves shown in the figure and the approval rate that can be achieved with this score is 57%. The primary reason for this relatively low performance is that the commercial score is designed to work with all size firms. It has not been optimised to deal specifically with small businesses.

A very different picture emerges when you look at firms with more than five employees. For these firms, it is the commercial score that delivers the best performance and the highest trade-off curve. If the commercial score is used to make credit decisions at a delinquency rate of 10%, the approval rate can be pushed up to 89%. With these larger firms, the blended score produces somewhat lower performance with a corresponding approval rate of 84%. Not surprisingly, the scorecard utilising consumer data only produces significantly lower performance with a corresponding approval rate of just 68%.

Knowledge-based decision systems

The specific details of a system designed to support credit decision-making will differ widely depending on the type of decision, data processing capabilities, organisational structure, management preferences, and a wide variety of other factors. Despite differences in operational details, it will generally be true that the most effective systems – the systems giving the greatest competitive advantage – will be those that draw on the widest range of information and utilise the most powerful analytical tools. Such systems are particularly critical in the process of extending credit to small businesses, where it is essential to make the decisions quickly, accurately, and at low cost.

Application Processing
A decision system designed to deal with new loan applications is outlined in Figure 2.8. Once the loan application comes in, the first step is to go to the information warehouse to gather every available piece of information pertaining to the loan applicant. That information is fed into the credit-scoring module which provides an objective, quantitative assessment of the risk associated with that particular application.

However, no matter how precise are the credit scoring models, they do not make decisions – they simply provide an assessment of risk. Business judgement now has to be applied to arrive at a decision. This judgement is expressed in the form of decision rules that specify which actions are to be taken on the basis of the nature of the loan application and the degree of risk associated with it.

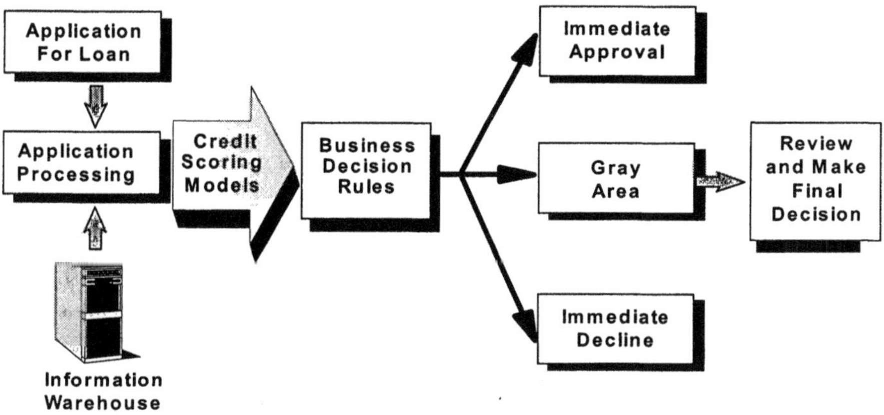

Figure 2.8 Decisions system for new loan applications

The goal of an efficiently designed system is to take immediate action on most loan applications. A substantial portion of the incoming applications will receive a sound credit score and will be given immediate approval. A second group of applications, and hopefully a much smaller share, will be evaluated as being too risky and will immediately be declined. The goal of the system is to have most of the applications fall into one of these two categories and thus be handled automatically. A third group of applications fall into a 'gray' area, where an immediate decision is not possible. This may occur because the information available is not conclusive; the amount of credit being requested is too large; or some sort of special circumstances are present. These 'gray' area applications have to be reviewed by trained credit analysts before a final decision can be made. The analyst may require the applicants to submit additional information or may change the terms under which the credit is being extended.

Portfolio Monitoring

A portfolio monitoring system incorporation credit scoring can be utilised to deal with the review and evaluation of an existing portfolio of loans. For all loans in the portfolio, information is drawn out of the information warehouse and credit scores are updated on a regular basis. Management reports are then generated to determine where there have been significant changes in the performance of the portfolio or in the performance of individual loan customers. The reports may, for example, show that there have been significant changes in the degree of risk associated with certain industries or regions or classes of customers. On the basis of these reports, management may choose to modify loan policies to make the appropriate adjustments in the portfolio.

The system also produces watch lists, which identify the individual loan customers that have had a significant change in their own risk characteristics. It may be appropriate to schedule an in-depth review with a loan customer that has experienced a significant deterioration in credit score. Conversely, customers that have shown appreciable improvements in credit scores may represent a marketing opportunity for offering increased credit lines or for cross-selling additional products or services.

Conclusions

Information technology has advanced to the point where it is feasible to build highly effective knowledge-based decision systems to manage risk. With vast amounts of information now available from diverse sources, the systems can deal with even the smallest businesses. In fact, with competition for the small business market intensifying rapidly, the only way to grow efficiently and profitably in that market is to automate the decision process. As has been shown here, the data, the information warehousing techniques, and the analytical tools necessary to manage risk in the small business market do exist and are being used with great success.

2.6 Trade credit in Europe today – Credit cultures, payment morality and legal systems

by Katarina Svensson Kling
Doctoral Student, Lund University

Late payments are becoming an increasingly important problem for companies in Europe. About 40% of their invoices are not paid on the due date, affecting liquidity, interest costs, and profits. Why do companies not adhere to one of the most basic rules in business – to honour contracts? Furthermore, there are significant differences between countries. Why are the contractual credit[1] agreements different? And why are companies in some countries more willing to adhere to contracts than in other countries? These are some of the questions examined in this article.

Culture, ethics and morality
Every person has a certain pattern of thinking, feeling and behaving. One part, human nature, is common to all. A second part, personality, is unique to the specific individual and a third part, *culture*, is a common feature of the group, e.g., family, school, or business community, to which the individual belongs. A culture manifests itself in different practices, symbols, etc., but the core consists of the values held by the individuals in the group. The values tell the group what is good or bad, normal or abnormal, rational or irrational, etc (see, e.g., Hofstede, 1991).

1 In this study a credit refers to a commercial credit used in business to business relationships as opposed to consumer credits.

We are not born with values. In our childhood we are told that there are certain things we ought to and ought not to do, since our acts influence other people. We learn what society expects of us. These deeply rooted values are usually referred to as *ethics*. The ethics function as the principles for our morality, i.e., how we actually behave.

There exist in business, as in life in general, some basic perceptions about how you ought to (and not) behave. For example, you should not deceive your business partner, you should not steal proprietary information, you should honour contracts, etc. These basic principles, that most people would agree to be desirable, could be called *business ethics (*see, e.g., Freeman, 1991; Solomon, 1993).

Business morality sometimes differs from business ethics; we do not always act according to our desirable principles. Morality is what is desired for oneself when confronted with a choice. Therefore, even if there is a basic understanding of what is desirable, e.g., that companies pay their invoices by due date, actual behaviour is different. When making a choice to pay its debt or not, a company may instead decide to use the money for other purposes.

Since there exists a set of principles – business ethics – it is possible to evaluate morality against these principles. The principle that is going to be discussed in this study is: 'you should pay your bills by the agreed due date' and the consequent moral issue, 'the *payment morality*',[2] revolves around to what extent invoices are paid in adherence with agreements. The morality of an individual could be understood as a function of the character of a specific relationship, the context in which a relationship exists and expected benefits and risks of certain behaviour. A relationship is different depending on, for example, frequency, intensity and power distribution. Some would argue that it is less important to act morally toward someone with whom you only meet once and will have no further interaction. The context of a relationship communicates what is considered good and bad. One important instrument for communication is the network of business contacts, which very efficiently may exclude a person or a company from further business. Another instrument is based on the transparency of an economy, e.g., available registrations of late payers. A third instrument is the legal system supporting good and punishing bad behaviour. In this study the design of the *legal process* concerning debt recovery is seen as a communicator of morality.

Many aspects of doing business are not easily classified as good or bad. The terms-of-payment, check-up of customers, different methods of speeding up and

---

2 The author is aware of the difficulties in using the term payment morality (a direct translation from Swedish), since morality in the English language is not easily applied to the problems and in the context as done in this study. Neither is there a similar word that could cover the studied phenomenon. The alternative terms that could be used are of a more neutral character, such as, payment performance or payment behavior. However, the purpose of this study is to add the sense of right and wrong (value system and principles for conduct) used by an individual or a company when confronted with a choice (in this case to pay by due date or not). Thereby, our understanding of the underlying factors affecting payment behavior can be furthered. Due to the lack of alternative terms, the author has decided to keep the term payment morality.

combat late payments are all a part of what could be called the credit culture of a specific business community, which has to be evaluated in relation to the values held in the culture of which a company is part and acts.

The general aim of this paper is to develop an understanding of the relationship between payment morality, credit culture, and the legal system and specifically;

- to describe and compare payment behaviours in different countries in Europe
- to define and measure credit culture and payment morality in a way that makes possible a comparison between countries, and
- to examine if there is an association between payment morality, respectively, credit culture, and a country's legal system.

The paper begins with a brief review of earlier studies of commercial credit. Thereafter the results from a survey of payment behaviour in 16 European countries in 1996/1997 and 18 interviews in a debt collection company during 1995/1996 concerning credit culture and legal structure in five European countries are presented. When referring to Europe in this study it is based on the results of the survey of these 16 countries. Finally the relationships between payment morality respectively, credit culture, and legal structure are analysed and discussed.

Two sides of late payments

When payment of a service or a good is made some time after the sale has taken place, the money due is credited for the intervening period. It is often assumed that a supplier of a commodity must have enough reserve capital to wait for the payment from the buyer. However, since the reserve capital could be used in different ways, there is a decision problem for the creditor if she/he should offer to wait for payment and, for the buyer if she/he should accept to pay in advance, at delivery or after a certain period. Three motives are discussed below based on marketing, transaction cost and financial arguments.

For the creditor, a basic reason for accepting credit is to sell more. If a supplier cannot match the terms of payment of its competitors there is a risk of a decrease in sales. From a *marketing perspective,* credit is one element in the marketing mix. For the buyer, credit cuts *transaction costs* by reducing the occasions for payment and making possible the planning of future payments. Finally, researchers have discussed *financial motives* for the existence of trade credit. The implicit interest of a credit, i.e., the price difference between paying in advance or after delivery and to pay cash at delivery, is used. Ingves (1984), identifies three situations. If the buyer's alternative interest rate is higher than the seller's both parties use credit. If the sellers' alternative interest rate is higher than the buyer's, it is motivated to induce the buyer to pay in advance. When no difference in interest rate exists the parties are indifferent to cash payment or credit.

The financial arguments assume an unlimited access to capital, yet for some access to capital is an important factor for the use of credit. Pettersohn (1976) found those companies' with a good access to long term financing is less dependent on commercial credit than companies depending on short-term financing, low liquidity, and keeping a long-term stock. Smaller companies also use more credit than larger companies.

The issue of overdue payments has been largely neglected. Larsson (1988) argues for the need to examine the total credit period and not only the terms of payment. During the latest decade most companies have learned a new concept – cash management. In broad sense cash management means that you should pay as late as possible and gets paid as soon as possible. The gain of the creditor is the loss of the creditee and vice versa. Numerous publications discuss credit management related to cash management with a focus on different techniques for analysis and day-to-day administration of accounts receivable (see, e.g., Hedman, 1991; Larsson, 1988).

Capital tied up in accounts receivable could be described by the different floats involved as illustrated in Figure 2.9. The reason for these floats being interesting to study is because they are causing estimated interest costs.

In the literature the expression 'hidden credit' is used (Dernroth, 1993, based on, e.g., Larsson, 1988; Neufeld, 1988; Hedman, 1991) for the difference between the contractual (agreed) credit period and the actual period between delivery and due date. The hidden credit period is due to internal factors in a company, such as the co-ordination between the sales and credit management departments (Sweica, 1989; Neufeld, 1988; Larsson, 1972; 1973). These problems are argued to be due to, among others, the historical positioning of the credit management in the administration department and not close to the marketing department and the difference in education with the consequent communication problems (Neufeld, 1988).

The overdue credit period is suggested to be due to both internal, e.g., organisational features, and external factors, such as, the customers' ability and willingness to repay a credit. Hagstad and Ljunggren (1980) argue that overdue payments are due to interest rates on overdue payments, which are too low, bad routines concerning reminders and demand for payment not being sent in time. Dernroth (1993) suggests two ways of affecting the overdue payment period. Either the creditor might enhance the credit assessment of the creditees or increase demand routines.

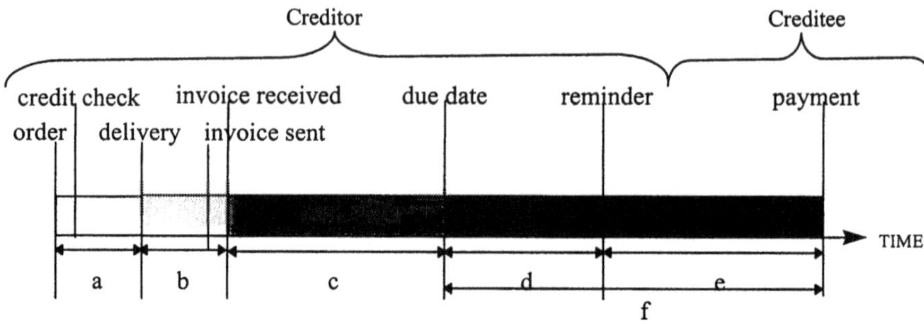

a = time between order and delivery

b = hidden credit period

c = contractual credit period

d = time between due date and reminder

e = time between reminder and payment

f =.overdue payment period

Figure 2.9 Capital tied up in accounts receivable (Dernroth, 1993 based on Larsson, 1988)

Consequently, existing research suggests that various factors affect the existence of commercial credit and the periods for the hidden, contractual and overdue periods of a credit. However, few studies have been conducted on the inter-cultural aspects of commercial credit and while many studies have focused on developing models for the ability to pay few studies have studied the willingness (and related motivational factors) to pay.

An interesting issue is to what extent overdue payment periods are governed by the credit culture, vis-à-vis payment morality and how the legal system affects these two dimensions.

Method

The study presented in this paper is based on a survey conducted in 1996/1997 on payment behaviour and interviews made in a debt collection company, Intrum Justitia (IJ), during 1995/1996.

Survey

The questionnaire used in the survey has been developed in co-operation with the head-office of Intrum Justitia and a market research company based in London. The questionnaire contains questions regarding terms of payment, actual payment periods, causes, consequences and trends of late payment, age analysis of late payments, methods used to speed up payment, desired measures for combat of late payment and attitudes towards the current legal system in the respective countries for collecting debts. All fieldwork was conducted using (Computer Assisted Telephone Interviewing) to ensure the accuracy of data collection.

The sample used for the survey was selected at random from the Dun & Bradstreet European Marketing Database to ensure a representative business sample.

The respondents were selected from different databases available in the respective countries (the countries participating are listed in Figure 2.11). Respondents were the day-to-day managers of credit at each company contacted, and the target response rate was set to 50% in each country (which was reached). The survey consists of 3001 responses (100 to 300 responses in each country). The sample was split evenly into three size bands (<50 Employees (997 respondents), 50-199 Employees (997 respondents) and >200 Employees (1007 respondents).

On average 80% of the companies' sales were made on credit, of which 87% was commercial and 13% consumer credit. 26% of the respondents exported to Europe and 17% exported to other countries outside Europe. The companies had a net margin of on average 14%. The industry sectors included in the survey were the following categories; retail and wholesale, business services, professions, transportation, distribution and logistics, food and drink manufacturing, chemicals, pharmaceuticals, communications, telecommunications, manufacturing, process, construction, utilities, primary industries and other. Banks and financial houses were excluded in the survey.

Interviews
Interviews have been made in five of the European countries participating in the survey; England, France, Germany, the Netherlands and Sweden. The purpose of the interviews was to get a better understanding of the cultural and legal differences between the countries.

The 18 semi-structured interviews have been conducted with individuals in Intrum Justitia, which is one of the largest debt collection companies in Europe. Intrum Justitia, established in 1923, is represented in 14 European countries, with around 1 400 employees and a turnover of over £80 millions. Intrum Justitia handles about 3 million cases a year and have a client base of about 45000 (Intrum Justitia, 1994a; 1995a; 1995b). Each interview lasted from 30 minutes to four hours. The interviews have for additional information been followed up by phone and fax and by the interviewees reading and commenting on the typed interviews and detailed summaries of time and costs constructed for the legal structure in each of the five studied countries.

Comments on the method used
The time and cost tables for legal proceedings constructed for each country involves some uncertainty (condensed versions are presented in this article). First, it is difficult to estimate and simplify time and costs for the legal proceedings since different cases can vary significantly. Second, the estimations are not done based on any internal statistics, but rather on the experience and perception of the experts interviewed. Third, the development of the tables is based on the experience of only a few experts in each country. It would be valuable to test these times and cost tables among more experts. One possibility of validating some of the data is through public statistics. However, public statistics has proven to be difficult or impossible to obtain for the different countries and therefore the author has not been able to obtain the statistics necessary to do this validation.

Payment behavior in Europe

In this section some of the results from the 1996/1997 survey of payment behaviour in Europe are presented. The companies were asked questions about terms of payment and how their customers comply with these. They were also asked about the reasons for and problems related to late payments.

Payment periods for domestic sales
The respondents in the survey give strong support for the seriousness of the problem of late payments. In average, about 40% of the respondents' invoices are not paid on due date. The respondents think that late payments lead to problems with cash flow (62%), loss of profit (56%), company growth (40%) and for company survival (33%). More than one third of the respondents think that the payment habits of their domestic customers have deteriorated during the last year. The responses by the companies regarding total payment, contractual credit and overdue payment periods for domestic sales are presented in Figure 2.10.

The Nordic countries (Norway, Finland, Sweden and Denmark), have the shortest total payment periods for domestic sales (in average 30 days), while the Southern European countries (Spain, Italy, Portugal and Greece) have the longest (in average 86 days). Central Europe (Austria, Germany, Netherlands, Belgium, France and Switzerland), UK and Ireland are in between these two groups (in average 45 days). The average for Europe is 53 days.

The contractual credit periods in the different countries follow the same pattern as the total payment periods. The Nordic countries have the shortest (in average 23 days) and the Southern European countries have the longest contractual credit periods (in average 65 days) while the Central Europe, UK and Ireland are in between (in average 33 days). The average for Europe is 39 days.

The pattern for the regions is not as clear for the overdue payments. For the overdue payments Spain has together with Norway the shortest overdue payment periods (in average 6 days). Portugal has the highest overdue payment period (in average 41 days), which is almost the double of the country that follows namely Italy (in average 22 days). The average for Europe is 14 days.

High versus low payment morality
When discussing payment morality, i.e., to what extent invoices are paid in adherence with agreements we look at the overdue payment periods. However, it is not fair to only look at the absolute number of days, since it is discriminating against the countries with a softer credit culture, i.e., which for example agree on a longer contractual credit period. It is more interesting to look at how the proportions of contractual credit and overdue payment periods differ between countries. If there were no differences between countries regarding payment morality the proportions of contractual credit and overdue payment periods would be similar even though the total payment periods would differ.

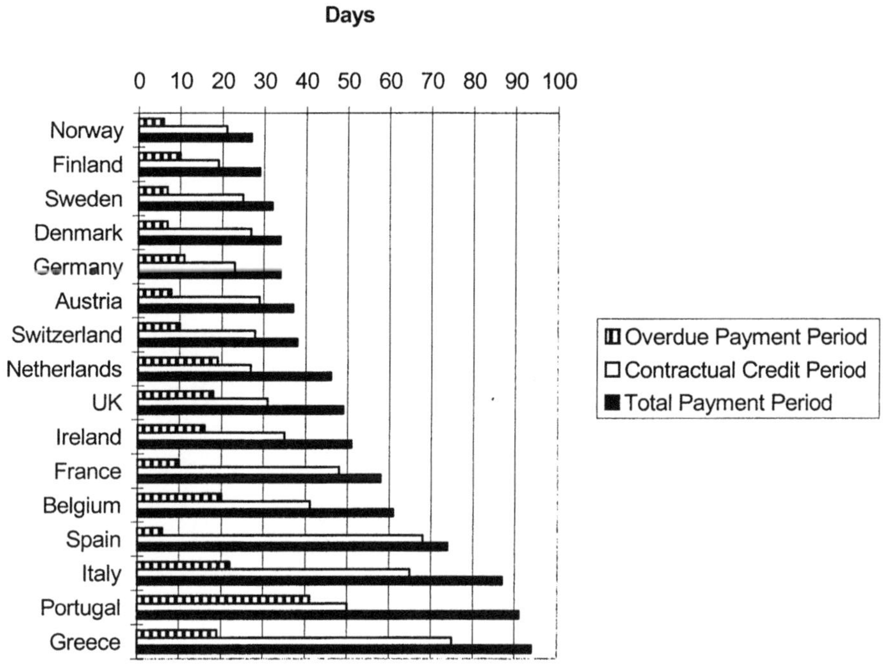

Figure 2.10 Payment periods for domestic sales

Interestingly, while Finland and Germany are among the top five countries regarding short contractual credit periods (19 respectively 23 days) they have at the same time relatively high overdue payment periods (10 respectively 11 days). This is not the case for the other three countries among the top five regarding short contractual credit periods (Norway, 21 days; Sweden, 25 days; and Denmark, 27 days). They have in average only about half as long overdue payment periods (6-7 days). Comparing the countries that have the longest contractual credit periods, Portugal still has the longest overdue payment period (in average 41 days) while Spain has the shortest overdue payment period (in average 6 days). In comparison, the overdue payment periods for Finland, Germany, the UK and the Netherlands make up for 32-41% of the total payment period, but only 8% in Spain and 17-25% in France, Greece and Italy. The irregularities of the proportions of contractual credit and overdue payments imply a difference in payment morality.

One purpose of this report is to allow for the differences in credit culture while still being able to separately study the payment morality. By distinguishing between contractual credit and overdue payment periods for domestic sales a payment behaviour index is calculated as: [total credit period/contractual credit period]. The average of *the ranking of the countries' payment behaviour index* and *their ranking according to percentage of invoices paid on due date* are used as a measurement of payment morality of the respective countries.

Table 2.2 Ranking of the European countries based on payment morality

Country	**Payment Behaviour Index** (Total/Contractual) Ranking	**Paid on Time** Ranking	**Payment Morality** (Average of Rankings)
Spain	1	1	1
Sweden	5	2	3,5
Denmark	4	3	3,5
Norway	7	3	5
Greece	3	7	5
France	2	9	5,5
Switzerland	9	5	7
Italy	8	8	8
Austria	5	11	8
Finland	13	6	9,5
Germany	11	9	10
Belgium	12	12	12
Ireland	10	15	12,5
Netherlands	15	12	13,5
UK	14	14	14
Portugal	16	16	16
Range	1,09-1,82	72%-39%	–
Average	1,4	61%	8,4

According to the data in the survey Portugal closely followed by the UK and the Netherlands, has the lowest payment morality in Europe, while Spain followed by Sweden, Denmark and Norway have the highest (see Table 2.2).

Tough versus soft credit cultures

Research on commercial credit suggests that different societies have their own cut-off points between toughness/softness in credit management and decrease/increase in sales. In this study the assessment of credit culture is aimed at estimating these cut-off points. Differences between societies in terms of tough or soft credit management could be identified through studying different patterns of the way companies manage credit, starting with the sales contract including, among others, the terms of payment, the use of cash discounts and invoicing of interest on overdue payments. Furthermore, it involves the use of collection agencies or lawyers for handling different phases of credit management, check-up of customers before accepting to give credit, and later how the payment is followed up, by reminders and legal proceedings when necessary. For example, in some societies it is common to invoice interest on overdue payments, while in others it is not at all accepted.

In this paper an estimate of a country's credit culture is calculated as an average of the ranking of the countries for each of the following factors (see Table 2.3):

- *terms of payment* (contractual credit period – days)

- *methods to speed up payments* (average of the rankings of 'sending own reminders' and 'using external actors such as debt collection agencies and lawyers', respectively the average of the rankings of 'offering discounts for prompt payment' and 'the rate of the discount used')

- *attitudes to measures to combat late payments* (average of the rankings of 'believing that there should be a statutory right for creditors to collect interest on overdue accounts' and that 'the statutory interest rate should be higher than the interest rate for borrowing money in banks', respectively the rankings of 'believing that debtors should compensate creditors for the administrative costs, such as reminders, debt collection costs, etc.')

The shorter the contractual credit period and the higher the percentage of the two other factors, the higher the country's ranking on credit culture. The averages ranking concerning these three factors are used as an estimate of a country's credit culture. The line between tough and soft credit culture has been drawn at 8,2, which is the average of the credit culture rankings.

Based on this analysis we find that the Nordic countries and some Central European countries have the toughest credit cultures, while Southern Europe, UK, Ireland and some of the Central European countries have the softest.

Integrating the two sides of late payments

Combining the payment morality – the behaviour of the creditee – and the credit culture – the behaviour of the creditor – gives us a matrix, which allows a categorisation of the countries participating in the survey into four groups. In Figure 2.11 the countries have been plotted into the matrix based on the average rankings in Table 2.2 and 2.3.

Most of the Nordic countries (except for Finland in group four) end up in group one having both a tough credit culture and a high payment morality. In group two we find the Southern European countries (except for Portugal which is in group three), which have a high payment morality but a soft credit culture. UK and Ireland are found in group three where the payment morality is low and the credit culture soft. The central European countries are found in all of the four groups. However, the more southern the more soft the credit culture.

Table 2.3 Ranking of the European countries based on credit culture

Country	Terms of Payment	Methods to Speed up Payments			Attitudes to Measures to Combat Late Payments			Credit Culture
	Contr. credit period Days	Own Rem. + External Actors	Disc. + Rate	Average Ranking	Inter. + > bank interest	Coll. costs	Average Ranking	Av. Rank.
Finland	*1*	5,5	5,5	*5,5*	3,0	6	*4,5*	**3,7**
Germany	*3*	2,5	7,5	*5,0*	4,0	3	*3,5*	**3,8**
Austria	*8*	3,5	5,5	*4,5*	5,0	1	*3,0*	**5,2**
Sweden	*4*	10,0	12,0	*11,0*	2,0	4	*3,0*	**6,0**
Norway	*2*	13,0	10,0	*11,5*	8,5	1	*4,8*	**6,1**
Denmark	*5*	9,0	8,5	*8,8*	8,5	11	*9,8*	**7,8**
Belgium	*11*	2,0	6,5	*4,2*	9,5	8	*8,8*	**8,0**
Netherl.	*5*	5,0	12,0	*8,5*	11,0	13	*12,0*	**8,5**
UK	*9*	6,0	9,0	*7,5*	7,0	13	*10,0*	**8,8**
France	*12*	8,5	10,5	*9,5*	8,0	7	*7,5*	**9,7**
Italy	*14*	9,0	5,0	*7,0*	9,0	8	*8,5*	**9,8**
Ireland	*10*	5,5	9,5	*7,5*	8,5	16	*12,3*	**9,9**
Spain	*15*	14,5	4,5	*9,5*	8,5	5	*6,8*	**10,4**
Switzerl.	*7*	15,5	11,5	*13,5*	11,0	11	*11,0*	**10,5**
Portugal	*13*	11,0	4,0	*7,5*	12,0	15	*13,5*	**11,3**
Greece	*16*	12,5	4,0	*8,2*	14,5	8	*11,3*	**11,8**
Range	19-75d	79-100	22-97%		63-100	63-94%		
		41-119	2-7%		29-95%			
Average	39d	94%	54%		91%	84%		8,2
		68%	4%		66%			

Certain characteristics regarding stated reasons for late payments for the respective groups' domestic customers, such as, financial difficulties, intentional late payments and administrative inefficiency, were found.

Group one finds administrative inefficiency to be a relatively important explanation. Group two explains the late payments with financial difficulties. Group three believes that the late payments are intentional, which is in accordance with expectations. Group four considers financial difficulties to be to be the most important explanation of their late payments.

Finally, patterns of perceived problems with late payments concerning their cash flow and profit or as being a threat to company growth or even survival, were found for the four groups. As could be expected, *group one* (high payment morality and tough credit culture) do not find the problems with late payments to be as

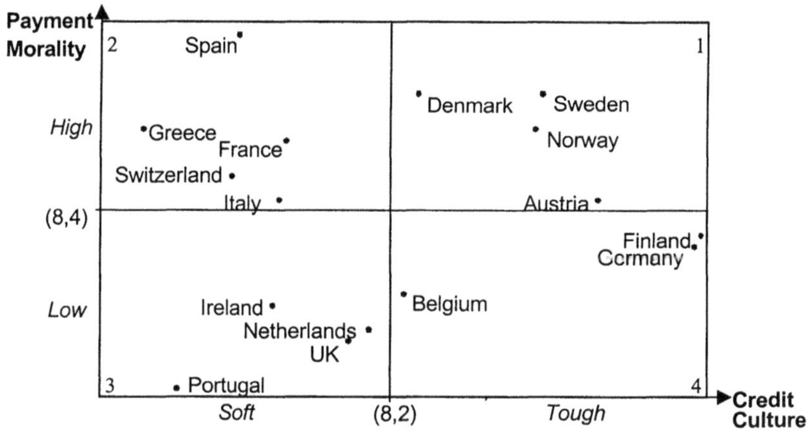

Figure 2.11 Integration of payment morality and credit culture

big threat as the other groups, while *group three* (low payment morality and soft credit culture) find all of the consequences to be a big problem. *Group two also* finds the consequences to be a relatively high problem. *Group four* finds the loss of profit to be a bigger problem than the consequences on cash flow, which is the biggest problem as stated by the other groups.

The legal system in five European countries

Different factors could be assumed to have an effect on credit cultures and payment morality. In this paper the design of the legal system concerning debt recovery is the focus. If the debtor does not pay its invoices it may become necessary to take legal action. A complex and/or inefficient legal system, defined as requiring a lot of time and money, is likely to lead to problems for a company to be taken seriously when threatening a customer of consequences (e.g., legal action) if not paying its invoices. The legal system is, therefore, assumed to influence both the credit culture and the payment morality. Furthermore, it could be assumed that countries which have a legal system supporting the creditor to charge interest on overdue payments and compensation for administrative costs or collection costs would make it easier to develop a tough credit culture. Thereby the payment morality would be enhanced by making it less economically valuable for the creditee to use late payments as an alternative financial source.

In this section the complexity, i.e., time consumption and costs involved, of the legal systems in five countries are analysed and connected to the results from the survey. Interviews have been conducted in France, Germany, the Netherlands, Sweden and the UK. The interviews have also been complemented with literature in this field (Datainspektionen, 1994; Intrum Justitia, 1993, Richardson, 1993).

Time consumption
The interviews consisted, among others, of questions aimed at generating a picture of the legal proceedings for a best, average and worst case. The best case could represent the true capacity of a legal system when a case is not complicated and if everything proceed as planned. The average case is where most of the cases end up and the worst case is when a case is complicated in various ways.

The persons interviewed were asked questions about both small (ECU1,000) and large claims (ECU10,000) in each country, since the legal systems in many countries look different for these two categories of claims (the amounts ECU1,000 and ECU10,000, were selected to cover these differences in each country). However, legal action for as small claims as ECU1,000, usually concerns consumer debts. Therefore, the data for the countries concerning the larger claims (ECU 10,000) is more relevant and therefore used for the results and conclusions in this article.

Differences in time between best, average and worst cases
In general there is a big range for each country between the estimated best and worst cases. The worst cases might in undisputed cases last up to two years and for disputed cases over four and a half years (Germany). Comparing the best and the average cases we find that the time consumption for the legal proceedings is about twice as high for the average cases as for the best cases in all of the studied countries. This indicates that each country has a potential to decease the time consumption within the existing legal structure.

In the estimated best-undisputed cases the time until the Bailiff receives the warrant is, in general, larger than the consequent execution. However, in most cases (i.e., average cases) the reality is the opposite. The time for the Bailiff to execute the warrant is the most time consuming phase. It is also this phase that consumes relatively more time when moving from the average to the worst case. It might therefore, be interesting not only to find ways to streamline the litigious phases but also to find ways of making the Bailiffs more powerful and efficient.

Differences in time due to the use of different courts and proceedings
Unless there is a fraud, a civil debt is not a criminal matter. The legal proceedings for debt recovery is, therefore, handled in Civil Courts, which do not deal with criminal matters. However, in Sweden the court does not handle undisputed claims. The same authority, the Crown's Bailiffs office, is used for all amounts. The other four countries have different courts depending on the amount of the claim.

A legal process is usually preceded by a demand letter (which is more strongly formulated than a reminder). However, of the five countries studied, it is only legally required in France. In the Netherlands and England a demand letter is sent to enable costs and interest to be claimed from the debtor, since the judges do not always accept these costs. In Sweden, Germany and England a procedure exist where the courts do not in advance review the application. In France a judge reviews the application beforehand and in the Netherlands there is usually a hearing where both parties are supposed to be present. The estimated average time taken for large (ECU10,000) claims is presented in Figure 2.13.

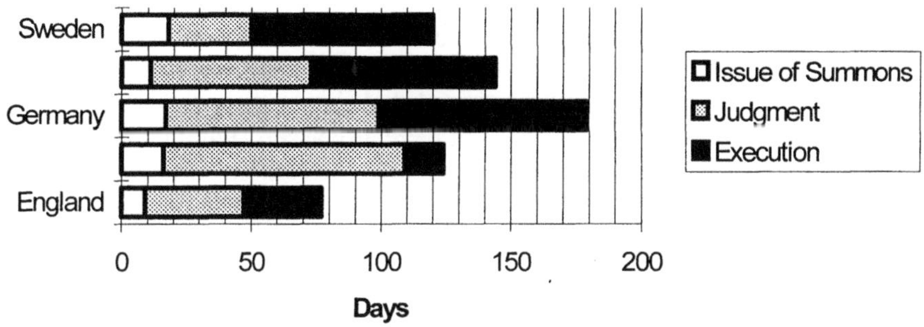

Figure 2.12 Undisputed large claims (ECU10,000)

Comparing the countries' average cases, England has the shortest legal proceedings, followed by Sweden and France. Germany and the Netherlands have the longest. While it takes around three months to receive the report from the Bailiff in England it takes twice as long in Germany.

When comparing the time until the warrant of execution is received by the Bailiff the differences between England, Sweden and France is large. It is the efficiency of the Bailiff that makes the difference. France seems to have very efficient Bailiffs compared with the other four countries. When looking at the larger claims where England uses Sheriffs, who are more efficient than their Bailiffs, England is closer to France in terms of efficiency in the execution phase.

When a Summons is disputed the legal proceedings become more complex. In general, when a claim is disputed (for the best, average and the worst case) the time is doubled in all of the countries. The legal proceedings for average disputed small and large claims are presented in Figure 2.14.

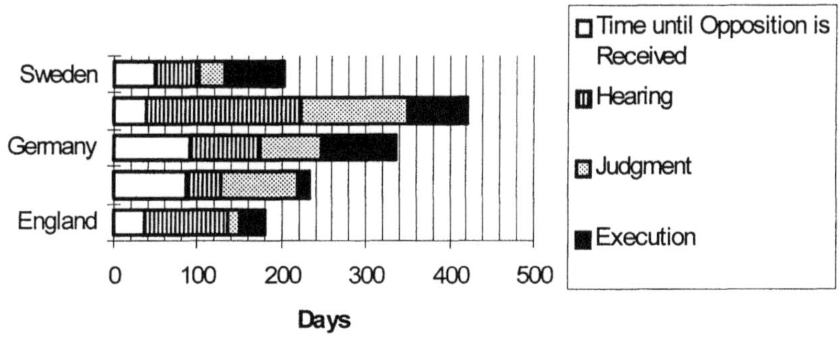

Figure 2.13 Disputed Large Claims (ECU10,000)

For the large disputed claims England (due to the Sheriff being more efficient) and Sweden has the shortest procedures (about 6-7 months). It takes almost twice as long in Germany (about 11 months) and the Netherlands (about 14 months).

Costs involved and chargeable to debtor
The interviewees were also asked to estimate the costs for an average case for undisputed and disputed claims and how much of the costs were chargeable to the debtor. However, it should be remembered that the creditor takes a risk since a debtors in financial difficulties might not have any assets, which could mean that neither the capital claim nor the other costs are recoverable, whereas the creditor ends up having to pay for the costs involved him/herself. The presentation below is based on the creditor doing all the work s/he is allowed to do her/himself.

Except for Sweden the countries use different courts depending on the size of the claim. Usually, when a higher court is used the costs are higher, because the parties have to be represented by lawyers. This is the case in England (above £5,000), Germany (above £10,000) and the Netherlands (above £2,000). In France different courts are used, but the costs are much the same, since no lawyer is required. In Sweden the same authority is used for both small and large undisputed claims. Consequently, the costs for undisputed claims in Sweden and France are lower. The costs are presented in Table 2.4.

For disputed large claims the parties in all the countries have to be represented by lawyers. Germany and the Netherlands are estimated to have the most expensive proceedings, while England and France the least expensive. The costs are presented in Table 2.5.

Consequently, the costs for both undisputed and disputed large claims are highest in Germany and the Netherlands.

Table 2.4 Costs (£) for undisputed large claims (ECU10,000)

	England	France	Germany	Netherlands	Sweden
Court	145,00	19,50	88,00	320,00	30,00
Bailiff	40,00	266,50	88,00	176,00	100,00
Lawyer	200,25	0,00	655,38	800,00	0,00
Total creditor	385,25	286,00	831,38	1296,00	130,00
Total debtor	375,25	286,00	831,38	1256,00	130,00

Table 2.5 Costs (£) for disputed large claims (ECU10,000)

	England	France	Germany	Netherlands	Sweden
Court	145,00	84,50	616,00	320,00	30,00
Bailiff	40,00	344,50	88,00	176,00	100,00
Lawyer	365,75	325,00	2296,14	1400,00	1250,00
Total creditor	550,75	754,00	3000,14	1896,00	1380,00
Total debtor	540,75	559,00	3000,14	1856,00	1380,00

Differences in chargeable costs
For the five countries studied it is possible to recover court costs and almost all of the Bailiff's costs from the debtor if s/he loses the case. However, for lawyers' fees the regulations differ. In Sweden and England the lawyers' fees cannot be recovered for smaller claims. In the other countries it depends on the judge if s/he considers the costs justifiable. Collection costs are in Sweden accepted up to a certain amount, which is regulated by law. In England and France collection costs are not chargeable to the debtor, while in Germany and the Netherlands it is up to the judge to assess whether the collection costs should be accepted. All of the five countries accept at a minimum a legal interest rate on overdue payments. However, the rates differ.

Germany has a lower legal rate[3] (5%) than lending rate[4] (10,62%), while the Netherlands' legal rate (7%) is almost corresponding to the lending rate 6,5%). In England and Sweden the legal rate (8% respectively 14%) is higher than their lending rate (6,75% respectively 11,29%). Data are not available for France. Consequently, the German legal system to a large extent allows the debtor to use late payments as a cheap alternative to, e.g., bank loans.

Association between legal system, payment morality and credit culture

Together the results of the five studied legal systems indicate that there might be an association between the complexity of the legal proceedings (time and cost) and the payment morality but not with the credit culture, as illustrated in Figure 2.14.

3 The data for legal rates was collected in March 1996.

4 The period for the latest registered average lending rate in the statistics from International Monetary Fund (1995) differs; England (November, 1995), Germany (November 1995), the Netherlands (December, 1995) and Sweden (September, 1995). No current lending rate exists for France.

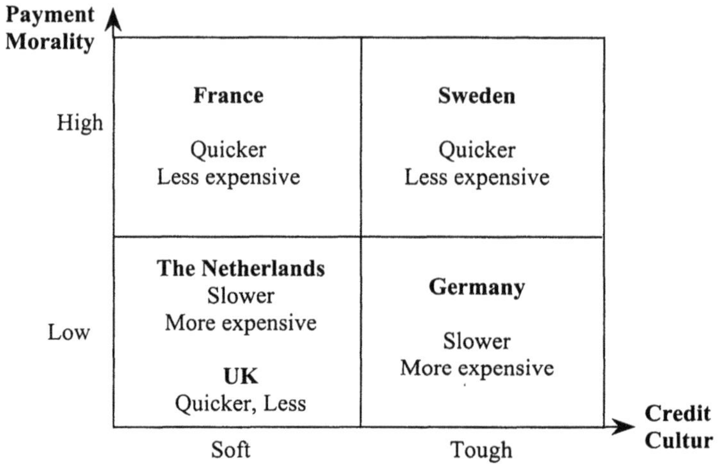

Figure 2.14 Association between legal systems and late payments

Both *Germany and the Netherlands* have for larger claims more expensive and longer proceedings, which makes the legal systems less efficient for communication of good and bad payment behaviour. The payment morality of these two countries was low.

Sweden and France had a less expensive and more expedient system than both Germany and the Netherlands, supporting their culture and morality. The French Bailiffs stand out as very efficient compared to the other countries. The payment morality of these two countries was high.

However, the results for *England*, being the country with, in many cases, the least time consuming legal proceedings, which at the same time was relatively inexpensive, was counter to expectations since England had a low payment morality. One possible explanation is that England lately has reviewed its system and made adjustments to make the legal proceedings more efficient. If this is the explanation and the results from this study concerning the association between the legal system and the payment morality is correct, we might soon see a change in the payment morality in England.

Conclusions

Looking at credit in the dimensions of credit culture and payment morality, reflects the two-way nature of any credit transaction, and brings new insights to the problems associated with late payments.

The results of this study show clear differences in payment behavior between different countries. However, counter to what might have been expected, the results suggest that countries with the longest total payment periods are not always the countries with the worst payment morality. The long payment periods are often explained instead by the credit culture in these countries.

Looking at the way countries map into these two dimensions of credit culture and payment morality it is especially interesting that all quadrants are occupied. It implies that having a tough credit culture does not necessarily make firms pay on time; nor does a soft credit culture prevent 'good' behaviour. This is also supported by studies at the Credit Management Research Group in Bradford which found that a majority of firms in England support statutory interest, but a majority also pay late (some of the time).

Furthermore, the results of this study indicate a possible link between the legal system and payment morality rather than with credit culture. This is partly counter to expectations since it was assumed that a tough credit culture would press for more efficient legal support. Similarly, an efficient legal system would be expected to give room for a harder approach.

The overall conclusion drawn from this study is counter to earlier research since the results do not support that suppliers to any large extent can affect the payment morality (willingness to pay) of the buyers. The payment morality seems rather to be affected by external factors such as the legal system. This suggests future research should focus on what motivates and restricts companies to pay on time or late. One interesting factor that might influence the motivation of the buyer to pay could be the information available about payment behaviour in a particular country.

Acknowledgement

The author wants to thank Barbara Summers at the Credit Management Research Group, University of Leeds Management Centre for helpful comments, Intrum Justitia for financial support and Université Paris-Dauphine for inviting the author as a guest researcher during the study.

2.7 Demand for credit and influences on payment behaviour

by Barbara Summers
Lecturer in Consumer Credit
and
Nicholas Wilson
ICM Professor of Credit Management, Leeds University

Credit is pervasive in the UK economy affecting financial transactions at all levels from an individual consumer to a multinational company. Surveys undertaken by Wilson, Watson & Summers (1995) and Wilson, Watson, Singleton & Summers (1996) show that most firms make the bulk of their sales on credit. What factors influence the extent to which trade credit is used and the payment behaviour of the firm when offers such as discounts for early payment are made?

Late payment is a current issue in Europe and policies aiming to address this issue need to be informed by research, which can shed light on the possible consequences of action. This paper summarises results from a major study designed to address that information gap.

Theories of trade credit demand

Transaction costs theory

Credit reduces the cost of engaging in trade by reducing the cost of making money available for the transactions. Firms incur costs when converting liquid assets to cash, although they can reduce this overhead, particularly on small amounts or where the timing of requirements is uncertain, by holding precautionary balances. Trade credit allows buyers to maintain reduced precautionary balances and to plan movements from liquid assets to cash in the most cost effective manner, Ferris (1981). This is the cash management motive for credit demand. A further motive arises from the reduced number of transactions on the buyer's bank account (the transaction volume motive); the buyer only writes one cheque per supplier per period and therefore reduces costs, as most banks charge businesses on a per transaction basis.

Financing theory

If we consider trade credit as one of several options for financing purchases, then the attractions of trade credit will depend on the relative costs and availability of other options. If credit market imperfections cause some buyers to have unsatisfied demand for finance, i.e. to experience credit rationing, then they will be willing to use trade credit even at a premium cost. If firms are cash rich then trade credit must be compared with the opportunity cost of other uses of the money.

Should credit rationing exist in a market then trade credit can be an attractive way of obtaining finance, even if the costs are high due to foregone discounts or late payment penalties. Suppliers may offer credit to borrowers which are unattractive to third party lenders because the firms have more in common than the financial transaction; the supplier benefits from future sales by helping a customer in difficulty to stay in business. The supplier is also in a better position to obtain information about creditworthiness than a third party lender; contact from the selling process can facilitate the monitoring of customers on an ongoing basis and, as Smith (1987) suggests, suppliers can also use two part terms to obtain ongoing information on creditworthiness. Buyers also save the fixed costs of arranging a loan.

Financial benefit
If a buyer is given credit terms then they have a period between receiving the goods and paying for them, during which time they may either earn interest on the money or avoid finance charges on borrowing. Unless the goods are offered at a sufficient discount for cash this represents a financial gain to the buyer.

Operational considerations
Firms have to incur costs before they make sales. The length of a firm's production cycle might therefore be expected to influence their demand for credit, as the firm would otherwise have to provide alternative finance. The extent to which a firm keeps stocks may also impact on demand, as these have to be funded.

Seller compliance
Trade credit can give information on seller performance. The idea that credit terms might provide signals of confidence in product quality by allowing the buyer an inspection period before payment is due has been put forward as a motivation for sellers to extend credit (see Ackerlof (1970), Smith (1987)) and credit can provide some protection against opportunistic behaviour by the seller after contract. Lee and Stowe (1993) also suggest that uncertainty on seller compliance can be a motive for foregoing early payment discount.

Credit as a marketing tool
The credit terms offered and the attitude the supplier takes to enforcing them are part of the price and can be used to achieve marketing objectives. (Schwartz 1974). Schwartz and Whitcomb (1978) suggest that credit terms and enforcement policy can be used to disguise price reductions from competitors and to facilitate price discrimination between customers, while Emery (1984) sees the setting of terms as a way for the seller to cope with variable demand, offering better credit terms (i.e. a lower price) when demand is low to increase sales and tightening up credit terms when demand is high.

Effects of the firm's environment
In an environment where trade credit is pervasive, a buyer would not choose to pay cash unless a cash discount of sufficient size is offered. One influence on demand is the credit demand of the firm's own customers as the firm has to finance the credit it offers. Larger firms may be in a better position to harness technology to take advantage of potential financial benefits whereas smaller companies may have insufficient staff time to organise payment around best utilisation of terms. Finally we need to take account of the firm's position in the value chain and the industry in which it participates.

Influences on payment behaviour

Late payment has been a subject of much debate recently in the UK press and various assertions have been put forward about late payment in these discussions including the exploitation of suppliers by dominant customers, credit rationing/ undercapitalised firms and poor financial/credit management. The use of net terms or the taking of extended trade credit (paying late), as opposed to payment after the discount period, is often seen as a sign of financial distress. There are, however, reasons to raise a note of caution to this somewhat sweeping assumption, as only a minority of firms offer discounts or impose interest on late payment. In our survey only 17% of firms offered discounts for early payment and only 44% had an interest clause in their conditions of sale.

Some insight can be gained by analysing the credit transaction from a game theory perspective.[5] When a firm purchases goods on credit it then has various options of payment behaviour as illustrated in Figure 2.15, although the terms of credit obviously affect the options available

Once the buyer has chosen its course of action the supplier has options to respond. What then might influence the firm's choice of payment behaviour? Anything that affects the value of the outcome for the buyer can be an influence. The value of the outcome has several components: financial, non-financial and future interactions.

value = f(financial, non-financial, future interactions)

The *financial component* can be evaluated with equations (1) and (2). Equation (1) computes the financial benefit of a combination of terms and payment behaviour relative to terms where a net period only is offered and payment made on time. Equation (2) completes the financial picture by taking account of the price of the goods/services, which may have been adjusted to include the cost of credit. The equation can be evaluated using variables at forecast or actual values, depending on whether it is the perceived cost/benefit of an option or its actual cost/benefit that is required.

The *non-financial* component is less homogenous and less easy to quantify. It might include the value of after sales service (less forthcoming after late payment), product quality (perhaps the possibility of supplier non-compliance) and the buyer's valuation of the seller's business ethics.

Future interactions embodies the repercussions of the choice of payment behaviour on future exchanges. Obviously defaulting on agreed terms can impact on the firm's future relations with the supplier but it may also affect those interactions with other suppliers by damaging the buyer's reputation.

---

5 This is based on the model developed in Summers (1996), which contains derivations of the equations.

$$P\left(t(d-I) - \sum_{n=0}^{F}(f-I)/365 - e\left(\sum_{n=0}^{L}(i-I)/365\right)\right) - c - a \qquad (1)$$

where:

P	price on net terms
F	number of days for which buyer has to finance transaction
L	number of days after net period date when payment is made (zero if payment is not late)
d	early payment discount percent
f	cost of finance to buyer on day n (annual percent).
i	interest rate on late payment on day n (annual percent)
I	inflation rate on day n (annual percent)
c	allocation of fixed costs associated with finance
t	probability an unearned discount can be taken without penalties
e	probability late payment interest will be enforced
a	administration charges associated with paying

$$\text{cost/benefit} = P - C^t \qquad (2)$$

where: C^t is the evaluation of Equation (1).

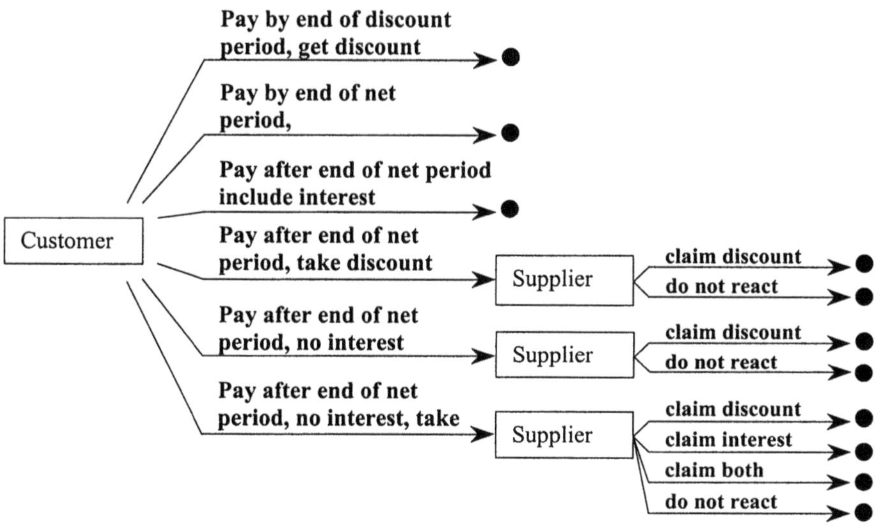

Figure 2.15 Payment options in the trade credit game

Circumstances where a customer might pay late and/or forego discount are:

1. If the value of the early payment discount does not exceed the additional costs (actual or opportunity) of paying in the discount period then the discount will be unattractive.

2. If the perceived probability of being able to take unearned discount is high and the expected repercussions are low, then the benefits of discount are achieved without the finance costs.

3. If there is no interest charge on late payment or the probability of being charged interest for paying late is low, then a financial benefit is gained from paying late. If this is not counterbalanced by concern over future interactions then late payment is attractive.

4. If a firm is credit rationed the cost of finance required to allow it to pay early or even on time is effectively infinite, so that forgoing discounts and/or late payment can be an enforced option.

5. Other factors may affect the attractiveness of the discount or even paying within the net period; for example if the buyer has doubts over product quality or supplier compliance.

6. Norms of behaviour in the firm's business environment will affect the expected impact of behaviour on future interactions. If paying late or taking unearned discount are commonplace they may be less likely to involve penalties.

Some of the indications above relate to theoretical considerations; 1, 2 and 3 come from financial benefit motivations, 4 links to financing theory, and 5 to seller compliance. 2 and 3 also link to the use by the supplier of credit as a marketing tool, in that this affects the probabilities of taking unearned discount and of late payment penalties being enforced. It is worth noting that firms will not display the same behaviour in every credit purchase interaction; it will depend on their evaluation of the utility of behaviour in each case. In some cases this is mentioned anecdotally, as in the suggestion large firms exploit small suppliers and pay those who are more powerful on time. We would expect firms to show behaviour patterns such as: paying suppliers who offer discounts early even if others are paid late due to financial pressures; preferentially paying firms on time where future interactions are most prominent: or paying suppliers late where the expected probability of penalties not being enforced is high perhaps because of poor credit management. The model is in fact not incompatible with any of the common assertions about late payment, but demonstrates that multiple causes are not unexpected. Firms are likely to juggle their resources to best advantage if they can.

Empirical approach & results

Data for this study are from 655 firms, which responded to a mail survey on trade credit practice conducted by CMRG in autumn 1994. The survey collected detailed data on the firm itself its organisational structure, products, markets, supplier relationships, credit policy, credit terms and credit management practices. These were then supplemented with financial and behavioural data from Dun & Bradstreet International. The firms were manufacturing companies. Details of the survey can be obtained from the authors and full details of the sample can be found in Wilson, Watson and Summers (1995).

Determinants of demand for credit
The dependent variables in this analysis were APTA (the ratio of accounts payable to total assets), and USETC (a binary variable set to 1 if the firm made 80%+ of its purchases on credit and to 0 otherwise). Univariate tests on both variables showed some support for transaction costs theory, financing theory and the use of credit as a marketing tool by suppliers, with a larger number of variables supporting financing theory and marketing being univariate significant for APTA than USETC. In addition, the relative size of the firm's trade debtors was significant with APTA.

Tables 2.6 and 2.7 show two sets of the multivariate models developed, those for USETC and APTA respectively. The first model in each set is based on work by Chant & Walker (1988) and Elliehausen & Wolken (1993), that was tested on a CMRG survey of small firms in Wilson, Singleton & Summers (1997). These models test primarily for the influence of the financing and transaction costs theories. The second model in each set is a parsimonious model developed from variables representing all the theories discussed above. USETC models were developed with logistic regression, while the APTA models were developed using linear regression with the errors corrected for heteroscedasticity (LIMDEP, 1995).

Significant variables in the USETC models provide some support for transaction costs and financing theories. The sign on MKT4R is opposite to that expected; it had been hypothesised that firms in industries with rapidly changing technology where ascertaining product quality may be more problematic might use credit periods to check on seller compliance. It may be that MKT4R is providing a measure of financial risk that affects suppliers as well as banks, in that firms with less stable technology may be more likely to fail and so default on payment. The industry variables suggest intermediate producers, who are suppliers of credit, make more use of credit themselves and those in consumer services use credit less.

Table 2.6 Model of demand USETC (0,1)

Variable	Description	Model 1	Model 2
STOCKTA	stock/ total assets	–0.5628	
STOCKTU	sales/stock	0.0001	
SUPPS	Number of active suppliers to the firm	0.2124***	0.2460***
LNSALE3	log of sales	0.0417	
RISK	credit rating	0.1203	
OWNMG	firm is owner managed	0.3125	
PYR	Number of years selling main product line (proxies age)	–0.0024	
TC2R	extent to which trade credit is seen as a cheaper form of finance	0.2542***	0.2060**
FINFAC1	Factor score for use of short term finance	–0.1457	
REC7R	extent to which credit limits set by banks have an adverse impact on the business	–0.0338	
INV6	extent to which firm's financial appraisal of investment is based on personal experience/ managerial judgement		0.2792**
TC6R	extent to which the payment profile of the firms customers makes trade credit a necessity		0.2569***
MKT4R	extent to which firm is in a market with stable technology		0.2157**
CLASS3	firm produces chemicals/petroleum		2.0803***
CLASS6	firm produces materials e.g. timber bricks		1.2223**
CHAIN7	firms primary business is consumer services		–1.6371**
	Model –2LL	**196.1292**	**217.5243**

The APTA models also have significant variables supporting transaction costs and financing theories. The significant variables also include the relative value of the firms' trade debtors, indicating that the amount of credit the firms extends relates to the relative value of credit it uses. The firms' financial condition, as opposed to more general conditions, also influences the relative value of trade credit the firm uses. Industry and supply chain variables are not significant in the APTA model.

Influences on payment behavior

Analysis of payment behaviour in the sample based on the Dun & Bradstreet Paydex Score[6] suggested that firms could be put into three main groups; those which paid promptly on average, those which averaged up to 15 days late and

6 The Dun & Bradstreet Paydex Score provides a measure of the average number of days the company pays either within or beyond agreed terms.

Table 2.7 Model of demand AP/TA

Variable	Description	Model 1	Model 2
STOCKTA	stock/ total assets	0.0404	0.0854**
STOCKTU	sales/stock	–0.0001**	
SUPPS	Number of active suppliers to the firm	–0.0064	
LNSALE3	log of sales	0.0072	
RISK	credit rating	0.0252***	
OWNMG	firm is owner managed	0.0422***	0.0216**
PYR	number of years selling main product line (proxies age)	–0.0005***	–0.2813***
TC2R	extent to which trade credit is seen as a cheaper form of finance	0.0027	
FINFAC1	factor score for use of short term finance	–0.0062	
REC7R	extent to which credit limits set by banks have an adverse impact on the business	0.0112**	0.0066*
QUICKRT	quick ratio		–0.0297***
OBJ6	extent to which improving profitability is an important company objective		0.0164***
DBTA	trade debtors/total assets		0.3008***
FIN9	use extended trade credit as a form of finance		0.0102**
CSUPP3R	extent to which credit limits set by banks have an adverse impact on the business		0.0092**
JITR	whether the firm uses a just-in-time production system		0.0281***
LTOTAS3	log of firms total assets		–0.0086*
	Model –2LL	**290.6632**	**437.5369**

finally those which averaged over 15 days late. On average, only 10.7% of respondents paid promptly, 46.5% paid 1 to 15 days late and 42.8% paid more than 15 days late.

The group paying 1 to 15 days late are significantly larger[7] than the prompt payers in terms of sales and total assets but they are also significantly larger (at the 10% level) than those paying 15+ days late in terms of sales. Those paying 15 plus days late are significantly larger at the 10% level than the prompt payers in terms of assets. In fact all three groups contain firms below the 5th percentile and above the 95th percentile in terms of total assets for the survey as a whole. Both groups, which pay late, have some common characteristics that distinguish them from the prompt payers. They are

7 Unless otherwise stated "significantly" different means significantly different at the 5% level.

- likely to have more active suppliers
- more likely to feel the payment profile of customers in their industry makes credit as necessity
- less likely to take early payment discount if it is offered
- more likely to use invoice discounting / factoring
- more likely to use government grants as a form of finance
- more likely to have a primary product in the engineering, metal processing or electronics industries
- more likely to buy in credit reference information.

Those paying 15 plus days late are also significantly

- likely to have a larger number of suppliers collectively supply 80% of their inputs
- more likely to feel late payment by customers puts them under pressure to pay late
- likely to be more reliant on short/medium term financing
- more likely to say they use extended trade credit as a form of finance
- likely to review payment periods to creditors more often
- likely to review financing of working capital more often
- likely to have a lower net operating income (adjusted for size)
- likely to export more of their turnover
- more likely to be intermediate producers and less likely to be retailers (at the 10% level).

Several of these characteristics are also significantly different between those paying 15 days late and those paying 1 to 15 days late.

The clear presence of at least two sub-populations of late payers suggest multiple causes for late payment. The group paying 1 to 15 days late are not more likely than prompt payers to feel late payment by customers puts them under pressure to pay late or to be reliant on short/medium term finance Given that the 1 to 15 days late are averages this group may be showing mixed behaviour, perhaps paying late where they have market power, or where they can exploit poor credit management. These firms are not significantly more likely to feel they use trade credit as a form of finance than prompt payers. This, along with the fact that such a small percentage of firms pay promptly on average, may suggest that the firms in the survey would not regard up to 15 days over terms as paying late. Although the firms in this group are larger than the other two groups on average, the spread of firm size in each group means this cannot provide clear evidence of the potential exploitative behaviour of large firms. Separate tests show that the larger firms in the survey actually have significantly better Paydex scores, although the size of the difference is too small to be significant in the non-statistical sense.

Neither late paying group is significantly more likely than prompt payers to feel late payment had had an important adverse impact on their business. This does not support the hypothesis that late payment as a whole is largely caused by a knock on effect from late payment by customers. However, the fact that all three groups show a substantial mix of those who did and did not feel they had suffered from being paid late suggests sub-population analysis based on this criteria may be indicated, and this is being pursued.[8]

The group paying 15+ days late show significant signs of financial pressure, feeling under pressure to pay late because of customers' payment behaviour[9] and making more use of short/medium term finances. Their characteristics are more similar to those identified for late payers in the CMRG small firm survey. Their reliance on short/medium term finance may suggest a finance gap with difficulty raising longer-term finance either through debt or equity. There is some evidence however that these firms are still trying to juggle their resources to best advantage; even among those paying over 15 days late 47% will always or frequently take early payment discount if offered, and only 7% never do.

Summary

The results of our analysis of trade credit demand generally support a non-exploitative view of the demand for trade credit, although the variables by which we might detect exploitation are all size related so a size based sub-population analysis may be called for. The evidence supports the influence of transaction costs theory, financing theory and the firm's industry on the percentage of purchases made on credit. The amount of trade credit used relative to firm size is also influenced by the extent of trade credit the firm provides, the firm's financial condition and perhaps the extent to which its suppliers use credit as a marketing tool.

In the area of influences on payment behaviour and the potential causes of late payment the evidence suggests multiple causation. The signs of financial pressure, particularly reliance on short term finance, in the group paying on average 15+ days late suggests the presence of a finance gap, while the apparent lack of such influences on those paying 1 to 15 days late suggests these firms may be either taking advantage of poor credit management or exploiting market power. The mechanism is not clear, however, as the range of firm size in this group versus other groups does not support the hypothesis that only larger firms are in-

---

8 Between 40% and 50% felt they suffered from being paid late in all groups.

9 This was a separate question to that discussed above. One question asked whether late payment by customers had had a severe impact on the firms business while the second asked whether late payment by customers put the firm under pressure to pay late.

volved in exploitation. A similar ambiguity is also reflected in the CMRG small firms' survey, where respondents cite both small and large businesses as slow payers. Although under a hypothesis of exploitation small firms might be expected to pay late as a knock on effect of late payment by their large customers, the fact that less than half of firms in the late paying groups see being paid late as having an important adverse impact on their business (and only those paying 15+ days late are significantly more likely to feel under pressure to pay late because of customer payment behaviour) suggests this cannot be the only explanation.

Other possibilities include suppliers allowing their customers to pay late for the long-term advantage of continued trade (i.e. help the customer stay in business). A second possibility is the presence of group norms accepting late payment behaviour; if a firm is paid late but pays equally late itself the financing requirement for intermediate points in the value chain is equivalent to prompt payment by all. Moves to prompt payment in this circumstance could cause a one-off increase in financing requirement for some firms, for example those with dominant customers who re-negotiate longer credit terms, and might change rather than alleviate the problem.

Late payment then seems to be a problem with multiple causes and where analysis of the impacts of potential solutions on all groups will be crucial to finding solutions, which do not cause adverse impacts on vulnerable but economically important groups such as small firms. CMRG's studies aim to address these issues.

Acknowledgement

Credit Management Research Group wish to thank Touche Ross and the DTI, who sponsored work on this survey, and Dun & Bradstreet International who supplied credit reference data. This paper is a summary of one of a series of papers on aspects of trade credit produced by Credit Management Research Group. For further information please contact the authors

2.8 The next property cycle: a survival kit for banks

by Mervyn K Lewis
National Australia Bank Professor, University of South Australia

This paper is concerned with the commercial property market and banks' involvement in it. Commercial real estate has always been a cyclical activity, but the boom and bust of the last ten years has been distinctive both in its global coverage and for the extent to which banks have got into difficulties with real estate lending. In considering the lessons to be learnt from this experience and how the mistakes of the past can be avoided in the next cycle, the paper first examines the character of fluctuations in commercial real estate. It then considers the attraction of real estate to banks and the peculiar hazards, which the cyclical features of the market pose to banks. Finally, the paper asks what can be done to prevent a repetition of past errors when the next boom unfolds.

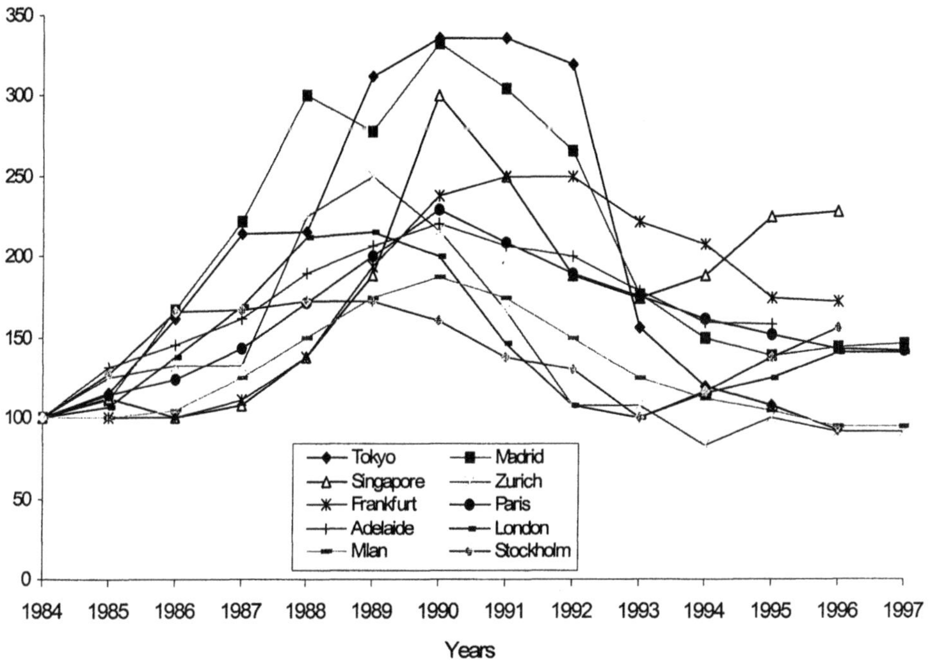

Figure 2.16 Office rental values in various cities[10]

The property cycle

Historians and others still speak of the 'roaring twenties', but this episode was largely confined to the United States. What has been different about the 'roaring eighties' and the bust of the 1990s is the universality of the cycle. Figure 2.16 illustrates the global character of the swing in commercial property prices with nominal rental values for offices in Frankfurt, London, Madrid, Milan, Paris, Singapore, Tokyo and Zurich. Stockholm and Adelaide are included too, although many other locations could have been used to illustrate the point that office rentals doubled (or tripled) in the upswing of the 1980s and declined almost as much in the first half of the 1990s. In fact, the Hillier Parker international property database from which the series in Figure 2.16 are drawn covers 75 cities in 25 countries. In 24 of the 25 countries, and in 74 of the 75 cities, property values declined in the early 1990s – mostly by substantial amounts. Some writers consequently talk of a 'one-world' property market (Baen, 1996), others of 'property as a global asset' (Baum and Schofield, 1991).

10 Source: Based on data supplied by Hillier Parker May & Rowden.

Examining the causes of the global real estate, Geoetzmann and Wachter (1995) opt for a 'simple' explanation in terms of the demand for office space: "global office markets move up and down with the global business cycles" (p.7). One difficulty with this explanation is that there is no global business cycle as such; instead, complex linkages exist between movements in economic activity in the United States, Japan, UK and Continental European countries (Artis and Zhang, 1996). The other problem is that commercial property prices are not always well correlated with conventional business cycles, as can be shown using the United Kingdom for illustration. Figures 2.17 and 2.18 explore the characteristics of the U.K. commercial property cycle.

In Figure 2.17 there are various 'real' measures: three indices of real rental values and an index of construction orders in real terms. Also shown are the dates of the peaks and troughs of the C.S.O. business cycle chronology. While new orders for construction correlate to some extent with each of the business cycle reference dates, the cycles for property rental values have wider amplitude and a longer period than construction.

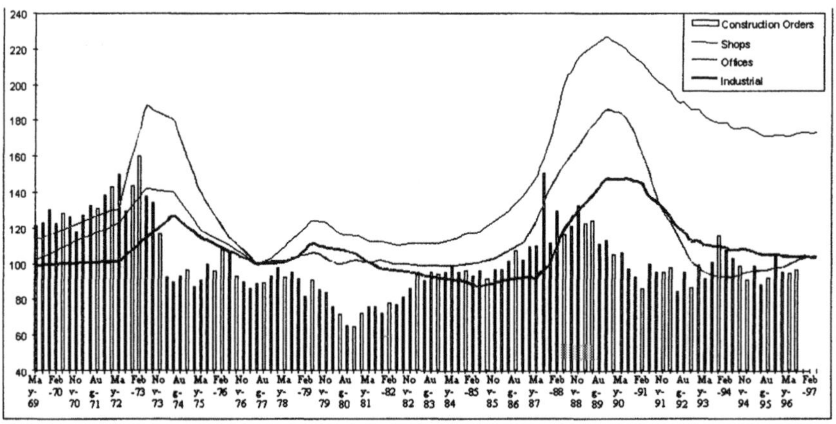

Figure 2.17 Activity in the UK Property Market [11]

Figure 2.18 compares fluctuations in commercial property values X with housing prices, Y equity prices and retail prices Z. Swings in the commercial property index have a lower amplitude than the equities index, although the property series relates to rental values and not capital values, and unlike the equity price and housing price indices, the property index thus excludes the element in

11 Construction. Index of value of new orders placed with contractors for buildings and works, at 1990 prices seasonally adjusted (index) 1990 = 100. Source: Economic Trends Annual Supplement (various).
Offices. Index of the real rental values of central London, suburban and provincial offices, index May 1977 = 100 Source: Hillier Parker May & Rowden.
Industrial and Shops. National indices of rental values of shops and new industrial buildings, index 1977 = 100. Source: Hillier Parker May & Rowden

capital values which reflects expectations of future movements in capital prices. Even so, during the latest cycle, the property series exhibited much greater nominal price falls than housing prices, and the downswing was much longer and deeper than for equities. Also, the periodicity of the cycle in property values appears to be much greater than that for equities.

It would seem from these figures that the cycles in the property market are not closely synchronised with the general business cycle. This aspect was well known to earlier researchers of business cycles. Kuznets (1930) identified long building-cycles, with a periodicity of 16-20 years, as distinct from the 4-5 year length of cycles in economic activity, and the 1-2 year cycles in inventories. In post-war years, an office-development cycle with a duration of 8-10 years has been estimated for the UK (Barras, 1983), and commercial building cycles generally are characterised by strong development activity and severe slumps in building production (McGough and Tsolacos, 1997).

Other writers (e.g. Ball, 1994) have emphasised developers' misforecasts, coupled with easy finance, as providing scope for an overprovision of space (especially in offices). A unique characteristic of property – i.e. land and buildings on it – is its longevity, and a feature of property development, in common with other construction, is a long delay between orders and completions. There also exist lags created by the need to acquire development sites, plan land use changes, evaluate the load-bearing and other capacities of the site, obtain access to finance, draw up plans, and obtain planning permissions. A typical project might take two to three years from beginning to end; for large projects, eight years can elapse between the initiation and the disposal stage.

The combination of a long time lag from planning to completion, optimistic expectations about future demand for space, and a short-run supply which is irreversible and specific to both location and use, creates the conditions for a classic 'hog cycle' whereby the market alternatives between famine and glut. The long delay before increased user-demands for office and shop floor space can be translated into additional property stock sustains space shortages, leading to rising rentals or property values. These rising prices induce developers to initiate new construction. But in the short run, the effects on demand and supply can even be perverse. Potential tenants may acquire properties ahead of time in anticipation of rising rents, while the increase in property prices enables property traders to increase their borrowings and purchase more property (Pratten, 1993). Eventually, the supply of new property responds to changing user and investment demands, but under perhaps very different economic conditions, producing an excess of supply of space and depressing rents and property prices. The consequences for availability in the City of London are shown in Figure 2.19. Most of the adjustment in office markets depends upon developers – the suppliers of office space – and as the market alternates between phases of over- and under supply, a tendency to cyclical fluctuations in development activity is thus generated.

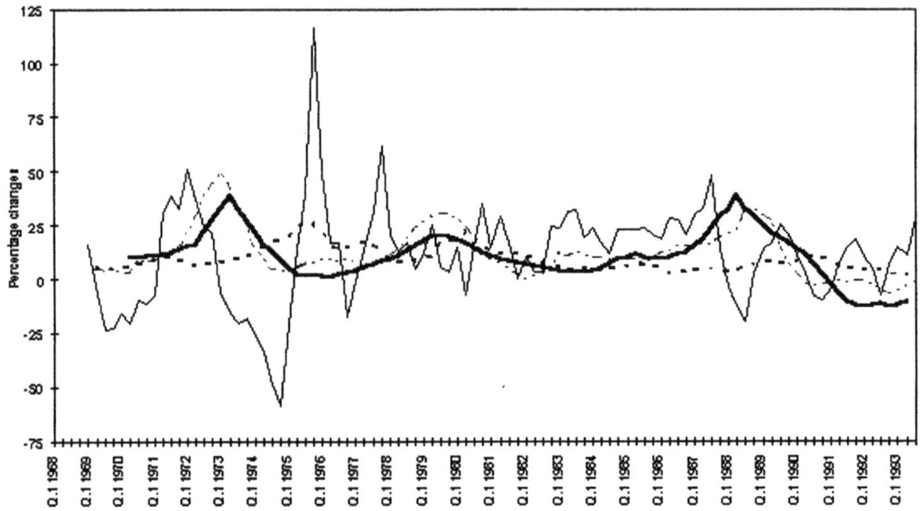

Figure 2.18 Asset price inflation in the UK[12]

Drawing these elements together, we might sketch the profile of a typical real estate cycle:

- rents begin to rise and capital values increase
- it pays to refurbish buildings and the volume of new construction expands
- increased funding and new sources of equity investment
- development sites and vacant land are absorbed
- a weakening of land use planning ensues
- optimistic forecasts of market growth and 'the boom that will not end' mentality sets in
- available supply begins to outstrip take up
- all real estate factors now at full stretch – **the peak**
- reduced take up and 'unstoppable supply'
- rent concessions and falling property values

12 Housing: Mix-adjusted house price index (second edition), 1990 = 100. Yearly percentage change. Source: Financial Statistics; Equities: Financial Times - Actuaries share index for all ordinary shares, index 1962 = 100. Yearly percentage change. Source: Financial Statistics; RPI. General index of retail prices (all items), 1985 = 100. Yearly percentage changes. Source: Financial Statistics; All property. An overall index of nominal rental values for all commercial property, constructed as a weighted average of component indices for shops, offices and industrial properties. Index 1977 = 100. Hillier Parker May & Rowden.

- tightened funding and foreclosures
- depressed real estate values and minimal construction
- banks reverse their boom policy and withdraw loans
- the 'wreckage' is cleared away and the market stagnates
- increased absorption and stabilising rents
- recovery and the readiness for another boom.

Despite this typical sequence its correspondence to events in many countries since the early 1980s, we should note that 'there is no new thing under the sun' (Ecclesiastes, Chpt. 1, V.9). Virtually the same catalogue of events featured in Homer Hoyt's classic study *One Hundred Years of Land Values in Chicago*, published in 1933.

Risks to banks

The distinctive character of the property cycle has the potential to create special risks for those investing in property, for those lending against commercial property, and for banks, which do both. In addition, in the case of banks, these risks are seemingly reinforced by their own frailties and collective behaviour.

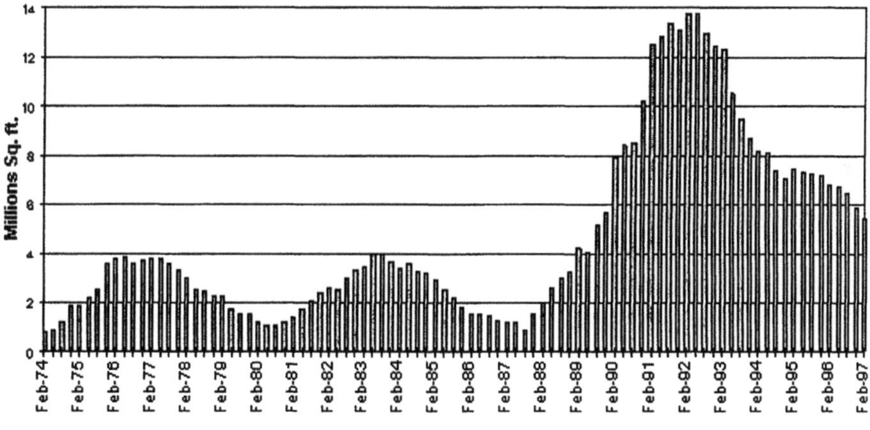

Figure 2.19 Availability of office floor space in city of London, 1974 – 1997[13]

Considering the latter point first, 'institutional amnesia' has been a feature of banks' involvement in the property market. For many UK and US banks, for example, a scenario of rising property values and increased lending, followed by falling values and a residue of bad debts, has unfolded twice over the past 20

13 Source: DTZ Debenham Thorpe Research.

or so years. There is another common thread in that bankers rushed in where others did not venture; as banks were expanding their exposure to commercial real estate, many traditional lenders to the sector were reducing theirs. In the US, life insurance companies' holdings of real estate and mortgages, as a% of total assets, declined from 30.5% in 1980 to 17.9% in 1992, while the share of commercial real estate in banks' lending increased from 9.3 to 15.6%. Funding for property in the UK is shown in Table 2.1. In 1980, life offices and pension funds provided over 80% of the new money going into property. Thereafter, 'institutional' funds fell in both relative and absolute terms, so that by 1990, banks were providing over 90% of the domestic funds flowing into the property market. Banks rapidly exited the market after 1991, but by then the damage had already been done.

Why did banks move so strongly into commercial property lending in the UK, US and in so many other countries? Loose monetary policy, deregulation and the competition for market shares have been widely cited as contributory factors; but some other factors appear to have been important. These were:

- poor risk assessment
- unfamiliarity with the market
- a sudden accumulation of risks
- balance sheet growth ambitions
- failure to control 'rogue subsidiaries'
- inappropriate incentive structures
- the 'feel good' factor and the herd instinct.

These elements of the lending experience were explored in Lewis (1994).

This increased exposure might not matter if banks' property lending equated with other forms of lending, but in fact this is not the case. The riskiness of property lending comes from its quasi-equity characteristics. Obviously banks have direct holdings of property due to the prime CBD locations which they occupy. But lending to property developers may involve a mixture of debt and equity, while there are important differences between property and other loans.

A bank's lending may be to the property company in the form of overdraft facilities or short-term loans secured against the assets. Or it may be against a particular development project in the form of non-recourse or limited recourse loans, often to special purpose 'off-the-balance-sheet' financing vehicles or to joint ventures which involve the bank and other financiers along with the developer in a subsidiary company.

Figure 2.20 illustrates an arrangement whereby a financing subsidiary of a bank and a developer form a joint venture to engage in real estate activities. Project financing of this type is relatively uncommon in lending to other sectors, and creates some special risks for the banks. Limited recourse loans provide some security for the bank, which may take the form, say, of certain pre-leasing commitments or guarantee of completion. In non-recourse loans there is no recourse to the parent company and the only security for the bank's debt is the property itself.

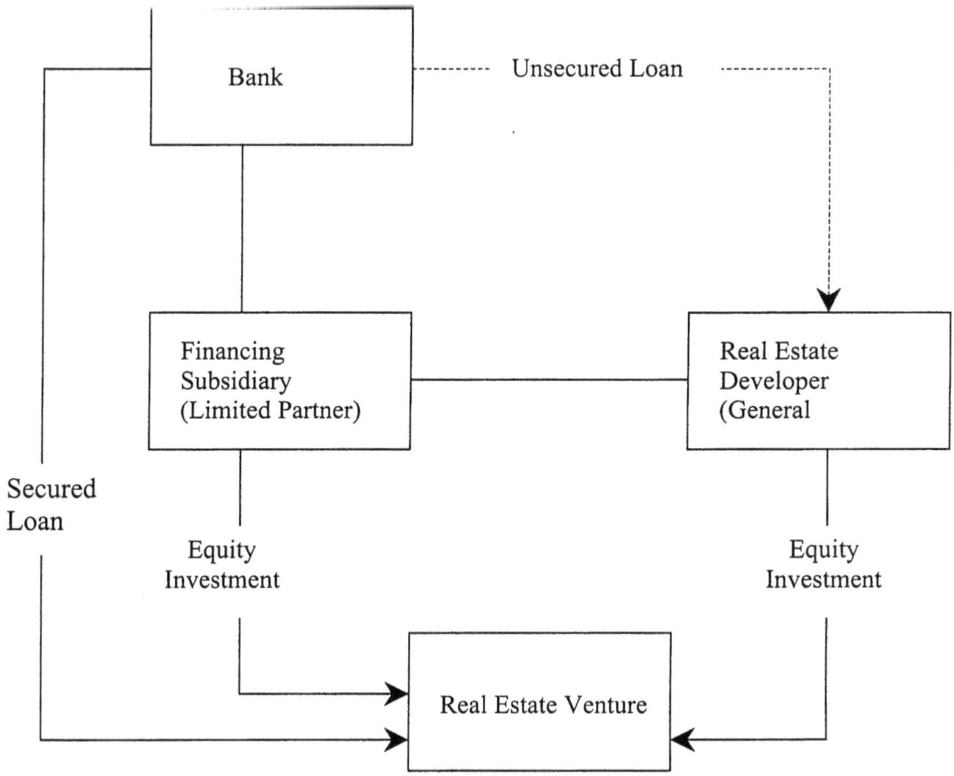

Figure 2.20 Special purpose financial vehicles for property development

Here the repayment source for loans assumes significance. In the case of residential mortgage loans, a borrower's ability to repay the loan is based on a cash flow from employment income, which is often largely independent of the value of the collateral, which then serves as a back up in case things go wrong. The same is true of most industrial and commercial lending, where conditions in the

Table 2.8 Funding for property in the UK, 1980-1996

£million

Year	Pension Funds	Insurance Companies	Banks	Capital Raisings	Property Unit Trusts	Overseas Investors	Total
1980	942	855	75	147	72	100	2,1
1981	843	1,074	468	97	108	70	2,6
1982	797	1,059	813	263	57	120	3,1
1983	680	845	930	83	-9	85	2,6
1984	906	744	967	237	47	65	2,9
1985	509	815	1,691	344	-5	90	3,4
1986	379	845	2,224	737	-101	150	4,2
1987	141	842	4,003	2,300	-516	290	7,0
1988	238	1,364	7,986	761	99	1,897	12,3
1989	135	1,877	10,639	1,647	30	3,217	17,5
1990	-491	1,080	7,033	178	-61	3,271	11,0
1991	484	1,665	688	1,270	22	1,607	5,7
1992	977	678	-1,726	279	-12	1,321	1,5
1993	155	274	-3,715	1,957	412	2,312	1,3
1994	-325	2,527	-2,068	1,402	421	1,737	3,6
1995	91	265	-1,449	1,166	-81	1,790	1,7
1996*	-272	860	158	859	na.	2,200	3,8

Latest estimates

Sources: Pension funds: Net investment in UK land and property by superannuation funds. *Financial Statistics* (various)

Insurance companies: Net investment in UK land and property by long-term and short-term insurance funds. *Financial Statistics* (various)

Banks: Lending by all banks in the UK to property companies. *Bank of England Quarterly Bulletin* (various)

Capital raisings: Amounts raised in all capital markets by property companies. 1980-1985. DTZ Debenham Thorpe. 1986-1996 Bank of England.

Property Unit Trusts: Net acquisition of UK property by property unit trusts. *Financial Statistics* (various).

Overseas Investors: Net acquisition of UK property from overseas. DTZ Debenham Thorpe Research.

borrower's industry, triggering the loan default, may be quite different from those in the collateral markets governing the ultimate recovery rates on the loan. With commercial real estate loans, by contrast, the borrower's ability to repay the loan is highly correlated with the value of the collateral, either because the property is acquired for re-sale or because increased vacancy rates and reduced rentals are quickly reflected in the price of the property and hence the value of the collateral.

It follows that fluctuations in available space and rental values on the scale shown earlier make property lending an inherently risky business and convert banks' property exposure into risks essentially equivalent to those of others undertaking investment in real estate (Twining, 1996). Factors governing those risks include:

- overly-optimistic valuations
- shrinking loan to valuation ratios
- cost overruns and late completions
- letting risks and voids
- planning and environmental restrictions
- convenants, indemnities and recourse
- illiquid secondary markets
- high leverage and sensitivity to interest rates.

These are, of course, the very factors with which bankers, as managers of non-performing property loans and property books in the early 1990s, have become acquainted only too well.

Avoiding the mistakes

It might seem that – like the third world debt saga of an earlier decade – the dangers of property lending would be seared into bankers' memories for years to come. Yet recent history is far from encouraging. Already, derivatives 'disasters' (Barings, Deutsche Morgan Grenfell, Daiwa, Sumitomo, Nat West Markets, Union Bank of Switzerland) have captured the headlines that were not so long ago filled with bank crashes due to bad property loans. Meanwhile, the fortunes of the commercial property market are once again on the ascendant. By the time the next boom arrives, bankers' memories will have dimmed and a new generation of lenders will be ready to repeat the mistakes of the past. What can be done to prevent another round of boom and bust?

Regulatory reforms – such as stipulated loan-to-valuation ratios, portfolio constraints upon property loans and higher B.I.S. capital adequacy risk weights for commercial real estate – are almost certainly doomed to failure (Lewis, 1996). For one thing, the momentum for regulatory change has undoubtedly been lost. For another, it is too easy for a determined bank to hide property loans through subsidiaries and other means. To give one example, how many are aware that increased lending by British banks to the shipping sector in the 1980s was in reality to the property market via the real estate operations of a well-known shipping company? Japanese banks' property lending via the 'non-banks' is another example.

Improved corporate governance is a more promising route. Looking at the performance of the banking industry over the last decade or so, it is difficult to resist the conclusion that there is something seriously awry in the market for corporate control in banking, and that insufficient checks have been exerted upon bank management. Corporate governance refers to the systems by which companies are directed and controlled, and governance structures arise whenever there is a potential agency problem which cannot be resolved through contracting arrangements (Hart, 1995). Since the *raison d'être* of banks is the presence of heterogeneous and costly information in financial transactions, it would hardly surprise if agency problems were important in banking.

Agency issues in banking firms are normally considered in the context of depositors and/or government deposit insurance agencies vis-à-vis bank shareholders, yet they seem likely to arise in the case of management and shareholders (Mester, 1989). Suggested solutions include executive remuneration's to align the interests of managers and shareholders, and external constraints upon managerial decision-making by non-executive directors and outside auditors. Yet all have their weaknesses. Executive pay schemes typically provide bonuses but do not allow for the docking of salaries or the repayment of bonuses when losses are recorded, while non-executive board members and external auditors may face the same information asymmetries as other outsiders, when assessing the riskiness of a bank's investments.

Self-discipline by bank management – albeit reinforced by regulatory and other external pressures – offers the best solution. Driven by market pressures and the force of events, banks have re-assessed the risks of derivatives and proprietary trading operations and have put in place compliance systems – constituting virtually a 'middle' office - to control the inherent risks (Aynsley, 1995). What is needed is a set of standards against which to evaluate risk-taking behaviour in conventional lending, and commercial real estate in particular. As a contribution, the following ten rules are suggested by the lending experiences of recent decades.

1. Know the sector status and the borrower, how the credit will be used and how it will be repaid;
2. Avoid an undue concentration of loans to single activities, individuals or groups, especially to the development/construction sector which is of a particularly high risk category;

3. Remember the adage 'turnover is vanity, profit is sanity': apply strict profitability criteria to each individual credit transaction and accept that the right lending decisions are not always the easy ones to make;
4. 'No news is bad news': invariably, late news and information from a borrower is bad news and information and a portent of worse to come;
5. Recognise that real estate sector downturns are inevitable, and conduct market sector sensitivity analysis and downside risk analysis to the loan book;
6. Focus on cash flow analysis and not 'rubbery' valuation figures, while nevertheless ensuring that the collateral is not vulnerable to the same shocks that weaken the borrower;
7. Avoid the 'feel good' factor and a 'romance' with the borrower: expand cautiously into new activities and never follow the herd instinct;
8. In good times, people tend to forget history: build up reserves and ignore those of the competitors who are willing to lend a little more for a little less margin and on easier terms and conditions;
9. Do not believe in eternal growth and the boom that will not end: e.g. it is virtually impossible to grow a loan portfolio faster than the rate of GDP without taking undue risk;
10. "The golden rule is that there are no golden rules!" (George Bernard Shaw).

Conclusions

Lending on commercial property – not derivatives – has been bankers' 'black-hole' of the 1990s. Faulty risk assessments, suspect valuation methods, lending on collateral not cash flows, and a lack of knowledge of the development pipeline were contributory factors, underpinned by managerial ambitions and a strong marketing drive, supported by incentive structures and selling techniques which did not translate well into banking. When the market turned and asset values collapsed, inexperience of a downmarket also played a role. Yet bankers ought to have been aware of the vagaries of the commercial property market in which fluctuations in demand, the complexity of the development cycle, long lags in supply, high gearing and illiquidity interact to produce the potential for a sudden build up of unsustainable capacity and, for banks, problem loans.

That is now all in the past. Market trends in a number of countries (East Asia excepted) suggest that the rental position remains subdued, but is rising, and that while speculative development is now underway, it is not excessive. Even Canary Wharf, that symbol of the 1980s, has begun a new phase of development. At the same time, there seems to be a long-term decline in institutional involvement in the property sector and when the next boom arrives, banks will again be encouraged to fill the gap. If a repetition of past experience is to be avoided, a survival kit is needed along the lines sketched out, the ingredients of which include a knowledge of the vicissitudes of the market, incentives to due diligence in commercial property investments, and the institution of lending policies which reflect the sector status, not competition and the euphoria of the times. Can bankers learn from history? Can corporate amnesia be overcome? Time will tell.

Acknowledgement

Tony McGough of Hillier Parker and Peter Evans of Deberham Thorpe kindly assisted with data and information. Judy Melbourne cheerfully prepared the figures and text. Ron McIver and Peter Rossini of the University of South Australia gave valuable advice.

2.9 Uncertainty in real estate appraisals

by Mats Ekelid, Hans Lind, Stellan Lundström and Erik Persson
Division of Building and Real Estate Economics, Royal Institute of Technology, Stockholm

After the real estate market crash people wonder how it was possible that prices reached such an "unreasonable" high level. How could the values of properties be so overestimated? The next question is then to ask about the profession that did the appraisals. Did they use the right methods? Did they give the right information to their customers? Or more generally: Did the appraisals have the quality that could be expected? This question has been discussed in a large number of countries in recent years. When trying to answer this question it is important to try to make a fair assessment of what is reasonable to expect from an appraisal. This must be judged from the knowledge and information that existed at the time. We must be very careful when we define what we mean by high quality in appraisals and appraisal reports.

Here we focus on the treatment of uncertainty in valuations of commercial properties. This choice is related to the criticisms that appraisers should have been aware of, and in some way informed their clients better, about the uncertainty in appraisals especially during a period when market values rise rapidly. An empirical investigation of a selection of appraisal reports from (primarily) the period 1980-1995 is presented.

In the next section we discuss more generally the quality and accuracy in valuations in order to put our study into perspective. Section 3 gives a short description of the methods used and the selection of the appraisal reports. In section 4 and 5 results are presented and analysed. Some more general reflections and comments on some limitations of our study are presented in the final section.

Quality in appraisals

One approach to judge the quality of appraisals is to ask whether different appraisers, confronted with the same information about a property, *will reach the same result when appraising the property*. Are the methods of the appraisers reliable in the sense that they produce the same result independently of the specific valuer? Britton et al (1991) presents a study of this type concerning the cost approach to valuation. Brown (1992) presents an overview of some other studies of this type related to the estimation of the market value of commercial properties. The general result of these studies is that there is a rather wide dispersion of the estimates of the value of a property, even though the appraisers used the same information about the property.

Brown et al (1997) argues that this should not be surprising. An appraisal is based on a *judgement* about the current market, and there will always be different views about how the market will develop. A rather wide range of appraised values should therefore be expected.

It is also important to note that if there were in fact a high degree of agreement between appraisals, this would not necessarily imply that the qualities of the methods are high. We can imagine a situation where a high degree of consensus among valuers is the result not of 'good' methods, but of very strict rules within a profession of how a value should be reached.

Another type of study is concerned with *the relation between appraised value and the price actually paid*. Matysiak & Wang (1995) and Brown et al (1997) present such studies. The result in the last study is formulated as follows:

"It shows that valuers have approximately 1 chance in 10 of achieving values within +/- 5% of the mean value. This improves to 1 in 5 if the range is increased to +/- 10%". (p 1)

They also show that appraisals tend to lag the market.

Again we note that a high correlation between appraised value and prices actually paid could also occur for 'wrong' reasons. If appraisers have a very strong position, the price actually paid could be the *result* of the valuation. Most of the time there would then be a strong correlation between valuation and price. Only in periods where the valuations get very much out of line would there be a period of differences, followed by a new realignment when appraisers have adjusted their methods and regained their position.

A third way to judge the quality of the appraisers is to ask the buyers and users of appraisals whether they are satisfied with the results that they get, along the lines of Mallinson (1994) and Crosby et al (1997). The result of the latter can be summarised as follows:

"Generally, UK clients are satisfied with valuation reports received from external valuers. ... However, there is a common criticism that valuers provide more information on the factual elements within a report – for example, the physical location and the layout and measurements of the building – than they do on the valuation methodology and the state of the market".

The problem with this type of study is that the buyer may not be well enough informed to judge what reasonably can be demanded.

We have chosen another approach and that is to look at a selection of appraisal reports and evaluate them from a number of different perspective. The focus is on *the treatment of uncertainty in the appraisal reports*. Our starting point is that a good appraisal not only uses the 'right' methods and produces the 'right' result, but should also convey the uncertainty of the appraisal. More specifically we look at two questions:

1. *How is the appraised value presented?* Is it presented as a single figure, or as some kind of interval? If there is an interval, how wide is it and on what is it based? An interval can both be seen as *an interval for the probable price,* suggesting that other valuers could reach other results, or as *an interval for actual prices*, giving information about the probability distribution of actual prices and not only about the probable price. We also investigated if some kind of sensitivity analysis was used. The data and analysis of these questions are presented in section 4.

2. Market values tend to change over time and in some situations the probability of changes might be higher. An estimation of the market value at time T might be uncertain, not in the sense that it is an uncertain predictor of price at time T, but in the sense that the market value at time T+1 might be very different from the value at time T. We could say that basing your decision on the appraisal at time T might be more or less risky, depending on how stable is the market value. We have therefore looked at *if and how the appraiser makes any suggestions about the stability of the appraised value.* If we had an experienced valuer, sensing that a boom is starting to reach a peak, we should perhaps expect some suggestions that it might be very risky to base a decision to buy on the result of the appraisal, even though there is no reason to doubt the estimation of the market value at time T. In section 5 we look at our material from this point of view.

The material

The first step was to clarify the aspects of an appraisal report under examination, namely:

1. For whom the appraisal is made
2. The purpose of the appraisal: value concept and how the appraisal shall be used

3. Time of valuation and date of value
4. Any special conditions that is assumed in the valuation (e.g. concerning use)
5. The data about the property and the market that are presented
6. The valuation method(s) used
7. More detailed questions related to the method used, e.g. sources, type of statistical analysis, time horizon in cash-flow analysis etc
8. How the conclusions are formulated: reservations, treatment of uncertainty, etc
9. Comments and reservations about the development of the value after the date of valuation
10. The 'volume' of the appraisal report

In this study we discuss mainly results related to items 8 and 9.

The next, and not uncomplicated, step in the study was to find appraisal reports. A random selection in the statistical sense was of course not possible as appraisal reports aren't collected in some kind of register from which a draw could be made. We contacted firms or individuals that we knew had been carrying out appraisals and asked them if we could use their archives. It turned out that the firms in general were very co-operative, given that their names and the results concerning their appraisals weren't published. The data presented here are taken from 8 different firms. As we believed that there were similarities in the valuations carried out by a single firm, we chose two appraisals for each year from each specific firm, one where offices and shops dominated and one where flats dominated. In this report we will not look at each of these types separately. We also had a minimum size for the property.

This type of process can be expected to lead to a selection of appraisal reports that are better than the average. Less serious appraisers and firms can be expected to leave the market after a crash and their appraisal reports will be difficult to find. We can also expect that some firm try to 'give a good impression' and not let us look at what they now think are 'old sins'. We don't think that these effects are important for our purpose. To look at a selection of better than average appraisals can be especially interesting if we, in a wider setting, want to discuss the role of the appraiser during a boom on a real estate market. The 'buyer' of an appraisal that choose a firm without a good reputation takes a risk, and that has nothing to do with the appraisal profession as such. Mistakes and some "faulty" products also occur in all times. Our general view is then that our selection gives a representative view of "good" appraisals over the time period 1980-1996. A small number of valuations from the period 1965-1979 are also included.

We have also made some rough checks to see that the changes over time that we report are not primarily the result of changes in the firms that the selections are taken from, but that changes of the reported type also can be found within specific firms.

This paper is based on an analysis of 79 appraisal reports from the period 1980-1996. All concern the estimation of market value.

Uncertainty in the estimation of market value

The data

In table 2.9 we present the data concerning how the value is reported. The division into periods reflect the property cycle in Sweden, with boom years 1985-1990 and a crash in the second half of 1991. The first thing that we can note is that there is no general trend over time. The share of cases where only a point estimate is reported grew somewhat in the period 1985-1990 (the boom years), but then it fell drastically after the crash in 1991. The type of interval also changed. The small intervals (1-4%) disappeared completely and there was a growth in 'unspecified' intervals.

Table 2.9 Point estimates and intervals

Period	*Point estimate only*	*Interval 1-4%*	*Interval 5-9%*	*Interval 10%-*	*Unspecified interval*	*Number of appraisals*
1980-1984	35%	12%	30%	24%	-	17
1985-1990	46%	14%	31%	9%	-	35
1991	25%	-	12%	50%	12%	8
1992-1996	10%	-	47%	16%	26%	19

The intervals presented were usually not explained, but it seems reasonable to interpret them as an *interval for the market value* and not for the actual price. No indications were given about the probability that the market value would be in the specified interval. Nothing was said about how the interval was arrived at. If there were any comment at all it was that the interval reflected the general uncertainty of real estate appraisals. The interval was not adapted to the specific appraisal.

In table 2.10 data on the use of sensitivity analysis are presented. By sensitivity analysis we mean that the appraisers described how different assumptions about the value-determining parameters affect the value, e.g. a change in interest rates or rent levels. The same pattern as in table 1 appears also in this table. The use of sensitivity analysis fell during the boom years, but grew dramatically after the crash. It should however be noted that it is still used in less that half of the appraisals.

Comments
How can we explain the pattern that can be found in tables 2.9 and 2.10? Let us first note that the 'methods' of handling uncertainty that we look at – presenting an interval, making a sensitivity analysis – are old methods that the appraisers knew about during the whole interval.

Table 2.10 The use of sensitivity analysis

Period	*Sensitivity analysis is presented*	*Number of appraisals*
1980-1984	18%	17
1985-1990	6%	35
1991	0%	8
1992-1996	47%	19

One possible explanation why these methods were not used more during the boom years could be that the users of the appraisal reports already knew about the general uncertainty of the appraisals. Therefore it was not necessary to make any explicit comments about uncertainty. The problem with this explanation is that it is not consistent with the fact that the use of these methods grew after the crash. If the users knew about the general uncertainty of the appraisals before the crash, they definitively knew about them after the crash.

Another explanation could be that the uncertainty of the valuations in fact was lower during the boom. When there were more transactions, there were more data and therefore the estimation of the market value was less uncertain. The problem during the boom years was not, according to this view, uncertainty in the estimation of the market value but that *the stability of the market value was over-estimated,* an issue to which we now turn.

Stability in the estimated value

Data
We also looked at different types of reservations and formulations about what the appraiser was prepared to take responsibility for. One type of formulation relates to the future development of the market value. The conclusion in the appraisal report is an estimated market value at a specific point in time. One way for the appraiser to signal uncertainty is to state that this should not be taken as an indication of what the market value will be *after* this point in time.

In table 3 we present data about how common was this type of reservation. We also report whether other types of reservations were made, but these mainly concern the quality of information about the property.

Table 2.11. Different types of reservations in appraisal reports

Period	*Reservations concerning future market value*	*Reservations concerning other factors*	*Number of appraisals*
1980-1984	-	-	17
1985-1990	31%	3%	35
1991	25%	25%	8
1992-1996	16%	32%	19

The data show a dramatic increase in reservations about the development of the market value during the boom years.

Comments

The data indicate that a number of appraisers were aware of the risk that the rising prices would not last. Even though they did not spell this out explicitly, they seemed to signal their uncertainty about future market values by explicitly saying that the appraisal concerns the market value at a specific time. The appraisal says nothing about the market value after that time. If we look at how the reservations are presented, they are mostly made by a single line and more in passing, like a matter of routine. This type of reservation became more common and perhaps was a signal about the stability of the market value, but for the user of an appraisal it would be rather difficult to identify this as a signal that the market value may change quickly.

Concluding comments

The general picture that emerges is that there was little explicit discussion of uncertainty in valuations during the boom years. In terms of presenting intervals for the estimated value and making sensitivity analysis, a smaller share of appraisal reports show an awareness of uncertainty than before. Even though more reservations about future market values are made, it was still only made in a minority of cases.

There are some 'objective' reasons for this lack of interest in discussing uncertainty, primarily more market data as the activity on the market was high. If we look at the drastic changes in the explicit treatment of uncertainty in the years after the crash, it is hard to explain these only from changes in the amount of market data. Some psychological or sociological aspects were probably important too. During an extreme boom there might be some kind of 'taboo' against talking about uncertainty. Everybody knew that the uncertainty was present, but talking about it or even thinking about it might affect air of market excitement. A discreet reservation about the future market value was then a rational policy for those appraisers who were most aware of the uncertainty and wanted to signal their uncertainty to the customer.

Some valuers said that the customers during the boom years did not want to hear about uncertainty. The characteristics of the appraisal reports might then have been at least partly 'demand-driven', and not be a reflection of what the valuer 'really' thought were best. The next question is then why the final user, for example a bank that should decide about a loan, did not demand an appraisal with a more thorough treatment of uncertainty. Perhaps we can explain the characteristics of real estate appraisals with the lack of risk analysis in the banks that used them - see the chapters by Per Lundberg and also Mervyn Lewis.

2.10 Leasing and property risk: The South Australian experience

by Wayne A Marano
Ph.D.
and
Mervyn K Lewis
National Australia Bank Professor
University of South Australia

The value of an investment in property is governed by current and anticipated future cash flows, the risks associated with receiving those cash flows and the possibility of future capital gains or losses. Increased risk associated with future cash flows should in theory, equate to diminished capital value, and visa versa. This relationship is important because changes in the way in which lease agreements can be structured and rentals reviewed have the potential for shifting the risk of future rental cash flows between the tenant and the landlord.

One of the principal means by which governments have intervened in the property market in Australia has been to influence the negotiation process between landlords and tenants. Our paper uses South Australia as a case study to examine the impacts on commercial leasing as a result of changes to government controls. The major changes made in 1995 under the South Australian Retail Shop Leases Act were: the abolition of ratchet clauses; a minimum five year term to be granted to the tenant, a condition that landlords cannot review rent to the highest of two or more methods of review, that the landlord must pay compensation to the tenant where the tenant's business is disrupted by the landlord, and that outgoings charged to the tenant be based on the ratio of the tenancy area to the total area of the premises occupied by the tenant.

In order to examine the impacts we studied a random sample of 111 leases comprising commercial and retail leases that were negotiated prior to and following the 1995 Act. Table 2.12 summarises the composition of the sample. It is immediately apparent that the statutory changes appear to have different impacts on two sectors. The commercial sector now has, on average, shorter lease terms, while for retail tenancies the term length has, on average, increased. The change in lease terms is displayed in Figures 2.21 and 2.22.

Table 2.12 Composition of leasing sample

	Mean		**Std. Dev.**		**Min**		**Max**		**Sample No.**	
Commercial	**Prior**	**After**	**Prior**	**After**	**Prior**	**After**	**Prior**	**After**	**Prior**	**After**
Term	7	5	4	3	2	2	15	10	23	16
Area (Sq.m.)	377	318	296	277	21	50	1037	1052	19	14
Retail										
Term	8	9	4	5	2	2	17	20	28	44
Area (Sq.m.)	132	161	102	103	25	22	379	360	24	38

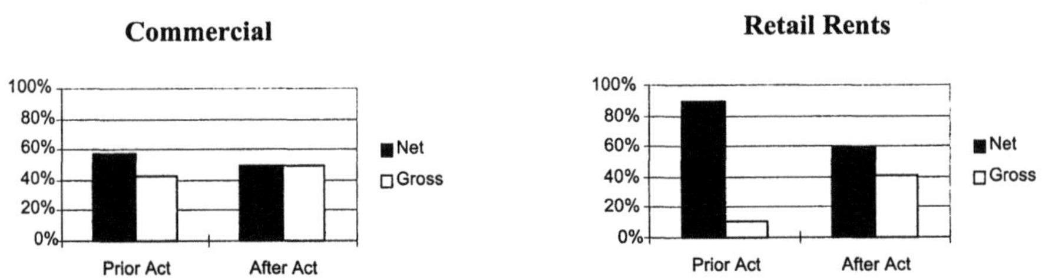

Figure 2.21 Percentage of Net and Gross Rents

Terms and conditions have also altered. With commercial leases there has been a small shift from net rent to gross terms, whereas with retail leases this shift has been much larger. Figure 2.22 shows that in tandem with gross leases, lessors have adopted a system of a fixed annual increase at the annual rent review based either on the CPI or at a predetermined rate. This dual strategy reduces the risk associated with variations that may occur in outgoings over the term of the lease and, at the same time, counters the impact of the prohibition of ratchet clauses.

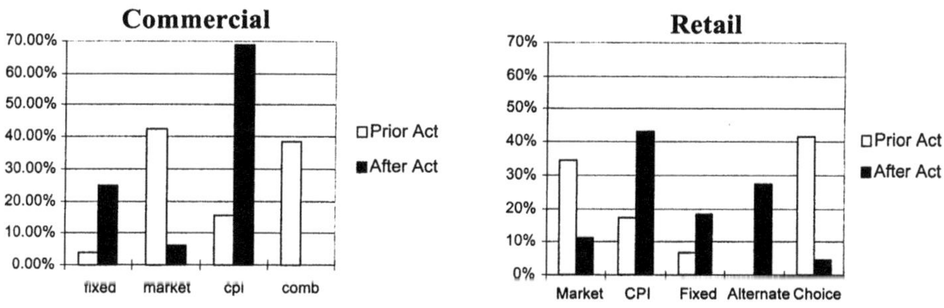

Figure 2.22 Rent review method

For both commercial and retail properties the dominant method of rent review used to be to market or to the higher of this and another method. Following the changes, market review is the least preferred. Commercial property rentals are mainly reviewed using the annual CPI. Retail properties display a similar tendency expect that alternating rent review methods are also used, e.g., Year 1-3 C.P.I, year 4 market.

Rent reviews are now being carried out almost entirely on an annual basis, whereas before the changes both market sectors had a significant number of two yearly reviews. In addition, since the changes the majority of retail leases determine rental using a base rental plus a percentage of turnover once a threshold limit has been reached.

Interviews with leasing agents

In the next stage of the research, additional information was sought from a series of 45 minute, structured face-to-face interviews. Seven senior leasing agents and property negotiation managers actively involved in the market were selected for these interviews. The seven participants each have on average 15 years of experience in property leasing and are actively involved in leasing on a daily basis. They also cover a sizeable segment of the market.

Most important changes

Each of the questionnaire respondents was provided with a list of 10 legislated changes and asked to rank them from a landlord's perspective in order of importance. Table 2.13 lists the responses.

Table 2.13 Most important changes

Change	Case 1	Case 2	Case 3	Case 4	Case 5	Case 6	Case 7	Average
Rent review method	2	2	1	4	2	2	2	1.9
Ratchet clauses	1	1	8	2	1	1	1	2.3
Compensation	0	5	3	3	3	3	5	3.7
5 year term	3	3	10	1	10	4	3	4.4
Lease administration	0	6	2	5	5	8	7	5.5
Mediation	0	7	4	6	8	7	4	6.0
Lease preparation	0	4	7	7	6	10	6	6.7
Premium on signing	0	10	6	8	4	5	10	7.2
Premium on assignment	0	9	5	9	9	6	9	7.8
Warranty	0	8	9	10	7	9	8	8.5

The prohibition of ratchet clauses, the method of rent review, and compensation provisions clearly ranked as having the greatest impact. At the other end of the scale, warranty of suitability and loss of premiums on signing a lease and approvals for assignments are ranked as having little importance. The minimum 5 years term and prospect of increased and more difficult lease administration fell in between. The results highlight those changes with cash flow implications as being the most important. The prohibition of premiums was not an important issue, suggesting that the practice was not widely used.

Respondents were asked what action landlords had adopted to overcome the changes made in the Act. Two major strategies emerged. One was 'grossing up leases' to offset the changes made to the recovery of outgoings. The other was the use of fixed rental reviews to overcome the loss of the ratchet clause.

Interviewees were then asked to rate how lessors' perception of risk associated with property investment had changed as a result the Act, ignoring as far as possible the confounding influences of other supply and demand factors. Generally, single property owners were rated as perceiving retail property investments as having greater risk and generally the overall ratings were skewed to the perceptions being slightly more negative. In a separate question, respondents were asked if the introduction of the Act had impacted on the market value of commercial and retail property. The answers suggested that the Act has impacted equally on both sectors. However, the extent of the impact was inconclusive with four responding that market values had been adversely affected while the other three indicated that there had been little or no effect.

In two open questions respondents were asked to comment on the positive and negative aspects of the Act in relation to property investment risk. The respondents made only 7 positive comments about the changes but had 20 negative ones. Positive comments generally related to there being a more informed market which may result in fewer tenancy failures and therefore fewer vacancies; e.g. "Forced people to be more professional, now everyone has to be aware of all terms and conditions" and "A fuller disclosure means lessees know what they are getting into". The negative comments generally related to landlords having increased risk. The loss of the ratchet clause was highlighted along with one observation that without it, "market review rents can go down, therefore financiers are devaluing property".

Conclusion

The research, while necessarily of an exploratory nature, has uncovered some interesting outcomes. There is no doubt that legislated changes to the way commercial leases could be negotiated had the potential to shift risk from the tenant to the lessor. The changes, which had the greatest importance to lessors, were the abolition of ratchet clauses, the prohibition of rent reviews based on the higher of two or more methods and the compensation provisions for the relocation of tenants. There was consensus among the respondents that the changes have been perceived as increasing risk to the lessor.

Lessors have responded by restructuring leases to include annually adjusted rentals based either on the CPI, a predetermined fixed annual percentage increase or a combination of both. The other major alteration in lease covenants has been the shift from net to gross lease arrangements. These two changes restore certainty to a major proportion of a lessor's cash flow. The responses appear to be similar for both the retail and commercial property sector. Across investor types there is some evidence, although far from conclusive, that institutional and multiple owner investors have been able to adjust to the transfer in risk more efficiently than single property investors, although this finding is far from conclusive. There are mixed views with respect to the impact that the Act has had up on commercial and retail market values. This would suggest difficulty in evaluating the lease variations adopted – a position that has been recognised in other research (Crosby et al, 1992).

Overall, it would seem that lessors have been able to adjust lease terms and conditions to offset risk and provide certainty of future cash flow in the new environment. However, these strategies may not have been sufficient to compensate lessors for all additional risks.

PSYCHOLOGY IN BUSINESS LIFE

3.1 Introduction

by James Shanteau
Professor/Director, Institute for Social and Behavioral Research
Kansas State University

The purpose of this chapter is to provide an overview of psychological research on decision making under risk. This research tradition has supplied many insights into how humans react to risk and uncertainty. These insights help explain why people take considerable financial risks under some circumstances and avoid smaller risks under other circumstances.

Background

Behavioural decision research began in the 1950s with analyses of how people make choices between gambles. In the 1960s, the emphasis shifted to probability revision and probability assessment. The decade of the 1970s produced a new line of work on risk heuristics (mental rules of thumb) and biases. The 1980s expanded this research through analyses of framing (context) effects and preference reversals (inconsistencies between choices and ratings). Finally, the 1990s yielded new ideas about models of risky decision making and alternate ideas about utility theory.

Today, the study of judgement and decision making is expanding in many exciting directions. The Society for Research on Judgement and Decision Making (JDM), begun in 1980 by the present author and several colleagues, has grown to over 1,000 members' world-wide. Meanwhile, the European Association of Decision Making (EADM) has developed rapidly from a 30-year traditional of sponsoring the Subjective Probability, Utility, and Decision Making (SPUDM) meetings.

Although initially dominated by psychologists, decision researchers now reflect a broad variety of disciplines including economics, statistics, management science, medicine, law, marketing, engineering, geography, accounting/auditing, nursing, computer science, and finance. It has truly become an interdisciplinary field.

Principles of risk behaviour

As noted by Slovic (1984), "it is extremely hard (for people) to think about . . . uncertainty, probability and risk". Indeed, repeated demonstrations have shown that most people lack a consistent understanding of probability and risk concepts. A number of principles have been uncovered, however, that describe how people think about probability and risk. Twelve of those are considered here.

1. Misperceptions of small probabilities. Obviously, people can only respond to risks they can perceive. One persistently reported misperception is an inability to react logically to low-probability events. People either ignore low risks or exaggerate their importance. In part, this misperceptions arises from the limited cognitive capacity people have for processing information. Simon's concept of *bounded rationality* contends that cognitive limitations force people to construct simplified models of the world. Thus, people's limited processing capacity frequently restricts human attention to rare events.

2. Focus on probability of loss. People don't like to lose money. This aversion to loss, however, seems more focused on probability than amount of loss: "It is not the magnitude of a potential loss that inspires people to buy insurance . . .it is the frequency with which a loss is likely to occur" (Kunreuther, 1979). Similarly, the criminologist Sir Robert Mark argues that the best deterrent to crime is not the severity of the punishment, but rather the likelihood of being caught. Focusing on the probability of loss can, of course, lead to non-optimal choices. In studies of choice behaviour, for instance, subjects preferred unfavourable gambles to accepting a sure loss, i.e.; people's attention is captured by the loss probability.

3. Risk aversion. It is commonly assumed that a person's propensity to avoid (or seek) risk is constant over gains and losses. For instance, a risk-averse individual would presumably avoid risk of any type. Empirical evidence nonetheless shows that most people are risk averse for gains and risk seeking for losses. People are often risk seeking when it comes to losses: they are willing to chance a loss even when they can insure against it. Many even decline to buy government-subsidised insurance in which the premiums are so low that buyers are effectively in a 'can't lose' position. Obviously, people have great difficulty thinking about risk.

4. Gambler's fallacy. Many people have a strongly-held, but false, belief that random events are self-correcting. If a couple gives birth to two girls, then a boy is viewed as likelier next time. A common sports example is the belief that a previously scoreless soccer (football) player is somehow 'due' to score a goal. This inability to appreciate the randomness of random events also shows up in low probability situations. If an unlikely natural hazard occurs, then people believe it is unlikely to occur again – *lightning can't strike twice.* Thus, the perceived likelihood of future events changes as a function of past occurrences.

5. Risk homeostasis. A general principle of human behaviour is that people try to remain at equilibrium levels, e.g., of motivation. This concept of *homeostasis* has been extended by Slovic (1984) to risk settings: There is "an optimal level of risk that people are comfortable in accepting". Efforts to reduce risk, therefore, are often met by even riskier behaviour by users. One example relates to farmers. When improved design made tractors more stables, farmers began using them on steeper slopes – the accident rate remained unchanged. This suggests that risk-reduction efforts may be offset by compensatory behavioural changes.

6. Overconfidence. Humans often operate under what has been labelled a 'certainty illusion' – a belief in their own invulnerability. People tend to underestimate their own vulnerability to certain sorts of risks. Similarly, people view themselves as invulnerable to hazards. Most believe they are better than average drivers, more likely to live longer than most, and less likely than others to be harmed by consumer products. Given such beliefs, it should not be surprising that many people refuse to take personal actions to reduce their personal risks.

7. Context effects. Psychologists have long been aware of the power of context effects on human judgement. One such class of effects has been labelled 'framing' by Kahneman and Tversky (1984) – a 'glass have empty' vs. 'glass half full' effect. They found that people are more likely to accept losses labelled as 'cost of protection' than 'uncompensated losses' – even though monetary consequences are the same. Researchers have reported that slight shifts in wording can have a pronounced effect on choice behaviour. This means that context effects can be used to manipulate the perceptions of risk.

8. Inability to conceptualise hazards. A major limitation to our ability to react to low-probability, high-consequence risk is the inability to imagine hazards that have not occurred. People who live in flood-prone areas are trapped by their own inexperience with floods. Thus, much of the difficulty in improving flood plans can be attributed to the inability of residents to conceive of floods that have not occurred recently. People are captured by their own experience. Consequently, they limit their view of the future to linear projections of their own past.

9. Individual differences. A common finding in psychology is the presence of wide differences between people in how they respond to risk. Studies of farmers, for example, report a relationship between willingness to accept risk and the types of crops grown. High-risk takers grow high-return 'cash' crops; moderate risk takers are more likely to be in dairy farming; lost risk takers are in general farming. Such behaviour, however, can be self-limiting. An unwillingness to take risks can keep farmers from engaging in more profitable efforts. Thus, those who practice 'safety-first' farming may be trapped by their own risk attitudes.

10. Training and education. Efforts to train people to think more effectively about risks have had limited success. While it is possible to learn to make better decisions in given situations, these lessons seldom generalise to other settings. People seem to have great difficulty in applying the wisdom gained from one risk setting to another. It is as if we have to relearn our lessons about risky decision making in each new situation we encounter. This may explain, for instance, why people who are risk averse with money may take great personal risks with drugs.

11. Experts. In part because of our personal inability to think about risks clearly, there is often a need to rely on experts to advise us. Thus, we now have experts in virtually every area of human endeavour from investment and banking to dating and marriage. Unfortunately, it turns out that these experts often disagree with each other – leaving the consumer with a difficult choice about whom to believe. In many high-risk situations, we are left with the question: How should we combine the opinions of experts with different opinions?

12. Resistance to change. Perceptions of risk seem quite stable and resistant to change. People's beliefs about risky events can show remarkable persistence, even in the face of contradictory evidence. One of the reasons is that we seldom receive feedback about the appropriateness, or inappropriateness, of our risk perceptions. Another reason is that through hindsight, we view past events as far more predictable than in fact they were. As a result, people have a tendency to deceive themselves about how well they can handle risk.

Some solutions

As a result of these misperceptions, investigators have proposed various approaches to help people make better decisions under risk. These include reliance on experts, use of training and/or education, access to better information, development of decision support systems, identification of high and low-risk personalities, and introduction of new technologies for making decisions.

In developing these solutions, the value of psychological perspectives along with those of other disciplines is evident. For instance, the authors writing in the chapters that follow have gained valuable insights by combining psychology with one (or more) of the following fields: economics, engineering, law, statistics, banking, sociology, accounting, education, finance, and marketing.

Implications

Let me offer some concluding observations. First, it is clear that economic theory by itself is not adequate to account for decision making under risk. "Utility maximisation is neither a necessary nor a sufficient condition for deducing who will buy insurance... If we wish to understand (such) behaviour, then we must determine the circumstances that attract the attention of (people)" (Simon, 1987).

Second, despite the problems people have coping with risk, humans are capable of improving their decision-making (Shanteau, et al, 1991). One suggestion is to change the time horizon for explaining risks – a 1-in-100 year flood can be presented as 'more than a 1-in-5 chance of flood damage in 25 years.' As this example shows, different phrasing can change risk perceptions dramatically.

Third, by working together researchers from different disciplines can provide new understandings of decision making, especially under risk. As an example, new insights into insurance buying have emerged in recent years due to the collaboration of psychologists, economists, management scientists, and statisticians (Slovic, 1984). The opportunity is there for researchers willing to work together.

The chapters that follow illustrate how psychological principles can be used to provide insights into human behaviour in risky environments. There are signs of clear progress in our understanding of managing risk in business environments.

In the following sections, Rob Ranyard, Janis Williamson, and Lisa Cuthbert describe their innovative efforts to apply novel *conversation-based methods* to evaluate decisions in their natural environment. Henry Montgomery's chapter provides a novel perspective on decision making by comparing two very important motivational styles of thinking: *reflective* and *nonreflective*. Leif Sanner offer a fascinating analysis of the *role of trust* as a key factor influencing risk judgements by entrepreneurs. In James Shanteau's chapter on *management of technological innovation*, psychologists, engineers, and management scientists combined their talents to analyse this most important problem. Lisbeth Hedelin describes an extensive study of *non-financial factors* on risk judgements by practising credit officers. In an insightful analysis by Fabian von Schéele, the concept of risk is extended to include *temporal factors* in addition to more traditional notions of probability and loss. The final two chapters both involve expertise: Anna Mette Fuglseth and Kjell Grønhaug explore the crucial role that *task characteristics* play in the performance of experts; and James Shanteau offers some answers to the question of *why do experts disagree*?

3.2 The development of conversation-based process tracing methods for the study of naturalistic decision making

by Rob Ranyard, Ph.D., Janis Williamson, Ph.D. and Lisa Cuthbert, Ph.D.
Psychology Subject Group, Bolton Institute

Cognitive approaches to the study of individual decision making began to develop from the late sixties. Some researchers regard final judgements and choices as the basis of the key empirical tests of a model's validity. Other researchers, however, have adopted process-tracing methods. In this approach, decision making is conceptualised as a process over time, and direct evidence is sought about temporal changes in processing, both before and after the decision. Techniques such as thinking aloud and information search have been employed and important insights have resulted. However, as Woods (1993) has argued, these formal process tracing methods are of limited value for the study of real world problems, and new techniques must be developed. As an alternative to the information board procedure, Oswald Huber and his colleagues (Huber, Wider and O.L. Huber, 1997; Huber, 1997) have devised an 'Active Information Search' (AIS) technique to investigate patterns of pre-decision information seeking.

The AIS method uses a very well briefed researcher who provides the information requested in a more informal, face-to-face setting. In a similar vein, we are developing an alternative to the think aloud technique based on a more natural, semi-structured interview. This builds on an interview approach we used in a study of decisions involving real instalment credit options (Ranyard and Craig, 1995) and uses a similar approach to Roth and Woods' (1989) 'Cognitive Task Analysis' (CTA) and elements of Klein, Calderwood and MacGregor's (1989) 'Critical Decision Method' (CDM).

Since the AIS method is at the core of the naturalistic process tracing techniques to be described here, its origins and recent development will now be described. As mentioned earlier, a substantial body of research has accumulated since the mid-seventies in which information search patterns have been monitored under controlled conditions to provide evidence of underlying decision processes. These studies have mainly used the information board paradigm, in which an attribute-by-alternative matrix of information cards is available for the decision task. Subjects must turn over the cards sequentially to reveal information about choice alternatives on different attributes, thus revealing their search patterns.

Despite its usefulness as a process tracing technique, the information board paradigm is inflexible and unrealistic in that attributes and alternatives are fixed in advance. Englander and Tyszka (1980) devised a more natural 'information-search tracing' method. They presented subjects with a set of letters, the labels of hypothetical choice alternatives, and subjects were allowed to ask any questions they wanted. An assistant provided answers verbally, with reference to pre-arranged descriptions of the alternatives, designed to anticipate all possible questions. In a later study, Tyszka (1986) added think aloud instructions to his standard information-search tracing task.

Huber et al (1997) recognised that this method was much more suitable for the study of naturalistic decision making, and developed the procedure for their current studies of (fictitious) decisions involving risk. They described the method of Active Information Search (AIS) as follows:

> "The subject is first presented with a minimal description of the decision situation. Then, he or she can ask the experimenter questions in order to obtain more information. The subject can ask any question, and also repeat questions any time. The question is recorded, and the answer is presented, printed or written, on a small card. This style of answering the questions was adopted in order to eliminate ef-

fects of verbalising the answer by the experimenter, and to avoid non-verbal influences. Please note that the subject asks the questions, not the experimenter".

They go on to point out that thorough preparation is essential if the AIS procedure is to be successful, in order to determine the optimal initial task description, and to prepare answers to as many questions as possible. Also, researchers have to train themselves to produce answers quickly, and to improvise answers to the (hopefully few) questions not anticipated.

Huber et al (1997) compared data from the AIS task with that from a condition where full information was provided, and found that some information was used more in the latter than in the AIS condition. They concluded that providing full information is reactive, in that it leads to information being used that would not be used naturally. On the other hand, they found that data from AIS alone was less useful than an AIS plus think-aloud procedure because some statements found in the think aloud component were not found in the AIS part. Therefore, the AIS method combined with think aloud instructions are likely to be the most effective variant of the method. Our own development of the AIS procedure is to provide spoken rather than written answers to respondents' questions. All variants of our process tracing methods, then, are set in the context of a natural conversation.

Conversation-based process tracing methods

It is useful to further contrast formal process tracing techniques with conversation-based methods. As indicated earlier, the formal methods originated from the experimental psychology framework in which experimenters take care to study their subjects in a strictly controlled environment. This certainly applies to research using information boards. In fact, most recent studies present boards via computer, thus facilitating the control of the task and reducing unnecessary variation. The use of the think aloud procedure is similarly controlled. Subjects are given information about a problem and are asked to think aloud as they work towards their decision. Experimenters try to avoid verbal responses or cues, which might influence the subject. Indeed, non-verbal cues are also avoided, with some recommending that subject and experimenter sit back-to-back.

Although our conversation-based process tracing techniques were developed from formal methods (and can be seen as variants of them), there are important points of contrast. Primarily, the former is grounded in the interview, rather than the experimental method. Thus, we refer to interviewer and respondent, not experimenter and subject; we use an office-type interview room, as opposed to a laboratory; we take standards of good practice from the research interviewing tradition, rather than the laboratory manual. We argue that the loss of control that inevitably results from the use of interview methods is more than compensated by gains in the quality of data and in range of applicability.

One of the main advantages of conversation-based process tracing methods is that a natural mode of social interaction is adopted. Researchers using the think aloud method often report that a number of participants talk very little, despite being prompted. This may be because non-interaction breaks the 'rules' of conversation, which may disrupt the participants' spoken language production and thought processes. Speakers need feedback from listeners in order to communicate effectively; for example, so that they can follow Grice's maxims of quantity, quality, relevance and manner. A skilled interviewer, who achieves good rapport, should facilitate the elicitation of respondents' questions and thoughts in a familiar social context in which they feel comfortable. The aim, then, is to capitalise on these advantages, while at the same time minimising potential errors of commission that may arise through interaction.

Table 3.1 presents an overview of conversation-based process tracing methods. As with all research interviews, they begin with orientation and end with debriefing (stages 1 and 4). At the heart of the method is the decision task simulation (stage 2). This stage often involves two or more decision problems and can be either structured or unstructured. Structured versions involve preliminary attribute elicitation, which primes the attributes on which decision alternatives vary. All variants involve active information search by the respondent in conversation with the interviewer. This may be accompanied by a conversational style of thinking aloud. Having made their decision, all respondents are asked to produce a free description of how they made it, without being probed by the interviewer (the non-directive post-decision interview).

Our pilot studies have found that the combination of respondent-led question asking and thinking aloud, with the interviewer remaining non-directive, usually creates a very productive conversational context. We have decided, therefore, not to include any concurrent probing by the interviewer, so as not to interrupt the respondent's thought processes. However, another optional elaboration of the basic method is an interactive post-decision interview during which the interviewer asks questions, which probe the simulated decision process. This follows the non-directive post-decision interview. Thus, there are six variants of the decision task simulation stage: conversational AIS only; conversational AIS with Preliminary attribute elicitation; conversational thinking aloud added to each of these; finally, the interactive post-decision interview can be added as well. We consider conversational AIS without any additional options to be the baseline condition against which the reactivity of other methods can be evaluated.

The next (optional) stage of conversation-based process tracing is the past decision interview (stage 3) in which the respondent is questioned about previous decisions they have actually made, or considered, which are similar to the stage 2 simulated decisions. Each element of the conversation-based methods listed above will now be described in more detail.

Table 3.1 The main components of conversation-based process tracing methods

Stage	Main aims
1. Orientation	to inform respondents about the task and their rights; to establish rapport
2. Decision task simulation	to elicit evidence of how decisions are represented and processed
3. Past decision interview (Optional)	to elicit recollections of past decisions
4. Debriefing	to monitor any problems that emerge; to give further information about the research

Stage 1. Orientation
The respondent is welcomed and offered refreshments. The general purpose of the study will have already been introduced prior to the interview. Nevertheless, the interviewer reiterates this, and explains his or her role in the research. The study is described as consumer research, focusing on people's thoughts about, and experience of, the topic in question (for example gambling, or consumer products and credit). Further preliminary information is then exchanged. In particular, confidentiality and anonymity are assured and permission to tape-record is obtained. The structure of the session is then summarised and it is made clear that the respondent will be asked to talk about their own experience of, in our example, gambling or consumer spending. Respondents are given a clear opportunity to withdraw before the main session begins. Then, the tape recorder is switched on, and a 'warm-up' conversation begins with the respondent being asked: "First of all, would you mind saying a few words about yourself?".

Stage 2. Decision task simulations
The aim of this stage is to present respondents with naturalistic and realistic decision problems in order to elicit verbal evidence of cognitive processes and mental representations underlying everyday decisions. Respondents should have some familiarity with the type of decision being studied. For each decision task in the series (not more than four in total), respondents are given a minimal description of the problem, and the interviewer takes the role of a helpful consultant who provides any factual information requested. Information is provided in spoken, rather than written form, and evaluative comments or opinions are not offered. A 'practice' decision task on a different topic can be used to explain what respondents are expected to do.

Preliminary attribute elicitation (optional). After being presented with the minimal problem description, respondents are asked to list verbally and in writing all the details about the decision alternatives they would like to know in order to reach their decision. If any attribute mentioned is unclear the interviewer asks for clarification. If the respondent pauses for more than 30 seconds the interviewer prompts them with the question 'anything else'? This open-ended procedure ends whenever the respondent wishes. It is adapted from the method used by Hershey, Walsh, Read and Chulef (1990) in their study of the effects of expertise on financial problem solving. Its role in process tracing is to obtain evidence on the respondent's 'mental information board' which can be useful in inferring their information search and decision making strategies.

Conversational active information search. The decision simulation proper begins when the respondent starts to ask questions about the alternatives. The interviewer's task is essentially that described by Huber et al (1997, quoted earlier) except that answers are given orally. Interviewers are careful to give only the specific information requested and no more. If the request for information is ambiguous the interviewer seeks clarification, or offers alternative clarifications for the respondent to choose. If the interviewer can't answer a question (which should be exceptional because of the pilot preparations) he or she simply says "I'm sorry, I don't have that information". If the respondent stops asking questions for 60 seconds and is not otherwise occupied (for example with reading or writing) the interviewer gives a question prompt, such as: "Is there anything else you would like to ask me?"; or "Don't forget you can ask me anything you want".

The AIS stage ends when the respondent makes their decision. The above interview strategy leads to a protocol containing the following types of conversational sequence: question-specific answer; question-clarification; prompt-question-specific answer; question-failure to answer. The content, order and organisation of such sequences can be used as evidence of the respondents' evaluation strategies in the same way as in information board research. Huber et al (1997) carried out a content analysis of their information search data which showed that risky decisions did not involve questions about precise probabilities and utilities to the extent predicted by traditional expected utility theory.

Conversational think aloud (optional). Rather than being a separate stage, this component of the simulation is, if it is used at all, integrated with the conversational AIS stage. This means that as well as asking questions, the respondent will make a series of statements. In the standard think aloud procedure, in controlled conditions, experimenters do not respond to these statements for fear of distorting or interrupting the thought process. However, this is unnatural and leads to the answerphone problem: people don't like speaking into an empty space. The conversational think aloud technique is an adaptation of the formal method for use in field settings. Interviewers take the role of non-judgmental listeners. They retain the formal technique's emphasis on achieving good descriptive validity of verbal data as evidence of thought processes, while at the same time creating a more natural, interactive social setting. The interviewer begins begin with these instructions, adapted from Russo, Johnson and Stephens (1989): "As soon as you begin working on the problem, please start thinking aloud. The best way to do this is to be as spontaneous as possible. Tell me what you are thinking as you are thinking it, even if the details seem insignificant or embarrassing. There is no need to explain to me why you are thinking what you are. You don't have to interpret or justify your approach. If you are silent for more than a few seconds I will remind you by saying 'Please keep telling me what you are thinking'". This, or alternative think aloud prompts ('What are you thinking now?' or 'keep talking') are given if the respondent stops speaking about the task for more than 20 seconds. In addition or instead, respondents can be given the question prompts described in the previous section.

The main differences between the conversational and the formal think aloud methods, then, are that in the former: 1) the instructions to think aloud stress that the respondent is speaking directly to a listener (the interviewer), rather than to a tape-recorder or an unknown person; and 2) the interviewer responds to the thinking aloud using conventional signals that they are listening and are interested: a) by non-verbal signals such as head-nods, direct gaze and attentive, interested expression; and b) by verbal acknowledgements and invitations to continue, such as "I see... yes... OK... uhuh...". We believe that, in general, these signals do not influence the course of information processing, but rather, they encourage the respondent to fully express their thoughts. The protocols resulting from this approach will contain sequences of uninterrupted statements and/or statement-acknowledgement sequences, which can be analysed in the same way as formal, think aloud data.

Non-directive post-decision interview. Once the respondent makes their choice the interviewer asks: "Can you say in your own words how you made your decision?". This is an open-ended question and the interviewer responds to the reply with the usual signals that they are listening and interested. They can invite more detail with a continuation prompt (e.g. 'Anything else?') but are otherwise non-directive. This retrospective report of the decision process is useful in checking the validity or internal consistency of process interpretations of the respondents' stage 2 concurrent questions and statements.

Interactive post-decision interview (optional). Here, the interviewer follows up the non-directive part of the post-decision interview with specific probe questions. For example: 1) *evaluations* of specific items of information can be requested, 'what do you think about aspect x?'; or 2) *reasons* for information requests or evaluations can be elicited, 'why did you want to know x?', or 'why is aspect x good (bad)?'. Such probes are used sparingly, since the interviewer is aiming to create the kind of rapport whereby as much information as possible is elicited spontaneously. On the other hand, it is natural to be asked such things in a normal conversation, and so the secondary function of these probe questions is 'conversational-repair-and-maintenance', to ensure that the flow of information disclosure proceeds smoothly. We are currently considering the inclusion of some of the probe questions developed by Klein et al (1989) for their CDM (see below).

The main purpose of this interactive component of the post-decision interview is to elicit from respondents more detailed accounts of the decision process if this seems necessary. During the earlier stages of the simulation the interviewer notes possible aspects of the decision process for post-decision probing. Thus, the interactive part of the interview is flexible, allowing the interviewer to pursue useful lines of inquiry as they see fit. They may decide, however, that further probing at this point in the interview is unnecessary.

Stage 3. Past decision interview (Optional stage)
In this stage, respondents are invited to describe and discuss past decisions of the type under investigation. The interview is semi-structured, in that a standardised interview schedule is followed. This is tailored to the specific topic and is developed in pilot work. However, the interviewer is permitted the flexibility of following up the prepared questions, where it is judged that this will enrich the interview. The procedures for this element of conversation-based process tracing are still being developed (see Kemdal and Montgomery, 1997, for a related approach).

Stage 4. Debriefing
The main aims of this are: 1) to provide the respondent with further information about the project if they are interested; 2) to thank them for their participation; and 3) to ascertain their willingness to participate in follow-up studies. If it emerges during the interview that the respondent has personal problems associated with the subject of investigation, for example, with gambling or debt, it is made clear that the interviewer is not qualified to advise. However, information is provided about how to seek help, via counsellors, advisors or self-help groups.

A study in progress

There have been several studies carefully evaluating the formal process tracing methods (e.g. Russo et al, 1989), and the study discussed earlier by Huber et al (1997) evaluated the AIS method. We are currently carrying out what seems to be the first study to evaluate conversation-based methods. The study in progress is based on the following everyday consumer decision problem. When people take out a loan for home improvements, a new car or hi-fi system, they run at least two kinds of risk: the risk that their future income may not be sufficient to meet their monthly repayments and the risk that the product may fail. Most personal loan arrangements offer the option of insurance against repayment problems due to unexpected loss of income through unemployment, ill-health or similar events, and most purchase agreements offer a warranty against product failure.

Our study investigates the processes underlying decisions concerning both types of risk, i.e. decisions to insure, or not to insure, personal loans of different amounts for different purposes and decisions to take out, or not to take out, an extended warranty. Each respondent is presented with two decision simulations, one involving the purchase of a car and the other a washing machine. A systematic evaluation of conversational process tracing methods will be presented in later reports. In the next section, protocol data from a pilot study will be used to look specifically at the two 'risk' decisions, i.e. warranty, and payment protection, and to illustrate the kind of information obtained from different techniques.

Example protocols and preliminary interpretations

We have been struck by how few questions some people asked regarding some of the decisions presented in our pilot study. For example, for the decision: Would you insure the item against mechanical breakdown?, one respondent in the baseline conversational AIS condition did not ask any questions at all, and simply said 'no'. This could have been because they did not know what to ask, or because they based their decision on prior beliefs or knowledge. However, AIS with conversational thinking aloud seems to provide useful information to clarify such issues, as Huber et al (1997) have reported. For example, one of our think aloud respondents said: 'No I wouldn't insure it against mechanical breakdown – do you want to know why? [Interviewer: OK] Because washing machines should be technologically advanced enough to last longer than 12 months and be fit for the purpose they are designed for'. This suggests that the respondent did not perceive a risk of mechanical breakdown because of the beliefs expressed, and consequently, saw no need to defuse the risk by taking out insurance. Sometimes, however, a respondent's reasoning process may be less clear without interactive post-decision probing. This is illustrated with the following exchange:

> *Respondent*: I don't know, it's a difficult one this, I usually do go for insurance. Anything of any reasonable cost, I do usually insure against breakdown, like my vacuum cleaner, I have insured that, and I always insure a washing machine.
>
> *Interviewer*: Why do you do that?
>
> *Respondent*: Because they break down so much and it costs so much to get repaired. It costs £20 to get someone to come out and have a look at it. Having said that the last one I've just had put in, I've had several appliances and I have not insured any of them. But usually I do, in the past I've always taken it out. But it's quite a lot now for five years. Last time I bought one I added it to the repayments.

Both of the above sequences suggest that respondents are treating the problem as what Klein et al (1989) described as a 'Recognition Primed' decision, with information search being limited to memory, as opposed to a search for new, externally available information. In the same vein, consider another example of thinking aloud about the extended warranty decision:

> No, I'd just take the 12 months guarantee on it... I've never had extra insurance on it. I know a very good man who is very reliable, who mends my washing machine. I've never had much trouble with washing machines. I wouldn't go for the extra expense.

This particular respondent seems to detect a risk that the washer may break down after the manufacturer's warranty had expired. The think aloud procedure, then, seems to have revealed the use of what Huber (1997) referred to as a 'defusing operator' in risk management. Huber made the assumption that people attempt to defuse the uncertainty of decision outcomes by applying one of the following operations (the examples given are from our pilot study protocols): 1) long term plans, e.g. 'I'm going to get a new kitchen in 2 years anyway so I could always replace the washer at the same time'; 2) worst case plans, e.g. 'the machine is unlikely to breakdown in the first 2 years, but if it did I could put the money saved by not taking out the warranty towards a new washer'; and 3) create new alternatives, as demonstrated in the protocol above where the respondent talks of getting a repair man out to fix the appliance if it breaks down. These examples demonstrate the main advantage of including think aloud instructions and interactive probes: more information is typically elicited about the decision process.

With reference to the preliminary attribute elicitation procedure, the inclusion of this stage allows a more precise analysis of the decision making process. For example, it allows us to examine how thoroughly respondents seek information concerning the chosen and non-chosen alternatives. In this analysis, the proportion of the factors listed in the preliminary attribute elicitation stage that are examined during the decision task is calculated for both chosen and non-chosen alternatives. To demonstrate, one respondent listed the following factors as important in choosing a washer: spin speed, water consumption, price, manufacturer's reputation and overall performance. She then only asked about two of these for all three of the machines, but asked about all these factors for her chosen alternative. This search pattern indicates a low thoroughness index, 0.4 for the non-chosen alternatives and a high one for the chosen alternative (1.0).

Concluding remarks

In this article we have described conversation-based process-tracing methods suitable for the study of a wide range of naturalistic decisions that people routinely make in their everyday business, professional and personal lives. We have outlined a study in progress intended to evaluate various methods in the context of personal consumer decisions involving financial risk. Our preliminary impressions are that conversational AIS with thinking aloud, followed by the non-directive post-decision interview is likely to be a most informative method with acceptable levels of reactivity. We are confident that the on-going investigation will show that our methods can reveal new insights into the processes underlying naturalistic decisions.

Acknowledgement

This research is supported by the Economic and Social Research Council of the U.K. (award L211 25 2051 of the Risk and Human Behaviour Programme).

3.3 Reflective versus nonreflective decision making: The case of credit decisions in business

by Henry Montgomery
Professor, Stockholm University

There are two psychological traditions, which are concerned with explaining the dynamics behind human behaviour. Motivational psychology is focused on how 'hot' factors like needs, emotions and different kinds of motivation lead to particular behavioural patterns. By contrast, judgement and decision making research is concerned with how various 'cold' information processes may explain how people choose between different courses of action. Another way of contrasting the two traditions is in terms of locus of control. Thus, motivational psychology views behaviour as controlled by factors inside the individual whereas judgement and decision making researchers attempt to understand how people's understanding of the world outside her/himself explain their behaviour.

Several attempts have been made to integrate the two research traditions. In particular, the ambition has been to understand how motivational factors influence predecisonal information processing (e.g., Janis & Mann, 1977; Kruglanski & Webster, 1996, Taylor & Gollwitzer, 1995). This topic is also discussed in the present paper. However, I will also discuss the reverse topic of how predecisional information processing may influence the selection of motivational factors in a decision situation. More precisely, it will be assumed that the extent to which and how the decision maker reflects on the motivational basis for his or her understanding of the decision situation is important for how the decision is made.

The outline of the present paper is as follows. I will first present a model of judgement and decision making – the so called perspective model (Montgomery, 1994) – which may be used as point of the departure for describing how motivational and information processing factors interact in a decision process It may be noted that the present description of the perspective model on some points updates and clarifies the earlier accounts of the model. Thereafter I will relate the model to the notion that thinking may be driven by different kinds of motivation. I will show how the resulting perspective-motivational model allows a distinction between reflective and nonreflective decision making. The distinction is illustrated by means of data from a naturalistic study of financial credit decisions. In a final section the distinction between reflective and nonreflective decision making is related to judgement and decision making models as well as to naturalistic decision making models.

The perspective model of judgement and decision making

The perspective model differs from other judgement and decision making models by assuming that there is a close analogue between evaluative judgements and visual perception. Evaluative judgements are assumed to follow from what an observer – the subject – sees in a mental object. Thus, evaluations are not computed in a more or less arbitrary way from given information, but follow directly from how the subject sees given characteristics of an object from a given viewing position. The perspective model implies that evaluative judgements of airily complex objects can be made quickly, in one step, and also that different viewing positions will result in gestalt switches in the evaluation of the same object.

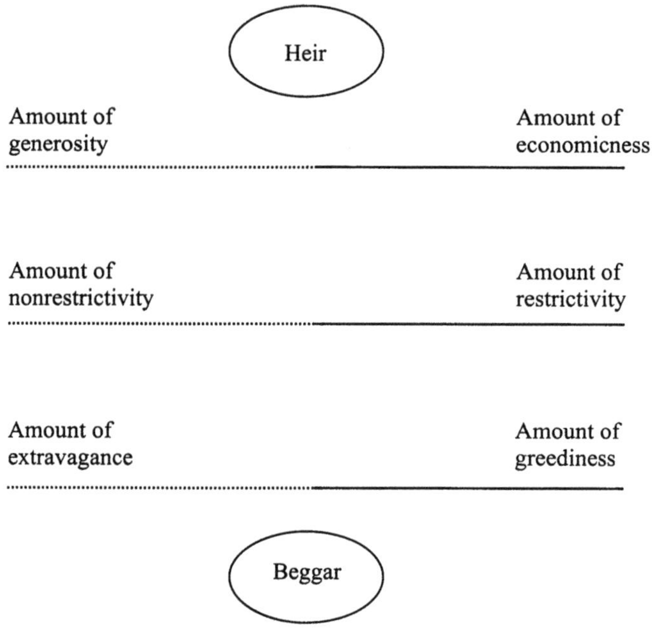

Figure 3.1A Overview of a mental space

The central idea of the perspective model is that an observer views an object with positive (attractive) and negative (unattractive) sides from a given position in a mental space (see Figure 3.1A). The subject is positioned outside the object facing either its positive side or its negative side.

The sides are assumed to be positioned in parallel to each other. On each side either positive or negative aspects of the object come together. Each aspect corresponds to a certain amount of a given quantity (e.g., amount of economicness). The positive and negative aspects are linked in pairs via the same descriptive aspects, which are thought to be positioned between the positive and negative side. For example, the positive aspect *amount of economicness* and the negative aspect *amount of greediness* are both linked to the descriptive aspect *amount of restrictivity* with money. Furthermore, the aspects on a given evaluative side are assumed to be located on bipolar dimensions, where each. dimension contains a certain amount of a given aspect (e.g., economicness) *and* a certain amount of its opposite (e.g., generosity).

In Figure 3.1A it is assumed that the amount of restrictiveness is about twice as great as the amount of nonrestrictivity (as reflected in the length of the black central line as compared with the length of the shaded central line). This relationship is paralleled by about twice as great amount of thrift than generosity on the positive side and by about twice as great amount of greediness than extravagance on the negative side (compare the lengths of the black lines and the shaded lines on the positive upper- and negative lower side).

It is not necessarily true according to the perspective model that the positive and negative aspects are 'objectively' equal as has been assumed in Figure 3.1A. What is necessarily true according to the model is that in some sense there exists an objective reality, independently of specific perspectives, with fixed amounts of positive and negative aspects (in our case assumed to be equal). However, depending on the viewing position, different aspects of the object will *appear* with different sizes, the general rule being that the closer the aspect is to the viewer the larger it appears.

This implies that if the object is seen from its positive side (see position of heir in Figure 3.1A) the positive aspects will tend to be seen as larger than the negative aspects (see Figure 3.1B, which shows what the heir sees from her or his perspective) and vice versa if the object is seen from its negative side (see the position of beggar in Figure 3.1A and what the heir sees from this position in Figure 3.1C). More specifically, in our example the heir will experience the object as more economic than greedy and also as more generous than extravagant (compare the upper and lower black lines or shaded lines in Figure 3.1B), whereas the opposite will be true for the beggar (Figure 3.1C). Moreover, the larger the distance is to the object, the smaller will the difference be between positive and negative aspects. That is, a longer viewing distance will yield a more objective view of the object.

The adoption of a given viewing position is assumed to imply that the subject identifies her/himself with an entity of some sort. This entity is denoted as a subject identification and may correspond to a role, a person or a group of persons. Each subject identification is located in one or several positions in the mental space surrounding the object. A subject identification is associated with certain interests, which determine how it is located in relation to the object. In general, the subject identification will be located close to the positive side of the object if the object is experienced as being congruent with its interests and on its negative side if the object is experienced as incongruent with its interests. In our example, the object is more restrictive than nonrestrictive with money. This is congruent with the heir's interests implying that she or he will be located on the positive side of the object and it is incongruent with the beggar's interests implying that she or he will be located on the negative side of the object.

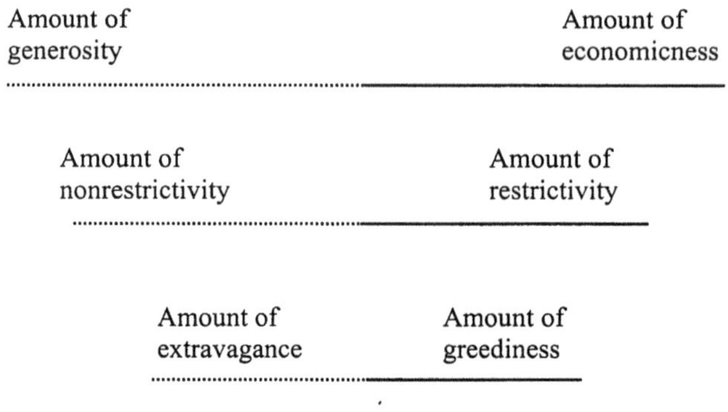

Figure 3.1B Heir's perspective

Figure 3.1A, 3.1B and 3.1C also demonstrates that 'gestalt switches' will occur if the subject shifts her or his attention (as a result of adopting a new subject identification) from one to another opposing evaluative-descriptive continuum. For example, a person who is 'very restrictive' on the descriptive dimension 'restrictive with money' could be seen as mainly 'economic' if the subject views it from its positive side (e.g., with the subject identification 'heir') or as mainly 'greedy' if it is seen from its negative side (e.g., with subject identification 'beggar').

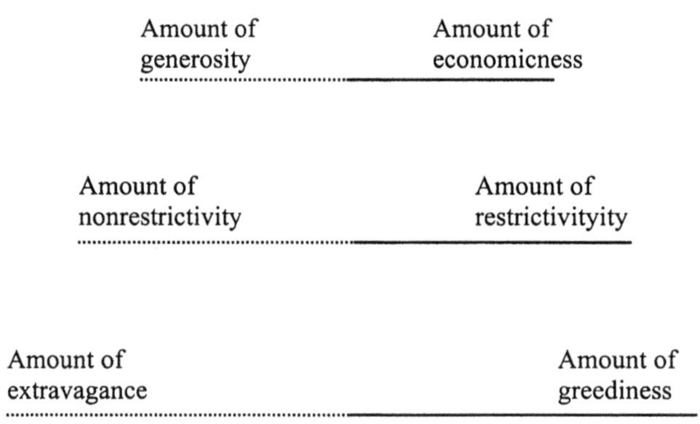

Figure 3.lC Beggar's perspective

Reflective and nonreflective thinking
Traditionally, motivation has been linked to external behaviour. However, recent research has stressed that there is a motivational basis also for internal mental processes, i. e., thinking in some sense. Typically, a distinction is made between two kinds of motivation for thinking , viz. a) thinking which aims at acquiring an accurate picture of the external world, and b) thinking which has goals other than accuracy. Non-accuracy goals include a desire to defending pre-established ideas, values or interests, or goals (defence motivation) or a desire that addresses the interpersonal consequences associated with expressing a given judgement in a particular setting (impression formation) (Chaiken, Wood, & Eagly, 1996). Various terms have been used for these two types of thinking. Type a) thinking has been labelled as accuracy oriented (Chaiken et al, 1996), open-minded (Rokeach, 1960), vigilant (Janis & Mann, 1976), or as being analytical (Epstein et al, 1996). Type (b) thinking is sometimes labelled by one comprehensive term, like close-minded (Rokeach, 1960) or, as exemplified above, is subdivided into different types of non-accuracy orientations like defence oriented and impression oriented thinking

In the present paper, the two types of thinking will be characterised and interpreted as reflective and nonreflective thinking, respectively. Reflective thinking aims at becoming aware of (reflecting) facts external to the thinking person. The reflective thinker is curious. He or she wants to find the truth and nothing but the truth. This implies that the thinker also wishes to uncover factors that may bias the thinking process. In nonreflective thinking there is the reverse motive of not becoming aware of all factors that influence the thinker. More precisely in this case, the thinker is not (and does not want to be) fully aware of those non-accuracy motives that bias her or his thinking (cf. Epstein's, 1989, notion of implicit values).

This is because awareness of non-accuracy motives may weaken their impact on the thinking and, hence, counteract the attainment of these motives. The reason for this, in turn, is that also nonreflective thinking has a reflective component in the sense that is oriented to external facts, but only to those facts that it may help the thinker to attain his or her non-accuracy motives. In other words, when a person is involved in nonreflective thinking, she believes that she increases her understanding of the external world (believed accuracy orientation) although in fact in her beliefs she uses certain aspects of the external world to serve interests beyond accuracy. In other words, there is always an ingredient of self-deception in what I have called nonreflective thinking.

Perspectives and reflective versus nonreflective thinking

We are now ready to relate the perspective model to the two kinds of motives in human thinking described above. As emphasised by G. H. Mead (1959) and many others, thinking always is oriented towards the external world from a given perspective. In the same vein, the perspective model assumes that people view the world from different subject identifications, each of which occupies a certain position in relation to an observed object. The perspective model further implies that non-accuracy motives always exert their influence in terms of the interests associated with the subject identification that is adopted by the individual at a given point of time.

Let us now examine in more detail implications of the perspective model for how reflective thinking works in a situation where an individual wants to understand and evaluate an object. For example, the object may be an alternative in a decision situation. Basically, in reflective thinking the individual is interested in getting a balanced and a comprehensive view of the object. To do so, it will be necessary to see the object from different sides, and, in particular from both its positive and negative side. This goal may be attained by means of the following mental moves.

First, the individual may adopt a subject identification, which is associated with interests that invite seeing the object from different sides. That is, in this case the individual moves the same subject identification into different viewing positions. For example, a businessman who identifies himself with his company's interests may aspire to view an economic prospect from both its positive and negative sides.

Second, the individual may also move between different subject identifications, which occupy certain positions in relation to the object. For example, besides identifying himself with his company a businessman may also identify himself with the interests of other economic actors.

Third, in order to get an overview of the object the individual will be interested in finding a suitable viewing distance. To attain this goal, the individual may move an adopted subject identification or find a new subject identification, which has the right distance to the object.

Fourth, the reflective individual will also be interested in seeing details of the object from a short distance. All viewing positions that may add new information are of interest to the reflective individual.

Fifth, the reflective individual will always be interested in focusing on the interests associated with different subjective identifications in order to avoid a biased understanding of the object. Put differently, she or he wants to understand and control her or his perspectives. To do so, she or he will not only focus on the to-be-evaluated object but also on the interests associated with different subject identifications that may be adopted for viewing the object. However, as is true for all mental focusing according to the perspective model, also this focusing will be done from a certain subject identification which makes it difficult or perhaps impossible to be completely unbiased when examining the interests associated with a given subject identification. In any case, the reflective individual is assumed to have a genuine ambition of becoming aware of how the interests associated with an adopted subject identification justifies her or his moving in the space surrounding the object.

Sixth, as a final step the reflective individual tries to synthesise what she or he has seen from different positions, where each position is associated with particular interests. In this step, the individual tries to find a balanced overview of the object and its relationships to interests associated with different subject identifications.

Let us now examine how nonreflective thinking works in terms of the perspective model. Generally, the nonreflective thinker tends to view the object from just one evaluative perspective, which implies that it will contrast to reflective thinking with respect to most of the characteristics of her or his thinking listed above.

In particular, the nonreflective individual is primarily interested in seeing the object from either its positive or its negative side. She or he has no genuine interest to balance out positive and negative features in order to get an accurate overview of the object. Her or his primary interest instead is to defend and consolidate her or his positive or negative evaluation of the object.

As discussed above, nonreflective thinking is assumed to involve a 'blind spot', i. e., to follow from interests which thinker is not aware of and does not want to be aware of. According to the perspective model, these interests must be based on a subject identification. Thus, nonreflective thinking is assumed to be driven by subject identifications, which are not clearly acknowledged by the thinker. Let us label such identifications as implicit subject identifications (cf. Epstein's, 1989, notion of implicit values). This influence is masked by having access to an additional explicit subject identification, which justifies the evaluation. For example, a credit manager may grant a large credit to a client because he identifies himself with the client's needs (implicit subject identification), but he justifies the credit decision in terms of external facts that are compatible with his company's interests (explicit subject identification).

Empirical illustration of reflective and nonreflective decision making

Using experiences from an ongoing study of decision making concerning financial credits (Montgomery and Lundin, 1998), I will now present a typology of different kinds of reflective and nonreflective decision making. The study involved interviews with credit evaluators (credit managers and salesmen) and clients related to a large Swedish wholesale business in plumbing. Five cases of credit decisions were investigated. All cases were selected to exemplify difficult decisions whether to reject or accept a credit request.

In our data, we found two basic types of subject identifications, which could be at work in both reflective and nonreflective decision making. On the one hand, the credit evaluator may adopt an *ego identification*, where the evaluator's interests are seen as separate from the client's interests. On the other hand, the credit evaluator may adopt a *we identification* implying that the evaluator and the client are seen as having common interests.

Both types of subject identification could be implicit or explicit. An 'implicit ego identification' concerns the decision maker's private fears and hopes. An 'implicit we identification' corresponds to being in a state of togetherness with the client. The credit evaluator takes for granted that his client forms a team with common interests. In both types of identifications the relevant object aspects may be related to how the credit evaluator perceives the social climate in the relationship to the client.

The 'explicit ego identification' is anchored in the credit evaluator's interests of being a good credit evaluator. As a rule, this identification will coincide with the selling company's interests. Relevant object aspects concern the client's economic status and his personal competence as a businessman. The explicit 'we identification' will be based on common economic interests and on aspects which make it possible to satisfy these interests.

Let us now relate the different types of subject identification to reflective and nonreflective decision making, respectively, in our data. In three out five cases we found clear evidence that the credit evaluator (credit manager or salesman) was influenced by the social relationship to the client. In two cases, which ended with credit losses and bankruptcy, there had been a preceding story of good social relationships between credit evaluator and client.

Moreover, the economic transactions between the selling company and the client had worked well. As a consequence, the credit evaluator focused on positive economic aspects and, apparently, failed to take warning signals seriously when they occurred. In both cases an 'implicit we identification' may have pushed the credit evaluator, when explicitly being in the role of credit evaluator, to adopt a perspective which brought positive economic aspects into the foreground and negative economic aspects into the background.

In the third case, a negative social relationship seems to have influenced the credit evaluator to reject credit, although it later turned out that the client would have been able to pay back the credit and be a good customer. Here a frustrated 'implicit ego' or 'we identification' seem to have been at work and influenced the evaluator. It should be noted, however, that there indeed were negative economic signals in this case although the economic situation apparently was still worse for the cases that were granted credit.

Let us now consider two cases where we found evidence of reflective decision making. One case (Case 4) may be seen as being based on an 'explicit we identification'. Here a firm in a bad economic shape was taken care of by an old friend of the credit evaluator, a lawyer who invested money in the firm. As a consequence, the credit evaluator re-evaluated the economic prospects of the firm. The credit evaluator believed in the lawyer's competence and honesty, and he appreciated the fact that the lawyer invested money in the firm. He was aware that his evaluation may have been influenced by his good relationship to the lawyer. He took a risk, but a calculated risk.

Another case (Case 5) exemplifies an 'explicit ego identification' leading to a decision to deny credit. In this case there were both negative and positive economic indicators, but with a perceived overweight for the negative indicators (estimated to be 70/30 or 60/40). There were no signs of close social relationships between the credit evaluator and the client.

Summarising the results across the five cases, the following observations can be made. In four cases (1-4) the personal relationship between credit evaluator and client influenced the credit decision. This seems to have been particularly true for the salesmen who tended to have a closer relationship to the client than was the case for the credit manager. In three cases (1-3) the credit decisions appear to have been based on nonreflective thinking inasmuch as the credit evaluator's economic judgements seems to have been pushed in a certain direction by his implicit subject identifications. In the remaining two cases (4-5) the credit evaluator was more clearly aware of his subject identifications and he deliberately tried to get a balanced view of the client's situation.

The data also illustrate how an object will be seen from its positive or negative side depending on whether it satisfies or not the interests associated with the adopted subject identification. In Cases 1 and 2 the positive side was in focus, due to the good fit of the implicit we identifications, and in Case 3 the negative side dominated, at least partly because of a frustrated ego or we identification. Case 4 illustrates a case, which started with a negative view but changed into looking at the object from its positive side as a result of new identification possibilities. In case 5 the dominance of negative aspects seen from an explicit ego identification led to a focus on the negative side of the object

Other accounts of decision making

How does the distinction between reflective and nonreflective decision making relate to other accounts of human decision making? First, it should be noted that the present distinction has a motivational rather than cognitive basis. In this sense, the distinction is close to the distinction between vigilant and various variants of nonvigilant decision making (Janis & Mann, 1976), action versus state oriented thinking (Kuhl & Beckman, 1985), implemental and deliberative mindset (Taylor & Gollwitzer, 1995, and need for closure versus need to avoid closure (Kruglanski & Webster, 1996). Common to all these distinctions is that they contrast an action oriented mode of thinking (i. e., thinking which aims at facilitating ensuing action) to a more passive, deliberative mode of thinking. The present distinction instead contrasts an ambition of to get a maximal knowledge (reflective thinking) versus an or ambition to avoid such knowledge that will threaten the attainment of certain interests (nonreflective thinking). Both types of thinking may be conceived as being action oriented or not. Although reflective thinking seems to be close to deliberative, non-action oriented thinking, our data exemplify how reflective thinking also may serve the reverse role of preparing the individual to perform actions which are grounded in more or less uncomfortable facts (Case 5). In the same vein, nonreflective thinking may serve the role of precluding action (e.g., to avoid an uncomfortable negative credit decision) as was true in several of our cases, but also serve the role of facilitating action once the decision maker has made up his or her mind (Case 3).

It may now be asked how our distinction relates to various cognitive decision making biases, such as the representativeness and availability heuristics, anchoring effects, framing effects etc.

Possibly, several researchers in this area would claim that cognitive biases may occur both in reflective and nonreflective thinking since these biases are due to cognitive limitations rather than being motivationally controlled (Kahneman, Slovic & Tversky, 1982). On the other hand, it is tempting to assume that nonreflective thinking is more vulnerable to cognitive biases than is true for reflective thinking since a reflective thinker would be expected to get rid of all kinds of biases. In particular, framing and anchoring effects may be motivationally controlled since these effects imply that one out of several possible perspectives, in some sense, is picked out as the salient perspective. Apparently, people can switch between different frames or anchorings (Maule, 1989). To the extent that this done in order to eliminate one-sidedness and increase awareness of possible biases, reflective thinking will be a means to reduce the impact of cognitive biases in our understanding of the world.

Finally, I will briefly consider how the reflective-nonreflective distinction relates to how decisions are conceived within research in naturalistic decision making. This research typically examines decisions made by professionals using their experience in situations calling for rapid action. Researchers within this tradition often stress the adaptive and reality oriented nature of naturalistic decision making. To the extent that this picture is true I would say that naturalistic decision making is reflective. 'Reflective' as this term is used here does not necessarily mean elaborate thought processes, but it means simply to be reality oriented, i.e., to reflect reality. On the other hand, also professionals may depart from reality in their decision making, being misled by their implicit subject identifications, as was exemplified in the empirical study described above.

3.4 Trust between entrepreneurs and external actors

by Leif Sanner,
Ph.D., Örebro University

The notion of trust

In the Merriam-Webster Dictionary (1976) trust is defined as "assured reliance on the character, ability, strength, or truth of someone and something". It has also a definition of trust in a commercial setting: "reliance on future payment for property (as merchandise) delivered". Central in both the general and the more commercially oriented definitions is that someone, a *truster*, believes something about someone or something else, a *trustee*. The truster has a belief about the trustee's ability to do something, about her/his character etc. This belief is somehow important for the truster who may be at odds if the trustee does not live up to what the truster expects from the trustee.

Trust as a more or less prominent issue has been studied in philosophy, psychology, sociology, economics, management, and marketing theory. A multifaceted phenomenon, lacking agreement on fundamental definitions and ways to define it, lends itself to be grasped and summarised by different views on it. Two main views concerning trust can be traced in the literature. In the first *expectation* is seen as the essence of trust. The second view also concerns expectation, but it is qualified against *risk*.

In the view of trust as expectation Luhmann (1979) is a common point of reference for many authors published in the field over the past 15 years. In any relation we put trust on another party, that she/he will meet with our expectations. Our action is often based on expectations that others will do things, which will favour us or at least not put us in a detrimental position. Trust builds on one's expectation that the other will act in some desired way. Expectation implies that this will not occur immediately but in a future time. Trust comes in as a form of complexity reduction involving a problematic relationship with time. "To show trust is to anticipate the future. It is to behave as though the future were certain" (Luhmann, 1979). That is to say: Man makes use of the present trying to reduce complexity of the future.

Different kinds of expectations underlying trust can be discerned in the literature: a) Expectation of the persistence and fulfilment of the natural and the moral order, b) Expectation of technically competent role performance from parties involved with us in social relationships and systems, and c) Expectation that partners in interaction will carry out their fiduciary obligations and responsibilities, that is, their duties in certain situations to place other's interest before their own (Barber, 1983).

Expectation between parties in a relationship includes reciprocity, mutual benefits, equity, fair exchange and distributive justice.

The debate indicated in the last section brings us to the view of trust as expectation qualified by risk. The essence of going into a risky situation can be seen like this: The penalty (disutility) one suffers if the other abuses one's expectation is greater than the benefit (utility) one gains if the other does not abuse that expectation. The main source of reference for this view is Deutsch (1962). If you trust someone, you give that person something that is or can be important to yourself. The trusted person acts on that but outside of your control. Risk is attributable therefore to the action of others, including the possibility that they will behave opportunistically, such as withhold information, create confusion etc.

Concerning the importance of trust for a business setting Arrow (1973) wrote that "virtually every commercial transaction has within itself an element of trust, certainly any transaction conducted over a period of time". Hayek (1948) meant that inadequate knowledge of available commodities and services is made up by our experience with the persons supplying them – competition is in a large measure competition for reputation or goodwill.

In the discussion above there are expressions concerning the truster's beliefs about the trustee; beliefs as a basis for trust. Trust is belief seen from the *truster's* point of view. Trust seen from the *trustee's* point of view is trustworthiness, i.e. to be worthy of trust in the eyes of truster. Trustworthy is in the Oxford Dictionary of current English defined as: "worthy of trust, dependable".

The concept of mutual trust denotes a set of expectations shared by actors involved in an interaction. Trustworthiness is then a set of expectations concerning one actor in the eyes of another actor. One question will then emerge: What can be clues for sensemaking trust? Or stated differently: When someone assesses another person's trustworthiness, on what will s/he base assessment? Using literature surveys of entrepreneurship and trust, the study formulated a set of concepts used for data collection and analysis for an empirical investigation. Actors can see trust as meaningful using the clues of person, enterprise and institutional environment (Zucker, 1986). Trust can be *person-based, enterprise-based and/or institution-based.*

A study of trust in action processes between two new ventures and external actors

Trust between two new business ventures and customers, a main supplier, financers and business start advisors were studied during five years. In all, six dyadic relationships between one new venture and an external actor were followed by recurrent interviews with the entrepreneur and with the external actors. Action processes and sensemaking concerning action was focused (Weick, 1995).

The analyses revealed that in action processes the entrepreneur can *use trustworthiness,* considered by the entrepreneur to exist in the eyes of an external actor as a precondition to an action process. The entrepreneur can also *build trustworthiness,* if existing trustworthiness as a precondition to the action process is considered by the entrepreneur to be inadequate in the eyes of an external actor for use in an action process. In the action processes there was often an alternation between use trustworthiness and build trustworthiness from one action/event to the next in sequence. Either that concerns the same trust base, for example build person-based trustworthiness to use it in next action, or a shift: use person-based trustworthiness to build enterprise-based trustworthiness.

The analyses of the six relations give a number of conclusions and indicate certain patterns of trust developement.

1. Trust can be built even if there is no trust at the start.
2. Institution-based trustworthiness was important either as pre-existing trust or as norms and values developed during the action process.
3. At the start person-based trustworthiness developed early by personal presentations in marketing etc.
4. Enterprise-based trustworthiness often developed after person-based (and possibly institution-based) trustworthiness.

Trust development patterns indicated:

- *Person-based trust can make sense for the development of enterprise-based trust*
- *A combination of institution-based trust and person-based trust can make sense for the development of enterprise-based trust.*
- *Person-based trust in combination with enterprise-based trust can make sense for the development of institution-based trust during the unfolding of the action process.*

The analyses presented above concern one actor's sensemaking of the other. Many situation are characterised by *reciprocity,* i.e. building trustworthiness for the entrepreneur in the eyes of an external actor is influenced by reciprocal building of trustworthiness concerning the external actor in the eyes of the entrepreneur. The collected data give indications of the characteristics of the reciprocal building of trustworthiness. It can be summarised in a sequence of six steps involving two actors' (A and B) reciprocal trustbuilding as follows:

1. A conceives trust to make sense in action involving B
2. A acts involving B
3. B pays attention to A's action and interprets its meaning for B

4. B acts involving A
5. A pays attention to B's action and interprets its meaning for A
6. Reciprocal reflections, i.e. reconstruction of each actor's meanings.

The action process may continue between the parties in a new sequence, i.e. as 1 - 6 above again. Action processes in the cases could also include *intermediaries* for trust between two actors: Person, group of persons, organisation or object can symbolise trust. In the study, many situations were identified where the entrepreneurs built trustworthiness in the eyes of some external actor by building or using trustworthiness in an intermediary. The entrepreneur conceived that the intermediary was trustworthy in the external actor's eyes and that the entrepreneur could benefit from this. From the interviews with the entrepreneurs as well as the external actors, a meaning with the use of intermediaries emerged: The trustworthiness of the intermediary in the eyes of the external actor may 'spill over' to the entrepreneur, which facilitates the entrepreneur's trust-building with the external actor.

The role of the intermediary is thus to actively or passively transfers trustworthiness to the entrepreneur. Identified intermediaries were grouped in a role dimension into active and passive. In a second dimension, type of intermediary, they were grouped as human or object. Intermediaries can thus be ascribed symbolic meaning concerning trustworthiness and trust. If the entrepreneur makes use of intermediary in some way this can be part of the entrepreneur's interpretative scheme about using and building trust. These interpretative schemes can be characterised in different ways. The entrepreneur enacts these schemes more or less consciously. The patterns may be simple or more elaborated, e.g. always to build trustworthiness the same way or in different ways. Finally, there can be variations in the extent they are repeatedly enacted.

The study coins the concept of 'trust strategy' *for an interpretative scheme implying a pattern or connected sequence of actions for trust, made sense by the new venture to promote an outcome.*

Conclusions

The study contributes to theory with the creation of a taxonomy of concepts concerning new venture trust. It also develops a process oriented view and methodology for studies of entrepreneurs in context. Suggestions for further research concern some different areas. Business failures could be studied to see how trust functions in a situation characterised by lack of trust, which would bring knowledge about obstacles for successful business start. The role of trust in processes of institutionalisation can also bring benefits for studying the role of entrepreneurs in the development of industries. Trust can also be a collective phenomenon and the taxonomy can be relevant for the study of trust pertaining to society sectors or industries. Practical implications may reside in the described action processes, where entrepreneurs, trainers/teachers and business advisors can find examples of the impact of trustworthiness and trust for new ventures. Described examples may contribute to learning concerning business action.

3.5 Social/psychological barriers to successful management of technological innovation

by James Shanteau
Professor/Director, Institute for Social and Behavioral Research
and
Clarence Rohrbaugh
Ph.D., Student, Kansas State University

Throughout history, the importance of innovation and discovery has been recognized. As expressed by the following writers, there has also been a concern for limitations or barriers to innovation.

> *He that will not apply new remedies must expect new evils; for time is the greatest innovator* (Francis Bacon, 1642)
>
> *There are three things, which the public will always clamour for, sooner or later: namely, Novelty, Novelty, Novelty (Thomas Hood, 1836)*
>
> *Discovery consists of seeing what everybody has seen and thinking what nobody has thought* (Albert Szent-Gyorgyi von Nagyrapolt, 1962)

The position taken in this chapter is that is not the absence of good ideas or lack of motivation that inhibits innovation in a business. Rather, it is the presence of social and psychological barriers that is the key problem for managers. The purpose of the research described here is to explore the sources and potential resolutions of the behavioural barriers to innovation.

This paper is organised into five sections. The first provides background and a model of the problem of innovation management. The next section presents an overview of our research approach. The third is a summary of the major trends in results. The fourth section looks at interpretations and connections to other lines of research. And the last section describes our efforts to help managers.

Background and a model of the problem

It is a truism that any company that does not innovate and improve will fail. Maintaining the status quo, either consciously or unconsciously, will inevitably allow the competition to catch up and gain the upper hand. For any business, therefore, innovation is a necessary part of survival (Cooper, 1994).

Yet when a company is at the height of success, the tendency is to keep doing the same things that led to success in the first place. That is, most managers assume, *if it ain't broke don't fix it.* One of the most difficult times to think about making changes is while in the midst of a hot streak.

A related problem is that success in business means that managers are under severe time pressure (Rubenstein, 1989). They are too busy getting the product out the door and satisfying customers to consider innovations. Later when things have slowed down, it is often too late to think about new directions. Thus, time pressure inhibits innovation.

It should not be surprising, therefore, to find that failure rates for innovations range from 40% to 80% for new consumer products (Mowen, 1995). The success rate for industrial products is somewhat better, ranging from 20 to 40%. These figures indicate the need for better decision making about innovation.

Research approach

To begin our research, we developed a generic eight-stage model of the innovation process. This model was derived from various ideas proposed in the literature on innovation. As such, this model can be considered an amalgamation. The stages in our model presented in Table 3.2 are not sequential. We do not believe the innovation process follows any set series of steps.

Table 3.2 Psychological model of the process of technological innovation

Generation of Ideas
Assessment of Ideas
Prioritisation of Ideas
Emergence of a Champion
Allocation of Resources
Research and Development
Prototype and Testing
Implementation of the Innovation

Although all stages of the innovation process are important, we decided to focus our efforts on the first four stages. These stages represent the steps in the process where we felt that psychological barriers have the strongest influence.

To study the barriers to innovation, our research plan involved five steps:

1. *Identification of the barriers to innovation.* To do this, we interviewed over 40 managers and/or owners of small manufacturing firms in Kansas. Most of the companies employ between 20 and 200 employees. In our interviews, we asked both about successful and unsuccessful attempts at innovation. We also looked at technical, economic, and behavioural factors.

2. *Assessment of the barriers to innovation.* We connected the barriers identified by the managers to the various stages in our model. In this process, we quickly discovered that it was vital to identify the 'choke points' in an organisation. These represent either the organisational or structural concentration of decision authority in one or two people.

3. *Gathering of stories about the barriers to innovation.* Our approach involved asking managers to tell us about actual cases where innovations either succeeded or failed. Specifically, we asked them to describe barriers that they had to deal with using real cases. These stories were then encoded and classified (see below).

4. *Development of decision-support tools.* Using a case-based approach, along with Bayesian influence diagrams, we are developing a set of 'tools' on how to deal with barriers to innovation. Rather than providing expert recommendations, these tools offer experienced-based suggestions on coping with financial, planning, marketing, technical, organisational, and managerial barriers. These tools operate in the same fashion as one friend talking to another.

5. *Evaluation of tool effectiveness.* We are presently trying out the decision-support tools with managers of small firms in Kansas. Our plan is to obtain feedback both on the managers' assessments of the tools and on the appropriateness for different types of companies and managers. We anticipate that evaluation and improvement of the tool will continue for several years.

To conduct the study, a team of researchers came together representing four disciplines: engineering, management, psychology, and computer science. This team has designed, implemented, and interpreted the results of the study. Some aspects of the research are still ongoing, i.e., the evaluation of the tool effectiveness.

Results and major findings

Preliminary research revealed that in most small businesses, there is a *choke point* in the decision making process. That is, there are one or two people in the company that control the decisions made by the firm. Everything passes through them – therefore the term 'choke point'. Even in moderately large sized firms employing several hundred workers, these choke points seem to exist.

The decision makers at the choke points are obviously busy people. They must handle many day-to-day problems that demand immediate attention, e.g., payroll, inventory, finances, personnel, suppliers, and customer demands. These problems must be solved quickly, or the company will be unable to function. Clearly, there is little chance for these decision makers to think about making major changes.

Managers must of necessity focus on short-term problems. That means there is little, if any, time to think about long-term concerns. Yet it is precisely these long-range issues that lead to major innovations and upgrades in the product or manufacturing process. One implication of this finding, supported by our observations, is that the changes that do occur are more likely to be *evolutionary* rather than *revolutionary*. Instead of making major changes in a product or process, managers only have time to think about making small adjustments.

After visiting with managers of over three dozen companies, some trends have become clear. Since these interviews lasted up to four hours, it is not possible to summarise all that the research team learned from visiting the managers. However, the results in the following two tables summarise the major findings. Table 3.3 provides a partial listing of typical comments made by managers of companies visited by the research team. These comments are presented in raw form, with no effort to interpret or classify these comments.

Table 3.3 Selected comments from managers; Reported barriers to innovation:

Most of my time is taken up by daily fire fights
Analysis, paralysis
I don't make a decision until I run out of reasons not to
I only make changes I can understand
The market is not ready
This new product (innovation) is not we – it is not what we do
We are too small to make big changes
If it ain't broke, don't fix it
My generation is analogue. Most innovations now are digital
Who has time? I am too busy getting the product out the door
We need to avoid over committing ourselves
We are making money – what's the problem?

These and many other comments about barriers were classified by the researchers in two ways. First, the comments were assigned to one of nine categories: *risk and uncertainty, time constraints, lack of fit to priorities, lack of resources, lack of economic payback, wrong decision maker, resistance within the organisation, lack of a champion or advocate,* and *a history of past failures*. Then the comments within categories were assessed for importance on three phases of initiation: *pre-initiation, initiation,* and *post-initiation*.

This two-way classification of the comments yields an ordinal impact of each type of barrier on the three stages of initiation. In Table 3.4 these impact assessments were either high (+), medium (0), or low (–).

As these results make clear, the first three barriers had an impact at all three levels of innovation. These are the 'big three' psychological barriers. Each of these barriers has important effects that inhibit innovation at multiple levels.

Table 3.4 Classification of reported barriers to innovations

Type of barrier	Impact on initiation phase		
	Pre-	During	Post-
Risk and Uncertainty	+	+	+
Time Constraints	+	+	+
Doesn't Fit within Priorities	+	+	+
Lack of Resources	0	0	+
Lack of Payback	–	0	+
Wrong Decision Maker	–	0	+
Organisational Resistance	–	0	+
Lack of a Champion	–	+	+
History of Past Failures	–	–	+

Perceived risk and uncertainty affects us all. Most people are risk adverse; that is, we prefer not to take chances. Instead, we like to play it safe and avoid risky situations. Of course, adopting an innovation is by definition risky. As the saying goes, *no one gets fired for staying with the status quo – but you may if you make a change.* This obviously creates a tension, since innovations are essential if a company is to survive.

It is possible for most managers to deal with perceived risk – if they have enough time and resources. They need time to think and reflect on the benefits versus the level of risk involved. And they need resources to investigate the pro's and con's of a proposed innovation, e.g., customer reactions, financing, and production capacity. Unfortunately, both time and resources are in short supply.

Time constraints and time stress are a consistent problem for managers. A successful manager is, by definition, a very busy person. There are numerous demands on his/her time, with little opportunity for contemplative thinking. Obviously, they have little time to spend on what may turn out to be a dead-end idea. If a manager has a list of 100 things to do today, thinking about innovation is probably going to be something like 95th on the list.

Priority setting is a constant problem for a manager. The day-to-day concerns of running a business must be addressed or the work product may not make it out the door. Thus, most managers are constantly *fighting fires*. These immediate problems threaten short-term work output and must be solved. However, adopting an innovation requires long range planning and thinking ahead. But that is precisely what most managers are unable to attend to.

Helping managers

To help managers cope with the barriers to innovation, we are developing a series of decision support tools. These tools are being designed around the observations and insights of the managers we interviewed in the research. In addition to asking managers to list barriers to innovation (see Table 3.3), we also asked them to describe how they dealt with those barriers. Specifically, we wanted the managers to tell us about 'success stories' where they overcome barriers to innovation. A partial listing of the comments generated appears in Table 3.5.

Table 3.5 Selected comments by managers on dealing with barriers to innovation

Innovation is the 'fun' part of the business
Think evolution, not revolution – but then make the changes
Innovation can't wait – do it now
We make money to buy new 'toys' so we make more changes
You have to take a chance – nothing ventured, nothing gained
The best time to make an innovation is when you are doing the best
Make everybody in the firm responsible for making at least one improvement
Listen to your customers – they have good ideas
Know your own strengths and weaknesses – play to your strength
Adopt a '1,000 flowers bloom' philosophy
Everyone in a company is a 'knowledge resource' – use them
Its more fun to build one new product than it is to sell 100 of an old product

These comments suggest many potentially useful coping strategies that can help managers deal with barriers to innovation. We want to use such comments by incorporating them into some easy-to-use communication tools. Although the tools are still in the testing stage, we can describe some elements and ideas behind their design.

1. In looking at previous efforts to help managers make decisions about technological innovations, we found that most were designed as decision support systems (DSS) using artificial intelligence (AI) technologies. For a variety of reasons, these computer programs have met with resistance from the decision makers they were intended to help. For instance, users dislike systems that are designed to 'think for them'; they are more favourably disposed toward systems that help them think (Shanteau, 1992).

2. To avoid the user-resistance problem of previous efforts, we decided to take a different route. Most DSS/AI systems in effect replace the decision maker and make a final recommendation. Our alternate approach is based on building tools that 'talks to' managers and offers advice. 'Story telling' is an effective means of communicating and understanding high-level knowledge (Schank, 1990).

3. The content of these tools comes from a database of comments made by practising managers (see Table 3.5). These stories and the lessons learned are constantly updated as new managers tell us about their successes and failures in using these tools. An important feature of the tools is a built-in feedback-and-upgrade algorithm to allow us to continuously add new stories based on the experiences of other users.

4. Interacting with the tools is analogous to communicating with a highly qualified and experienced manager. This manager-in-the-tool reflects a composite of the different types of advice received. From the user's perspective, it seems as if another manager is helping them make decisions about innovation.

5. The tools are designed to be portable and easily accessible by a manager in his/her office. We do not want a system that requires extensive hardware or software. Instead, we want a system that is highly portable, interactive, and easily updated. Fortunately, some recent developments in interactive software development have simplified our task.

6. The tools are intended to be customised for every user. The specific preferences of each manager will be reflected in the way that he/she interacts with the tools. If a visual input is preferred, then that is the way the information will be presented. If verbal interaction is preferred, then that is the mode that will be used. These preferences will be entered initially and then be used later.

7. The tools are being compartmentalised so that managers can get as much or as little advice as they want or need. If the user only wants to have financial input, then that tool alone will be made available. If the manager wants a complete breakdown for the proposed innovation, then many different tools will be used.

Discussion and interpretation

Based on these findings, we believe that it is not the inability to come up with technological innovations that is the problem. In our research, we have seen lots of creative ideas generated within these businesses. Instead, the problem is the ability of managers to know when to adopt and when not to adopt these ideas. The choke point arises because busy managers do not have the time or resources to compensate for the perceived risk of going ahead with an uncertain innovation. Thus, there are many missed opportunities for implementing new technologies.

In previous papers on decision making expertise, the first author presented a list of domains categorised by whether good performance or poor performance was reported in the literature (Shanteau, 1992). (A reduced version of this chart appears in Table 3.10) For instance, weather forecasters have been reported in many studies to be reliable and well calibrated when making short-term forecasts. In comparison, research on clinical psychologists has consistently revealed low levels of validity as well as low levels of between/within-reliability.

As observed in Shanteau (1992), there is a pattern to those domains. Most of the good-performance domains involve decisions about physical properties or stable systems. In contrast, most of the poor-performance domains involve decisions about human behaviour.

This distinction may be used to explain why managing innovations are the limiting factor. Since generating an innovative idea is generally more physical, it is often done well – just like the other high-performance domains. However, managing an innovation is more about behaviour, and is generally poorly done. This may help explain the *paradox of innovation* – how can managers who are so good at coming up with new ideas have such difficulties in managing those ideas?

Final comments

The National Science Foundation (NSF) in the United States is presently sponsoring over 30 projects looking at management of improvement. Eleven of these grants have been to examine Management of Technological Innovation and 20+ projects are looking at Transformations to Quality Organisations (Woo, 1997). The topics being investigated range from *cost modelling for engineers* and *evaluation of environmental costs* to *innovation in retail banking* and *improving quality in a dual workforce R&D environment.* As such, these 30+ projects investigate a variety of perspectives on management of improvement.

Nonetheless, an analysis reveals that only two projects focus on small-to- medium-size companies. Yet it is these companies that are the source of a disproportionate high proportion of innovations (Cooper, 1994).

The project described in this paper is unique in that we are the only NSF-supported research study looking at the behavioural barriers faced by small-to-medium-size companies. Moreover, we are attempting to reduce the impact of these barriers using a flexible, case-based approach to developing decision support tools to help mangers. In essence our approach is based on letting experienced managers tell their stories to other, less-experienced managers. We are not trying to be experts in an AI system. The experts in our research are the managers who are leading small-to-medium-size businesses. We believe that practising managers are more likely to listen to and follow the advice of their colleagues. Our job as researchers is to provide the means for this to take place.

Acknowledgements

The research described in this paper was supported, in part, by a National Science Foundation Grant # DMII 96-12126 from the Division of Design, Manufacture, and Industrial Innovation, Program on Management of Technological Innovation, Directorate for Engineering. We most gratefully acknowledge the patient and helpful Cupertino of the many small business managers in Kansas who contributed their time to make this project possible.

The other members of the research team working on this project include Farhad Azadivar (Advanced Manufacturing Institute), Sharon Ordoobadi (Department of Industrial and Manufacturing Systems Engineering), Jeffrey W. Tucker (Manufacturing Learning Center) and Nancy Mulvancy, Amarnath Poola, and Yan Xue (graduate students in Engineering) at Kansas State University.

3.6 The impact of non-financial factors on the decision making by credit assessors dealing with the threat of insolvency

by Lisbeth Hedelin
Assistant Professor, Gothenburg University

The present paper presents results from a questionnaire study and a follow-up interview study that have focused on non-financial factors in the credit granting process occurring during a threat of insolvency and/or bankruptcy situations of small firms. Forty-three executive assessors in small business enterprises and their owners (EOs), 13 of their credit assessors (CAs), and 21 of their accountants (ACs) participated in the questionnaire study. Out of these individuals 21 EOs, their 21 CAs, and their 21 ACs participated in the follow-up interview, thereby enabling these 21 cases to be seen from these three perspectives. Two years later, data for the 21 cases were also available from the Swedish Patent and Registration Office (PRV) concerning whether or not bankruptcy did occur or not.

The concept 'EO' means a person who is either a family owner or a majority owner of a limited firm, who apart from possessing the firm (as sole or part owner) also runs the firm as her/his main business. A limited firm implies a limited financial risk (in the form of registered shared capital) for the owner inasmuch as he or she has not guaranteed the security of the loans to the firm (in Sweden this guarantee is a very common demand from the banks before granting loans to small firms). In addition to this guarantee from the firm, the EOs can also put their personal assets at risk if they do not fulfil their duties to establish a balance sheet for liquidation purposes in time.

The main purpose of the study was to identify the consequences of the causal and critical events leading to bankruptcy for the decision making by the credit assessors in granting or not granting credit. We were also interested in EOs' reactions and behaviours (i.e. coping strategies) during the crisis arising as a consequence of the firms' financial crisis situation, and wished to examine to what extent these factors can have an impact on the decision making by the credit assessors in the process of granting (or not granting) credit.

Theoretical Basis

The behavioural perspective on the role of the EO has met with a great interest in the research field. In Bass and Stoghill's Handbook of Leadership (1990) over 7 500 references were presented in the subject. Despite this extensive research there is no consensus as to what extent the managers at the top actually influence their firm's development. Several different theoretical perspectives have been used in this context. Within one perspective, the research has focused on the relationship between successful firms and the role of the EOs. This study reports about 50 per cent of the variance among firms regarding performance (profit and turnover) has been attributed to the leadership of the firm (Day & Lord, 1988).

Investigating CAs' credit decisions for new ventures, Hedelin and Sjöberg (1995) found however only a few personal characteristic to be of decisive importance. One explanation by Hedelin and Sjöberg (1995) for this result was that the decision making in the credit granting process is very rapid, superficial and simple. Other research findings have also showed judgement processes to be very simple. Even though experts identify up to ten cues as having relevance, for example, for a diagnosis, they actually use very few – usually only two or three – and the process tends to be purely additive (Rasmussen, 1995). Another problem identified by Hedelin and Sjöberg (1995) was that CAs is not very good at describing in what way they make their credit judgements. The conclusion that people are not very good at describing the way in which they make judgements has also been arrived at in Brehmer in other contexts (1981). Such judgements can also be affected by difficulty in assessing the personality characteristics, which characterise the entrepreneurial success. Most studies in the field have failed in this respect (Sexton & Bowman, 1985).

From another perspective, there are studies which connect the EO, her or his personality, her or his way of managing the firm, and the way decisions are made, with the risk for insolvency or bankruptcy (Keasey & Watson, 1991). Argenti (1986) showed that there are three fatal ways EOs can fail leading to bankruptcy: a) the EO lets the firm expand faster than its capital basis, which will lead to an increase in bank loans: interest costs increase depending on weak financial 'management' which the firm's liquidity basis or profit will not increase to the same extent; b) the EO lets the firm engage in a project which has such a size that it can cause the firm to go bankrupt if the project does not succeed; c) the EO lets the firm take such extensive bank loans that it will not leave some operational possibility if the investment goes wrong and they cannot obtain further loans. Only one of these fatal mistakes is needed for the firm to be threatened by insolvency. Another aspect is that the relationship between the EO and his/her CA can be strained since there is a potential conflict of interest between the EO and the bank in this situation (Rose-Ackerman, 1991).

Crisis reactions, behaviours in crisis, and coping strategies

The difficulty of correctly judging the realism in the EOs' possibilities of handling the financial problems might be related to the EOs' *psychological state* at the time of the judgement. A consequence of emotional stress is that even though an EO who experiences a crisis situation may be aware of that situation, he or she might not adhere to the relevant information, but instead distort this information in order to gain support for his or her own preference. Neglecting information not only happens in situations where emotional stress can be present but is common also in other situations of assessment (Hedelin & Sjöberg, 1995).

Based on this, we were interested in which coping strategies EOs use in a crisis or stress situation like the insolvency situation, and also in which way these coping strategies have an impact on the decision making by the credit assessor in the credit granting process. According to earlier research, coping strategies have been divided into those that are emotional focused and those that are problem focused coping (Erera-Weatherley, 1996). It would be seen that initially emotions have an impact on the coping strategy used (Cox, 1997), and then the problem to be solved affects the coping strategy. Oakland and Ostell (1996) found however that personal and situational factors have an impact on what kind of coping strategy is used, the emotional based or the problem based strategy.

Acute/evolving events and the psychological development of crisis reactions and behaviours

D'Aveni (1989) discusses three ways for firms to go from being healthy to being insolvent and bankrupt. Slowly, often over several years, gradual decliners become less and less compatible and finally bankruptcy is a fact. Sudden decliners, on the other hand, have a very short time period (less or about one year) from when decline first occurs until bankruptcy becomes a fact. The third kind, lingerers, are firms that for an extended period of time live on the verge of bankruptcy, but in some way are able to avoid actual bankruptcy. D'Aveni (1989) found that even the most successful firms suddenly become candidates for bankruptcy. A critical event can cause also a seemingly healthy firm to go bankrupt (Mitroff, 1988).

The psychological crisis can develop successively when a combination of critical events and the effects of those successively appear. In this case, it is probable that the reactions entailed in the crisis are strengthened. If the bank acts, for example, with a statement that the credits are going to be withdrawn, then it is probable that this can strengthen the crisis reactions further. The development of 'vicious circles' (see Senge, 1992) can also cause a critical event which from the beginning did not seem to have such serious consequences. These 'vicious circles' through their psychological dynamics lead to serious consequences in the form of crisis reactions and crisis behaviours.

It appears probable there is a connection between personal characteristics, reactions and behaviours of crisis, on the one hand, and which events the EOs point out as critical, on the other. The EO with an external locus of control (Rotter, 1966) or a low self-efficacy (Bandura, 1982) can be assumed to see and to point out external critical events as causes. What the EO sees, that is, attributes as a cause, can however even be an expression of the crisis.

The outcome: Bankruptcy or survival
After insolvency or bankruptcy has occurred a period of uncertainty frequently follows. This period can imply cloudiness concerning what possibilities exist for reorganising a firm and for obtaining new financing (Gilbert, Menon, & Schwartz, 1990).

The phase of reorganisation may imply a very ambiguous situation for the EO and this can affect his or her crisis reactions and strategies of coping. The situation can also be ambiguous because the available information is incomplete. This is due to the fact that such information may not be noticed or may convey a wrong message or is incomplete. The EO is dependent on upon external expertise of various kinds (credit assessors, accountants, financial advisers, financial or legal authorities etc) to provide notice that the firm is approaching a situation of insolvency. These persons however often react and become involved too late (SIND 1985:7). A contributing factor which may explain why CAs and ACs do not get involved until a late phase, may be that EOs often have too much confidence in their ability to manage the situation by themselves and therefore do not ask for help. This may also be due to the fact that the EOs deny the seriousness of the situation or possibly take a chance. The use of this strategy may consequently have a negative impact on the decision making by the creditor in the credit granting decision process.

Method

Subjects, Firms
We acquired financial information about small firms in Western Sweden from 'Upplysningscentralen': an organisation owned by the banks in Sweden monitoring the financial status of Swedish firms. Based on the information from UC we selected the EO participants. The parameters used for selection of firms were the number of officially registrated no-payments and zero or near zero profits. We selected the firms who had between 3 and 5 failed payments. The reason to use the parameters of failed payment and zero or near zero profit were to involve firms near or just experiencing the state of insolvency or bankruptcy. We did not exclude any commercial branch from the study. The maximum criterion at the selection of the number of employees was 20 (but was exceeded by one firm that had 23 employees). The owner of the small firm should be the executive (EO). The EOs were informed that we wanted a written note that admitted us to contact

their CA and their AC in order to get their views of the executive and the firms under study.

The selection using these parameters resulted in a sample of 328 firms. However, only 43 small management executives and executive owners (EOs), 13 of their credit assessors (CAs), and 21 of their accountants (ACs) participated in the questionnaire part of the study. Twenty-one EOs (out of the 43), their 21 CAs (7 further than in the questionnaire study), and their 21 ACs participated in the interview.

We were not able to contact 106 (32%) of the EOs for any one of the following reasons: letters were sent back because the addressee was unknown or the telephone had been withdrawn. In the former case, it is likely that they had had their telephone connection withdrawn due to unpaid bills. Further 72 (22%) of the EOs did not answer our letters.

One hundred and seven (33%) EOs refused to participate for the following reasons: 32 EOs stated that their firms' financial situation had changed to the better, or never had been bad, and thus they refused to participate. Eight EOs refused to participate because a lack of time. The remaining 67 EOs refused to participate without giving a reason.

Design and procedure
The design of the study is a multi-method one. The questionnaire[1] was divided in three parts: background information, questions related to business activities, and ratings of own attitudes about risk behaviour, risk management, and personal characteristics. In total, the questionnaire consisted of 204 items. Only the responses to some of these questions are reported here; the rest will be reported elsewhere.

The questionnaire data were followed-up with semi-structured interviews.[2] Only two out of 86 follow-up interview questions have been so far analysed. These two questions were: 1) 'Can you describe the causal and critical events in relation to the state of the firm during the last six months?'; and 2) 'If you would blame something or somebody for the problems of the firm, what or who would it be?' Two years later we also received financial information from PRV (the Swedish Patent and Registration Office) about the status of the firm.

Results

Main causes of and attitudes toward (i.e. blame) the financial problems in firms
The questionnaire data indicated that the three specific subjects of investigation (EOs, CAs, and ACs) showed the same response pattern in their views of the

---

1 The questionnaire can be ordered from the author.

2 The interview questions can be ordered from the author.

main causes of the firms' financial problems. The majority of the EOs, the CAs, and the ACs attributed 'decrease in market to be a cause to the firm's problems. Many of them also attributed 'too little operating capital' to be a cause.

The EOs was more defensive in their attitude than the CAs and the ACs. For example, only few of them attributed the problems to 'absence of a good business idea', while more of the CAs and the ACs did this. The same pattern appeared with respect to 'absence of a good management', and an inverted pattern appeared with respect to 'societal problems and political activities'.

The EOs, whose firms showed *an evolving sequence of events* in the way problems developed (according to the interview data), rated the personal characteristic 'good ability to communicate' (according to the questionnaire data, and confirmed with interview data) as depicting them (r = 0.48, $p < .05$). No such significant relationships were to be found among the CAs, or the ACs.

The CAs who considered the firms to have *an acute event related to development* of the problems (according to the interview data) also stated that the EOs 'put demands on their business relationships' (r = 0.60, $p < .05$; based on the questionnaire data, and confirmed with interview data). They also judged the EOs' less likely to be 'methodical' (r = 0.64, $p < .05$), 'purposeful' (r = 0.61, $p < .05$), 'persistent' (r = 0.63, $p < .05$), or 'straight to the point' (r = 0.63, $p < .05$). No such significant relationships were to be found among the EOs, or the ACs.

The ACs who attributed the EOs' problems to *internal causes* (according to interview data) also attributed 'nervousness' (r = 0.54, $p < .05$), 'increased aggressiveness' (r = 0.60, $p < .05$), 'withdrawal from other people' (r = 0.58, $p < .05$), 'dejection and uneasiness' (r = 0.58, $p < .05$), and 'increased alcohol consumption' (r = 0.65, $p < .01$) to the EOs (according to the questionnaire data). No such significant relationships were to be found among the EOs, or the CAs.

Response patterns from the EO, the CA, and the AC is interesting to compare since they deal with the same case. The following firm A is an example.

> EO: *The problem started during 1989-1990. In 1991 the whole market turned downwards. Nothing was sold, the only thing to do was to close the business. Nobody invested during the bank crisis. Nobody was allowed to borrow from the banks.*
>
> The CA: *Too low profit margins, too extensive need for capital, both liquidity problems, and profitability problems. The firm is bound to go to liquidation, too many persons have been involved, the business was financed by loans, and there was a decrease in the size of the market.*
>
> The AC: *The firm got into problems, confidence in the firm decreased. The bank became very cautious. They looked at their total financial engagement of the concern. The business idea was actually very good. The firm had a large and relevant experience of the business field. A number of critical events caused the problems. One event was the divided management. Another event was that the bank*

was worried about their total financial involvement. They withdrew their credits. There were no other special events. The firm had a number of orders, and the deliveries functioned well enough.

These interview data showed that the EOs, the CAs, and the ACs did show that they take three different perspectives when they make their pronouncements as to the financial crisis situation of the firm and as to the future possibilities existing for the firm. The CAs more often did show a more pessimistic view of the firm. The ACs were more informed, careful, often closer to the EO, and attempted to assist him or her in saving the firm at the same time as they did warn the EO from taking further risks. One explanation to these different viewpoints is that they do not have the same information available as to the business opportunities. Another explanation is that they simply have different roles to play.

Reactions and behaviours (i.e. coping strategies) during the crisis
Within the context of the questionnaire, the EOs was asked about the extent to which they had taken steps to cope with the financial problems. 'Enlarge field of business' and 'sell to lower prices' seemed to be the most frequently used strategies of coping. It thus seemed to be easier to use money rather than giving product development or competence development of the staff as a moderating factor. Also the CAs and the ACs were asked about the steps and measures the EOs took. The CAs agreed that the EOs use the coping strategy 'to enlarge field of business'. The ACs showed a somewhat more informed response pattern. They indicated that the EOs uses the strategies: 'accept customers with lower payment ability' and 'sell to lower prices'.

A stepwise regression analysis showed that in the latest step 21% of the variance of problem focused coping by the EOs was explained by one variable, denoted as 'knowledge of the economy' ($R^2_{adj} = .207$, $F(1, 31) = 9.07$, $p < .01$).

This kind of analysis was also carried out on the strategy of emotional focused coping. Here the analysis showed that 51% of the variance was explained by two variables, 'decreased self-esteem', 36%, and 'feelings of shame', 15% ($R^2_{adj} = .512$, $F(2, 31) = 17.25$, $p < .001$).

Frequency (questionnaire data) of the psychological symptoms appears as far as we can see to be relative to their seriousness. Several subjects experienced more severe symptoms such as 'muscle pain' (26 persons), 'binge eating' (22 persons), 'headache' (22 persons), 'fits of crying' (11 persons), 'pain in neck and shoulders' (7 persons), and 'digestion troubles' (7 persons). Seven persons reported 'feelings that their life was meaningless'. Three persons reported 'suicide thoughts' and one person refused to answer that particular question.

In spite of this, half of the EOs (50%) indicated that they had enough 'personal strength and will to continue to run the business', in spite of the present problems in their firm. They (50%) also indicated that they had 'personal ability to run the business'. The two variables 'personal strength and will' and 'personal ability to continue to run the business' were strongly related ($r = 0.92, p < .000$).

The perceptions of 'a decrease in self-confidence' was negatively related to sufficient 'personal strength and will to continue to run the business', that is, the EOs who experienced a decrease in self-confidence, felt less 'personal strength and will to continue to run the business in future' ($r = -0.55, p < .04$). Nor did they feel 'a personal ability to continue to run the business' ($r = -0.54, p < .05$).

Awareness of the firm's acute financial problems
Fourteen EOs (33%) indicated that they became 'aware of the firm's acute financial problems' a year ago. Only one of the 43 EOs indicated that he or she became aware of the problems six months ago. Twenty-seven (63%) EOs did not report any given point in time when they became aware of the problems.

Impact on decision making by the credit assessors
Among the CAs, significant relationships were found between their ratings of 'the business opportunities' and their ratings of three variables. These were specifically their rating of 'probability that the firm would survive' ($r = 0.71, p < .01$); their rating that 'their bank had taken initiative to positive steps with the purpose to save the firm' ($r = 0.61, p < .05$); and their rating of EOs' 'knowledge about products and markets' ($r = 0.67, p < .05$). Among the ACs, no such relationships were to be found, but the last mentioned one ($r = 0.55, p < .01$).

Only a quarter of the CAs (25%) found it probable 'the firm would survive'. More of the ACs (40%) found it probable 'the firm would survive'. Only among the CAs, a significant relationship was found, namely between 'the firm will survive' and 'bank had taken initiatives to positive steps with the purpose to save the firm' ($r = 0.64, p < .02$).

Two years after the questionnaires had been filled in and the follow-up interviews had been completed, information from the authorities (PRV) was obtained as to whether or not a bankruptcy had occurred for the firms whose owners participated in the study. We received data for only 38 firms. Seventeen (45%) of these 38 firms had been living on the verge of bankruptcy, but were still regarded as going concerns. Four of the 38 firms were under new ownership. For 11 (29%) of the 38 firms bankruptcy had become a reality, three of the 38 firms had closed on own demands, three of the 38 firms were liquidated or had made an amalgamation. More than 84% of the firms had had problems for longer than two years.

Discussion and conclusion

The most underlying reason behind the financial problems was a down-swing in the market. Structural changes and activities within the societal and political activities were also considered to be a hindrance by the EO. The EOs tended to see the problems as external and denied their own responsibility. These EOs also did show serious personal crisis reactions. They often felt betrayed, cheated and let down. Many of them attempted to avoid bankruptcy at any cost. Many of them also felt that they had been very naive, they did not think that they would be so 'completely disregarded' by their creditors as they were. This is in line with the results by Rose-Ackerman (1991).

In particular, the interview data showed that the EOs, the CAs, and the ACs did show that they take three different perspectives when they make pronouncements as to what has actually caused the financial crisis situation of the firm and as to future possibilities for the firm. Based on a superficial analysis, the CAs did more often show a more pessimistic view of the firm and its future possibilities. This in turn probably influenced them in their credit granting process. This superficial analysis can be compared to the summaries decision making made by creditors when new ventures apply for loans (Hedelin & Sjöberg, 1995). The ACs were more informed, careful, often closer to the EO, and attempted to assist him or her in saving the firm at the same time warning the EO from taking further risks. The CA and the AC differ in this respect. The creditor wants the EO to earn more money on behalf of the firm if there is a slightest chance to do it. An explanation of these different viewpoints is that they do not have the same information available. Another explanation can be that they simply have different roles to play and these roles are unclear regarding their responsibility in warning the EO from taking further risks. The results imply that the long-term consequences of these distinct perspectives are neglected with serious personal as well as socio-economic consequences for the EOs, and the society as a whole.

As the number of subjects in our study was small, there was no real basis for firm conclusions. Nevertheless at this phase of the investigation, the very occurrences of symptoms and crisis-reactions and their impact on the decision making by the creditor in the credit granting process, are clearly interesting and point to giving directions for further research.

Acknowledgements

This paper is based on a more substantial research project presented at the Second International Seminar on Risk Behaviour and Risk Management, Stockholm, Sweden, June 9-12, 1997, "Entrepreneurs' Reactions and Coping Strategies in an Insolvency Situation: Critical Events".

The author wishes to thank Programme Director Bo Green and Professor James Shanteau for valuable comments about how to abridge the original article for this publication. Thanks also to Dr. Adrian Parker for a language check of the manuscript. The author also gratefully acknowledges Karin Hedelin (business school graduate from School of Business), and Martin G. Erikson (doctoral student in Psychology) in collecting data. Thanks also to NUTEK, Dun & Bradstreet Soliditet AB, and Föreningsbanken who contributed to the financing of the project.

3.7 Business risks in service companies due to poor temporal assessment

by Fabian von Schéele
Doctoral student, Luleå University of Technology, Dept. of Engineering Psychology

Distinctions of risk, contract and time

This paper presents a field study focusing on time and temporal assessment in service organisations. The aim was to assess the risks due to misjudgement of time and the economic implications that follow.

Any organisation can be regarded as a system of formal and informal contracts. According to Coase (1991), all deviations from the contracts increase the transaction costs of the system. The ideas of Coase are applicable to this field study due to the assessment of temporal deviation from various contracts.

When trying to define the word 'risk', people often refer to unwanted outcome (Fisher, Chitose & Gipson, 1993). If, however, we accept the definition of 'risk' as a *function of the probability and the seriousness of possible losses* (Vlek, 1992), this concept applies to a system operating with monetary values as well as temporal values.

The *customer contract* is the agreement between the service supplier and the customer. It regulates the activities that shall be performed by the service supplier in order to satisfy the customer. At the same time, it regulates *how much time* the service supplier shall spend on each activity. Failure to fulfil the agreement affects the behaviour of the customer and the market. The transaction cost may be regarded as a cost between the service supplier and the market. Accordingly, the customer contract forms an external risk.

Deviations from contracts are measured in terms of *time*. 'Time' is regarded as an entity that permeates the service company and flows through the service process. Furthermore, 'time' cannot be defined from the perspective of the service supplier only, but must incorporate the temporal norm of the customer. Finally, focusing on time as a carrier of value to the customer, a cognitive model of psychological time will be discussed. There is a distinction between *objective* time and *subjective* time. Objective time is entirely linked to the mechanical clock time and this time paradigm serves as a ruler to the individual for the subjective time. On the other hand, subjective time is an assessment by an individual of a time duration. The subjective time of an individual varies greatly during a day. It also exhibits differences between individuals (Campbell, 1990).

Temporal misjudgement and risk

The differences between the subjective time and objective time are substantial. Individuals do not pay attention to the anomalies between their subjective time and their objective time. Burt & Kemp (1993) demonstrated that simple tasks, well known to the subjects, can lead to misjudgement in the assessment of the task duration. Furthermore, the error varied, depending on whether the subjects made the assessment *before* or *after* the activity. The size of their misjudgements varied from 20% to 112% in relation the expected task duration. In order to see how stress influenced control of time, Burt & Kemp (1993) repeated the experiment. The size of misjudgement of the retrospective assessment was now rated from 67% to 143% in relation to the expected task duration.

The misjudgements between the expected estimation and retrospective estimation of task duration are consequently of *considerable size.* These estimations can be transferred to the situations of time budgeting when planning a project, and registration of worked time of each individual in a service company. The work of Burt & Kemp (1993) deals with simple, everyday tasks. It is worthwhile to point out that the present survey deals with *complex tasks,* well known to the people who perform them. Also, my research indicates the accumulated result of task assessment during a period of one year. Accordingly, one can assume that assessment of complex tasks during a long period of time may affect the results of my empirical findings in a manner that the *precision of the task time assessment is deteriorated.*

Method

Five health care units participated in the field study. The health care units supply health care services on fixed-price contracts to companies and organisations. All contracts were signed on a yearly basis.

The working time of all employees was recorded with the exception of the administrative staff and the managers. In order to assess the risks, 233 fixed-price contracts were analysed. The value of each contract was transferred into an equivalence in time, denoted normtime T(n).

T(n)	=	(CV) x (W x E)/ (C x M)	(Hours)
CV	=	Contracted Value	(SEK)
W	=	Total time worked	(Hours)
E	=	Efficiency	(%)
C	=	Total costs of the service supplier	(SEK)
M	=	Margin of profit	(%)

In order to assess to what extent the service supplier fulfilled the terms of the contract, a quality dimension that is called *precision of service delivery*, P_{sd}, was defined.

$$P_{sd} = \frac{T(d) \times 100}{T(n)} \%$$

T(d) stands for time delivered by the service supplier. This time was registered by the suppliers' employees, who kept a record of their activities. T(d) represents a *subjective* time dimension recorded by the employees. T(n) indicates the time the customer has actually contracted and represents the normtime. The normtime is to be regarded as the ruler for *objective* time. Accordingly, P_{sd} assesses deviations from normtime and is an expression for the psychological mechanisms linked to temporal assessment.

One can say that precision of service delivery expresses how well the service supplier fulfils her/his temporal obligations to the customer. If the ratio equals 100%, the customer receives the amount of time she/he actually has purchased. If the ratio is less than 100%, there is an under deliverance of time – the customer has a right to have more time delivered according to the signed contract. If the ratio is more than 100%, the supplier has made an over deliverance of time. To keep the ratio close to 100% is an objective of the service supplier, since it is an expression of good economic management.

Results

Table 3.6 indicates that health care unit B supplied its largest customer with *57% more time in one year than contracted* (precision of service delivery similar to 157%), while health care unit D supplied its largest customer with 83% less time in one year than contracted (precision of service delivery similar to 17%).

Table 3.6 Precision of service delivery to the three largest customers

Customer	*Unit A*	*Unit B*	*Unit C*	*Unit D*	*Unit E*
Largest	115%	157%	94%	17%	133%
2nd largest	257%	195%	126%	119%	0%
3d largest	61%	107%	110%	71%	416%

The results gives us two important findings:

1. There are *significant deviations* from norm time indicating a *poor precision* of delivery
2. The deviations are of a *substantial volume*

These findings create a hazard to the service supplier when budgeting the business, and pricing the services. These findings also form an obstacle for a successful negotiation, since they form a kind of *uncertainty* linked to the service and its price.

Accordingly, all customers, whether large or small, have to negotiate and make decisions dealing with the same uncertainties. This indicates that one can expect all *customers of services to behave as decision makers under risk.* The only differences between the customers are their personal biases, risk aversion and point of reference.

When the *total output of time* for each health care unit was related to the *total norm time*, it was evident that all units had a performance far beyond the contracted value. Each unit delivered much more time than they actually credited their customers. The situation seriously hampered the economy of the units. The accumulated over delivery of all five service suppliers exceeded 6.000 hours in one year. This equals almost four man years of service production.

In Table 3.7 the probability for receiving a certain level of precision of service delivery are presented. The deviation from norm time exhibited as precision of service delivery is in the left column, the number of customers corresponding to the service supply is in the central column and the probability of receiving a certain service level is in the right column.

Table 3.7 Probability for receiving a certain level of precision of service delivery

PRECISION (%)	CUSTOMERS	PROBABILITY
0 - 40	65	0,27
41 - 80	20	0,09
81 - 120	***37***	***0,16***
121 - 160	23	0,10
161 - 200	27	0,12
201 - 300	25	0,11
301 - 400	15	0,06
> 400	21	0,09
TOTAL	**233**	**1,00**

The population was split into stratas, corresponding to a bandwidth of 40% of precision of service delivery in each stratum. In my opinion an acceptable 'normtime' should be equal to 100% +/- 20% which is indicated in Table 3.7 with a darker area. The reason to select a bandwidth of this size emanates from the knowledge that precision in temporal assessment in general is poor. Accordingly, one has to accept a larger bandwidth.

One might assume that a deficient temporal assessment in some sense should be regulated due to 'selfmending mechanisms' on a long-term basis. The communication within the service companies should presumably prevent the aggregated outcome of temporal assessment to attain 'extreme values'. The present survey, however, cannot support these assumptions. By adding up the result displayed in the intervals in Table 3.7, the probability that a certain number of customers receives 'wrong' amounts of time is assessed. Accordingly, there is a probability equalling to 0,84 (0,27 + 0,09 + 0,10 + 0,12 + 0,11 + 0,06 + 0,09) to erring temporal assessment by the service supplier. There is only a small probability – 0,16 – that the time of service delivery is within an interval of-80 – 120% of norm time. This might lead to the conclusion that *temporal assessment does not tend to level around 100% of the normtime,* even after one year of service delivery.

The survey leads to the following conclusions:

- Large discrepancies in temporal assessment *affect the market price*, thereby affecting the profit of the service supplier.
- The effects of deficient assessment of task duration *accumulate* in a manner indicating that under delivery, as well as over delivery, seems to multiply itself with time, thereby creating an impediment to a successful contractual negotiation. There is no indication that a service delivery on a long term basis will approach a level that balances the time contracted.
- The *size of the customer does not affect the precision of service delivery.* The importance of a customer has no effect of the temporal assessment of the service supplier. All customers, whether large or small, have to negotiate and make decisions dealing with the same uncertainties. This indicates that one can expect *all customers of services to behave as a decision maker under risk.* The only differences between the customers are their personal biases, risk aversion and point of reference.
- The *risk of erring in temporal assessment is substantial* and the economic consequences severe . This survey demonstrates that this risk concept applies to the single service provider.

Discussion

During the period of the field study I was active as a consultant and participated in many contract negotiations. Accordingly, the qualitative analysis relies on my experiences from this time.

The deregulation of the health care unit market in Sweden in 1992, combined with a deep recession has generally been used as the explanation why the market price of the services decreased sharply resulting in thousands of people losing their jobs There might however be other explanations. A health care service customer has to optimise the utility and make a decision between the following alternatives.

1. Prolong the contract with the health care unit and receive their service one more year.
2. Decide whether a competing health care unit should be contracted.

All alternatives present outcomes linked to certain probabilities. The outcome can be expressed in terms of cost for a contract compared to cost for sick employees. In order to make a successful decision the customers relied to several strategies referred to below. The market displayed different categories of customers (von Schéele, 1996):

1. the ones that tried to reduce the costs inferred by active health care policy decided by the company, below as *risk seekers*.
2. the ones that tried to gain something from the active health care policy decided by the company, below denoted as *risk averse*.

The *risk seekers* (to which the majority of customers belong) preferred to reduce the value of the long-term contract, thereby risking to be *charged extra* if the company should need urgent assistance from the health care unit.

- If this category had received an *over deliverance* of time last year, they could argue that they accepted to sign a new contract, provided that the time delivered *and the price will be decreased* by x%.
- If this category had received an *under deliverance* of time last year, they could argue that they had paid y% too much for each hour last year. Consequently, they preferred a new contract of less value the coming year, but to a price per hour, which is y% lower than the one suggested by the health care supplier.

The situation applies to the value function of the Prospect Theory (Kahneman & Tversky, 1979). The value function V(p) is supposed to describe the value of a choice by a customer as a function of expected gains or losses. In general, the X-axis describes volumes or perceived gains or losses, while the Y-axis describes the perceived value of a certain choice.

In this study the x-axis symbolises precision of delivery with a large under-delivery of time far out to the left, and over-delivery far out to the right. The y-axis symbolises the value function V(p) here indicated by two curves. Origin is the point where the customer has received contracted value, that is 100% precision of delivery, and his attitude for compensation when bargaining a new contract is assumed to be neutral.

I suggest that the poor precision of temporal assessment may influence the utility function and the value function to display certain interesting properties.

a) The value function may *display a 'knee' close to origin* due to the poor temporal assessment. This "knee" is due to the abstract properties of time; it is believed to be more difficult to follow up the precision in time delivery than it is to control the precision of payments. Therefore, the customer supposedly is more lenient to minor temporal deviations from norm time.

b) The shape of the utility function and value function may differ *if the utilities and values are expressed in a temporal instead of monetary values.*

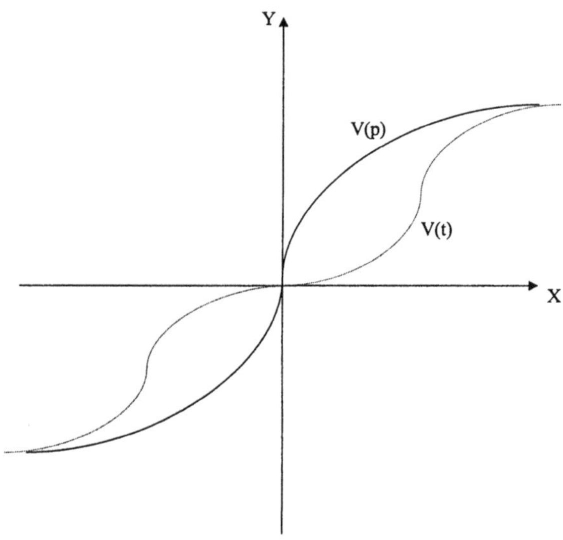

Figure 3.2 The value functions V(p) and V(t).

The implication of my suggestions can easily be transferred into a business setting. Many service companies attempt to increase the perceived service quality by giving the customer some extra attention. This may prove to be a hazardous strategy, due to the fact that the customer too has a poor temporal assessment and, accordingly, will not appreciate the service effort to its proper value. Furthermore, some extra attention tends to be very difficult to control, since time has no borders and temporal rules of thumb are *fuzzy*. As soon as time is translated to a figure, it has been given a cognitive dimension, which will affect the negotiation and the business outcome.

My suggestion applies to a negotiation setting. In service negotiations focus varies between task, price and volume (time). The value curve indicates that over-delivery as well as under-delivery put the service supplier in an awkward situation during the negotiations. The compensations asked by the customer are not proportional to the production costs. The curve explains why a customer, who has received an immense delivery of overtime, will not experience a 'gratitude' proportional to the service effort of the supplier. The situation of the customer is to be compared to a static decision and the value curve here is a theoretical modification of the Prospect Theory (Kahneman & Tversky, 1979).

Similarly, the *risk averse* preferred to sign a prolonged contract, which guaranteed them status quo, that is the same service as last year from the same service supplier. But they signed a contract only if they could be convinced that they would *gain* something from it.

- If this category had received an *over deliverance* of time last year, they could argue that they accept to sign a prolonged contract, provided that they receive the *same amount of time and the same price* the next year.
- If this category had received an *under deliverance* of time last year, they could aspire to prolong the contract, provided that the price and the time supplied was the same as last year – but that a *compensation was paid* for the under deliverance of service time.

Accordingly, any solution to this problem always comes out to be in the favour of the customer.

The risk seeking customers as well as the risk averse customers usually succeeded to decrease the value of the long term contract. For the five health care units in this survey, the *fixed-price* contract decreased from the level of 1.100 SEK/ client and year in 1992 to 600 – 800 SEK/client and year in 1994. I suggest that the risk averse as well as the risk seekers contribute to decrease the price level. This is mainly attributed to the substantial misjudgement of temporal assessment on behalf of the service providers. In accordance with Prospect Theory (Kahneman & Tversky, 1979), the customers evaluated the *changes of welfare*, rather than the *final states*. Thus, a customer having received a great over deliverance of time was more apt to notify a reduction of time, than if the service was actually levelled out according to the contract.

Are the results representatives for any service enterprise? Presumably yes. However the temporal behaviour of an organisation is dependant of several factors; management, task motivation, temporal feedback and average age of employees, just to mention a few. The conclusion of *time as a hidden psychological mechanism* gearing the price level will be applicable to any service enterprise. The deviancies from normtime may vary, due to the reason that the customers in the study used the contract as a *combination of service contracts and a social security.* In another field of service business, I assume fewer customers to receive as little as 20 – 40% have contracted time. However I do expect the deviance from norm time to be substantial – especially in terms of over-delivery. It is an unforeseen fact that one does not have control over time in an enterprise just because one seems to have a satisfactory control over the money.

3.8 Task characteristics and expertise

by Anna Mette Fuglseth, Professor
and
Kjell Grønhaug, Professor
The Norwegian School of Economics and Business Administration, Bergen

Expertise is considered important in society. "Expert judgements" are obtained in critical situations, such as the public concern over the spread of radioactivity from Chernoble and the "mad cow" disease being conveyed to human beings. Reviews of the literature show, however, that experts often fail, and that conflicting perspectives on expertise are presented in different research disciplines (Shanteau, 1992). The purpose of this paper is to examine such conflicting perspectives. We argue that expertise is dependent on task characteristics, and that different types of tasks demand different types of expertise.

First, the notion of expertise is discussed and inconsistencies from the literature are described together with possible explanations. Next, tasks are characterised along two dimensions, degree of uncertainty and degree of complexity. The two dimensions are dichotomised and cross-classified, and the resulting four ideal-type tasks are taken as the starting point for a discussion of different types of expertise. Three theories/perspectives are applied to understand the expertise needed in various tasks: automatic/controlled processes, development of knowledge structures, and primary/secondary decisions. The discussion is summarised in a framework for expertise, and implications are highlighted.

The concept of expertise

Definitions of expertise and its derivative expert are multiple. Most definitions refer to special knowledge or skill. For example, The Random House Dictionary claims that an expert is "a person who has special knowledge *or* skill in some field". The definition shows, as commonly agreed upon, that expertise is domain specific. This raises the problem of how to define the domain. The definition also raises another ticklish problem: "Is it possible to demonstrate skill without having knowledge?" This problem will be addressed later on in the discussions regarding automatic processes.

It is commonly believed that expertise is acquired through training or practice in a task (Ericsson et al., 1993). This belief assumes that expertise is, or should be, related to performance, but also raises the questions whether expertise presumes experience of a specific task, similar tasks, and to what extent expertise can be transferred (Singley and Anderson, 1989). The task aspect of expertise will be examined in more detail later.

Some inconsistencies and explanations

The literature on judgement and decision making and on cognitive science presents inconsistent views of the *performance of experts*. Within the cognitive science literature, the common belief seems to be that experts possess superior abilities to perform better than novices do (Anderson, 1995). Empirical research reported in the behavioural judgement literature shows in contrast that experts often fail to perform better than non-experts do. An example is Goldberg's (1959) study comparing the ability of psychiatrists and their secretaries to diagnose brain damage. He found no difference. Another example is Armstrong's (1985) review of the literature on expertise in forecasting. He concluded that expertise beyond a minimal level is of little value in forecasting.

Diverging opinions of the *possibilities to study expertise* are also reflected in the literature. This particularly relates to differences in views regarding experts' ability to verbalise their knowledge and skills. Some researchers claim that experts lose awareness of what they know. Johnson (1983), for example, in what he terms "the paradox of expertise", claims that "the very knowledge we wish to represent in a computer program as well as the knowledge we wish to teach others, often turns out to be the knowledge that individuals sometimes are least able to talk about". Other researchers in contrast argue that expertise can sometimes be communicated to others, e.g. Shanteau (1992).

Review of the literature also shows that experts have been studied by employing *different methodological approaches* that may tap into different aspects of the phenomenon studied. Thus inconsistency with regard to reported expert performances may reflect methodological biases, e.g. differences in operational definitions of expertise and experts. Studies have defined "experts" both based on ex ante and ex post criteria. In a series of studies, particularly in the literature on judgement and decision making, experts have been included based on criteria assumed to reflect expertise, e.g. experience (Johnson, 1988). Such an approach may be questioned, as the predictive ability of the selection criteria may be absent. Other studies have included experts based on their performance, e.g. in studies of chess players (Chase and Simon, 1973). Such differences in choice of assumed experts, may be a possible cause to at least some of the contradictory findings reported in the literature.

Expert performance relates to the handling of a task, which is influenced by the knowledge and the problem solving processes of the individual. Differences in handling a specific task thus reflect differences between e.g. experts and novices. Tasks vary, however, and we assume they can be characterised by objective criteria, such as Shanteau's (1992) distinction between decisions about something relatively constant and a moving target, and Johnson's (1988) distinction between tasks having a certain or uncertain relationship between inputs and outputs. Variations in observed expert performance may thus also be explained as *variations in task characteristics*. In the following we will emphasise the importance of task characteristics on expertise.

Task characteristics

A task is a piece of work that has to be done, often within a certain time. Handling a task implies solving problems of a certain kind dependent on the task domain. As noted above, tasks can be characterised in several ways. Here we will focus on two dimensions, degree of uncertainty and degree of complexity. Task complexity is some times defined relative to the capabilities of the problem solver (March and Simon, 1958, p. 55), and uncertainty can be seen as an aspect of complexity (Campbell, 1988; March and Simon, 1958, pp. 139-149). For the study of expertise, however, we believe that it is useful to define complexity in terms of objective task qualities (Campbell, 1988) and to make a distinction between uncertainty and complexity:

Expert task performance often relates to predicting outcome. The tasks to be handled can vary considerably with regard to outcome predictability. Degree of predictability relates to the relationship between input and output. In most real-life tasks the relationships between inputs and outputs are not known with certainty. In some cases the relationship can be described by a known/estimated probability distribution, i.e. the case of risk. An example is calculating the insurance premium of motor car damages. In other cases it is not possible to generate an 'objective' probability distribution of the relationships between inputs and outputs, i.e. the case of uncertainty. Often, however, it is possible to combine empirical data with personal knowledge to arrive at subjective probabilities, e.g. medical diagnosis. In real life, sudden and dramatic changes often take place. Tasks in such turbulent situations are characterised by unpredictability. Still, in many situations it is possible to identify critical variables and get an understanding of cause-effect relationships. For example, in 1979 Saudi-Arabia changed its oil strategy almost overnight, which caused an increase in crude oil prices of as much as 176% during a period of 18 months. It is not possible to foresee such events. From analysis of historical data it is possible, however, to develop a general understanding of the effects of dramatic changes in critical variables. Such an understanding allows for advance formulation of strategies to handle alternative states of the world so that the organisation can react fast and appropriately even to unpredictable environmental changes.

Within the literature on human problem solving and decision making a distinction is often made between structured and unstructured/ill-structured problems (Simon, 1977). People differ, however, in their ability and ways of representing problems. To what extent problems are conceived as structured or not, may thus be influenced by the person's knowledge. We also believe it might be influenced by the complexity of the task. Complexity refers to the number of elements and their interrelationships. The number of elements does not necessarily relate to complexity, but – in general – the greater the number of elements, the higher the possibility of complex relationships among the elements. In the simplest task there are two elements and one direct relationship. As the number of elements increases, multiple (direct and indirect) relationships will increase the complexity of the task.

Dimensions of expertise

Experts can be distinguished from non-experts in a great variety of ways (Johnson, 1988; Shanteau, 1992). Here we will focus on three dimensions of expertise of importance for performing different types of tasks, i.e. automatic and controlled processes, knowledge structures, and primary and secondary decision processes.

The distinction between *automatic/controlled processes* has been termed "one of the foremost developments in experimental cognitive psychology over the last decade" (Newell, 1990, p. 136). Controlled processes require attention, they are serial in nature and depend strongly on memory load. On the other hand, they are easily established, altered and even reversed by the subject. Automatic processes are initiated by appropriate inputs and then proceed automatically. They are difficult to alter, ignore, or to suppress once learned. Combinations of automatic and controlled processing are of special interest for the development of expertise in complex and new tasks. In complex situations both controlled and automatic processing are utilised. In novel situations controlled processing may be adopted to perform accurately, though slowly. As such situations become familiar, requiring the same sequence of processing operations, automatic processing will develop (Schneider and Shiffrin, 1977).

Experts and non-experts have been found to vary in *knowledge structures*. Kelly (1955), in his descriptions of the development of knowledge structures, sees man as a scientist with the ultimate aim to predict and control his environment. "Man looks at his world through transparent patterns or templates which he creates and then attempts to fit over the realities of which the world is composed" (Kelly 1955, vol. I, p.8-9). Such patterns are called *constructs*. According to Kelly, individuals seek to improve their constructs by increasing the repertory, by altering the constructs to provide better fits, and by subsuming them with super-ordinate constructs or systems (ibid. p.9). An important notion by Kelly is permeability of super-ordinate constructs. A construct is permeable if "new experience and new events can be discriminatively added to those which it already embraces" (ibid. p.80-81). Permeable constructs allow individuals to generate alternative interpretations of even new events in order to get a better understanding and thus better ability to handle them. The theory of cognitive complexity (Schroder et al., 1967) also emphasises the usefulness of well-developed cognitive structures in such tasks. Well-developed knowledge structures imply that experts have developed permeable, super-ordinate constructs that allow them to interpret new events, and that they have knowledge along different dimensions (differentiation). Flexibility implies that knowledge can be combined in various ways allowing experts to discriminate finely among events (discrimination) and generate new and discrepant interpretations of an event (integrative complexity).

We also believe that the distinction between *primary and secondary processes* (Stabell, 1978) is important to understand expertise in uncertain tasks. A primary decision relates to the key decision task, for example the shipping company's decision whether or not to buy a tanker. Secondary decision processes concern search, evaluation, and choice of information sources, methods for analyses, and decision aids in connection with the primary decision. As argued by Edwards (1983), experts are never unaided in real-life tasks, but adopt and exploit useful aids. The quality of decision-makers' secondary decisions is expected to influence the quality of their primary decisions.

Expertise in different tasks

The two dimensions, degree of uncertainty and degree of complexity are more or less continuous. For the discussion to follow, we will, however, dichotomise the two dimensions, cross-classify them, and relate our discussion of expertise performance to the four ideal-typical situations as shown in Figure 3.3.

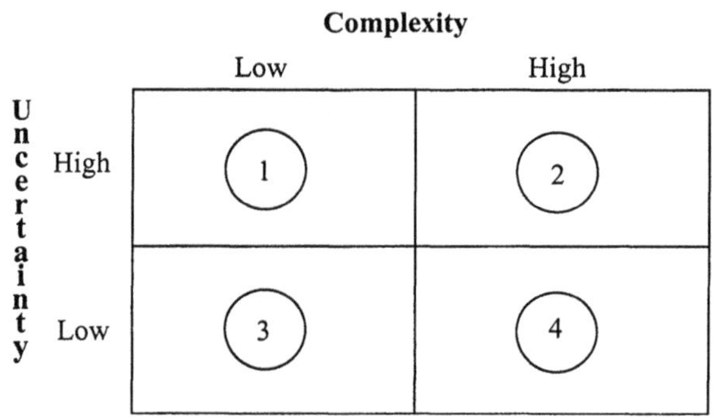

Figure 3.3 Tasks by degree of complexity and uncertainty

The number of the four cells refers to the order in which they are discussed below. Expertise is described in terms of cognitive structures, problem solving/decision making processes, and performance.

Expertise in Simple Tasks under Certainty

Simple tasks under uncertainty have single relationships between input and output. Examples of such tasks are changing gear, doing addition, and type writing. Because conditions do not change, they can be repeated. They are also the types of task for which automatic processes are developed through experience because consistency and training are key factors in the development of automatic processes (Schneider and Shiffrin, 1977). In the development of automatic processes, general problem solving procedures are gradually replaced by task-specific productions (Anderson, 1983; Newell, 1990).

Expert performance in simple tasks under certainty implies that the tasks are performed faster than do the non-experts and with no errors. An intriguing example is the sorting of chickens according to sex. For the egg-producers it is of great economic importance to sort out the hen as soon as possible because it can lay eggs. For the untrained person this is difficult, even though the task as such is simple, and the relationship between genital characteristics and the outcome determination, sex, is stable. Japanese experts have been reported to sort – almost perfectly – 6,000-8,000 chickens an hour, which has made their expertise valued and sought by egg-producers all over the world.

Expertise in Complex Tasks under Certainty

Examples of complex tasks under certainty are found within the domains of physics, geometry, computer programming, and chess. These are tasks handling problems that do not repeat, but components of the problems do repeat, and automation of such sub-problems takes place also in domains that are perceived as more complex.

One dimension of expertise is representation of problems according to deeper principles that enable more effective problem solving procedures (VanLehn, 1996; Anderson, 1995). In a study by Chi et al. (1981) novices and experts were asked to classify a large set of physics problems into similar categories. The novices chose surface features such as rotations or inclined planes as their bases for classifications, whereas the experts saw problems that were completely different on the surface as similar because both problems involved conservation of energy or both used Newton's second law. This shift in classification from surface features to deeper features has been found in a number of domains (Anderson, 1995).

Differences between novices and experts also relate to the way problems are solved. Larkin (1981) describes differences in novice and expert solutions to a physics problem. Novices work backwards from the desired conclusions using general search strategies (controlled processing). Experts are able to work forwards because they have developed productions that allow them to associate their representation of the problem to productions that solve the problem (automation of sub-problems). According to Anderson et al. (1984) this shift from backward to forward problem solving does not take place in all domains. Computer programming is mentioned as a counterexample. Their research indicated that expert programmers work in a top-down manner, which is basically working backwards. Domain differences have been proposed as an explanation of the observation that experts not always work forwards. Physics and geometry are formal domains characterised by a set of principles logically sufficient to solve problems in the domain (Larkin, 1981). Within computer programming problem statements do not indicate principles to solve the problem. Programmers usually solve new problems and work backwards until they reach a stage where they have productions that can solve the problem. Then, however, they shift to a forward solution procedure in the same manner as the expert physicists.

The purpose of the above description has been to indicate how expert processes in complex tasks may partly be explained by more permeable constructs (deeper principles) and by the combination of controlled and automatic processing, the degree of automatic processing being dependent on the domain. Expert performance in such tasks is characterised by the ability to solve problems faster than non-experts. The quality of the solutions is better as well. For example, the programs of expert programmers are more robust, easier to maintain, and have modules that can be reused in other programs.

Expertise in Simple Tasks under Uncertainty

The term 'simple, uncertain tasks' refers to the handling of events that repeat making it possible to collect data. Such tasks are also characterised by simple relationships between inputs and output; i.e. no intermediate variables are assumed. The relationships between event and outcome in such tasks, however, are not known with certainty.

Results from laboratory studies on judgement under uncertainty in relatively simple tasks (e.g. tosses of a coin, brief personality description) indicate that most people perform badly as intuitive statisticians (Tversky and Kahneman, 1974). In some studies of expert judgement probability assessments have been validated against external, objective standards (Bolger and Wright, 1992). This research also indicates that the accuracy and consistency of expert judgements is quite variable.

Some of the above studies have resulted in conclusions that experts have difficulties in coping with uncertainty and are thus inadequate decision-makers. Based on our research on decision processes within shipping (Fuglseth, 1989), we partly disagree. In shipping management, the sub-task of evaluating the effects of a change in bunkers prices on the supply of transportation services is an example of a simple task under uncertainty. Both managers and novices know that an increase in bunkers prices will cause an upward shift in the supply curve. Findings from our research shows that experts had a more detailed mental image of the form of the curve and estimates of the parameter values describing the curve as well. This finding indicates that the experts studied make use of statistical analysis to understand the relationships between freight rates and supply.

In tasks under certainty training and experience with the domain might be sufficient to develop both the knowledge and skill to become an expert. In uncertain tasks, however, it seems that expert performance also requires formal knowledge about human biases and statistics – and skill to use such knowledge effectively. As observed by Tversky and Kahneman (1974, p.18), statistical principles are not learned from every day experience, and people usually do not detect the biases in their judgements of probability. In uncertain tasks it is difficult to acquire understanding of cause-effect relationships through daily observations. Because the relationships between the independent and the dependent variables are stochastic, a large number of cases is needed to evaluate co-variation, and without the use of written records and statistical tools, the ability of individuals to judge co-variation is severely limited (Brehmer, 1980; Jenkins and Ward, 1965).

The processes of experts in simple, uncertain tasks, therefore, comprise data collection and analysis – or access to and evaluation of data collected and analysed by others. Phelps and Shanteau (1978) report on livestock judges who keep written records of prior decisions to reduce biases. As described above, shipping experts use statistical analyses to increase their understanding of cause-effect relationships. According to our observations, expert evaluations of uncertainty are a controlled process, but also that some secondary processes become automated. The shipping expert performing analyses himself, browses his usual databases, extracts data, and applies a statistical software package in an automated way, concentrating on the interpretation of the results.

Performance of experts compared to non-experts in simple, uncertain tasks is expected to be more accurate predictions, and thus – more adequate actions.

Expertise in Complex Tasks under Uncertainty

Complex uncertain tasks comprise the handling of events with direct and indirect relationships among a large number of variables. Furthermore, such tasks refer to the handling of events that are non-repetitive, and that may be characterised by uncertainty not only of cause-effect relationships, but also of identification of appropriate causes. As noted above, both Kelly's theory of personal constructs (Kelly, 1955) and the theory of cognitive complexity (Schroder et al., 1967) emphasise the usefulness of well-developed cognitive structures in such tasks.

Complex, uncertain tasks imply a comprehensive phase of problem identification and definition, which actually consists of many problem definition, problem solving, and choice processes (Simon, 1977). Because of their domain knowledge, experts are able to be aware of possible problems at an early stage, i.e. they are sensitive to subtle environmental changes (discrimination). They are also able to generate more causes and consequences to explain an event because they interpret the event from more perspectives (differentiation) than do novices. Experts also generate more complex interpretations of an event, i.e. generation and integration of alternative interpretations (integrative complexity). An example of a complex interpretation is the development of how a price change for crude oil may effect economy, trade, chartering, demand and supply of transportation services, both short-term and long term consequences. In addition, experts may interpret an event from several points of view. For example, the above-mentioned change in crude oil prices may be interpreted from the OPEC point of view, from the oil companies' perspective, or from the perspective of different trades, i.e. tank, dry bulk, combined carriers. The different points of view are then integrated in the evaluation of what is rational behaviour from each point of view, and this evaluation is used to predict what will probably happen.

The interpretation of an event is essential for the development of alternative actions to handle it. For example, how decision-makers perceive and represent an event, will influence the solutions they are able to generate (Kelly, 1955; Raaheim, 1961). Because of their complex interpretations of an environmental change, experts generate more actions, and they have a broader perspective of their actions. Experts also have more complex evaluations and choices of actions. Effects of alternative actions are evaluated considering the uncertainty of environmental changes, and actions are moderated in order to increase the possibilities to make flexible adjustments.

In addition to complex interpretations of an *actual* event, experts also consider possible future events. They generate alternative scenarios and develop strategies for handling such scenarios in order to be 'proactive' instead of putting out fires. When developing organisational strategies, experts take a portfolio point of view, i.e. they consider how their business activities covary, e.g. that liner traffic in the Middle East is cycling with oil drilling in the North Sea, whereas tank shipping and oil drilling are counter-cycled.

In our opinion it is important that the judgement processes of experts in complex uncertain tasks are seen in connection with their secondary processes. Because they are able to generate more complex interpretations of an event or a scenario, experts are also more aware of uncertainty. In order to handle this uncertainty they perform a comprehensive monitoring of the environment, and they use and evaluate a wide variety of information sources to support the detection and interpretation of weak signals. This environmental monitoring does not replace, but complements the routine data collection and data analysis from well-known sources described for simple uncertain tasks. In addition, experts use and evaluate computerised models to support the understanding of complex interrelationships among groups of variables, e.g. shifts in both supply and demand for transportation services as a consequence of a change in crude oil prices. For analysis of actions they have models of their organisations, e.g. spreadsheet models developed by themselves or their assistants.

In sum, due to well-developed and flexible cognitive structures, experts are able to develop primary and secondary decision processes that are highly effective in handling complex, uncertain tasks.

Discussion

Figure 3.4 summarises our above discussion. The table is to be read as follows. The two dimensions, degree of uncertainty and complexity are dichotomised and cross-classified, generating four ideal-type situations. In each cell superiority of expertise is characterised according to three dimensions, i.e. knowledge structures, decision making/problem solving processes, and performance.

Figure 3.4 illustrates the combination of controlled and automatic processing when experts handle complex problems that do not repeat. The table also illustrates the importance of well-developed and flexible cognitive structures for handling complex, uncertain tasks. Furthermore, the table indicates the need for knowledge about human biases and statistics in addition to domain knowledge, and the increasing importance of secondary processes when experts handle such tasks.

The framework-underlying figure 3.4 may be useful to explain some of the inconsistencies found in research on expertise within human decision making and cognitive science. The examples of expertise mentioned by Anderson (1995), i.e. cigar rolling, changing gear, geometry, physics, and chess, vary along the complexity dimension, but are all positioned at the certainty pole of the uncertainty dimension. These are domains where the performance of experts is considered good. Also most of the domains mentioned by Shanteau (1992) where good performance has been observed, are positioned towards the certainty pole, e.g. mathematics, physics, livestock judging, soil judging. One reason for the e.g. mathematics, physics, livestock judging, soil judging. One reason for the inconsistent findings may be variations in domains, and thus the characteristics of the tasks studied.

Uncertainty \ **Complexity**	**Low**	**High**
Low	*knowledge structures:* task specific productions *processes:* automatic processes *performance:* faster less errors	*knowledge structures:* well-developed domain knowledge task specific productions for sub-problems *processes:* effective representation of problems automatic processing of sub-problems *performance:* faster higher quality solutions
High	*knowledge structures:* knowledge of human biases knowledge of statistics task-specific productions for secondary processes *processes:* controlled evaluation of uncertainty automatic secondary processes routine use of information sources/decision aids *performance:* more accurate predictions more effective actions	*knowledge structures:* well-developed and flexible domain knowledge knowledge of human biases knowledge of statistics task-specific productions for routine sec. processes *processes:* controlled primary processes environmental monitoring complex interpretations actual and imagined events controlled secondary processes evaluation of information sources/decision aids automatic secondary processes routine use of information sources/decision aids *performance:* more accurate predictions more effective actions proactiveness

Figure 3.4 Task characteristics and expertise

Another reason for inconsistencies reported might be that 'experts' often have been selected based on their experience. In repetitive tasks, performed in a stable environment, performance will improve through experience (Larkin, 1981). In complex and uncertain tasks, however, the relationship between performance and experience seems to be more complex. Formal training emphasising knowledge and skill that are difficult to obtain in complex and ever-changing environments, may be a prerequisite for development of expertise.

The reported discrepancies concerning experts' ability to communicate their expertise may be due to the fact that different types of expertise have been studied. It might be difficult for experts to communicate their automatic processes, even if access to the "source code" may not be lost when the processes are 'compiled' (Anderson, 1983). In uncertain tasks requiring reflective judgements where proceduralisation of primary decision processes does not take place, experts are probably able to communicate their perceptions of the problems and their plans for action (Shanteau, 1992).

The framework outlined above has implications for research on expertise. In future research adequate attention to definition and selection of experts should be given. Task characteristics should be considered of importance for selection of methods and data collection, as well as choice of theoretical dimensions and what aspects of expertise to be studied. In order to enhance the understanding of expertise in uncertain tasks, we believe it is particularly essential to include secondary decision processes in the research design (Edwards, 1983).

3.9 Why do experts disagree?

by James Shanteau
Professor/Director, Institute for Social and Behavioral Research,
Kansas State University

Researchers are often perplexed when they observe sizeable and consistent disagreements between subjects. This is particularly true when the subjects are experts. As shown by the following quotations, however, disagreements have been viewed historically as important.

> *By different methods different men excel* (Churchill, 1764)
>
> *The history of scholarship is a record of disagreements* (Hughes, 1936)
>
> *The tough-minded... respect differences* (Benedict, 1940)

The position taken here is that disagreements between experts are a normal part of their jobs.

The purpose of this paper is to explore why it is natural for experts to disagree with each other. The material is organised as follows. First, there is a review of the literature on disagreement between experts and a discussion of a commonly held hypothesis about expertise. Second, 10 structural and functional factors behind why experts often disagree are presented. Third, domain differences in the extent to which experts agree are considered. Fourth, an alternate hypothesis is offered that more closely corresponds to how experts view tasks. Finally, the paper concludes with a discussion of research implications and future directions for analyses of experts.

Background to research on experts' judgement

Since the start of systematic research on decision making in the 1950s, researchers have expressed dismay at the extent to which experts disagree. For example, if we ask two financial experts to assess an investment, the expectation of most investigators is that they will make the same recommendation. If they arrive at different recommendations, we wonder whether they are as skilled as they claim.

In a seminal paper, Einhorn (1974) argued that *consensus* (between-expert reliability) is a necessary condition for expertise. He reported, however, sizeable differences in the diagnoses by three expert medical pathologists. The average between-expert correlation (r) was .55 (where .0 is chance and 1.0 is perfect).

Similar evidence was presented in a study of expert livestock judges evaluating overall breeding quality of swine (Phelps & Shanteau, 1978). Despite a high level of internal consistency (average r = .96), the consensus was much lower, r = .50. Apparently, livestock experts have internally consistent strategies, but do not agree with each other about what those strategies should be. Comparable results have been reported by researchers for other domains, e.g., consensus values of less than .40 were found for judgements by professional stockbrokers and clinical psychologists.

Several studies of professional auditors have reported greater between-expert consensus. Three studies of audit judgement revealed correlations of .76, .70 and .68 for assessments of financial profiles, internal controls and control reliance, respectively. Several studies have explored the question of whether agreement increases with experience. One of my students compared 11 accounting students with 10 audit seniors and 10 audit partners; the mean between-judge correlations increased from .66 to .76 to .83, respectively. Other studies have generally reported similar trends. (For more information, see Shanteau, 1992).

These results suggest three conclusions: First, experts in a variety of domains frequently disagree; the consensus correlations range from .40 to .55. Second, the agreement between financial experts is higher, with correlations ranging from .68 to .83. Third, there is some evidence that increased experience may lead to greater consensus. Before making too much of these findings, however, it is important to note the wide range of tasks and skill levels studied.

Experts-should-converge hypothesis

The unimpressive consensus correlations for non-financial experts and somewhat better results for auditors lead many researchers to question the abilities of experts in general. Following Einhorn's logic (1974), these investigators assume that agreement is a necessary condition for expertise. The lack of agreement, therefore, suggests that 'experts are no damn good'. This analysis and interpretation of reliability data are based on an implicit hypothesis about experts. The hypothesis, labelled the *Experts-Should-Converge* (ESC), is based on the following five arguments:

1. For most tasks performed by an expert, there is assumed to be a 'gold standard' or unique 'ground truth' that can be identified. If this truth is easy to access, we could get it directly. For expert tasks, however, it is outside the realm of common knowledge or direct sensory experience of most people. Thus, unique correct answers exist, at least in theory, but they are difficult to obtain.

2. Because of their special skills and experience, experts should be able to figure out and tell the rest of us about this ground truth. That is, experts can access what others cannot.

3. Since by definition there can be only one ground truth, all experts should give us the same answer. The special abilities of experts should allow them to obtain a single truth.

4. If experts disagree, then someone is wrong – they cannot all be correct. Some or all of them must not be experts, i.e., disagreements are a reflection of ignorance or incompetence.

5. Since non-experts do not know which of the so-called 'experts' are correct, the only safe course of action is distrusting all of them. That is, disagreement between experts implies that we should be suspicious of their claimed special abilities.

This hypothesis, of course, is not a formal chain of logic. But, it is implicit in the way that most researchers reason about findings reporting disagreements between domain experts.

Contributing Factors

The ESC hypothesis is supported by two disconnected lines of thought, one of which affects theoretical reasoning and the other influences empirical research. First, research on decision making has been linked historically to theories from economics (e.g., expected utility theory) and statistics (e.g., Bayes theorem). When applied to well-specified problems, such theories lead to unique solutions. Given a specified set of antecedent conditions, these formalisms provide point estimates of the optimal decision strategy. Interestingly, a great deal of laboratory work has been devoted to showing the inadequacy of such theories. Nevertheless, economics and statistics continue to provide a point of reference for much of decision research.

This reasoning has also been applied to analyses of domain experts. Although most experts work on problems that are not well specified, researchers nonetheless assume that unique solutions exist – just as they do for simpler cases. Many investigators have recently questioned the relevance of economic/statistical theories as a basis for making real-world decisions. While economic and statistical theories often cannot be applied to the domains where experts work, it is nonetheless assumed that point solutions exist.

Second, nearly a century of experimental psychology (particularly in America) has been focused on analysis of the *Generalised Normal Human Adult Mind* – GNHAM. This emphasis dates to the beginnings of experimental psychology, particularly Wilhem Wundt and Edward Titchener: "Titchener's interest lay in the generalised, normal, human adult mind that had also been Wundt's main concern." (Heidbreder, 1933).

In fact, there is no evidence that Wundt ever used this term. References to the concept, however, are common in Titchener's (1916) writing, e.g., "psychology is concerned with the normal, human, adult mind." Modern historians of psychology now believe that Boring created a 'myth of origin' to provide a justification for Titchener's (who was his mentor) place in psychology.

According to GNHAM, the goal of behavioural researchers should be to investigate commonalties among humans, not differences between them. That is, the focus of psychology belongs on the generalized mind, not on individual minds. Because the Titchener-Boring view dominated (at least in America), research was directed to the search for 'universal truths' of behaviour. As a result, psychology has not developed paradigms to deal with outlier behaviour. And expertise, by definition, is outlier behaviour. (See Shanteau, 1988 for further background.)

Research, therefore, has been influenced by two research streams that assumed 1) that decision problems should have unique correct answers and 2) that differences between individuals are not importance to empirical investigations. The persistence of observed differences between experts provided evidence inconsistent with these views. Thus, disagreements between experts lead to the conclusion that something must be wrong. In the next two sections, I explore 5 structural factors and 5 functional factors behind why researchers should not be surprised when experts disagree.

Structural Factors

Analysis of the context in which most experts work provides five structural factors behind why experts may disagree.

1. In most contexts where experts work, the 'ground truth' is a fiction. Single-point optimal solutions do not exist. Despite the tremendous analytic ability of master players and the incredible computation speed of computer programs such as *Deep Blue*, the game of chess still does yield optimal solutions. If this is true for a well-structure game such as chess, how can it be possible to find a 'correct answer' in an ill-structured setting? In fact, the reason we need experts in the first place is because they offer us answers that we could not obtain any other way.

2. A distinction should be made between the different levels of decisions made by experts. Using terminology from medicine, it is possible to distinguish between three levels: The first is *diagnosis* (what is it?) based on categorisation and/or classification. The second is *prognosis* (what is the likely outcome?) based on forecasting future scenarios. The third is *treatment* (what to do about it?) involving selection of a course of action. There are thousands of diagnoses and hundreds of prognoses, but relatively few treatments. It should not be surprising to find that experts may disagree at one level (diagnosis), but agree at another (treatment).

3. Despite the assumption behind the ESC hypothesis, experts are seldom asked to make single-outcome decisions. The concept of a 'point prediction' is largely a fiction created for the convenience of the researcher and is not descriptive of the tasks that experts do. As Golde (1970) noted, although "an expert does sometimes make decisions, his (her) role is usually much more of an advisor". In other words, the job of the expert is to clarify alternatives and describe possible outcomes.

4. Experts generally work in dynamic situations where there is frequent updating with evolving constraints i.e., the problems faced by experts are unpredictable, and in such situations there are rarely any best or correct answers. Therefore, while the ESC model assumes a stationary target, the reality faced by experts is generally more like a moving target.

5. A long-term perspective reveals that experts frequently work in realms where the basic science is still evolving. For instance, the rapid changes in medicine mean that the current 'best answers' are soon obsolete. Why should we expect experts to agree on a single 'correct answer' today, say for the treatment of AIDS, when new knowledge will likely provide better solutions tomorrow?

Functional Factors

An analysis of the strategies used by experts to make decisions reveals at least five functional or process factors behind why experts may disagree. These factors have to do with how experts think about the choices and judgements that make.

1. While most researchers view an 'error' as any deviation between behaviour and the 'correct answer', experts have a different definition of error. Experts are usually more concerned about avoiding big mistakes, whereas researchers

are looking for perfection. Thus, the same outcome could well be called an ‘error’ by the researcher and a ‘success’ by the expert.

2. Most experts operate as if they have flat loss functions for deviations from optimality. They see small deviations as having minor consequences. But researchers often operate as if they have steep loss functions. That is, they view any deviation from optimality, no matter how slight, as having large consequences. A similar argument can be made for how disagreements between experts are viewed.

3. In many (most?) settings, experts expect to disagree with each other. In a discussion among two experienced academics, for instance, we know that they invariably will find something to argue about. Even when they agree on 99% of the issues, they will quickly find the last 1% and argue about that. Similarly, experts in most any field will bypass items of agreement to focus instead on disagreements. Thus, experts view disagreements as a normal part of their job.

4. Disagreements are often a route by which experts increase understanding of their field. By seeking out areas of disagreement, experts examine the limits of their own knowledge and stretch their range of competency. Therefore, experts see disagreements as a key step for maintaining and increasing their grasp of their field.

5. Once a domain has advanced sufficiently to the point where all the issues are resolved, there are few disagreements among experts because there is nothing to argue about. When a field has developed to that degree, however, the answers are known and agreed upon. Thus, total agreement among experts would be an indication that there is no longer much of a role for experts to play in a domain.

Domain differences

We all know that experts in different domains perform different tasks. Yet researchers persist in treating all experts alike, so that the term ‘expert’ is used generically. Nearly all researchers are aware that at least some experts, e.g., weather forecasters (see Stewart, et al, 1997), show little sign of bias or ‘cognitive illusions.’ Thus, despite the generalisations often drawn about experts, we know there are (many) exceptions to the rule.

In an effort to account for these domain differences, I constructed Table 3.8 to differentiate between those domains where experts do well and those where experts do not. The table is based on a continuum from high to low competence. In the left column are those domains where expert make aided judgements using Decision Support Systems (DSS) or other computerised tools, e.g., in weather forecasting. The next column contains domains where experts make skilled but unaided decisions, e.g., livestock judges. The third column lists domains where experts show limited competence, e.g., clinical psychologists. The behaviour of 'experts' in the last column is close to random, e.g., stockbrokers.

Table 3. 8 Progression of domains from high to low performance

Highest levels of performance ⟵⟶ **Lowest levels of performance**

Aided Decisions	*Competent*	*Restricted*	*Quasi-Random*
Weather Forecasters	Livestock Judges	Clinical Psychologists	Stock Forecasters
Astronomers	Chess Masters	Parole Officers	Polygraphers
Test Pilots	Grain Inspectors	Psychiatrists	Astrologers
Insurance Analysts	Photo Interpreters	Student Admissions	Parole Officers
Physicists	Soil Judges	Intelligence Analysts	Court Judges

There are many ways to describe the differences in this table. For present purposes, it makes most sense to note that domains to the left side possess more stable (*static*) properties. That is, the stimuli and the problem 'hold still' for experts to evaluate. The domains to the right side, however, involve more changeable (*dynamic*) properties. Thus, the stimuli and problem are less stable, harder to specify, and more like 'moving targets.' It makes sense, therefore, that expert agreement will be higher for the left side and lower for the right side.

Table 3. 9 Reliability (Consensus) values for experts

Highest levels of performance ⟵⟶ **Lowest levels of performance**

Aided Decisions	*Competent*	*Restricted*	*Quasi-Random*
Weather Forecasters	Livestock Judges	Clinical Psychologists	Stockbrokers
r = .95	r = .50	r = .40	r = .32
Auditors	Grain Inspectors	Pathologists	Astrologers
r = .76	r = .60	r = .55	r => .0

To test this idea, Table 3. 9 lists reliability values obtained from studies of domain experts fitting the four categories in Table 3.8. Two domains are listed under each category, with the between-expert agreement (consensus) given as correlations. As can be seen, the average consensus *r* value for weather forecasters is .95, whereas the average values for livestock judges, clinical psychologists, and stock forecasters are .50, .40, and .32, respectively. Comparable results appear for other domains in the second line. The trend supports the prediction outlined above – better structured domains lead to higher consensus and less structured domains lend to lower consensus.

For comparison, the within-expert reliability (consistency) correlations for these domains are listed in Table 3.10. Again, the trends are similar. With one exception, the consistency values are higher than corresponding consensus values in Table 3.9 .

Table 3.10 Reliability (Internal Consistency) values

Highest levels of performance ⟵⟶ Lowest levels of performance

Aided Decisions	*Competent*	*Restricted*	*Quasi-Random*
Weather Forecasters r = .98	Livestock Judges r = .96	Clinical Psychologists r = .44	Stockbrokers r = <.40
Auditors r = .90	Grain Inspectors r = .62	Pathologists r = .50	Astrologers r = ?

Researchers' view of experts

Compared to other fields of inquiry, decision researchers have taken an idiosyncratic view of the abilities of experts. Investigators in artificial intelligence, expert system design, cognitive science, and computer science have all concluded that experts are superior problem solvers worthy of emulation. This is why knowledge engineers build computer simulations (expert system) around what experts know and do. Further, most domain-specific researchers (such as in medicine, weather forecasting, and financial assessment) view experts as possessing unique information essential for making good decisions. In short, investigators in these fields see human expertise as something to be emulated.

In contrast, researchers, especially in America, have concluded that experts are flawed and prone to making simple errors. Moreover, experts and novices are viewed as sharing the same shortcomings. For instance, Tversky (quoted in Gardner, 1985) stated: "whenever there is a simple error that most laymen fall for, there is always a slightly more sophisticated version of the same problem that experts fall for".

Investigators have overlooked the fact that in most real-world problems, unique solutions do not exist. Instead, there are multiple solution paths. For instance, in medicine there can be many ways to treat an illness – when one approach does not work, a physician seeks out another. It should not be surprising, therefore, to find experts disagreeing about the recommended approach to take. Other inquiry systems, therefore, accept multiple points of view across experts as inevitable. In contrast, researchers with their simplified, single-answer view of the world seem to find a multiple-solution perspective difficult to understand.

Multiple-solution hypothesis

The position taken here is that previous researchers have unknowingly adopted the ESC view of expertise. According to ESC, disagreement between experts is a sign that something is wrong. This in turn leads to the conclusion that experts are not as skilled or as competent as they claim to be. In this section, I will propose an alternate hypothesis that is closer to the view of how experts see themselves. This is labelled the *Multiple Solution Model* – MSM. There are five arguments behind this hypothesis:

1. To begin, the primary job of an expert is not to make decisions but to help clients reach a broadly defined goal state. For example, the goal of the client may be to design a better investment portfolio or to find a better loan strategy. These goals do not involve single answers, but instead require something more elaborate from the expert, such as a strategic plan.

2. To reach the client's goal state requires dealing with multiple, constantly changing factors. The situation faced by experts is different and more complex than the simplified settings studied in research laboratories. Thus, experts work on problems that are considerable more complex than those studied in lab settings.

3. Using their knowledge and experience, the role of the expert is to recognise patterns and find consistencies in a dynamic problem space. The expert's job is to clarify the issues for the client, i.e., make sense out of chaos.

4. Based on their experience and insights into the nature of the problem, experts help clients clarify their thinking. For instance, an expert will often identify several alternate paths to the client's desired goal states. The expert's role is to lay out the options and the consequences in a clear and comprehensible fashion for the client.

5. In the end, it is the client, not the expert, who actually makes most choices. The expert offers insights and observations, but the client makes and implements the final decision(s). Thus, the responsibility generally rests on the client, not the expert.

The issue is nicely summarised by Golde (1970): "We seem to expect too much and the wrong things of our experts". As expressed by MSM, experts generally act more like knowledgeable consultants. Rarely do they function as the 'all-knowing' single-answer decision makers envisioned by most researchers. Instead, experts help clients by giving them the insights and information needed to make their own judgements.

Conclusions

By relying on comparisons to economics and statistical analysis and by incorporating GNAHM assumptions into their research designs, investigators have unknowingly adopted a restricted view of what experts do. By drawing a parallel to economic/statistical theory, researchers have adopted a 'single correct answer' approach to assessing expertise. When an expert (or anyone else) gives an answer different from the 'correct answer', he/she is said to have a 'bias' (Tversky & Kahneman, 1974). And when two or more experts give different answers, their claim to special competence is questioned (Einhorn, 1974).

The position here is that researchers have relied on an incorrect view of how experts function. For instance, the environment in which experts work is much different from that incorporated into traditional laboratory research. The complex, changeable environment that experts operate in is considerably more complicated than the small, stable environment constructed by investigators. In reality, problems rarely are simple enough to lead to a single correct answer. Instead, there are multiple answers (or at least multiple routes to answers). If so, it should not be surprising to find that experts often take different approaches (as envisioned by MSM) to making recommendations.

The underlying problem is that researchers misunderstand what experts do and what is expected of them. Investigators seem to think that experts should see the world as they do. However, experts generally have another view of the world – with many complexities and contingencies, but few optimal solutions. From the MSM perspective, disagreements between experts are to be expected. Although researchers view disagreements as evidence of incompetence, experts see disagreements as a more-or-less inevitable part of the job.

By adopting the GNAHM approach to research, most investigators have largely ignored individual differences. Average results are emphasised, variances are not. More important, researchers almost never look at the distribution of responses over subjects. Consequently, exceptions are overlooked and statements are made about results that imply that all people follow the same pattern.

The dangers of reliance on GNAHM thinking for researchers have been recognised for some time. However, the warnings have not been heard. What should be done? Edwards (1983) offered two messages: "One is that psychologists have failed to heed the urging of Egon Brunswik that generalisations from laboratory tasks should consider the degree to which the task… resembles or represents the context to which the generalisations is made". The other message is that "experts can in fact do a remarkably good job of assessing and working with probabilities".

Therefore, disagreement between experts should not be viewed as a source of concern about the competence of experts. It is time for researchers to rethink their views about the lack of consensus leading to a supposed incompetence of experts. Persistence in such beliefs at this time says more about the biases of investigators than it does about experts.

Acknowledgement

The preparation of this chapter was supported, in part, by *National Science Foundation* grant DMII 96-12126 from the Program on Management of Technological Innovation and, in part, by support from the *Institute for Social and Behavioral Research*, Kansas State University.

INNOVATION, GROWTH AND ENTREPRENEURSHIP

4.1 Introduction

by Frédéric Delmar
Ph.D., Entrepreneurship & Small Business Research Institute

Entrepreneurship is a key to economic development, because it has to do with the combination of new or old resources in new ways in order to create a business opportunity. These new ideas and innovations are often created by newly founded and small firms that engage in rapid growth. These firms even create new industries (Storey, 1994). Therefore, entrepreneurship, small firm growth and innovations are closely connected to each other.

During the last decade the role of small and medium sized enterprises (SMEs) has received more and more attention from both policymakers and researchers. The major reason is that SME create a majority of new jobs. This fact has recently been illuminated in a study of job creation by company size class in Canada (e.g., Picot & Dupuy, 1998). Hence, the employment creation ability of SMEs is now a central focus. Put simply, new jobs can be created in two ways: either by the creation of new firms or by the expansion of existing firms. Both the process of organising a new business and the process of expanding it, are part of the entrepreneurial process.

One question for researchers and policy makers seeking to expand the economy is thus whether the importance of SMEs as job creators is mainly a result of many small start-ups and incremental expansions, or if a small minority of high growth SMEs contribute the lion's share of new employment. This is known as the 'mice vs. gazelles' or 'flyers vs. trundlers' debate. Storey strongly advocates the position that the small group of high growth SMEs in the EEC countries are the 'real' job creators (Storey & Johnson, 1987; Storey, 1994), whereas, Davidsson, Lindmark and Olofsson (1996; 1994) in their study of the dynamics of the Swedish business sector research in Sweden give more support for the 'mice' hypothesis.

In addition, growing businesses are important, not only as carriers of new employment opportunities, but also as carriers of new innovations. Business growth is needed at an economy-wide level in order to achieve economic development.

But at the business level, the issue is more problematic. Many entrepreneurs abstain from growth because they do not see expansion as a goal or the need for the business. The major cause of this refusal to expand their business is the belief that expansion is difficult and risky, and personal and financial gains are insecure. Also note that many governments create disincentives for growth by making laws apply to larger firms in a manner more stringent than for the smallest firms. On the other hand, previous research about the small firm dynamics in the US economy suggest that growing businesses double their chances of survival compared to non-growing businesses (Phillips & Kirchoff, 1989). As a consequence, all entrepreneurs face simultaneously the risk of not expanding, and the risk of launching an expansion and not being able to manage the transition.

In order to address this problem, a plenary session was organised at the Seminar, thoughts about challenges in innovative management and problems associated with business growth were in focus. It was concluded that human capital, rather than financial capital, was the most critical element of a successful expansion. In this context, human capital means both finding an entrepreneur motivated to expand, and also acknowledging the need to complement her or his own competencies with external expertise. Experienced venture capitalists illuminate the art of matching inventors and capitalists.

Furthermore, the structural problem of unemployment was also addressed, viz., that one of the major barriers to fast expansion was the lack of a competent work force. Despite the high unemployment rate, it is difficult to find people with the right competence profile so that the supply of labour does not match the demands of labour made by expanding businesses. In other words, the supply side of the work force do not match the demand that rapidly expanding firms have. Experienced business managers attending the Seminar pointed out the need for professionalism in managing business growth.

A suggested remedy targeted specifically towards small business policy is the to the problems with the creation of various public as well as private organisations with the specific purpose of helping businesses to expand. These organisations provide entrepreneurs with competence in order to encourage and support their growth intentions. Once the needs of human capital are assessed and satisfactorily resolved financial matters tend to solve themselves, although there are some special features of venture capital and the financing of innovation.

Even if financing tend solve itself once the need for human capital is fulfilled, different providers of financial resources are needed to meet the different needs of new, innovative and expanding firms. Venture capital is finance provided to firms unable to raise funds in conventional capital markets. Funds are typically provided to finance the starting-up of a new company or of a growing enterprise broadening its capital base, along with management-led buyouts. Since the subscription of money involves a combination of a fixed return instrument, such as fixed coupon preference shares or loan stock, with ordinary shares, quite different risks are involved in venture capital financing as compared with many other forms of finance.

These special risks come from the degree of uniqueness of each venture along with the need for the financier to be concerned with, and involved in, the management of the company. The consequences are high evaluation and monitoring costs, and greatly complicates decision-making criteria was considered in the open discussions at the Seminar.

This chapter offers an overview of the current problems facing politicians and practitioners dealing with the problems of high growth firms.

The first paper in this chapter written by Per Davidsson and myself on 'The characteristics of high growth firms and their job contribution' deals with the employment creation and dynamics in Sweden during the 1987-96 period. The paper is based on census data and encompasses all firms having more than 20 employees in 1996. The development of these firms is traced back ten years to 1987. We found that young firms dominated among high growth firms. Furthermore high-growth firms were predominantly to be found in young and growing industries in the service sector.

The second paper written by Jan P. Warhuus entitled 'Towards a better understanding of risk in entrepreneurial decision making' deals with one of the classic problems in entrepreneurship research: risk and the entrepreneur. In contrast with previous research which was based on personality traits and gave little of relevance, this paper focuses upon the perception of the situation and how it affects the decision to start or expand a business or not made by the entrepreneur. Thus, Warhuus departs from the traditional view of risktaking in the entrepreneurship literature and focuses instead on decision making. He suggests that entrepreneurs are moderate risk takers and that the complexity surrounding the decision to start a business or expand is not taken account by decision theories such as the Prospect Theory (Kahneman & Tversky, 1979). More complex decision models are needed. Warhuus concludes even more complex decision models are needed in order to understand the start-up and processes.

The third paper written by Hans Landström on 'The assessment of business opportunities' explores the differences between the decision-making of informal and institutional venture capitalists. It was found that informal venture financiers emphasised the role of the entrepreneurs and the future opportunities that could follow a positive development of the relationship between the parties involved. Landström also found that institutional venture capitalists tend to focus on the present situation and try to assess the product's viability on the market, and focus relatively lesser on the role of the entrepreneur. Consequently, the entrepreneur seeking finance should be aware that different investors utilise and weigh the decision criteria differently. In other words what could be wrong from one investor's point of view, could be right from another investor's point of view.

The fourth paper entitled 'Innovation strategy and management control systems: linking long-term objectives with short-term actions' is written by Istemi Demirag and Andrew Tylecote. The two researchers chosen to focus on the functioning of accounting and financial control systems when faced to long term investments decisions about an innovation. Based on a case study, they conclude that *short-termism* is not only due to outside pressure, but also to internal miscommunication. Consequently, decisions on new investments have to be based on the best possible data available, and these data must be shared with parties of interest both inside and outside of the organisation.

Reflections

Overall, the papers emphasise that a number of factors contribute to the successful evaluation of an entrepreneurial venture. An understanding is needed of how innovations and new ventures are diffused in a market economy, while the nature of the relationship between the entrepreneur and the investor needs to be reorganised. Researchers and practitioners attending the seminar pointed out that in order to minimises the risk of failure the entrepreneur or the entrepreneurial venture has to provide a full and transparent assessment of the venture's possibilities. This information is utilised by informal investors tend to evaluate the entrepreneur's development potential, whereas formal investors tend to evaluate the present achievements of the entrepreneurs and her or his product or service. Nevertheless it is clear that the expansion of a firm is a decision to be made by the entrepreneur alone. However she or he needs to gather the necessary resources to expand the firm which can, in the majority of the cases, only be achieved by an open discussion with providers of the necessary resources for the survival and prosperity of new and expanding firms.

4.2 Towards a better understanding of risk in entrepreneurial decision making

by Jan P. Warhuus
Ph.D., Centre for Small Business Studies, Southern Denmark Business School

Risk-taking has played a prominent role in the literature on entrepreneurship. The rationale is that starting a business is assuming business-risk a high level of risk when measured in monetary terms. As a consequence of this reasoning, it has been assumed that acts of entrepreneurship will only be performed by relatively risk-seeking individuals. Research, however, has failed to detect this risk-seeking propensity among entrepreneurs' (Cooper, Woo, & Dunkelberg 1988) and vis-à-vis comparable managers (Brockhaus 1980). If entrepreneurs do not exhibit heightened risk-taking propensities why do they start ventures that others, such as bankers (MacCimmon & Wehnung 1986), find more than moderately risky? There are reasons to question the traditional view and to utilise models of decision-making that can cope with the complexity of entrepreneurship. Entrepreneurship is the process of organisation creation (Vesper 1982). This process is characterised by a high concentration of critical incidents where decisions are made under uncertainty. Studies of the decision-making behaviour of entrepreneurs can help us to understand "what individuals do to enable organisations to come into existence" (Gartner 1988).

Principal topics

The venturing team or individual is at the time of start-up important in understanding the risk behaviour of young growing firms and remains important later. Kahneman & Tversky (1979) challenged rational choice theory when they introduced 'Prospect Theory' (Tversky & Kahneman 1986). Prospect theory suggests that 'reference points' and the 'outcome range' is very important in understanding decision behaviour. Guided by prospect theory and rival empirical findings specific to business, attitudes towards-, risk by managers and organisations (Lopes 1987; MacCimmon & Wehnung 1986; March & Shapira 1987; Sitkin & Pablo 1992), these two areas are explored in the phases of start-up, growth, and distress of six young growing firms. When decisions are complex and hard to decompose, people *edit* alternatives before making a decision. In editing, the *framing* of a prospect is important because a decision can often be framed in more than one way (Li and Adams 1995; Lopes 1987; Tversky and Kahneman 1981). Hence, gains and losses of the same numerical size have different subjective values.

Establishing a *reference point* is important because the reference point can alter both the situation and the outcome. There are at least two reference-point positions for the decision to start-up a new firm: focus on 'the current asset position' *(status quo)* before venturing, or focus on the possible gains of starting a business *(aspiration-level)*. In the early life of a firm the critical decisions are related to growth and periods of distress. After starting a company, the entrepreneur's *status quo* changes fast due to the high level of information feed-back. Hence, it is expected that *decisions about growth are perceived solely as positive; and decisions related to distress are perceived solely as negative.*

The width and content of the perceived *outcome range* is important according to prospect theory because people tend to overweigh 'certain' and 'extreme' outcomes. This suggests that the outcome range is a major component in the perceived risk at start-up due to the overweighing of extreme outcomes and lack of certain outcome components. Alternatively, Lopes (1987) suggests that the focus on the opportunity produces a narrow, less uncertain outcome range which in turn limits the entrepreneur's perceived risk. Yet, according to March and Shapira (1987) it is the magnitude, not the range, of outcomes which is important, suggesting that the entrepreneur's understanding of risk is not based on the rational choice idea of probabilities but on the magnitude of *negative* outcomes. As mentioned, in after-start-up decisions the reference point is expected to adjust continuously. In this case, prospect theory suggests that the positively framed outcomes of growth situations will yield moderate risk behaviour, while negatively framed decision situations in periods of set-backs will yield more risk-seeking tendencies. Alternatively, Lopes (1987) argues for a 'safety first principle': risk aversion until survival is secured, which suggest that *when the focus is on survival, risk-taking in distress situations be replaced by risk-averse behaviour.*

Method and Data

The six cases include three Danish and three American firms that by 1995 were 4 to 15 years of age and had grown to employ at least 50 people. The cases have an even spread of low, medium, and high technology manufacturing industries with both team and individual start-ups of three types: *de novo*, purchase, and spin-off. Guided by Marshall and Rossman (1989), Silverman (1993) and Yin (1994), in-depth semi-structured, audio-recorded interviews with each entrepreneur are supplemented with visits to the company, and interviews with the entrepreneur's choice of 'important' advisor and the entrepreneur's present banker. Through the pattern-matching methodology of Campbell (1975), refined by Yin (1994) and others, the guiding propositions are used to analyse the rich and exploratory interview data and to plot emerging patterns.

Major Findings

The life situation prior to start-up (*status quo*) is a strong component of the entrepreneurs' pre-start-up reference point. All entrepreneurs report some degree of frustration with regard to prior working experience. Yet, the frustration reported indicates that the reference point is higher than the *status quo* as suggested by theory. The expected gains from starting a business are important in all of the cases. However, it is only in half of the cases that the gains are closely related to the business opportunity. In the others, any opportunity would serve the purpose. A hope for more fun in working life is expressed by five of the six entrepreneurs. In summary, neither prior situation nor the expected possible gains are dismissable and the cases indicate a different reference point than suggested by theory. As predicted by theory, in critical situations after start-up, the *status quo* is often the point of reference. As soon as the firm had tested and adjusted its initial strategy for a market position, the start-up reference point is adjusted in line with this experience.

Start-up decisions provide plenty of opportunities to outweigh extreme outcomes and conditions regarded as certain, yet the considerations investigated in the present cases do not follow this predicted pattern. The outcome range seems to shrink rather than widen as the initial phase progresses. In addition, the editing by the entrepreneur is far more complex than a comparison of a pre start-up situation vs. a specific start-up opportunity. The fact that time and cost dimensions of the start-up phase had been overlooked or underestimated, despite the fact that the advisors see the entrepreneurs as competent and thorough individuals, indicates that the focus on the opportunity produces a narrow outcome range. Although understanding of risk is articulated at a very aggregated level and this group of entrepreneurs decline single-construct risk-measures, this study does not support the importance of magnitude. After-start-up decision behaviour on growth represents the most consistent pattern; entrepreneurs do exhibit moderate risk behaviour. On distress the personal reasons for starting a firm seem to determine whether the entrepreneur will take risky decisions or focus on survival and cut losses. The differences are illustrated in the following two remarks: 'smaller size... that was not what it was about' and 'you don't gamble with your own child'.

Implications

At start-up, the reference point of the entrepreneur is somewhere above the survival point of the firm. Frustrations with pre-start-up conditions are often resolved by the decision to start. The entrepreneur engages in portfolio-like considerations about the start-up opportunity; where the desire to change the current situation affects decision behaviour. Unless the entrepreneur expresses a clear aspiration reference point, an adjustable *status quo* reference point is employed in subsequent decisions.

The outcome range at start-up is skewed to the right. Thus, despite knowledge of the possible negative outcomes of the decision, the perceived risk at start-up is correspondingly quite low. The results indicate that the subjective value of the funds at stake is lower than the subjective value of the start-up experience. During early growth, the entrepreneur is above the *status quo* reference point and moderate risk-taking choices among growth options are observed. During distress, the entrepreneur looks for temporary explanations and, if found, adjusts the reference point accordingly. If more fundamental issues seem to account for the incidence, the decision behaviour is affected by the entrepreneurs' perception of a threat to survival.

With regard to the applicability of the results, the findings are limited by the small number of cases and their (intentional) success-bias. The purpose of this study has not been to test theory, but to understand entrepreneurial decision-making and, as such, the results may serve to direct attention towards sensible decision behaviour. For example, a very high level of detected frustration in start-up decisions, or a lack of attention to survival factors in times of trouble, could serve as warnings to both providers of credit and other business partners.

The study suggests that entrepreneurship can benefit from employing modern decision-making theory. As for future research, the study suggests that models incorporating the dynamics of social influence and interaction could be successfully applied, and calls for replication on nascent entrepreneurs.

Acknowledgement

I am grateful to the Center for the Study of the Enterprise, San Francisco State University for hosting me during part of this project, and to William B. Gartner for his comments and encouragement. I am also grateful to William D. Bygrave and the Center for Entrepreneurial Studies, Babson College for hosting me during part of this project.

4.3 The characteristics of high-growth firms and their job contribution

by Per Andersson
Professor, Jönköping International Business School
and
Frédéric Delmar
Ph.D. , Entrepeneurship & Small Business Research Institute

Largely as a result of mass unemployment problems in many European countries, the dynamics of job creation has in recent years attracted increased interest on the part of academics as well as policy-makers. In connection to this, a large number of studies carried out in various countries have concluded that SMEs play a very large and/or growing role as job creators (Birch, 1979; Baldwin and Picot, 1995; Davidsson, Lindmark and Olofsson, 1993; 1994; forthcoming; for further reference to studies carried out in a large number of countries see also ENSR, 1994; Loveman and Sengenberger, 1991).

While most researchers agree on the importance of SMEs, there is some controversy as regards whether this is mainly a result of many small start-ups and incremental expansions, or if a small minority of high-growth SMEs contribute the lion's share of new employment. This is known as the 'mice vs. gazelles' or 'flyers vs. trundlers' debate. Storey strongly advocates the position that the small group of high-growth SMEs are the 'real' job creators (Storey, 1994), whereas, e.g., the Davidsson *et al* research in Sweden (cf. above) gives more support for the 'mice' hypothesis.

The different views may in part be due to real country differences. For example, Blixt's (1997) recent investigation of high-growth firms in Sweden did not attribute very impressive absolute amounts of new employment to them. It must also be understood, however, that the differential results are to a great extent built into the methodology (cf., Davis, Haltiwanger and Schuh 1996). When reading this and other reports on the importance of high-growth SMEs, it is therefore important to realise that the results are in part an effect of study design and definitions.

At any rate, most researchers and policy-makers are likely to agree on the following; firstly, a small group of high-growth firms are very important for total employment creation, or at least would be so if the development of a large enough such group could be stimulated. Secondly, our current knowledge about the economic contributions and management practices of high-growth SMEs are at present insufficient for strong theory-building as well as for the development of optimal policy measures.

The primary objective of this study is to make a contribution to the needed knowledge by exploring the dynamics of high-growth enterprises from more of a 'macro' perspective. This entails: a) their contribution to employment; b) their industry and size class affiliations; and c) their (aggregate) development trajectories

Method

Data were taken from *Statistics Sweden* (i.e., the official 'Bureau of Census'). Their registers are complete in the sense that all legal commercial activity is represented, whether run as sole proprietorship, partnership, limited liability company or some other legal form. Data originate from different sources such as tax authorities and mandatory surveys. Updating is frequent and generally speaking the registers are of a very high standard by international comparison. Data from three different registers, and ten annual versions of each, have been utilised in developing the data set.

The data set comprises *all enterprises that in November 1996 were in the private (non-government) sector, that were commercially active in Sweden and had at least 20 employees.* With respect to that category, we are dealing with a census study. There are 11 748 such enterprises, 233 of which were start-ups in 1996 and therefore excluded from all employment change analyses below. Annual data for all enterprises have been compiled for the 1987-1996 period. In existence for the entire period were 8 562 firms. Start-ups during this period are included if they fulfil the size criterion for the final year, as are previous government sector firms that by the final year have transferred to the private sector. Firms that dissolve during the period are excluded regardless of their previous size and growth, as are surviving firms that previously may have had more than 20 employees but do not reach that number in 1996. No upper size limit has been employed.

In total 1.25 million people were employed in 1996 in this sample. This represents approximately 60% of total employment in the private sector. The remaining 40% are employed in firms that have fewer than 20 employees.

The most important purpose of this paper is to examine the contribution of high-growth firms to employment. It was concluded that changes in absolute employment would be the best performance criterion, since we are primarily interested in how much employment is actually created in the economy and not in the relative development over time. We define HGF as *those 10% of the valid cases*

(11 748 minus the 233 that only appear in the last year of the database) *that display the highest annual average absolute employment growth.*

Being a SME is not part of the HGF definition, so 'High-growth SMEs' will only constitute a sub-set of HGFs. Compared with a growth-rate based definition, the chosen definition favours larger firms. Compared with a definition based on total employment growth over the entire period, the chosen definition favours younger firms, i.e., those that are started during the period. The average annual growth for all firms during the 1987-96 period was 0.1 people. The 90th percentile, i.e., the cut-off point for high-growth firms, was 7.75 new employees annually. This means that we do not demand extreme growth figures for inclusion in the HGF group. The sample has been split in two groups, high-growth firms (HGF) and the rest of the sample (the control group).

Three different variables were used to break down the analysis by sub-categories: firm size (six size classes), industry (16 industries), and age (number of years in the register). In some analyses we collapse data into more aggregate categories than those indicated within parentheses above, e.g., SMEs vs. large firms.

Results

Categorical affiliations

An important first question is how the HGFs are distributed across size-classes, industries, etc. compared with firms in the control group.

As regards size classes, we can observe first that HGFs are strongly underrepresented in the smallest size class but markedly over-represented in the 50-249 employee size class, i.e., medium-sized firms. While 76% of the HGFs are (still) SMEs (i.e., have <250 empl) the HGF group has an over-representation of large firms (i.e., >250 empl): 24% of the firms in the HGF group have more than 250 employees compared to 4% in the control group. This may seem to run counter to widespread beliefs that SMEs are the most important for job creation. However, to some extent this result is a consequence of our HGF definition; a definition based on growth rates would have favoured smaller firms. To a very great extent the over-representation of large HGFs is simply a result of their growth. Among the 24% that were large firms in 1996, almost half were classified as SMEs earlier in the period. Hence, 87.6% of the HGFs were SMEs at some time during the 1987-96 period.

As concerns industries, the broad picture is that HGFs exist in all kinds of industries, but that they tend to be over-represented in young and growing industries and under-represented in traditional ones. The over-representation is especially pronounced in knowledge-intensive services and in education & health care, i.e., precisely those industries that grew in the most absolute and/or relative terms during the period (cf. Davidsson *et al,* forthcoming). Blixt (1997) and Storey (1996), who studied Sweden and the UK, respectively, both use sales growth in their definition of high-growth firms and therefore arrive at results that differ in some details, but the general pattern that the occurrence of HGFs is related to the relative growth of industry sectors comes through in their studies as well.

Concerning age, there is a very high representation of firms that were created during the period in the HGF group: 62% of the firms in the HGF group were created during the period compared to 27% in the control group. This is methodologically a tricky issue. Since we have a lower bound of 20 employees' end size for inclusion and most firms are born very small; it may justifiably be argued that young firms, if included, by definition have a high probability of being classified as high-growth firms. It may therefore be helpful to know that the Swedish economy comprises about half a million firms in total; that during this period 18-28 thousand 'genuinely new' firms were created annually, and that the five year survival probability for such firms is close to 60% (Nutek, 1996; Statistics Sweden, 1997). We have also taken steps in our methodology in order not to unduly favour young firms (i.e., the absolute growth criterion and our non-acceptance of zero initial size, cf. the Method section). Blixt (1997) and Storey (1996) also find a clear over-representation of young firms among the HGFs, and the same age-growth relationship has been established in a number of other studies as well (cf., e.g., Storey, 1994). We therefore feel we can safely conclude that the high representation of young firms in the HGF group is not merely a statistical artefact. Instead, the message is very clear: HGFs are to be found primarily among young firms.

In sum, most HGFs are SMEs. They are markedly younger than the control group, and while present in all industries they are clearly over-represented in young and growing ones.

The contribution of high-growth firms to absolute employment

In this section we will analyse HGFs contribution to new employment, in total as well as broken down by size and industry. We will for each sub-analysis display a table, which gives the job contribution by HGFs and the control group in the final analysis year, i.e., from November 1995 to November 1996. This table will be accompanied by a chart that shows the development over the entire 1987-96 period. In the 'over time' charts, sub-category affiliation, except HGF vs. Control, is based on data for the actual year in question.

Table 4.2 displays the absolute employment and absolute employment changes for HGFs and the control group 1995-96. As can be seen, both groups display positive net employment change figures. However, during this period the much smaller (in numbers) HGF group generated almost 80% of all new jobs, when employing only just over 30% of the total sample's work force. 80% is an impressive share, but do HGFs contribute a large amount of new jobs in absolute terms? In one sense, yes; the HGFs added almost 40 new employees each, on average. However, 45 000 new jobs is a small number compared with unemployment figures of several hundred thousands. Further, the total figure is of the same magnitude as what is ascribed to the formation of 'genuinely new' firms annually in Sweden (cf. Statistics Sweden, 1995; 1997). According to another source, birth and expansion of 'small firms', defined as firms with 0-200 employees, contributed with more than 70 000 net new jobs in 1994. A large share of this is attributable to firms with less than 20 employees, i.e., a category that is excluded completely from the last year of the present study.

Considering also that we have employed a rather permissive lower bound for HGFs (7.75 new jobs annually on average) and that 1995/96 was their 'top year' (cf. table 4.1) the conclusion must be that HGFs as we have defined them are an important source of job creation, but not one that outshines other categories of job creators such as the formation and incremental growth of new and very small firms.

Table 4.1 Changes in employment in HGFs and the control group 1995-96

	Change	**Frequency**	**Employment**	**Frequency**	**N**
High-growth firms	45 294	79.7%	400 917	32.0%	1 153
Control group	11 537	20.3%	851 498	68.0%	10 362
Total	56 831	100.0%	1 252 415	100.0%	11 515

The most important finding in Figure 4.1 from a methodological standpoint is that the HGF group, despite their small numbers and varying business cycle conditions, outperforms the control group in every single year. This is also in spite of the fact that the number of cases decreases more rapidly for HGFs than for the control groups, as one moves from 1996 backwards (n_{1987}= 437 and 7736, respectively). A very interesting result is that the performance difference is especially pronounced in the worst recession years, i.e., 1992 and 1993. HGFs were apparently much less affected by changes in the general economy. In fact they tended to have a fairly stable development over time, when in the same time the rest of the economy lost a great number of jobs. Thus, high-growth firms seem especially important during a recession period. This is a result we will revert to towards the end of the paper.

The cumulative total growth of HGFs over the entire period was 185 000 new jobs, which is a significant figure but far from making up for the 255 633 net job losses in the control group (plus even more jobs lost via dissolutions not captured by these data).

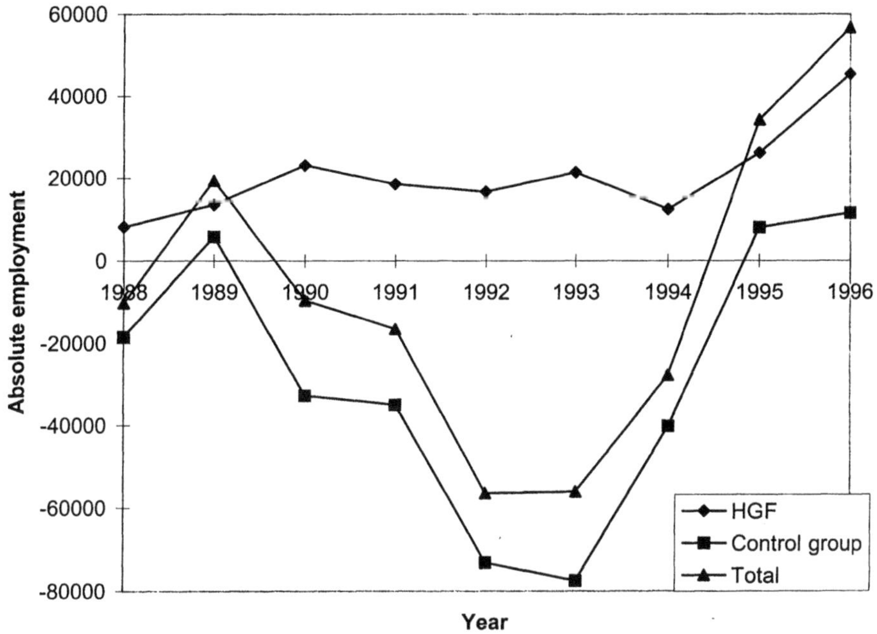

Figure 4.1 Changes in absolute employment by performance category, 1987-96

We have concluded that high-growth firms have a significant – although not sufficient – impact on employment. We will now turn to the employment contributions by HGFs in different size classes. Table 4.2 displays the changes in absolute employment by firm size in 1995-96. As a group small and medium sized firms (firms with less than 250 employees) contributed the majority of jobs (53.8% of net jobs).

Table 4.2 Changes in employment firms by firm size 1995-96 (percentage in parenthesis)

Firm size	High-growth	Control group	Total
Firms with less than 250 employees	13 867 (30.6%) n = 874	16 735 (145.1%) n = 9 929	30 602 (53.8%) n = 10 803
Firms with 250 or more employees	31 427 (69.4%) n =279	-5 198 (-45.1%) n =433	26 229 (46.1%) n =712
Total (n= 11 515)	45 294 (100%)	11 537 (100%)	56 831 (100%)

Figure 4.2 displays the changes in absolute employment by size class, 1987-96. However, when we also include growth performance, we can conclude that large firms had the highest variance. That is, among HGFs they were the greater job creators, while in the control group large firms actually lost jobs. The difference in growth performance was far less pronounced for small and medium sized firms. This pattern was enhanced when examining the historical development. We can clearly see the difference between the two size classes, where small and medium sized firms constantly outperformed large firms. Only during the last two years had large firms a non-negative development of employment, while during the recession year's large firms in the control group lost very large numbers of jobs. High-growth firms were relatively more important as employment creators for the large firm class, whereas there was relatively little difference between the two performance groups in the small and medium sized firm class. Differently stated, large firms exhibited a greater variance in performance than did small and medium sized firms during the period examined.

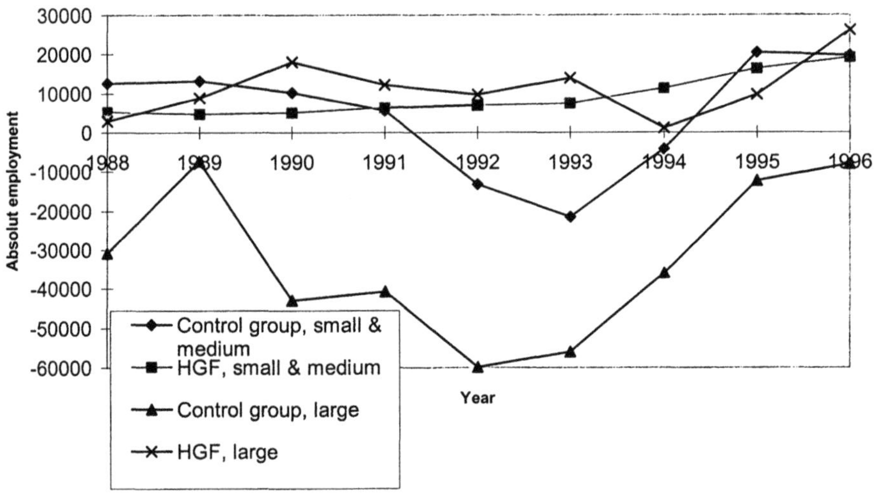

Figure 4.2. Changes in absolute employment by size class, 1987-96.

Table 4.3 displays the changes in employment and their distribution by industry 1995-96. We use very broad industry sectors in this analysis, viz. manufacturing (incl. construction) vs. services (or, rather, 'non-manufacturing'). Almost 60% of all new jobs were created by high-growth firms in the service industry. This is yet another clear indication of the growing importance of the service industry as employment creator. This was also the trend when the development over the ten-year period was examined.

Table 4.3 Changes in employment and their distribution across industry 1995-96

Industry	High-growth firms	Control group	Total
Manufacturing	11 213 (24.8%) n = 288	8 425 (73.0%) n =3 783	19 638 (34.6%) n = 4 071
Service	34 081 (75.2%) n = 865	3 112 (27.0%) n = 6 579	37 193 (65.4%) n = 7 444
Total (n= 11 515)	45 294 (100%)	11 537 (100%)	56 831 (100%)

The high-growth firms in the service industry were steadily above the development of other groups. At the same time, the manufacturing industry control group displays a dramatic decline. In brief, the service industry had the most positive development and this development was largely due to high-growth firms creating the absolute majority of new jobs.

Discussion and conclusions

In this paper we have analysed non-government high-growth firms across all industry sectors in Sweden during the 1987-96 period, using a high quality data set that has been carefully developed for this purpose. We have restricted the study to the firm level, and to firms that had a minimum size of 20 employees in the final year, 1996. No upper size bound was used. As our primary interest is in employment creation, we defined high-growth firms as those 10% of all firms that contributed most in annual average absolute employment growth.

It turned out that firms that had an average annual employment increase of 7.75 people qualified among the 'high-growers'. This we may also regard as a first result: it does not take extreme growth figures to be among the top 10% growth firms. Their average contribution during the last year in our analysis (1995-96) appears more impressive. During this 'top' year, the high-growth firms added close to 40 new jobs each on average. However, even this does not look very impressive in the aggregate. It sums up to a contribution of the same magnitude as that annually provided by genuine start-ups, and even doubling the contribution by high-growth firms would not mean a quick solution to the current unemployment problem.

We found that there was an over-representation of high-growth firms in certain sub-categories. Importantly, young firms dominate among be high-growers. No less than 62% of our high growers was created during the period and thus are less than ten years old. As young firms are on average smaller firms, and large growing firms on average add more jobs annually than small growing firms, the over-representation of young firms is lesser for number of new jobs than for number of firms. As regards industries, we found an over-representation of high-growth firms in young and growing industries, in particular knowledge-intensive business-to-business services, education, and health care. Altogether, some 70% of the high-growth firms' employment contributions were in services.

An over-all picture that emerges from our data is that genuinely new jobs to a great extent are created by young and small firms, often in young and growing industries. Large, established firms, often in mature industries, account for relatively more of total job changes, but the net result tends to be negative in terms of number of jobs. The latter categories do comprise, however, a group of growing firms that account for a relatively large share of total net job creation, but most of this represents re-structuring rather than the creation of genuinely new jobs.

There are two other extremely important issues that we have not been able to deal with satisfactorily. Firstly, many firms may choose to pursue growth not by expanding the original firm (only), but by creating a company group. Secondly, many firms may pursue growth in sales but not in employees, and handle this by increased outsourcing or sub-contracting. An employment-based definition would not capture these firms, yet they create new employment outside the boundaries of their own organisations.

Finally, one striking feature of our 'over-time' analysis of high-growth firms is their relatively stable development over time. This is in spite of the fact that the economy has been through, during the analysed period, the most dramatic business cycle shifts since the Great Depression. This is, as we see it, a highly suggestive result that in a way gives some input to the 'population ecology' vs. 'strategic adaptation' debate (cf. Low & MacMillan, 1988). That is, do firms shape their destiny, or are they powerless victims of changes in their environment? Our result that high-growth firms are more common in growing industries lends some support to the population ecology view. Otherwise in our analyses the high-growth firms very much appear as a category of firm which is capable of shaping its destiny. One can infer, arguably, that their aggregate development is a result of pro-activeness, goal-directness and opportunity-orientation as described in the entrepreneurship literature. When the economy turns down, they continue to develop much as before. When it turns up, they do not necessarily (on a per firm basis) start to grow much more. It is as if regardless of the environmental situation, they find ways to achieve their goals.

By contrast, the control group – and especially large firms in company groups in traditional industries – appear much more as victims of their environment. When the economic conditions worsen they start to lose huge amounts of jobs. When it turns up, they follow suit. In a way, the behaviour of this numerous group of firms is both cause and effect of business cycle patterns, whereas the high-growth firms seem to shape their development relatively independently from the development of the general economy. At the same time, as a group they serve as a cushion that makes a downturn somewhat less dramatic than it would else have been.

Acknowledgement

This research project was funded by grants from Ruben Rausing's Foundation for Research on Innovation and New Enterprise, the Swedish Employer's Confederation (SAF), and the Swedish Council for Work Life Research (RALF). An earlier version of this paper was presented to the OECD Working Party on SMEs on September 30, 1997.

4.4 The assessment of business opportunities – A comparison between informal investors and institutional venture capitalists

by Hans Landström
Professor, Halmstad University

It has been widely recognised that small firms play an important role in any European economy. Interest among policy-makers in stimulating start-ups and small firms has therefore increased during the last decade. In this context the lack of risk capital has been an ever-recurring theme in the economic debate. It is however probably the case that access to capital cannot in itself generate growth in firms but that scarcity of capital is very likely to hamper potential growth.

In Sweden we have traditionally relied on the institutional supply of capital to small firms, from banks, institutional venture capital companies, government subsidies, etc. In recent years, interest in the informal risk capital market has grown, i.e. private individuals who invest their own capital in small unlisted firms.

Despite the growing interest in the informal risk capital market, our knowledge about how this market operates is relatively limited. Earlier studies (Haar, et al., 1988; Landström, 1992; Mason & Harrison, 1994; 1996) are united in demonstrating the importance attached by informal investors, in their assessments of new investment proposals, to the entrepreneur's management team's competence and capability, and to the firm's market potential. Financial considerations also seem to be significant for informal investors' assessments. Thus, in this respect the informal investors seem to display certain similarities to the institutional venture capitalists (Tyebjee & Bruno, 1984; MacMillan, et al., 1985). The examination of earlier research shows, however, that there are lack of studies that in a more comprehensive fashion rank the decision-making criteria that informal investors consider to be important when it comes to new investments.

Against this background the purpose of this study is to 1) describe the criteria for decision-making used by informal investors, and 2) compare the similarities and differences in decision-making criteria between informal investors and institutional venture capitalists.

The results of the study can help give those involved in the informal as well as the institutional risk capital market a more systematic picture of the investors' decision-making and give those involved the opportunity to learn from each other. The results will also give entrepreneurs seeking external capital an idea of what factors are important in the investors' assessments, which should make it easier to obtain capital. For policy-makers, better knowledge of the criteria used by the investors can allow the development of more effective instruments to facilitate the financing of new and expansive firms. Finally, the study is relevant to research in the field in that the study adopts a more analytical method than that used in several of the earlier studies.

In the study, a conjoint method is used in order to measure quantitatively the relative importance of one decision-making criterion in relation to another. The method is described in more detail in Emory & Cooper (1991) and Riquelme & Richards (1992). From earlier research and a number of explorative interviews, 34 decision-making criteria were identified. A subjective sample of 44 informal investors in Sweden was made, in which they answered a questionnaire relating to the decision-making criteria. The data from the questionnaires were coded into a conjoint model in order to process the relative ranking between the decision-making criteria for each respondent, which are then assembled in mean values, in turn reflecting the ranking of the decision-making for the whole group of respondents.

Informal investors decision-making criteria

The characteristics of the informal investors

One characteristic of the respondents is that they are men aged between 45 and 64 years. A large proportion of them (42%) have an academic degree in economics or business administration, but approximately one quarter have no university education. It is interesting to note that nearly all have entrepreneurial experience, in that they have established one or more firms themselves. They also have a good deal of management experience, for example 78% of the respondents have managerial experience of small firms. Considered as a group they are thus investors with a great deal of entrepreneurial and managerial experience, and with experience relating primarily to the board and/or managing director level.

During a five-year period the respondents carried out on average 5 informal investments, i.e. one investment per year. The contacts with new investment opportunities occur primarily via business colleagues, the entrepreneurs themselves, and friends. As for the size of investments, each investor invests in median 1.5 million SEK in informal investments. The investments occur to a large extent in the early stages of development, for example 55% of the investments are made in the seed or start-up phase. There is a wide distribution as regards the industries in which investments are made, but firms with high-tech products in the manufacturing industry seem to be popular investment objects, followed by firms with industrial products in the manufacturing industry. The respondents mainly make their investments within their own regions. Approximately 60% of the investments are made in firms, which are located less than 80 km from the investor.

Decision-making criteria
Which qualities do informal investors value in the investment opportunity? The results of the study show that it is not possible to identify one or more specific criteria that stand out as particularly important for the informal investors in general. Analysis of the responses from each respondent shows quite clearly that the decision-making criteria are specific to the individual and that the investors appear to use different decision-making criteria in their assessment of new investment proposals. It is clear from the results, however, that the informal investors attach considerable importance to the leadership behind the investment proposals, which means that the assessment of the entrepreneur/management team in the firm is an important factor criterion for the investor.

Apart from this very strong focus on the assessment of the entrepreneur/management team, it can be worth noting that the informal investors look for the potential in the firm's market and products rather than existing strengths and weaknesses. In this connection, important criteria are 'market growth and attraction', 'uniqueness of product', and 'ability to create post-entry barriers in market', rather than 'sustained share competitive position', 'nature and degree of competition', and 'degree market already established'. The economic criteria seem to vary in importance. The short-term economic returns are of minor importance for the investors' assessments. At the same time, it is important to them to obtain a long-term economic return on their investment and it is important to be able to sell their ownership interest.

Finally, it can be noted that the investment phase does not seem to be of importance. The informal investors tend to invest during different phases of the firms' development. It can also be noted that the Swedish informal investors attach little importance to the fact that additional input of capital may be required in the firms in which they are investing. This may be due to the fact that many informal investors in Sweden appear to regard their informal investments as a 'business idea', whereby they make use of their earlier experience as entrepreneurs by making informal investments in small unlisted firms. The result is that they are prepared to venture relatively substantial amounts in the firms in which they invest.

The results clearly show that the informal investors feel much more dependent on the people with whom they invest as compared with other types of financiers. Thus, the results suggest that the informal investors in general attach considerable importance to the entrepreneur/management team, followed by the market potential of the firm. The results also verify that the decision-making criteria seem to a high degree to be specific to the individual. There are not criteria, which stand out as important for a large group of investors. Another result of the analysis is that the informal investors in Sweden seem to work very seriously and professionally with their informal investments, and that, to them, their investment activities are a kind of business idea.

The empirical conclusions that can be drawn from the study can be summarised as follows:

- Informal investors have their roots in the business process itself and, in this connection
- Business potential is of greater importance than existing strengths and weaknesses.
- Moreover, the informal investor wants to be able to influence the future development of the firm.
- The informal investors appear to attach great importance to the economic returns of the investment – they are not philanthropists.
- Informal investors expect the entrepreneur to be able to show that he has the ability to lead the firm. The informal investors invest 'more in the entrepreneur than in the firm', and a great deal of importance seems to be attached to assessments of the entrepreneur's entrepreneurial competence and ability to take action.

A comparison between informal and institutional venture capitalists

What are the differences and similarities between informal investors and institutional venture capitalists when it comes to their use of decision-making criteria?

One result of the present study is that the informal investors can be regarded as entrepreneurs themselves. Taking this view, there seem to be certain significant differences between informal investors and institutional venture capitalists. These differences reflect differences in their view on the investments. Informal investors see their investments primarily as 'subjects' where the prime motive is the chance to create business (business creators) and a desire to participate in the process (co-creators). On the other hand, the institutional venture capitalists can be regarded as financiers who tend to see their investments as 'objects' – a financial project – where central concepts for their operations are to financially 'package' the firms they enter, to supplement the resources of the firms, and to solve the problems that arise in the firms. Furthermore, seen from an agency theoretical approach, the informal investors act as 'principals' in that they invest their own assets and must take all the consequences of their investment decisions, whereas the institutional venture capitalists are employees and act as 'agents' for the owners of the venture capital companies. This means that the principal-agent relation is different, which could imply differences in decision-making behaviour. In addition, it can be expected that informal investors and institutional venture capitalists will tend to use different strategies in order to deal with uncertainty, both as regards the decision process, and the decision-making criteria used to reduce uncertainty.

The informal investors can be expected to possess the ability to deal with uncertainty, for example by: a) working with a relatively focused investment strategy; b) making use of their personal network in their assessment; and c) using relatively few decision-making criteria in their assessment. Such a way of handling the investment situation seems to lead to a reduced experienced uncertainty in the decision-making (Brunsson, 1976; 1985), and thereby a greater propensity to invest. For institutional venture capitalists the situation seems to be the reverse. Experience from the Swedish venture capital market has shown (Landström, 1990) that most venture capital companies work with a diversified investment strategy, where the portfolio firms operate in many different industries and as well are in different stages of development. The institutional venture capital companies have also access to a staff who can analyse the investment proposals. In other words they have both the time and resources necessary to carry out in-depth 'due diligence', as well as the competence to work with sophisticated analytical instruments to assess the business and financial risks. This in-depth analysis also means that the assessment of new investment proposals takes into account many different aspects. Such an analytical *modus operandi*, according to Brunsson (1975; 1985), leads to the experience of an increased sense of uncertainty in the decision-making situation, which does not create a propensity to invest, but instead a strong focus on decision-making, i.e. decision rationality.

The institutional venture capitalists' view of the investment as an object, and their focus on decision rationality, also means that other decision-making criteria are used in their assessment of new investment proposals. There is, for example, a good deal of empirical evidence (Fiet, 1995; see also Tyebjee & Bruno, 1984; MacMillan, et al., 1985) to show that venture capitalists regard uncertainty concerning present-situation conditions, and the product-market situation as more 'threatening' than conditions relating to the entrepreneur. This is not to say that the entrepreneur is not important for the assessment, but the venture capitalists often have contractual opportunities to protect themselves from 'mismanagement' and have developed techniques to monitor their investments. On the other hand, informal investors see the chance to create business opportunities and seem to attach a great deal of importance to the business potential of the investment by focusing on decision-making criteria involving the market and the technical potential of the investment (focusing on the future). Thus, the informal investors have a desire to participate in the creation and development of the firm, but at the same time, the informal investor must to a large degree rely on the entrepreneur's ability to promote the development of the firm, which means that informal investors will focus on decision criteria related to the relationship with the entrepreneur in the portfolio firm.

Finally, differences can be expected to exist between informal investors and institutional venture capitalists as regards their view of the entrepreneur, inasmuch as institutional venture capitalists seem to attach greater weight to their own possibilities of supplementing the entrepreneur's qualities and abilities. Gelvan (1995), for example, argues that the institutional venture capitalists tend to focus on supplementing resources in their assessment of new investment proposals. Therefore, the venture capitalists attach great importance to how their own 'unique' resources fit in with the firm's need of supplementary resources. Such a line of reasoning means that venture capitalists would attach greater significance to the aspect of supplementing resources and look for firms in more mature stages of development, where the venture capitalists' unique resources would be more fully utilised. The result is that the venture capitalists look for entrepreneurs who can be characterised as 'resource-dependent administrators', where the entrepreneur's functional administrative abilities are more important than his entrepreneurial ability. Focusing on the informal investors, as indicated above, they must to a considerable extent rely on the entrepreneur's own ability to develop his firm himself – they must have an entrepreneurial ability, at the same time as the informal investor has a desire to participate in the development of the firm and supporting the firm. As a consequence the informal investors are looking for 'co-operative entrepreneurs', i.e. entrepreneurs with entrepreneurial capacity who have the social competence needed to make use of the informal investor's competence and experience. A comparison of informal investors and institutional venture capitalists is given in Figure 4.3.

Dimensions	**Informal investors**	**Institutional venture**
	Investor characteristics	
Characteristics	Entrepreneurs themselves	Financiers
View on investment	Subject (managerial acumen)	Object (financial project)
	Uncertainty reduction strategies	
Decision process	Action rationality	Decision rationality
Decision-making criteria	Future opportunities Relationship focus	Present situation Product-market focus
	Entrepreneur characteristic	
View on entrepreneur	Co-operative entrepreneur	Resource-dependent

Figure 4.3 Comparison between informal investors and institutional venture capitalists

Implications

The results of the study show that the decision-making criteria vary to a large extent among different informal investors. The criteria that one investor considers as important may be considered less important by another informal investor. This implies that it may be sensible for entrepreneurs to attempt to answer as many standard questions as possible regarding, for example, market requirements, the competence of the entrepreneur, the uniqueness of the product and the firm's financial situation. Furthermore, a refusal by one informal investor does not necessarily mean that the proposal is a bad one – another informal investor may have other preferences and the personal relationship may function better for him.

The problem in Sweden is mainly that the informal risk capital market is too small; there are too few individuals who make informal investments. In this connection it could be important to teach potential informal investors to make investments, for example with the help of mentors, in the shape of experienced informal investors. In such a learning process, knowledge of what decision-making criteria are used by other informal investors is of great importance.

4.5 Innovation strategy and management control systems: Linking long-term objectives with short-term actions

by Istemi Demirag, Ph.D.
and
Andrew Tylecote, Ph.D.
Sheffield University Management School

Background to the case

This case study highlights the problems of accounting and financial control systems for new investment decisions in the electronics division of a company called Chantrey. It also helps to identify how external financial market pressures can be instrumental in administering strict financial control systems in companies, resulting in short-termism (see Demirag 1995a, 1995b, 1996).

Until 1986, the control style and culture of Chantrey company was not financial, the emphasis was on sales growth rather than profit, and the new acquisitions were not tightly integrated into the group. All this changed after the new group CEO took over in 1986. All managers were put through a training programme inculcating new financial objectives. There was a rigorous Strategic Business Unit (SBU) approach, giving clear profit and loss responsibility to each operating company and encouraging detailed, separate costing for each product line, pruning where necessary. The new Group CEO also encouraged a closer, less complacent relationship with the customer, a culture driven by markets rather than a simple reliance on engineering capability: this could be expected to help improve profitability, particularly in civilian markets. The sharpness of the break with the past is indicated by the fact that around 130 of the 200 directorships within the Group changed hands within the first 18 months of the programme. Financial measures were the only methods used on a systematic basis to monitor performance – hardly surprising, given the complexity of the company. There were, however, as there always are, other, informal flows of information. We were told how on two occasions major investments had been agreed for strategic reasons – a major product development, a step-change in process technology – and it had been accepted that as a result there would be a sharp fall in the ROCE of the SBU involved.

The case study

The case study examined the investment decision in a new product called ZB within the electronics division of Chantrey. The ZB had been a notable, if relatively small-scale success, winning a Queen's award for exports. It was developed at Chantrey Search Technology Systems (CSTS), an operating company within the Marine Technology subdivision, which is in turn within Chantrey Electronics. CSTS was acquired by Chantrey in 1986. It is located in 'Dorbay', on the South coast of England; it was formerly known as Scott Electronics, a private company. Scott had been a small, specialised innovative firm, which grew out of one-off small development and manufacturing jobs, largely for the UK military, and became focused on one type of military equipment. In the early 1980s research was carried out on a necessary adjunct to this equipment, and the ZB was developed for the purpose, a prototype being ready by 1984 – basically a ruggedised version of a recently introduced technology adapted to serve Scott's specialised market. The ZB was a success in its own right in the UK and US and is now sold to other manufacturers of the equipment; by 1991 it comprised 25% of the company's £9m turnover. This was an unforeseen bonus to Chantrey, which acquired Scott for its expertise in the core equipment, not the adjunct.

Scott had the common strengths and weaknesses of fast-growing small private companies. On the positive side was its innovativeness, technical excellence, inter-functional co-ordination, closeness to the customer. But on the negative side was its lack of effective accounting systems – which was not resolved for several years after the take-over. The SBU-centred approach adopted by the parent group from 1987 only really percolated to CSTS in 1989. Once it did, it was generally well suited to maintaining the entrepreneurialism and competitive spirit (inspired by the struggle for survival) of the small firm. If the firm had slipped up on any major contract they were under no illusions that the Group would be there to bail them out. The effects of this are very clearly visible when we look at the case of the ZB.

The Success of the ZB

The growth of the ZB business was from the outset an impressive story of inventiveness, improvisation, speed, determination and, on occasion, inspiration. The winning of the large order on the other hand did take place under the new regime, and clearly demonstrates the performance pressures engendered: CSTS was fighting for its survival in the ZB sector and yet unable to count on significant financial support from its parent. If it had seriously underestimated its costs at the end of the reverse costing exercise, its management expected the company to be wiped out just as it would have been if it had been a small company. The most obvious gain from its membership of a large group was that it had at length acquired up-to-date systems for working out what those costs were – there was no cross-subsidisation, no 'deep pockets' to enable it to establish itself in what might become a highly profitable sector. Nor was there any hint in what we were told of synergies with other parts of the group, through the Technology Centre or otherwise. However, these were early days: we were equally interested in current policy and strategy regarding further development of the ZB.

Where Next?

Our electronic engineer co-investigator pursued two lines of questioning regarding the ZB: Firstly, what was the likelihood that it would be superseded? He believed it inevitable at some stage that ZB technology would be threatened, given the current pace of development and level of interest in this field. Fundamentally, the Chantrey product was dependent on a key Japanese component. When something came up that outperformed this component, Chantrey would not necessarily know about it in good time.

Whilst the ZB's success had been impressive, the Research Manager agreed that since 1984 success had been based upon 'a real incremental approach'. The worry was that, in focusing on development work and working from one contract to the next, there was no room or resources for preparation for another step change necessary to maintain CSTS's position in this market area. Some work had been done on the development of a more advanced product, and a few sales made, but the market had proved disappointing relative to expectations. The Engineering Manager described the 5-year strategy discussions:

> *"where ideas are bounced around as to what we do as a site, but they are somewhat tongue in cheek*".

The Research Manager was clearly concerned:

> "*I'm the R&D manager and I've got no idea where we go after the ZB*".

The second Director argued that even in the case of the medical ZB, the centre had failed to provide the resources to exploit the available opportunity. These accounts, from the CSTS Research and Engineering Managers and the second

Technology Centre Director, seem to us, taken together, to provide damning evidence of short-termism and sectionalism in Chantrey. An established technological capability with obvious potential in the original defence market, and one or more civilian markets, should have been supported both with a) central funding and b) co-operation from other companies in the Division and elsewhere in the Group. Moreover c) CSTS should not have been so leanly staffed that it was unable to take initiatives and undertake exploratory work without reference to higher authority. On all three counts Chantrey are in this case found wanting. We now proceed to consider how far these deficiencies were general to the company and how far the management accounting practices contributed to them.

An overview

We can identify that management accounting practices did indeed create short-termism and sectionalism in Chantrey, but that this was due as much to what they omitted as well as what they included: in other words, because financial information was freely available, and used by the centre for evaluation and resource allocation, and non-financial information was much less freely available and used. That doomed the company to a degree of short-termism, at least so far as the less-visible elements of innovation were concerned (how far the more visible elements were affected, like capital expenditure and R&D, would have depended on the resources allocated from the centre, about which it is more difficult to generalise). It did not necessarily condemn it to sectionalism. Had the Technology Centre been given more resources it might have been able, at least in this respect, to counteract the 'destructive rivalry between SBUs'. But much must also depend on more organic determinants of relationships. The barriers to communication across the company were not only financial. Account must be taken of the fact that the electronics division had been brought into existence out of a series of acquisitions the earliest of which was made in 1977. Whilst the grand vision of technological convergence and synergies may have been logical, the difficulties of achieving this through the meshing together of a large number of previously separate companies appear to have been underestimated. The second Director, who had previous experience of managing acquisitions, felt that too little effort was put into deciding 'exactly who was going to do what with what' before purchases were made.

Another physical barrier, commented on by all the interviewees, was the inability exacerbated by the constraints of the British labour market to develop a company-specific workforce, facilitating mobility within the group, and thereby creating internal networks for technology transfer. As the second Director put it:

> *"Moving people is by far the most efficient way of moving technology".*

A Central Personnel register was kept for top managers only, who were moved around within the Group. The same was *not* done for technical personnel. This would, admittedly, have been difficult given the geographical spread of the Group and the traditions of external (geographically-specific) rather than internal (company-specific) labour markets which exist in Britain, exacerbated by severe skill shortages. A proposal was made by the Technology Centre for a directory of technical personnel, outlining their areas of expertise:

> *"But the decision came down from Board level, 'we will not publish that booklet, because if it gets into the hands of a competitor, or an executive search agency, we stand to lose an awful lot of people'. So there was a very positive decision on security grounds not to have that sort of publication. You may not agree with it, but it's a reason, a valid reason".* (Second Director)

We agree that this was indeed 'a valid reason'. If indeed a company has to keep secrets from itself in order to prevent poaching it is a serious reflection on the side-effects of a 'competitive' labour market. As long as these constraints exist in the British labour market, management in the UK will need to be aware of the difficulties this creates in devising realistic plans for integration of their acquisitions. Nonetheless, we do not believe that it would have been impossible to collect, hold and disseminate information in a less dangerous way, which would have achieved the required result.

Conclusions

The case study merely confirms and illustrates what we had already hypothesised from the literature. What had we actually learnt from it that was new? We believe it is one example - though clearly not conclusive – which supports the view that short-termism is at least as much to be put at top management's door as at that of the City of London. As we saw, the CEO blamed the City for inhibiting him in both acquisitions and R&D. Yet so far as acquisitions were concerned, it had let him have a good run for his – its – money before it began to conclude that the money had not been well spent. The inhibition there arose not from a lack of understanding of the strategic benefits but from a belated understanding that – whether from overpayment before or incomplete integration afterwards – the strategic benefits were not enough to justify the cost. With that in mind, we are entitled to be sceptical about the inhibition on R&D spending. Could that and the other inputs required for technological innovation not have been justified to the City? If the group was so incoherent that the City could not understand its technological strategy, it was its own fault. Even treating previous acquisitions as a *fait accompli*, parts of them could have been better integrated, other parts could have been sold. There was no sign in the location, the funding, or the influence of the Technology Centre of real determination: to create or project any technological coherence; to encourage inter-SBU co-operation within or across divisions; or to monitor innovative effort by SBUs in a way which would have allowed the evaluation of their managers by current profitability to be balanced by an evaluation by technology (and therefore profit) -in the pipeline-.

The failure to put real 'beef' into the Group Technology Centre was paralleled by a failure on the management accounting side. The management accounting system could and should have incorporated measures of spend on training, R&D,

market research, etc. – revenue investments to set alongside capital investment. These are measures of inputs, which could have been complemented by the output measures recommended by Bromwich and Bhimani (1989) and Johnson and Kaplan (1987), such as total launch time for new products, customer satisfaction, and key characteristics of new products. These output measures are rather specific to a given technological area and cannot be understood without a knowledge of the product and market environment; which in this high technology area was fast changing. Nor could they have been commensurable across the diverse range of Chantrey's divisions, subdivisions and operating companies. Therefore they could not have provided an effective set of measures for control by corporate HQ, without a thorough mapping of the differences within the company; but just such mapping needed to be carried out, by units such as the Technology Centre, if the group was to realise the synergies it aspired to. Given the deficiencies of the group's management accounting systems, it was scarcely surprising that Chantrey perceived short-term pressures from the City which inhibited their innovative spend. What they did not know they could not explain; what they could not explain they could not defend. The Chantrey case study has shown, then, how external and internal short termism can interact, and how management accounting systems are involved in this interaction.

LOAN GUARANTEES SCHEMES IN RISK MANAGEMENT

5.1 Introduction

by Robert Cressy
Professor, Warwick Business School

Banks and other lending institutions have to find ways of pricing risk if they are to ensure survival and to maximise profits. It is now known, however, that small businesses are more risky than large - such risk being measured by income and capital variability (Cressy and Olofsson, 1997). The differential risk of small and large enterprises, however, presents difficulties for loan pricing by way of the well established credit market phenomena of *adverse selection* and *moral hazard*. Both these phenomena occur in the context of what economists call asymmetric *information*, essentially a market situation where one signatory to the contract knows more about the parameters relevant to the credit decision than the other.

In the case of adverse selection, the bank is usually assumed to know less about the firm's survival chances than the firm itself. Adverse selection occurs typically when, in the face of excess demand, a bank attempts to raise price and finds that it attracts more risky borrowers. This produces an incentive for the bank to ration credit by non-price means. In other words, to offer credit to (say) the *first n applicants* that arrives at its doors. Moral hazard, on the other hand, arises when (for example) the bank's attempt to price the perceived extra risk of a small firm into the loan contract by means of a higher interest rate reduces entrepreneurial effort, thus making the project more risky than before. If effort is unobservable to the bank (the informational asymmetry) without expensive monitoring, the credit contract may involve the bank lending less than is socially optimal.[1]

Another important issue for the banks' pricing policy is that the *unit fixed costs* of lending are higher for smaller loans(firms), implying that higher prices (interest rates) are already on the agenda for smaller firms regardless of their relative

[1] This is a technical term used by economists to indicate that the expected return to the 'last' $ lent to the firm (probability of success *times* the interest margin) should equal its cost (prime rate) to the bank. If this is true then the last $ contracted with the firm represents a 'fair' bet between firm and bank.

riskiness. Of course, economically such costs should be priced into the loan or the bank cannot break even and no lending would take place. However, the attempt to do so may make small firm loans unattractive to borrowers, especially when they are aware that the bank apparently has little interest in or knowledge of their business's prospects. Finally, from the banks' viewpoint, the perceived lower return to small firm lending combined with higher risk makes them reluctant to acquire information about the firm's prospects. This, needless to say, is a condition required for economically efficient lending.[2]

As a result of these two categories of problem banks largely resort to collateral-based lending and credit scoring. In the former case, a loan is made conditional on the provision of assets that can be turned over to the bank and cashed in if default occurs. This proactive helps solve the moral hazard problem since by having a stake in the success of the venture by way of business/personal assets the entrepreneur will be more likely to put in the economically appropriate level of effort. However, rationing is not thereby necessarily avoided, even though its severity may be lessened, since collateral may not always be forthcoming from would-be borrowers in appropriate amounts (Evans and Jovanovic, 1989; Cressy and Toivanen, 1997). Thus, not all borrowers with viable projects may have collateral available to the required amount, and some will in consequence receive less than they need. The problem is likely to be most acute in the case of smaller, service-based firms, and those in the hi-tech sectors, whose characteristics make them particularly vulnerable.[3]

To combat the problem of asymmetric information and the consequent 'excessive' requirements for collateral, two alternative financial instruments have evolved, one government-based, and the other largely market-based Rudy Aernoudt's paper on 'European policy and loan guarantee schemes' provides an extensive overview of the European Commission's policy stance and initiatives in this growing area. These schemes fall broadly into two categories, the government loan guarantee scheme (LGS) and the mutual guarantee scheme (MGS). A mutual guarantee scheme, the structure of which is detailed in Rudy Aernoudt's paper 'European loan guarantee schemes', is a private grouping of companies, often in a particular trade, and which in aggregate, possesses greater knowledge of the creditworthiness of its members than the bank from which a loan is sought. It offers to provide insurance to the bank against loan default by its members for a premium (membership fee) paid by the membership to the organisation. In general, firms are more willing to reveal information about their business to the MGS organisation than they are to the bank. This helps solve the asymmetric information problem, and bridge the gap between financier and business. The only role for government is in the assisting of setting up of these organisations

---

[2] Another term that economists use to describe the need for the bank's return on the last $ lent to represent the marginal product of the funds to the firm (the probability of success *times* the firm's project return).

[3] Hi tech start-ups frequently suffer from low asset base, negative profits, and products that the typical bank manager will find baffling in complexity. Despite often illustrious academic credentials these features make bank loans difficult to obtain except as part of a wider funding package.

where there is no tradition of them, and in re-guaranteeing the societies themselves against default. This however, is a lower level of risk in general than direct government guarantee due to the diversification that has already occurred by MGS risk-pooling.[4]

Government loan guarantee schemes are discussed in Rudy Aernoudt's paper on European policy and subjected to critical evaluation in Robert Cressy's paper on 'Government guarantee schemes in Europe'. They are, by contrast with MGS, guarantees provided by the government to the bank against loans to firms (usually small and young) in return for a premium paid by the firm (or the bank) to the government. The apparent advantage of the LGS is that it does not require local knowledge and a 'co-operative mentality' for the granting of the loan. This means that loan decisions may in theory be more timely. Also, such loans can, and often are, larger than the typical MGS offering. The disadvantage of LGS over MGS is the higher degree of losses incurred by the government, and this may itself result from the very absence of local knowledge that we have cited above.

Governments in Europe, the United States Japan and many other countries now play a significant role in supporting smaller firms in the credit markets via such guarantee schemes. It is important to recognise what the public sector is best at and what should be left to the market. In the European Union, the majority national governments run their own schemes, and, particularly in the South, mutual schemes are popular. There is also a growing interest at European level in the role of these schemes in rectifying perceived credit market deficiencies. In this context Rudy Aernoudt's paper on policy provides an valuable enunciation of the principles behind the European Commission's role in the Union countries credit markets, and in particular their role vis-à-vis loan guarantee schemes. Government schemes are placed within the context of Industrial Policy more generally. Rudy Aernoudt enunciates some important principles limiting the commission's involvement in this area, namely, 'market solutions first'[5] and 'subsidiarity'. The former refers to the need to allow the private sector to do what it does best. The latter refers to the need to allow national and regional devolution of decision-making where appropriate. An interesting example of the implementation of this principle can be found in the European Parliament's recent rejection of the European Investment Bank's proposed pan-Union 'ELISE' loan guarantee scheme. Apparently, this scheme infringed the principle of market solutions first, and the emphasis of policy has now moved towards support for mutual schemes where government plays a more 'at arms' length' role.

---

[4] It is possible to show that under a wide range of assumptions the risk of a portfolio of loans is lower than the risk of any individual loan and that this decreases with the number in the portfolio. This creates an argument for large mutual guarantee scheme than small.

[5] This phrasing is mine rather than Mr. Rudy Aernoudt's. The terminology is intended to indicate that what can be done efficiently by the market should so be done.

Governments, then, would seem to be justified in intervening in the economy if by so doing they can help rectify (at reasonable cost) a market deficiency. This principle has been enshrined in economic folk-lore for more than a century. However, it is important to be aware that even this seemingly minimal government role has loopholes, since it is not inconceivable (the former Eastern European block countries being a case in point) that such intervention may sometimes make things worse, e.g. by 'crowding out' the private sector, transforming profitable lending by the market into unprofitable losses. This is a government-induced misallocation of resources (reminiscent doctor-induced or *iatrogenic* illness in the patient) that we can well do without. In short, it is crucial to believe that government intervention will *remedy* a market failure, and that this is the *best* alternative use of public resources.

This is in fact the principle issue addressed in Robert Cressy's paper on government guarantee schemes, where, on the basis of existing (imperfect) evidence, he evaluates the UK's Loan Guarantee Scheme. Whilst the UK scheme has been around for some 16 years, and can thus be regarded as quite well established, he finds himself arguing the case for its abandonment. It is not sufficient, he argues, to tinker with the scheme's parameters in the hope that this will produce the right mix of government loss and private gain. This is merely re-arranging the deckchairs on the Titanic. The criteria Cressy uses for making this judgement are precisely the two discussed in the last paragraph: intervention seems to be designed in this case to make things worse, and nor is funding the LGS the best alternative use of resources. In consequence, he proposes a range of alternative policies to help small firms, including training for managers, human capital restrictions on self-employment, and a call for macro-stability measures.

5.2 European union enterprise policy and loan guarantee schemes

by Rudy Aernoudt
Professor, Hogeschool Gent[6]

The paper aims at giving insight in the EU-policy related to guarantee schemes. As a guarantee policy as such doesn't exit, but is integrated in the enterprise policy, it seems necessary to start from a broader context. Therefore, the paper is divided into three main parts. Firstly, I discuss the scope of the European Union's enterprise policy in general and examine some of the limitations under which it operates. Secondly, I summarise the EC's specific policy on guarantee schemes. Thirdly, I discuss mutual guarantee schemes as an alternative to government-based ones. The final section concludes the scope of EU policy in the field of guarantees.

---

6 Official at the European Commission, where he is dealing with enterprise policy. This paper expresses his personal view rather than the views of the European Commission.

European union enterprise policy

Without attempting to detail the different aspects of European Union policy towards enterprises, in this section I outline the general framework of that policy and explain how the specific policies mentioned above fit into the global framework.

Limitations to policy

Probably the best way to understand the European Union's role is to start by identifying its limits. In this regard the following principles of operation are relevant:

- *The private sector's responsibilities:* What can be done efficiently by the private sector and by the market, has to be done by the private sector.
- *Subsidiarity:* What can be done in an efficient way on a lower regional level, should not be done at a European level. Linking this to enterprise policy, we must take into account that Member States have their own individual enterprise policies.
- *Unanimity:* There must be unanimity (complete agreement) in Community decision making. In most of the fields relevant to enterprise policy, the unanimity rule is 'still' in force. This often makes it hard to take decisions. The fraught process of tax harmonisation demonstrates this amply. Whilst different proposals have been made to alter the unanimity rule, to date no Council summit has resulted in agreement to be taken by unanimity on the topic.

This set of principles leaves limited scope for enterprise policy. In fact, we could summarise enterprise policy in the field of financing, by two kinds of interventions: those aimed at improving the financial environment and those aimed at increasing the financial resources available to SMEs.

Interventions aimed at improving the financial environment

Again this set of actions can be summarised under five headings. I shall provide some comments on those areas that seem most relevant to the present analysis.

- *Late payment*

  Studies have shown that 43% of all payments are intentionally late (see Wilson, 1997). Based on these perceptions, Svensson (1997) ranked the different countries on the basis of 'morality' criteria, which reflect the actual payment practice in each state relative to its own standard.

  In 1995 the European Commission launched a recommendation on late payment. In 1998 it proposed a directive on late payment in response to the serious obstacles to cross-border transactions and to the opening up of public procurement markets that this had created.

- *Bank-SME relationships*
  Although venture capital, together with special purpose vehicles, and other financial engineering techniques, has attracted much attention, and doubtless we can each make our own *aggiornamiento,* most of the external funds for SMEs still originate from classical bank loans.

  As has been shown in Summers (1997) the main source of external finance for enterprises is overdraft. Hence it is clear that the relationships between banks and SMEs are crucial. In that context the European Commission launched a 'round table' discussion of bankers and SMEs with a clear objective: the identification and exchange of best practices in the area of bank/SME relationships. The 1995-1997 Round Table has been successfully concluded and the report has become available.[7]

- *New financial instruments*
  The European Commission is promoting various new financial instruments. A pilot seed capital action succeeded in launching 23 seed capital funds all over Europe, and a new action in the field is to be launched in 1998. Another action is the above mentioned mutual guarantee scheme promotion. The promotion of business angels is another example of new financial instruments.

- *Access to stock market*
  In the United States of America, the National Association of Securities Dealers Automatic Quotation (NASDAQ) electronic stock market provides suitable smaller companies with ready access to long-term equity capital, through the medium of a public offering of their shares and a subsequent listing on the market. Based on the proven need for stock markets for SMEs by different studies, and the success of the NASDAQ market, the European Commission financed a feasibility study to examine the setting up a similar stock market for SMEs in Europe. Subsequently, the EASDAQ was set up and 23 companies in Europe were quoted on that market by the end of 1997.

- *Taxation*
  Though the mainstream of taxation is a national matter, in some fields the Commission has taken initiatives. However, this topic is rather tangential to the present subject, so I shall just illustrate with one example, namely, that the European Commission pleads for the limitation of taxes resulting from the transfer of enterprises in order to guarantee their continuity.

Interventions to increase financial resources to SMEs
Three kinds of actions have to be considered here. First of all, there is the role of the European Investment Bank in giving global grants to banks with priority for SMEs. Nowadays, on average, 12.000 SMEs a year benefit from these extremely cheap loans.

---

[7] Report on the second Round Table, Bankers and SMEs, February 1997

Secondly, there is the European structural policy. Through that policy, the European Commission co-finances financial engineering techniques, which fit into the development programmes proposed by the Member States. For the period 2000 – 2006, the new regulation stipulates that priority should be given to those actions, in the framework of structural policy. A special Community initiative called SME has been created in order to finance any measure aimed at helping SMEs to get better access to credit facilities.

Finally, different Community programmes aim at helping SMEs to develop in the open markets. They are mostly linked to certain fields of intervention. Some examples are the 4th R&D programmes which finance research projects in SMEs and the programmes which finance the setting up of Joint Ventures with Eastern Europe (JOP) or with Mediterranean, Asian and Latin American countries (ECIP). A similar programme to facilitate joint ventures between European SMEs – Joint European Venture (JEV) – has been operational since November 1997.

EU policy towards guarantee systems

We can summarise the EU policy on loan guarantee systems, government and mutual, under three headings.[8]

The European Investment Fund

The European Investment Fund was created in 1994 with a capital of ECU 2 billion in order to give guarantees for SME loan portfolios of banks and to guarantee special investment funds. The capital is owned partly by public institutions such as the European Investment Bank (40%) and the European Commission (30%), and partly by the banking sector (67 financial institutions holding the remaining 30% of the capital).

Guarantees are mostly issued indirectly in favour of specialised financial institutions. By analogy with the global grants of the European Investment Bank (EIB), mention should be made of the global guarantees of the European Investment Fund (EIF). After two years of activity (mid '96), the EIF has signed transactions for MECU 1,129 related to 17 projects.

In addition, in the framework of the 'growth and employment' initiative, which was adopted on April 98 by the European Council, the European Commission will allocate a complementary amount of MECU 150 over 3 years. The objective is to cover the costs of guarantees and counter-guarantees issued by the EIF in order to promote an increase in the availability of loans supported by guarantee schemes operating in the Member States in the public or private sector.

---

8 A detailed analysis can be found in my paper 'Loan guarantee systems in Europe', presented at The Second International Stockholm Seminar on Risk Behaviour and Risk Management.

The growth and environment program
A good illustration of the functioning of the EIF, and how this may be combined with the EC programme, is the role of the programme called 'The Growth and Environment programme'. This programme aims to facilitate access by SMEs in the EU to bank loans for new investments that produce environmental benefits. The scheme works through a network of especially selected financial intermediaries who provide the investment loans. The EIF issues guarantees to these financial institutions covering up to 50% of the loan. These guarantees are issued at no cost to the borrowing SMEs or to the financial institution since guarantee premiums are financed through the European Commission. The EIF covers its own share of potential losses under the scheme.

The Growth and Environment scheme first became operational in the second half of 1996. The EIF has so far signed contracts with 11 financial institutions in 9 Member States for a total guarantee volume of approximately MECU 350.

The mutual guarantee system
Government-based loan guarantee schemes as described by Dr. Cressy in the paper that follows in section 5.4, are an arrangement for the sharing of risks between the lending bank, the borrowing firm and the government. Another type of loan guarantee scheme, frequently found in Europe, and with no direct government involvement, is the mutual loan guarantee scheme (MGS).[9] The mutual system of guarantees functions on the basis of 'solidarity' between enterprises. The philosophy behind this practice is that through more detailed knowledge of the sector and the enterprises in it a better understanding of the firm's prospects can be obtained. Government intervention is therefore in this case either completely absent or, as for example in Germany, its role is limited to re-guaranteeing the system that makes the loans.

Linked to the above discussion of market efficiency, the EC has given priority to the development of mutual guarantee systems throughout Europe. The EC does so by backing the European mutual guarantee association whose role is to stimulate the setting up of mutual systems. In addition to this, feasibility studies are funded – as for example in Finland – and pilot projects are set up – as for example in the UK and Greece.

Mutual* versus *government guarantee systems

Turning now to the structure of the mutual guarantee system and its relationship to government schemes, we note that the mutual guarantee society functions as a third party inserted between the bank and the SME. The MGS is illustrated diagrammatically in Figure 5.1.

---

[9] See also Robert Cressy, chapter 5, 'Finance', in the Fourth Report of the European Observatory for SMEs, commissioned by DGXXIII.

This alters the relation between the latter two in providing a degree of security which, as mentioned above, is not only of a financial nature. However, this third party does not intervene in the loan and repayment procedure. This continues to be handled by the bank and the SME, with the latter now also operating as a member of the mutual guarantee system.

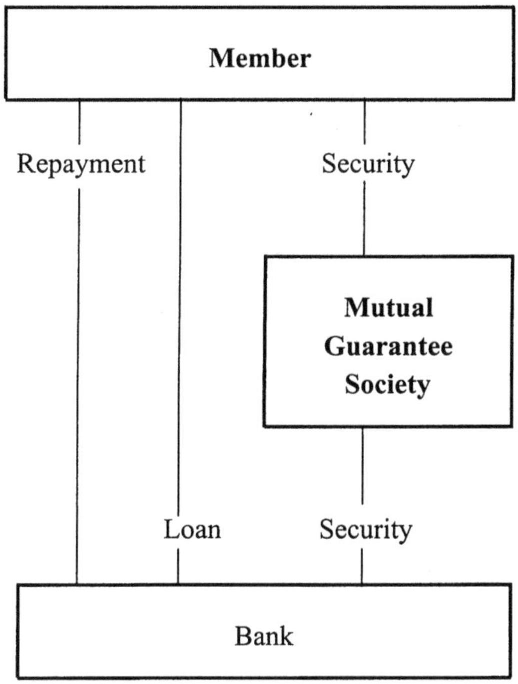

Figure 5.1 Mutual guarantee systems

As regards the functioning of MGS as compared with government schemes, MGS involve a new organisation inserted in the lending relationship. Nevertheless, for banks 'small remains beautiful'. This has been attested by some studies showing that a surcharge of 2 to 5% is levied on credits for SMEs in comparison to rates charged to large enterprises.

These studies have one glaring defect; namely, they do not compare like with like. The amounts lent on mutual basis are smaller than those lent to large businesses. Therefore administrative costs, rather than the profit rate of lending are the primary influence factor on margin size, and any valid comparison must therefore take this into account.

In this context, therefore, I am inclined to adopt the Schumpeter standpoint and assert that 'small *is* beautiful' here. Thus, the market deficiencies, which Cressy (1997) has described so well, can, to some extent, be overcome by such mutual organisations where government involvement is minimal. The MGS are by their nature closely linked to industrial sectors and thus based on a deeper understanding indigenous borrowers' prospects through 'local' knowledge of the borrowing firms. The advantages of the guarantees provided by these mutual systems are therefore not simply of a financial nature. They constitute a package that helps bridge the information gap between lender and borrower, reduces the moral hazard in lending and thereby inspires the confidence of the banks.

To highlight the importance of this mutual system we simply note that the proportion of total guaranteed lending from public sources in the OECD countries is 58%. This implies that the mutual schemes in the OECD countries account for 4 ECUs in every 10 guaranteed.

Conclusions

Although the scope of EU policy in the field of guarantees seems to be limited at first sight, a whole range of activities has been developed. These activities involve as well the financing of guarantee schemes through the structural policy or via the European Investment Fund, as the exchange of best practices, through the round table, as the establishment of new systems, such as the pilot action on mutual guarantee schemes.

Although no overall cost benefit analysis of those interventions has been conducted, I am convinced that, in order to be efficient, any EU policy has to be market-oriented and in completion to national or regional interventions. The more market-oriented the scheme is, the less it will distort the functioning of the market. In this sense, where possible, mutual guarantee schemes are preferable, as they inspire the confidence of banks. And isn't confidence what it is all about when we discuss finances?

In this context, it is hoped that within the new Growth and Employment initiative, priority will be given to existing mutual guarantee schemes and to the setting up of new ones.

5.3 European loan guarantee schemes

by Rudy Aernoudt
Professor, Hogeschool, Gent [10]

We are all familiar with the statement to get a loan you've got to prove you don't need it. In fact, the meaning of this sentence, is in its use, as Ryle would say. And in this respect it is usually insufficient to prove the cost-effectiveness and the pay-back capacity of a project in order to get a bank loan. Sticking to the you never know principle, and arguing that money lent comes from the savings of accountholders, banks are reluctant to grant loans, unless sufficient collateral is provided. Although we live in a financial environment with a high profile given to capital market funds and venture capital, the fact is that 70% of SMEs are still financed through traditional bank loans. The refusal to grant such a loan is, in many cases, a major impediment to the creation of a company and/or the financing of an investment.

Even more damaging for SMEs is the fact that banks, if they agree to finance, prefer short-term financing. A recent study carried out in he United Kingdom[11] showed that in a number of countries, such as Denmark, Greece, Italy, Portugal, and Spain, small enterprises do have a very limited access to long-term loans. This implies that long-term investments are often financed through short-term, commercial credits. Needless to say, such financing violates the rules of sound financial management and results in balance sheets unable to comply with the acid-test criterion. Moreover, the firms receiving such finance are often characterised by negative working capital.[12]

We can thus appreciate the importance of developing financial instruments other than mortgages that can provide guarantees to banks, enabling SMEs to obtain loans on the right terms for the prevailing market conditions. One of such instrument is the loan guarantee scheme. Before analysing the different types of loan guarantee scheme, let us have a closer look at the general concept. What's in a name?

What's in a name?

A *Loan Guarantee Scheme* is a scheme providing guarantees to banks lending to SMEs. Such guarantees range from 30% to 80% of the loan value. The schemes

---

[10] Official of the European commission, where he is dealing with enterprise policy. This paper expresses a personal view rather than the views of the European Commission.

[11] Bank of England (1996).

[12] The acid-test is an accounting ratio measure of the liquidity of a firm. It raises the question of whether stocks can be financed through the permanent capital (equity capital and long term loans), with a deduction being made for fixed assets. If the remaining capital at least equals the stocks, the acid test is positive, indicating a liquid firm.

can be organised (and funded) by governments and so through public funds: so-called *Government Loan Guarantee schemes*. In this case the government provides a guarantee to the bank against a premium paid by the borrowing party to the bank or government. This third party, coming between banks and their clients, provides a guarantee 'of the last resort'. By contrast, another type of scheme, the *Mutual Guarantee Scheme*, involves private groupings of companies, often linked to sector-specific interest groups, to provide loan insurance to the banks. Before analysing these two systems in detail, let us examine some data at world- and EU-level.

In 1997 85 countries in the world had a loan guarantee scheme (Doran and Levitsky, 1997). Of these, 23 were in the OECD, 7 were in Central and Eastern Europe, 15 in Latin America, 11 in Asia, and 6 in Africa.[13] There is a great variety in these systems, which vary, e.g., according to stage of economic development. In OECD countries, only 58% of the loan guarantee schemes function on a funded basis (i.e. based on government support), while in the developing countries 78% are funded schemes. Apart from their funding role, governments are very active in organising loan guarantee schemes. At world level, 70% of guarantee systems are government-based, with 25% private-sector-organised and 5% co-operative-based.

In the European area, we can see that loan guarantee schemes differ between the South and North of the region. In the South of Europe, mutual guarantee systems, based on the co-operation idea, are well developed. Mutual systems already exist in Belgium, France, Italy, Portugal and Spain. Austria and Germany have a bank-based system close to the mutual system. Feasibility studies on the setting up of a mutual system, financed by the European Commission, have been launched in Finland and the UK. In the North of Europe, in some countries such as the United Kingdom, Ireland, and the Netherlands, the system is more government-oriented. France and Belgium, located between North and South, have both systems. Here again, however, the classification will have to be modified, as we examine both systems in detail.

Before doing so, let us take note of some statistics. For 1994, the latest year for which figures are available, in 6 Member States of the European Union, 32,472 SMEs benefited from a public guarantee scheme, to the value of 3,342 MECU, whilst 51,548 SMEs in 5 Member States benefited from the mutual guarantee system to the value of 3,379 MECU.[14] The average amount for guarantees by SMEs is bigger in public guarantee systems (103,000 ECU) than in mutual guarantee systems (67,690 ECU). This is due to the fact that the target group for the latter is primarily the craft industry. Before looking closer at both types of loan guarantee system, and to obtain a more global view on the way Europe copes with the problem of insufficient collateral, it is worthwhile noting that in a

---

[13] Dovan and Livitsky(1997).

[14] An explanation and detailing of those figures will be found later in this paper, respectively in Tables 1 & 3. Figures are partly derived from ENSR (1996), pp. 212 to 219. MECU denotes million ECU.

number of countries a *risk loan system* exists which helps fills the gap that guarantee systems would otherwise attempt to cover. As the name suggests, risk loan systems provide loans rather than guarantees, and in practice function in two different ways. On the one hand, public credit institutions can refinance bank credits, as is the case in Spain, Italy and Germany. On the other hand, they can directly grant loans, as in the Scandinavian countries. In some cases, in addition to the risk loan, guarantees are granted by these institutions, but this happens only to a very limited extent.

The mutual guarantee scheme

The philosophy of the system

The philosophy behind the mutual guarantee system is that closer links between the interest groups in SME-dominated industries, namely, craft work and commerce, can result in a better knowledge by the banks of a companies' standing, and of the markets in which it operates, and that this in turn allows a better *ex ante* evaluation of the project by the lender. Credit risk is thereby considerably reduced.[15] The fact that the mutual guarantee organisations trust the enterprises and their projects, and express this trust by offering the lending bank a partial guarantee, makes it easier for the latter to grant loans. In a certain sense, guarantees offered by the mutual system are not merely financial in character, but also technical and moral, since through the operation of the system banks become familiar the technical and moral capacities of the borrowing firms.[16]

If such schemes are well-implemented and designed, additional bank lending may also be considered, and the costs of such lending controlled for.[17] So, through the medium of 'solidarity' (mutual co-operation), SMEs are able to obtain better access to loans and to loans under better terms. In order to understand the various systems prevailing in Europe, it is of value to trace the phenomenon back to its historical roots.

Almost 100 years before the European Union was created, or more precisely, in 1848, Belgium created the *Credit Union of Brussels* aimed at attracting capital for the benefit of its members with a view to using them as guarantees vis-à-vis third parties. The first transformation of the co-operative principle into law took place in France after the first world war. The *Société de Cautionnement Mutuel* was set up as an instrument to reconstruct the economy. Other countries followed suit. Belgium created the *Caisse Nationale du Crédit Professionnel* in 1929, whilst Germany developed their credit guarantee legislation in 1954, and Italy

---

15 A nice illustration of this point is the case of the Italian region Emilia Romagna where insolvency rates for loans granted by mutual guarantee schemes are lower than 1%. The average default rate on ordinary loans in the region is by contrast 10 to 11%. See E. Tubia, The system of credit guarantee consortia in Emilia Romagna, in perspectives, #19, March 1997.

16 This triple guarantee approach has been retained by the Economic and Social committee in its resolution on the role of mutual guarantee schemes in 1992, ESC-document 492/92 of 29 April 1992.

17 See Dovan and Levitsky, op. cit.

created its co-operatives for mutual guarantees in 1956.[18] Although most of these were created in the post-war climate, they really took off after the economic crisis of the early 1970s. Along with their increasing activities, the organisations became increasingly professional, and in many member states, were assimilated into the financial institutions.

In Italy, to date, more or less 600 mutual guarantee societies have been established. In Spain, where the creation of *Reciprocal Guarantee Societies* (RGS) only became possible after 1978 as a consequence of the Moncloa agreements, these societies mushroomed. However they achieved true professional status only after mergers and recapitalisation operation had occurred. They were then able to function rather like credit institutions. Also, in Germany, after the creation of the federation of mutual guarantees in 1990, the societies began to function like traditional banks. Finally, in France, the SCM were converted into financial institutions in 1984.

Benefiting from the support of the EU, this convergence of the societies towards greater professionalism led to the creation in 1991 of the *Association Européenne de Cautionnement Mutuel* (AECM). The objective of this institution was on the one hand to represent the mutual guarantee system at European level, and on the other, to help disseminate the system elsewhere in Europe.

Following a pilot-phase, the mutual system was established in Portugal. A feasibility study was launched by the European Commission in several other countries, including Finland and the United Kingdom. In the first of these two countries the setting up of a mutual guarantee system was postponed, though the study revealed a potential difficulty in doing so, since in the interim public guarantee schemes had been established.[19] It is worth noting that the study revealed that 80% of companies were willing to co-operate with other entrepreneurs. However, nearly 70% stated that they were not willing to guarantee loans for other companies, even though this could lower the cost of finance and improve access to finance. In the United Kingdom, the chances are growing for the development of mutual guarantee systems. This is enhanced by the recent change of government, since the new government is particularly in favour of the idea. Characterised by a well-functioning public loan guarantee scheme in the UK, a national association of mutual guarantees has been set up and a pilot mutual guarantee project launched in the Lancashire area. This pilot-project recently received the support of the Co-operative Bank. A second project has been launched in county Durham.

Some recent additions to the AECM include Austria, upon joining the European Union, and Hungary, following the setting up of the Hungarian credit guarantee association in 1995, grouping together three mutual guarantee funds that had

---

[18] See Comparative analyses of mutual guarantee societies , AECM, Hamburg 1993.

[19] Feasibility Study on the introduction of the Mutual Guarantee Societies to Finland, Small business institute, Turku school of economics, Helsinki, 1997

specialised in micro-enterprise related activity. Even more recently Morocco joined the AECM, assuming the status of Associate member.

Other countries where public loan guarantee schemes prevail have experimented with mutual guarantee systems and are negotiating membership with AECM. In Greece. a new law dating from 1995 made the establishment of mutual guarantee companies (MGC) possible. Two pilot projects were launched, one in Athens and one in Thessaloniki. Neither project, however, is operational at the time of writing. The main shareholders of the system in Greece are the Chambers of Commerce.

Present structure of mutual guarantee systems

This brief historical overview should of course enhance our understanding of the present structure. Before turning to this analysis, however, and to provide a feel for the scale of the system, we in table 5.1 present a few key-statistics. We limit our analysis to the 6 most significant countries (in alphabetical order) : Austria, Belgium, France, Germany, Italy, and Spain.

Table 5.1 Operational data on mutual guarantee schemes

Country	Number of MGS	Number of SMEs	Value (MECU)	Average (000 ECU)
Austria	8	8 346	812	97
Belgium	17	2 860	42	39
France	157	28 387	549	19
Italy	578	ND	ND	ND
Germany	24	7 886	1559	198
Spain	19	4 069	417	76
Total	803	51,548	3,379	67

Source: Report of AECM; 1997 and ENSR(1996) (data for 1994).

In order to make an accurate comparison of these figures, it also seems important to understand the different structures, which govern them. These differences can be summarised under four criteria: a) the capital providers of the organisation – giving an indication of their 'mutual' character; b) the links the organisations have with financial and/or public institutions; c) the existence or otherwise of associations of mutual guarantee; and d) the operational domain of the relevant societies.

The systems are different. Those in Belgium, France, Italy and Spain are alike as far as the shareholders or the beneficiaries of the guarantees are concerned. These systems may be regarded as examples of mutual systems, *stricto sensu*. The German system is slightly different from these, as the shareholders are corporations and associations. Moreover, in Germany guarantees given by the system of guarantee banks, the *Verband der Bürgschaftsbanken*. Guarantees are normally up to 80% of the value of the loan, but the state re-guarantees these to a level of 65%. We could say that the German system is close to public guarantee funds, but still closer to the mutual system since the State is merely re-guarantor and only covers a part of the partial guarantees offered by the banks.[20] This is however not the only difference in the operation of the 'solidarity' principle to be found in Europe. Companies also have to pay an large entry fee to the system in Italy, at the point of obtaining the loan in France, and neither entry nor loan granting is free of charge in Germany – where membership of the Chamber of commerce is also encouraged. Moreover, public institutions in the last resort back up operations in Italy and Germany.

Although the systems are very different from one country to another, we should emphasis that it is not the aim of the European Union or of the AECM to harmonise existing systems. Nevertheless a best practices approach can be a useful adjunct to existing and newly-created schemes both in, and outside, the European Union. Special attention should be paid here to Central and Eastern Europe. A number of countries there, including the Czech Republic, Hungary, Slovakia and Poland, have established guarantee systems with the assistance of the PHARE program.[21] In line with this thinking it is possible the European Commission will update its 1991 Communication on mutual guarantee schemes and propose a new initiative in this field.[22]

Public loan guarantee schemes

Whilst it is not my intention in this paper to discuss public loan guarantee schemes at length,[23] I mention them in passing to show how the two concepts may (as exemplified in the French case) be combined.

The philosophy of public loan guarantee schemes

The philosophy of public loan guarantee schemes is that the government, being a solid financial body, provides grants to banks in return for a premium paid by the SMEs. The justification of spending or even losing public money, is that through guarantee schemes, viable SME projects will be financed with loans, thus creating employment and contributing to economic growth; in other words, assisting

---

20 This point of view is confirmed by the practise as the German organisation is part of the AECM (see above). A system, which is quiet close to the German system, is the Austrian one, where the mutual Structure of Mutual Guarantee guarantee association ARGE joined the AECM.

21 For more details on those countries, I refer to the rapport on the seminar Supporting SME with credit guarantee schemes in central and eastern Europe, hold in Budapest in October 1996.

22 The role of mutual guarantee schemes in the financing of SME's in the EU, SEC(91), 1550 final, Sept. 1991.

23 See Robert Cressy's section of this chapter for an extensive discussion.

in the creating of additional economic wealth. Especially countries from Northern Europe, such as the United Kingdom, Finland and the Netherlands, are active in this field, but the system also exists in Greece, and though Belgium and especially France rely on a mutual guarantee system; they also have a public guarantee scheme. Both are all the more interesting for the purpose of our study and I will focus on the example of France later on.

Nevertheless, on the whole, we can claim that public guarantee schemes remedy the lack of mutual guarantee schemes. The guaranteed amount varies from 70% to 40%: 70% in the UK, 50% in the Netherlands and 50% in Ireland. In Greece, where the Loan Guarantee Schemes operate at regional level, the rates vary from one region to another. The amounts involved are considerable.[24] Key figures on public loans scheme are presented in table 5.2.

Table 5.2 Key figures on public loan scheme guarantees

Country	Number of SMEs	Value of guarantees (MECU)	Average Value of guarantee (000ECU)
Belgium	1 052	59	56
Finland	1 036	252	243
France	6 647	2 010	302
Greece	15 002	472	31
Netherlands	3 533	287	81
United Kingdom	5 202	262	50
Total	32 472	3342	103

Source : 4th Observatory for SMEs. All data are for 1994.

Combining public and mutual schemes: the French case

Of particular interest for here is the French case. While a mutual guarantee system originates in this country, and is functioning rather well,[25] in 1988 the State decided to create *SOFARIS*,[26] a society whose mission was to guarantee SMEs credits for the banks to facilitate the management of public guarantee funds.

24 E.g. in the UK up to 90 million £, for details see Cressy and Cowling (1997).

25 See Table 5.1

26 SOFARIS stands for Société française de garantie des financements des PME. In 1996 SOFARIS became part of the Banque de Développement des PME.

In France Public guarantee funds have been created since 1979, with the purpose of guaranteeing subordinated loans,[27] creation and transfer of enterprises, innovative projects, the craft industry, foreign investment,[28] and so on. Only in 1993 was a special fund created to guarantee credits of SMEs. Such guarantees cover 50% of investment-credits or working capital-credits.[29] In 1995, a special fund was created aimed at micro-enterprises. This highlighted a conflict of interest with the pre-existing mutual guarantee systems, specialised in the craft industry, and mainly offering guarantees to micro-companies.

The crucial question in this discussion is, of course, why should a public loan guarantee scheme for SMEs be established? According to official public documents, it seems that the French State, inspired by the successful promotion of mutual guarantee systems, decided to use the guarantee scheme as a component of industrial policy.[30] In the case of SOFARIS the argument used was that the mutual guarantee system, based on solidarity, was especially active in craft and commerce and its proven efficiency should be extrapolated into industry. In the latter area direct government involvement was required due to the absence of the market solidarity principle underlying the functioning of MGS in craft. In order to appreciate the importance of the SOFARIS system, it is worth comparing it quantitatively with the mutual guarantee system. In 1994 the mutual systems realised 7.5 billion ECU of Guarantees, while the public schemes realised 15 billion ECU. With regard to stocks of guaranteed loans, the mutual systems have a portfolio of 60 billion ECU, whereas the public systems equivalent is only 13 billion.

The official rationale for a dual system is that the market is sufficiently large to permit the coexistence of both public and private (mutual) guarantees, with separate fields of operation. However, in practice these fields become progressively ill-defined.[31] Moreover, the obligation of a mutual guarantee society to respect the Cooke prudential rate (8% solvability ratio) limits its activity.

In practice, there exist two kinds of mutual guarantee systems, namely, the 'captive' one, where the society is linked exclusively to one bank; and the independent one. The latter system has suffered enormously from recent developments, and its volume of activity has shrunk.[32] The fund specialised in building and public works actually had to cease its activities altogether. In fact, out of a total of 7.5 billion, FF 0.7 billion were realised by the 3 'captive' societies alone. The volume of activities of the public guarantee system, created long after the mutual

---

[27] Inspired by the UK-approach, this fund was created in 1979 but no longer exists.

[28] With special funds for investments abroad in Central and Eastern Europe.

[29] Respectively relying on the budget of 600 MF for investment and 300 MF for workcapital credits.

[30] Les notes bleues de Bercy , économie et conjuncture, October 1993, p.3, France.

[31] The potential of the SME market in France is estimated at a 200 Million FF. SOFARIS and the mutual guarantee schemes supply only 10% of this market.

[32] A special decree exempts mutual guarantee societies from respecting the 8% solvability ratio if they are legally bounded to one bank for the whole of their operations.

system, is twice as big as that of the mutual system. But this does not allow us to jump to conclusions concerning its relative efficiency.

We must not forget that the public scheme is based on public money used as guarantee, while the mutual guarantee system is based on the contribution of the members. Hence, the latter system is much more expensive for SMEs. The question is rather whether public money could not have been better used in support of the existing network of market oriented mutual guarantee scheme (so far as necessary) instead of offering similar services to similar clients. A risk sharing agreement between the state and the private sector in which the state guarantees 65% of the risks assumed by the mutual guarantees system, as is the case in Germany, seems more consistent with an efficient use of public money.[33] An alternative would be a market-sharing rule where mutual guarantee schemes concentrate their activity on micro-enterprises (craft), and public schemes on industry.

Anticipating on the assessment of EU-intervention in this field, two observations have to be added regarding the implication of the EU in the French system. Firstly, the public guarantee scheme will be co-financed by the structural policy of the EU under the SME community initiative. Secondly, regarding the mutual guarantee system, a request has been forwarded to the European Commission to modify existing directives relating to the weighting coefficient applied to assets guaranteed by mutual guarantee funds[34]. But let us have a close look to the EU-interventions before concluding.

The European approach towards loan guarantee schemes for SMEs

Subsidiarity

Every EU-policy has to respect the principle of subsidiarity. This means that the policy has to take place on the lowest level, provided that it is still appropriate. In this context, we can wonder whether the European Union has any direct role to play in guaranteeing loans. The answer is not simple, as attested by the miscarried launching of the ELISE programme in 1996. In order to understand that programme, we first need to analyse the functioning of the European Investment Fund, which is the European instrument for the providing of guarantees.

The European Investment Fund and its role towards SME

The European Investment Fund (EIF) was established in 1994 following the decision made at the Edinburgh Summit. It is a financial institution bringing together the European Union, the European Investment bank and 76 financial institutions from all 15 Member States. The European public shareholders own 70% of the capital. The Fund supports medium and long term investments in two fields regarded as essential to the development of the European economy: Trans-

---

[33] A further analysis of this matter seems necessary, but this goes beyond the object of this paper.

[34] The request concerns a demand for attributing a weighting of 20% for credits guaranteed by mutual funds, as is actually the case for credits towards regional and local authorities and to multilateral development banks, as stipulated by article 6 of the directive 89/64 7/CE of 28 December 1989.

European networks (TENs) and Small and Medium sized Enterprises (SMEs). The EIF's essential business is to provide guarantees to banks and financial institutions funding investments in these two fields.[35]

For the purpose of this paper, let us highlight the EIF's activities linked to the mainstream activities towards SMEs. The EIF offers partial guarantees for SME loan portfolios of banks and for private sector capital contribution to specialised investment funds for SMEs. Guarantees may either be issued indirectly in favour of specialised financial institutions or by way of exception directly to the final beneficiary. They may either be guaranteed to individual SMEs or to portfolio of SMEs' loans held by financial institutions, which will then share the risks with the EIF.[36] The EIF operates on a commercial basis and sets prices to reflect risk. Price decisions will allow for an adequate remuneration of shareholders' capital. In practise, no individual operations on guarantees take place and the fund work only through financial intermediaries. As a general rule, the commitments of the Fund with respect to any other project may not exceed 50% of the cost.[37] An important advantage for the intermediaries is that the EIF is classified as a multilateral development bank, which permits a 20% weighting for transactions, covered by the EIF.[38]

As far as concrete actions are concerned, only a small part of EIFs guarantees activities are in favour of SMEs. In fact, most of them concern the transeuropean networks (TENs). After 2 years of activity, (in the first half of 1996), the EIF signed a contracts for 1,129 MECU related to 17 projects. Only 2 projects concerned the SME programme and amounted to 89 MECU or 7.82% of total guarantee activities. The first project, to the *Groupe Banque Populaire* of France, was the guarantee of an SME loan portfolio, to the value of 54.18 MECU with a maturity of 15 years and involving a 'last call' clause. (This means that indemnities can only be claimed for when the guaranteed party has exhausted its remedies against the principal debtor). The second operation related to guarantees on the private sector financing of loan funds in the UK, granted to the Merseyside Special Investment Fund. This was to a value of 13.71 MECU with a maturity of 10 years and involving a 'first call' clause. (This means that in case of default payment, direct appreal can be made to the party granting the guarantee.) This last operation was realised in collaboration with the European Regional Fund, a participant in the Merseyside Fund.

---

35 The European Investment Fund provides, besides its mainstream activities, equity capital for Venture capital funds.

36 EIF, rules of procedure, Luxembourg, 1996.

37 The 50/50 risk scheme proportion in some studies considered to be the worst solution. See f.e.Dovan & Levitsky, op. cit.

38 In conformity with article 6 of the directive 89/647/CEE. See also above mentioned problem linked to the mutual guarantee system and the Cooke rates.

Some specific EU-projects
Since the EIF works on a commercial basis, the fees it charges represent a potential barrier to SMEs. Therefore, some initiatives have been launched by the European institutions to offset the SMEs for their fees. These are the programmes, Growth and Environment, and *ELISE*. The first programme, Growth and Environment, aims at facilitating access for SMEs to loan producing environmental benefits. The EIF provides 50% residual loan guarantee and the EU-budget pays the EIF fees. Companies interested must contact participating institutions. So far, 22 institutions from 13 Member States have been pre-selected.[39] It is intended that through this programme, contracts be signed for an equivalent of 900 MECU, guaranteeing 1.8 billion ECU.

A second programme, initiated by the European Commission, was ELISE which stands for European Loan Insurance Scheme for Employment. The idea, was that the European Union would finance the EIF for guarantees accorded in favour of SMEs up to a total credit volume of 1 billion ECU. Only credits given to small enterprises linked to employment intensive investments would benefit from the free guarantee. The European parliament was fully in favour of the programme but it was not approved by the Council, who had to vote with unanimity, as it was claimed that the subsidiarity principle was not respected. An possible decision by the intergovernmental conference to decide enterprise-linked items with qualified majority might give new prospects.

Conclusions

To summarise, we need to keep in mind the co-existence of two main systems of guarantee schemes, either government-led or mutual guarantee systems. The latter, based on he subsidiarity principle, are especially active in France and Italy, where a total of 1.5 million small enterprises benefit from the system; but they are also to be found in other countries such as, Austria, Belgium, Germany, Hungary, Spain and Portugal. Pilot-projects have been launched in Greece and United Kingdom. An accurate legal translation of the subsidiarity principle and the increasing professionalism of the system make it a reliable instrument of SME's financing, profitable for every party involved. Bankers can rest on their laurels, backed by a stable guarantee society, allowing SMEs to obtain loans more easily at a reasonable price and avoiding a burden on the taxpayer. Except for this last element, we obtain the same advantage from public guarantee schemes, which we find essentially in Finland, Greece, Ireland, the Netherlands and United Kingdom. But also in Belgium and France, both countries with a huge experience in mutual guarantee systems.

Nevertheless, credit guarantee schemes have been subject to criticism. In the first place this has come from bankers, who are driven under the schemes to finance projects which would be rejected by a credit scoring analysis. And as all bankers are aware, granting credits on the grounds of good guarantees is, in the long run,

[39] of which 2 AECM members from France and Germany.

bad policy.[40] Secondly, economists do not generally like guarantee schemes because good projects should be self-supporting. If a project satisfies this criterion, it needs no guarantee. Thus, the argument goes, through the provision of guarantees only weak projects are financed. Of course, empirical analyses need to be conducted to determine the validity of this position. In the meantime, if economists can convince bankers that a good project needs little guaranteeing, and if bankers can convince economists that many *ex ante* weak projects became profitable ones, the leverage effect of the loan guarantee schemes will increase and become more efficient. Isn't Plato's ideal world one where bankers, economists, SMEs and co-operations work together, and only make an appeal to tax-payers and public money when the market co-operative solution is inadequate?

Indeed, government should not compete with private systems in the same field. Such competition, with disparate strengths on the two sides, will rule out a market-driven system as demonstrated in France. Government action can, however, be complementary to the market-oriented-system by re-guaranteeing risks initially guaranteed by the mutual funds, as is well-illustrated in Germany. Only when the mutual system does not exist should the government generate a substitute. In that case, where the public system is well functioning, no mutual system will ever see the light of day.[41] Perhaps, therefore, it is preferable for government to offer incentives to set up mutual systems.

EU governments are aware of the importance of SMEs in the European economy, and of the need to facilitate access to credits, as shown by the ratification of the 3rd Multiannual Programme.[42] A Swedish commentator has (and others) have recently pointed out that there are two broad categories of SMEs. Those that have no wish to grow, and those willing and able to expand either domestically or internationally.[43] The latter contribute considerably to the increase of the welfare in Europe, which already depends on SMEs for almost 50% of its value measured as GDP. In light of the above remarks, I believe the EU should outline its policy of subsidiarity and pursue financing initiatives in order to stimulate the co-ordination between mutual systems (e.g. by financing AECM), and should foster the exchange of best practice. Furthermore, it should pursue the launching of feasibility studies in countries considering the setting up of systems (as exemplified by its support for Finland and the UK) and stimulate financing possibilities via the use of Structural Funds.

As regards its direct granting of guarantees, it is doubtful whether the European Investment Fund concentrates its actions where the market fails. Driven by a cost-effectiveness approach, it guarantees AAA funds, which could normally

---

40 This argument is known as the negative selection argument.

41 As is the case for the Netherlands, see rapport of second Round Table of Bankers and SMEs, European Commission, 1997.

42 The third multi-annual program for SME's was adopted by the Council at 9 December 1996, and approves the European SME program for the period 1997-2000 with a budget of 127 MECU.

43 Transnational development of SMEs and the role of the bank, S. Delis, perspective, n°19, op.cit.

have no problems to pass through the open market. One assess, guided by a cost-benefit analysis if the role of the EIF should not be reoriented towards backing (associations of) mutual guarantee funds. This could happen in full respect of the subsidiarity principal and complementary to national or regional policies on the matter. On the eve of the introduction of the EURO this would allow loan guarantee systems to benefit from the single market and stimulate the European activities of the system, which for the moment are all active in their own countries, regions, or even localities. Regarding guarantees, a real use of the European market schemes has still a long way to go.

5.4 Government guarantee schemes in Europe: Who has them? Who pays? Who gains?

by Robert Cressy
Professor, Warwick Business School

The paper reviews the theory and practice of government loan guarantee schemes (LGS) in Europe, using the UK experience to provide indications of the likely effectiveness of the schemes. It concludes that there is little evidence to date to justify their continued expansion on the grounds of credit market deficiencies, or job creation. On the contrary, such schemes seem to be an expensive way of subsidising the banks to take on uneconomic lending.

What is a loan guarantee scheme?

A loan guarantee scheme or LGS is a financial instrument for sharing the risk of lending to small businesses between the borrowing firm, the bank and the government. It is effectively an insurance policy on a loan with the insurer the government, the amount insured a proportion of the loan, and the insurance premium paid by the firm. The most important requirement for eligibility is that the firm has no collateral for the loan.[44] The conditions under which this insurance contract is agreed vary, but usually there are at least four components.

1. *The loan amount.* This is the amount that the lender (the guarantee bank) will lend to the firm. There is usually an upper limit placed on the size of the loan to ensure that it only attracts smaller firms. The term of the loan varies (in the UK between 1 and 7 years) as also does the margin paid to the bank over its cost of funds.
2. *The guarantee percentage.* This is the proportion of the loan that the government agrees to pay to the bank in the event of the firm's default. In some

[44] In the case of existing firms this requirement is often that a *proportion* of the loan is uncollateralised in the absence of the scheme. It is this proportion that is then eligible for LGS lending.

countries this is as low as 50% (e.g. France) and in others as high as 100% (e.g. in the US). In the UK the figure is currently 70% for existing firms and 85% for new firms.

3. *The premium.* The premium is the insurance premium on the loan guarantee, usually expressed as a percentage of the loan. This varies considerably between countries.

4. *The target group.* This is usually small firms defined according to some suitable criterion, usually including smaller start-ups, smaller existing firms and often including a maximum age. Sometimes economically depressed regions of an economy are targeted or a particular type of activity, such as exporting.

Why do we have them?

Loan administration costs

There are fixed costs associated with lending that imply the unit cost to the lender declines with loan size. Since these costs must be covered to break even, the bank cannot charge less than the unit admin. cost, and if there is to be a profit the loan margin must be larger than that charged to larger businesses for this reason alone. The LGS guarantee increases the expected return (margin) from such lending so allowing the bank to make a higher expected. profit. From the firm's perspective, this reduces the chances of rationing (loan refusal)[45] from this source.

Project risks

In addition to higher loan costs SMEs are more failure-prone. This means that if the bank prices in risk into the loan contract, the margin paid by smaller firms will be larger than that paid by large firms. However, smaller firms' risk proneness *is itself influenced* by the margin charged: a higher margin will eventually make failure certain, producing a self-fulfilling prophecy (Cressy and Cowling, 1994;1996)! The role of the LGS scheme is to reduce the risk of smaller borrowers to the bank, and so induce more lending.

Lack of collateral for lending

The problem faced by most small firms is that they are young and in the service sector. This means they have, especially at start-up, few collateralisable assets, and being often young enterprises, little track record. Lack of collateral would not matter if lenders were able to assess accurately borrowers' net present value. However, most banks feel that they cannot do so. Their lending decisions, whilst incorporating information on the human capital of the entrepreneur(s) (Cressy,

---

[45] Rationing' in the economics literature refers to a situation where there is *market failure*. Typically, the market is assumed to suffer from informational asymmetries. The bank is assumed (debatably) to be less informed about the viability of the business than the business itself. This combined with certain assumptions about the risk and return of the firms' projects results in a situation where the bank will not raise the interest rate iini the face of excess demand for funds. Under these circumstances, society could be made better off if financial resources were reallocated by government intervention, e.g. fiscal regulation of the credit markets.

1996a,b), rely substantially on fixed assets, or collateral. If these are not available, loans may be refused. LGS allows lending to firms without collateral by increasing the lenders expected profits from such loans though the agreement to pay a percentage of the loan under default.

"Banks don't understand us"
A charge often laid against banks is that they have a hands off approach to SMEs. This means, it is claimed, that they do not understand their businesses (especially if they are hi-tech) and do not have the ability to assess their Net Present Value (the discounted sum of future profits from the business). LGS lending in the UK was introduced partly with the idea of increasing the banks' confidence in lending to smaller business, by increasing their familiarity with the sector as a whole. Recent UK research (Binks and Ennew, 1996) has indicated that firms with a 'relationship' to the bank has better lending terms offered them. US evidence (Peterson and Rajan, 1994) suggests that greater availability of credit is the main advantage of an enduring relationship.

Information-based credit rationing
As a result of collateral based lending, asymmetric information (the firm is claimed to know more about it's success chances than the bank on this theory), banks will not expand lending to equate demand and supply for fear of worsening the quality of their loan books. Smaller firms have no power to influence this decision.

Guaranteeing jobs?
'Them entrepreneurial votes'. Governments, starting with the UK's Mrs. Thatcher in 1979, have found that subsidising the SME sector has certain political advantages: small business owners are conservative in their political aspirations, and thus conservative governments have reasons to treat them well, encouraging growth in their numbers. The expansion of the small business sector also has appeal to governments desirous of reducing unemployment levels in their own countries if it is judged that such expansion has little 'crowding out' effects.[46]

How often, how much and where?[47]

A statistical summary of guaranteed lending in the Europe 19 (E-19) countries (see Cressy, 1996c) indicates that LGS schemes exist in about half of E-19 countries, mainly concentrated in the Northern states of the Union. In 1994 some 50,000 loans were made by the 10 member states operating LGS, with numbers increasing at around 8% across the board. These loans had a total value of some 6.6 billion (thousand million) ECUs, again increasing at around 25% per annum. This is partly due to the secular increase in the average loan size offered by the

---

[46] Crowding out occurs if for example, the extra jobs generated by the new small firms (or expanding existing small firms) simply displace those of pre-existing firms, e.g. by driving them out of business.

[47] Observatory 2 dealt with certain aspects of guaranteed lending and the reader is referred to that document for additional material.

schemes. Typical loan size in 1994 was 130 000 ECUs, an amount that has increased in nominal terms at about 10% per annum over the last three years - a figure above the rate of inflation. This real increase may reflect the move by national governments away from subsidising start-ups and towards helping larger, established enterprises – following the experiences of the last recession that saw large numbers of the smallest firms going bust. There is also considerable variation in the loan size across member states with France, Finland, and Norway offering significantly larger loans (average ECU 200-300 thousand) than the whole the sample (average 130 thousand).

The fraction guaranteed varied considerably between 30% and 82.5% of the loan with a premium of less than 2.5%. There are significant differences in sectoral coverage of the schemes and in the maximum length and amount of loan. In some countries the maximum loan guaranteed has increased in recent years with seemingly dramatic effect.[48] Default rates also varied considerably across countries, with rather high figures recorded in the UK (about one quarter of the loans issued per annum).

Supply, demand and the target group

Crucial to understanding the role of LGS schemes is information on the supply of and demand for loans by the relevant target groups. There is little reliable data here but a crude analysis of the relationship between supply and demand for loan guarantees for seven European countries indicates the following. The assumptions underlying the calculations are: a) the target group for LGS is start-up businesses; and b) all businesses in that group that meet the criteria are offered loans.[49] This then enables us to represent the proportion of total start-ups that receive LGS loans by the ratio of actual LGS lending to the country's birth rate.[50] Typically, the proportion of the target population demand covered by LGS loans turns out to be less than 5% of that population. The total number of loans to SMEs from all sources in a given year is many times larger than this. For example, in the UK in the first quarter of 1993 no less than 2,767 SME loans were made to SMEs by NatWest alone. For a crude estimate, annualising the NatWest figure, and taking published figures for the market share of NatWest in the UK small business sector of 30%, this implies 1993 LGS lending numbers as

---

48 In the UK a rise in the ceiling from ECU 127k to ECU 212k has resulted in a 50% increase in loan take-up and a 100% increase in total value in the last three years This suggests that if a debt gap exists in the UK it may be at a higher level than previously anticipated. However, in the UK it also reflects the reduction in the insurance premium from 1.5% to 0.5% of the value of the loan. It should be mentioned that the changes in the UK scheme refer to lending to existing enterprises rather than new enterprises.

49 This needless to say is not entirely accurate, since some LGS will target existing businesses as well as start-ups. Indeed, whilst originally much lower, in the UK existing businesses constitute currently constitute about half the total demand. By making this assumption we get the *maximum* percentage of the target groups covered, and hence the *maximum* impact of the schemes.

50 Strictly we should be comparing the *stock* of businesses demanding loans to the outstanding stock of loans in the same period. The data for this comparison are unfortunately unavailable. Instead we are comparing the flow of loans to the flow of new firms who would be potential users.

a proportion of total SME loans are 0.064% or less than one tenth of one per cent of total SME lending numbers.

It is thus a tiny fraction of total lending to SMEs. But 'Nothing is either good or bad, but thinking makes it so': If the target group figures represent an upper bound to the magnitude of the debt gap it is small beer indeed, and something that governments should lose little sleep over.[51] However, it is still important to evaluate the return on this social investment. Also, within that group of borrowers are some important hi-tech businesses. It is known that these are big job generators (in proportion to their size) and their success has potentially big knock-on effects in terms of technological diffusion.

Do they work?

Despite their widespread use, little attempt has been made to evaluate the contribution LGS in Europe. However, a number of studies from the UK have indicated that the LGS schemes are of limited usefulness and their achievement of there stated objectives generally questionable. The criteria of evaluation are several.

Do they plug the debt gap?
We need first to impugn the presupposition of the question, namely, the proposition asserting the general existence of debt gaps. Several studies indicate that there is little evidence of *general* debt gaps in the UK. If they exist at all they may have a macro economic component (i.e. they are more likely in recessions), and may be confined to particular sectors of the economy (e.g. hi-tech businesses). From some of these studies, the main problems facing small firms in the early years is the *level of demand* in the economy, together with adequate human capital resources and government policy that affects macro-economic conditions is therefore critical to survival (Cressy, 1996b).[52] There is limited evidence of debt rationing in the UK fast growth sector, but little evidence for the hi-tech sector.[53] Thus the premise of the UK scheme is questionable. In some other European countries, for example Germany, evidence is available for the existence of debt gaps and these seem to be worse for smaller firms(Egeln-Hornle and Licht and Steil 1997; and Audretsch and Elton, 1997). In the United States, the empirical evidence is again mixed, with some authorities (e.g. Berger and Udell, 1991) indicating that there is little evidence of general rationing, whilst others (e.g. Hall, 1992) claiming the opposite.

---

[51] Another way of looking at the statistics is of course as showing the *virtues* of the financial system: if the debt-gap problem is *this* small, we have little to worry about, even if the LGS schemes do not contribute to solving the problem.

[52] The growing leverage of the 1980s in the UK, in particular in the small firm sector, led inevitably to the bankruptcies of the early 1990s. SMEs were the main casualties.

[53] This partly reflects the activity of certain UK banks, most notably NatWest and Barclays, in developing innovative financial instruments that combine debt and equity in ways that address market needs of Hi-Tec firms.

Economic Additionality?
To be valid as a policy instrument LGS must be able to add to economic output by offering funds that would not otherwise have been made available, rather than substitute for privately provided funds. Studies indicate, however, that this may not be the case. If debt gaps do not in fact exist this is not in the least surprising. However, some top bankers in Europe argued that borrowers on LGS were in fact *more* risky than they would lend to without LGS. This may mean that the projects financed would not be viable on normal criteria (the level of return would *not* compensate for the risk involved even if full collateral were provided).[54] The result is that the provision of public funds is actually causing a resource misallocation, as funds are being diverted from other uses artificially.

A move away from start-up loans in UK
Since its inception in 1981, when the proportion of loans to start-ups was 55% (still only about a half of LGS lending) the proportion to this group has steadily fallen, currently standing at less than 30%. In principle, such a move may be considered legitimate, since there is reason to believe that if debt rationing exists it will also be a problem for *existing younger* firms, especially in the service sector (Cressy and Olofsson, 1997). However, other European and US evidence (Egeln-Hornle, Licht and Steil, 1997) suggests that debt gaps are a *declining* function of size. Thus smaller firms (in particular *start-ups*) are *more* likely to experience debt gaps than larger. Thus the government, or the banks, is shying away from the more risky businesses in the earlier stages of their lifetimes, towards the firms with lower risk through developed track records. In fact, we believe that the change in the composition of UK LGS lending is primarily at the instigation of the banks (Cressy and Cowling, 1997).

The score: 1. Higher default rates.
Evidence from a survey of European bankers (Cressy, 1996c) and UK econometric research (Cressy and Cowling, 1994) suggests that LGS loans are in general more risky than comparable small business loans not made under the schemes. In the UK the relative riskiness (13% p.a. vs. 8%).is in the ratio of 1.5:1. If this risk could be justified by the returns made by the firms, we should not regard this as a matter of concern. Can LGS loans demonstrate higher returns to equity investors?

The score: 2. Bandwagon effects
A feature of LGS lending identified in recent UK research is the bandwagon effect. The observation is that LGS numbers are positively correlated with failure. The explanation for this seems to be the following. The bank allocates a fixed sum of money per period to LGS lending in its loan portfolio. Borrowers arrive in fixed pools per period and their quality evaluated (quality assumed in this theory to be observable[55]). The 'queue' is then offered funds in order of quality with the best-

[54] Full collateral does not mean in general that the bank loses no money in the event of default.

[55] There are detailed reasons for questioning the usual asymmetric information theory advanced in the literature, as recent empirical studies of UK term loan data have shown.

offered funds first. The last borrower in any period is then the *lowest* quality, and if the bank's budget is expanded, the quality of borrowers will be *lowered*, *raising* the aggregate default rate. This account of the phenomenon implies a kind of rationing but not of the asymmetric information variety.

The score:3. Bank-driven lending: papering over the cracks

As alluded to earlier, there is reason, in addition to the bandwagon effect just discussed, for believing that the numbers on the LGS scheme in the UK are determined by bank policy rather than variation in demand from the small business community. A recent UK contribution shows that the numbers on the LGS scheme in the UK are highly sensitive to two things: a) macro events measured by GDP, and b) the loan guarantees percentage set by the government. By comparison, they are highly *in*sensitive to the LGS premium and the bank's cost of capital.

This suggests, two things. Firstly, as argued in Cressy and Cowling(1997), the role of demand in the economy is *negatively* related to lending under the scheme, so that as the economy moves into recession lending under LGS *increases*. This cannot plausibly be firm-driven, since a fall in demand would from the firm's perspective be a reason for cutting back fixed investment.[56] Thus it simply evidence of the banks using the system to protect their dubious decisions of the preceding boom and their new (more risky) decisions in the recession.

Secondly, LGS numbers are positively correlated with the guarantee percentage. Since they would be at most negatively correlated with the guarantee if this were a firm-driven phenomenon, the relationship again indicates that it is the expansion of loan supply by the banks that determines the variation in LGS numbers in response to guarantee changes. Thus, this avenue leads to the same conclusion: the motion of the system is bank-driven, but this time it is because the banks find that they can now take on more loans for the same risk exposure (expected loss).

Little additionality

Both NERA(1990) and Aston(1991) indicate that there is some degree of crowding out implicit in bank lending. NERA show that the effects on employment are also negligible. Cressy (1996a,b) produces results that implicitly support this proposition also, though from a different angle.

Debt-rationing: myth or reality?

The *prima facie* case for credit rationing made in the theoretical finance literature has found both proponents and opponents in the subsequent empirical literature. But the empirical work in the area suffers from the same problems. This partly reflects the criteria for rationing employed, which differ between studies; but it also reflects different variables defined in the datasets, different methodologies

---

[56] It might be associated with borrowing to cover liquidity crises. However this would typically be associated with increased overdraft borrowing rather than term lending, which is the purpose of LGS money.

and indeed different ideologies. A representative study finding for credit rationing is Evans and Jovanovic(1989), Hall(1992); Egeln, Licht and Steil (1997). Representative studies finding against this thesis are Berger and Udell(1992), Cressy(1996a,b), Hughes(1997).

"On yer bike": the ***cyclical*** *phenomenon of rationing*
A recent UK study of start-up businesses and their banks found that the collateral requirements of small firms for one UK bank were significantly different in a boom from a recession. The bank was more likely to waive collateral if demand was high. Thus the 'fixed' admin. costs of the loan were effectively not independent of macro conditions, but *instead moved procyclically*. This means that in a boom in particular, the argument for rationing is weakened still further by the well known profit -motive of rational (rather than rationing) bank behaviour.[57]

The real issues: Identification criteria

One of the main problems in evaluating the existence of rationing or otherwise is the variety of theoretical criteria, statistical methodology and datasets used by researchers. These differences include (a) Theoretical criteria (switching Self-employment to Wage employment; stickiness in loan rates; ratio of commitments to total lending; windfall gains and start-ups).(b) Methodology (static vs. dynamic; questionnaire vs. econometric techniques; the range of variables controlled for in the models). (c) Datasets (time periods, coverage, variables included, panel datasets vs. cross section vs. time series). All this, of course, calls for more research, a topic in which I have no personal interest! But more seriously, given the not insignificant volume of funds being disbursed in this direction, a pan European programme of research should be inaugurated to evaluate the effects of such schemes: the argument from fortress Europe is not a solution in the long run to the forces of competition. If we are to compete, there is little point in diverting public funds to this end if there are better uses elsewhere.

Making headway

Very briefly, we feel the following are useful steps forward.

Firstly, there is a need for more informed financial micro policies. To achieve this requires more research evaluations – these are cheap and insightful – and these should be done by independent researchers; there is very little point in asking the baker to evaluate his own bread. Secondly, to make these findings effective, we need as a follow-up a commitment by governments to implement findings. Thirdly, an attempt to raise the general quality of European small businesses is needed. This will reduce default rates generally and under existing LGS in particular, and thereby reduce the burden on the taxpayer. This means, for example, stricter entry qualifications to trades (cf. Germany) and possibly the

[57] It may be said that the argument for rationing in a recession is by the same token also strengthened.

equivalent of the UK's Financial Management Certificate linking owner-manager training and interest margins of the banks – but again the effectiveness of this instrument needs evaluation. Fourthly, critical environmental support is required through greater policy co-ordination, both in the micro and macro domains, and at the national and international levels, to ensure that what is implemented in the micro domain (LGS) is not contradicted in the macro domain (e.g. by expansionist monetary policy and the consequent high debt-equity ratios). This leads on to the fifth and final point, that we need an emphasis on the creation of macro stability. We must not forget that small businesses are the flotsam and jetsam on the tide of GDP.

INSOLVENCY RISKS AND THE ROLE OF INSOLVENCY LAW

6.1 Introduction

by Theodore Eisenberg
Henry Allen Mark Professor of Law, Cornell Law School

Insolvency law plays a prominent role in the area of commercial risk and risk management. All commercial contracts must be drafted against the background of insolvency law. And all lenders, at the time of evaluating and extending credit, must consider the bankruptcy implications of their loan decisions. The efficacy of a lender's decisions is tested only when a borrower is in financial distress and bankruptcy is one of the likely outcomes. So study of insolvency laws and their operation must accompany studies of commercial risk and risk management.

The Seminar provided a unique opportunity for international bankruptcy scholars to report their findings and to interact. The opportunity was not wasted. The papers summarised in this Chapter represent state-of-the-art research on how insolvency laws operate. The papers illustrate the need for a multidisciplinary approach to risk research in business life. They draw on expertise from the fields of banking, law, economics, accounting, corporate finance, and statistics. Thanks to the opportunity provided by the Seminar, we are much closer to reaching a consensus on several important questions of insolvency policy and bankruptcy research methodology.

Together, the papers in this Chapter cover three separable stages of transactions relating to insolvency laws: the first stage cover the pre-insolvency behaviour of banks and their customers that contributes to some firms becoming candidates for bankruptcy. The second stage cover the factors that lead some firms to file for bankruptcy while others do not, and the third stage cover the insolvency system's treatment of firms that do file for bankruptcy. Barry Howcroft addresses the pre-insolvency behaviour of banks and their customers. Clas Bergström et al. study the forces that lead some firms to file for bankruptcy, and Timothy Fisher and Jocelyn Martel, Stefan Sundgren, B. Espen Eckbo, and Karin Thorburn study how insolvency systems work for those firms that use it.

The papers operate at both the policy and methodological levels. The papers by Fisher and Martel, Sundgren, Eckbo and Thorburn, and Thorburn, while employing excellent methodology, have clear policy implications. The paper by Bergström et al. is more purely methodologically oriented. The keynote speech given by Howcroft provides important insights into how the risk of business failure influences pre-insolvency behaviour and the lessons to be learned from sacrificing quality for quantity in lending decisionmaking.

In sum, the Seminar enabled a diverse group of academic insolvency experts to meet and exchange research results. This cross-fertilisation has helped move analysts towards a consensus of how this important branch of societal risk management actually functions. At the end of this chapter, Bo Green, this book's editor, reflects on the need for a comprehensive inquiry into how the bankruptcy system as a whole functions. In the next chapter, he considers banks' role in the financial system in a paper discussing the environment for a new Swedish reorganisation law.

Measuring the performance of insolvency laws

One important insolvency policy question is whether insolvency laws perform well. The most general test of an insolvency law's performance is whether it increases net social welfare. There are empirical claims, for example, that U.S. Chapter 11 reorganisations decrease social welfare (Bradley & Rosenzwieg 1992). But to date these claims appear to be empirically flawed (e.g., Bhandari & Weiss 1993, Eisenberg 1993). Assessing a net social welfare effect of a law like Chapter 11 is difficult because one would like to conduct a controlled experiment in which two societies exist, equivalent in every way, except that one has an insolvency law and the other does not. Such a controlled experiment is unlikely to be available in the real world. Second best methods of evaluating insolvency laws will have to suffice.

The papers by Sundgren and Fisher and Martel each address the performance of reorganisation laws. The countries studied, Finland and Canada, respectively, have important historical, economic, cultural, and regulatory differences. Yet both papers find evidence that reorganisation laws function well in one important respect. Fisher and Martel conclude that Canadian creditors receive more in reorganisation than they would in liquidation. Sundgren finds that Finnish creditors receive more in reorganisation than from sales of businesses as going concerns in liquidating bankruptcies. To these results one may add the prior findings of Eisenberg and Tagashira (1994) that Japanese creditors receive more in composition than they would in liquidation. Studies on three continents thus all conclude that, in one important respect, insolvency reorganisation laws serve the useful function of preserving a firm's going concern surplus and allocating some of it to creditors. Because all estimates of liquidation value are subject to error, as the paper by Eckbo and Thorburn notes, caution is necessary before concluding that creditors in fact receive more in reorganisation.

These findings do not suggest that occasional large reorganisation proceedings cannot go badly awry. Weiss and Wruck (1998) have shown the questionable handling of the Eastern Airlines case in the U.S. But if one is evaluating an insolvency system across many cases, rather than evaluating the system's performance in an individual case, the three studies finding preservation of a going concern surplus suggest that reorganisation laws systematically achieve beneficial results.

Papers by Eckbo and Thorburn and Thorburn have different implications. Eckbo and Thorburn provide a useful overview of the question whether mandatory auctions are superior to reorganisations and a brief review of the literature. Relying primarily on the findings in Thorburn's paper, they conclude that auctions, at least as conducted in Sweden, represent an economically efficient mechanism for reconstructing bankrupt firms that may be superior to the U.S.'s Chapter 11. Thorburn's analysis of Swedish firms suggests that returns to creditors be enhanced by mandatory auctions of troubled firms. This suggests that reorganisation laws should be curtailed in favour of mandatory auctions. These Swedish results are at least partially in conflict with the results presented in Sundgren's paper. He also studied how bankruptcy cases were resolved and found that creditors receive a better payoff in a reorganisation than in a going concern sale in liquidating bankruptcy.

Two methodological points are worth noting with respect to Thorburn's findings. First, all three studies confirming preservation of a going concern surplus by reorganisation laws cover legal regimes in which both reorganisation and liquidation are possibilities. Thorburn's data are from Sweden, where reorganisation possibilities are severely limited compared to Canada, Finland, and Japan. Swedish law contains powerful deterrents against using reorganisation. These deterrents include high minimum amounts that must be paid to creditors in a reorganisation compared to what must be paid to creditors in a liquidating bankruptcy, inability to effectively deal with secured creditors in a reorganisation, and the Swedish Wage Guarantee Act's powerful incentive to use bankruptcy instead of reorganisation (Eisenberg 1995). So the superiority of mandatory auctions over reorganisations must be inferred not from a comparison with Swedish reorganisations, but rather from a comparison with U.S. reorganisations under Chapter 11.

This reliance on U.S. data leads to the second methodological point. The data available on the mass of U.S. Chapter 11 cases is probably inferior to the data available on reorganisations in Canada, Finland, and Japan. There are excellent studies of large, public U.S. Chapter 11 cases. These Chapter 11 cases are not directly comparable with Thorburn's Swedish firms because the public U.S. firms are so much larger than the Swedish firms are. And firm size is known to profoundly influence Chapter 11 outcomes (Eisenberg 1995). Aggregate data covering all U.S. Chapter 11 cases are dominated by the mass of small, unsuccessful Chapter 11 cases that U.S. law attracts. But these data also are not directly comparable with Thorburn's Swedish firms because the data are dominated by firms smaller than Thorburn's. Poor results in many U.S. Chapter

11 cases may not reflect poor results in firms that are close in size to Thorburn's. Recent findings by Maksimovic and Phillips (1998) suggest that Chapter 11 impose little in the way of indirect bankruptcy costs. Chapter 11 bankruptcy status is relatively less important than industry and plant-level productivity in assessing firm performance. Their study, which includes firms not in Chapter 11, suggests the need to be cautious in relying on Hotchkiss' (1995) finding of significant below-industry performance following Chapter 11 proceedings. In addition, Pulvino (1998) provides evidence that financially constrained airline sell their aircraft at lower prices than their unconstrained rivals do. He states that his findings "suggest that immediate cash liquidation of insolvent firms may result in socially inefficient outcomes" (p.973). The bottom line is that we still just do not know enough about the performance of U.S. Chapter 11 for the bulk of salvageable firms that use it.

When U.S. firms are comparable to foreign firms in size and industry, there is little evidence that U.S. Chapter 11 performs poorly compared to foreign reorganisation laws. In the one such empirical study, which compared Finnish and U.S. firms, U.S. unsecured creditors were shown to enjoy better results than unsecured Finnish creditors (Eisenberg & Sundgren 1997). And the favourable treatment of U.S. creditors survived comparison with several other countries as well. This suggests caution in concluding that mandatory auctions are superior to reorganisations based on a comparison of unmatched Swedish and U.S. firms.

If U.S. Chapter 11 firms in fact subsequently perform more poorly than Swedish firms subjected to auctions, it may indicate that, contrary to popular belief, Chapter 11 extracts too high a price from debtors in favour of creditors. This is consistent with the existence of the absolute priority rule (whereby all creditors must be paid in full before junior interests may participate in the reorganised firm) in the U.S. but not in some other countries. While it is widely recognised that the absolute priority rule is often breached, all studies suggest that violations are small (Eisenberg 1993). Thus, the absolute priority rule may well be routing going concern surpluses away from debtors and towards creditors.

The methodology of bankruptcy prediction

Turning to methodological issues bearing on bankruptcy prediction, studies of insolvency have always relied on sampling. The practical reality that imposes the need to sample raises a methodological point emphasised in the paper by Bergström et al. The fullness of their sample of Swedish firms allows them to test the effect of sample size on bankruptcy prediction statistical analyses. Bergström et al. shows that sample size can influence both the coefficients in a regression model and the model's predictive behaviour. The predictive inaccuracy of unweighted samples in which one group is disproportionately represented is well known (Maddala 1983:90), even in studies in which samples are matched. Their results also suggest the importance of precisely matching two samples in two-sample studies, such as those involving active and bankrupt firms. For their results show that even the behaviour of regression coefficients, and not just predictions, can be affected by sample size where unmatched random sampling is used.

Pre-insolvency lending practices

Barry Howcroft's paper focuses attention on the pre-insolvency lending practices that profoundly affect the nature and rate of subsequent insolvencies. His paper reminds us that the insolvency process studied in detail in the other papers comes in to play only when lending criteria and practices have not led to the desired results. The effects of the U.K. economic recession led him to assess the lessons that might be learned from pre-recession lending practices that contributed to subsequent high insolvency rates. He finds evidence of changing practices and attitudes among banks and their customers. Banks engage in more determined quality control than before and seek greater uniformity in the credit granting process. He also finds a greater willingness of banks to attempt to rescue businesses rather than to place them in liquidation.

6.2 Does a reorganisation law improve the efficiency of the insolvency law? The Finnish experience

by Stefan Sundgren
Professor, Swedish School of Economics and Business Administration

Several countries such as Germany, France, Britain and Finland have adopted reorganisation directed insolvency codes during the last twenty years. Chapter 11, the U.S. procedure for rehabilitating firms, has served as a model in many of the countries with its purpose of maintaining companies as operating units instead of liquidating them. Among lawmakers, there seems to be a belief that effective insolvency procedures are characterised by reorganisation provisions.

Simultaneously, however, the fundamentals of reorganisations have come under extensive attack. Critics claim that reorganisations save firms that ought to be shut down and that the direct costs of often-lengthy proceedings are high. Baird (1986), Jackson (1986), and more recently, Bradley & Rosenzweig (1992), argue that market based insolvency procedures are more efficient, and that financially distressed firms should be 'auctioned' in the open market instead of reorganised. The idea behind this is that auctions allocate assets to the highest value user for a price equal to the second highest fundamental valuation. If the first and the second highest valuation are reasonably close, then the auction price will be close to the value of the assets in their best use. Can one trust the markets? Sales of assets can involve significant costs, if assets are traded in a thin market. Assets can be sold below their 'fundamental' values, leaving creditors with a smaller payoff than what they could receive in a reorganisation of the firm. (e.g., Aghion,

Hart & Moore 1992). Schleifer & Vishny (1992) predict that prices received are particularly low during periods of time when an industry or the whole economy suffers from financial distress. Strömberg's (1997) empirical results provide support for the prediction.

As a consequence, studies suggest there is a net gain to creditors in reorganisations. Eisenberg & Tagashira (1994) compare the estimated proceeds to creditors in liquidation with the discounted value of promised payments to creditors in reorganisations for a sample of small and mid-sized Japanese firms. It was found that creditors on average receive more in a reorganisation than in an immediate liquidation, although only 34% of the reorganisations would be successful. That is, the debtor pays the creditors according to the terms in the reorganisation plan. Alderzon & Betker (1995) studied a sample of public U.S. firms that reorganised under the provisions of Chapter 11, and also found that creditors on average were paid more in a reorganisation than what they would have been paid in an immediate liquidation.

This paper presents Finnish empirical evidence on the issue whether creditors enjoy a net gain in reorganisations. Furthermore, it studies whether the administrative costs of the proceedings differ. The study is based on a sample of 362 firms that filed for reorganisation during the first year after the effective date of the Finnish reorganisation law, i.e., February 1993 to February 1994. For comparative purposes, the study also reports on a sample of 83 firms that filed a liquidation bankruptcy petition prior to the implementation of the reorganisation law. Before the reorganisation law, liquidation bankruptcy was the single route in practice for financially distressed firms in Finland. Although the law had originally been designed for piecemeal liquidations, going concern sales had become increasingly common. Many firms that reorganise under the new code probably would have been sold as going concerns to a party that continued the operations under the old code.

The study is focused on small firms: the median assets are only about FIM 3 million (ECU 0,5 million). Studies of small and medium-sized enterprises (SMEs) are important for several reasons: although the vast majority of all insolvent firms are small, most empirical studies on bankruptcy are focused on large, publicly owned firms.

The organisation of the paper is as follows: section 1 gives an introduction to the Finnish insolvency laws. Section 2 presents the data. Sections 3 and 4 include the main findings of the paper: section 3 provides an analysis of payoffs to creditors in reorganisation and liquidation. Section 4 investigates the direct, or administrative, costs of reorganisations and going concern sales, and section 5 of the paper provides a conclusion.

Finnish insolvency laws

Understanding the empirical results requires an introduction to Finnish insolvency law. The Finnish insolvency procedures underwent a major transformation in 1993, when the new reorganisation law was adopted. Prior to 1993 liquidation bankruptcy was the single route used in practice. Although the liquidation bankruptcy code originally had been designed for liquidations, going concern sales had become increasingly common. Under current laws, an insolvent firm can either file for liquidation bankruptcy or for reorganisation. Reorganisations under the revised laws have probably changed practices for failing firms. In essence, many firms that were sold as going concerns under the old code are probably reorganised under the new code.

Reorganisation proceedings can be grouped into three basic phases: a) initiation and screening of cases for eligibility; b) the preparation of a reorganisation plan; and c) voting and confirmation of a plan. A reorganisation can be initiated both by the debtor and creditors. In practice, however, the debtor mostly files the petition. For the firms in the sample in this study, creditors filed the petition in only 5% (17/362) of cases, and the debtors in the remaining ones. In many cases, a reorganisation petition was filed by the debtor in response to a liquidation bankruptcy filing by a creditor. About 17% of the cases that eventually emerged with a confirmed reorganisation plan, and 35% of the dismissed cases had a liquidation bankruptcy filing pending when they filed for reorganisation. That debtors file for reorganisation in order to avoid a liquidation is not surprising, since a reorganisation is a much better outcome for managers and owners than a liquidation. Debtors have the incentive to try to initiate a reorganisation, even though the firm has only a remote chance of survival.

Thus, mechanisms to filter firms eligible for a reorganisation from those not eligible are necessary. The Finnish reorganisation law screens cases rather tightly. Shortly after the filing, the court must send a notice to the major creditors of the debtor. If any of the creditors opposes a reorganisation, the court makes a determination of the eligibility of the case. Reorganisation proceedings continue only if the court finds that the case does not meet any of the ineligibility criteria listed in the code (see Finnish Reorganisation Law, hereinafter FinRL, § 7). Key ineligibility criteria are that: a) it is likely that the insolvency cannot be avoided by a reorganisation plan; b) it is likely that the debtor will be unable to pay debts arising after the initiation of the reorganisation; and c) it is likely that the debtor's assets do not suffice for the administrative expenses of the case.

Let us consider next the preparation of the reorganisation plan. As in France and the UK an outside official, here called an administrator, has the main responsibility for the construction of the plan. Competing reorganisation plans can be prepared by secured creditors, unsecured creditors, or share-holders, each holding at least 20% of the debt- or equity-claims in the corresponding class. The debtor's management can also construct a plan (Fin RL § 40). The reorganisation plan should include terms of the debt restructuring as well as the restructuring of the operations (FinRL § 42). Moreover, estimates of what creditors would receive in liquidation should accompany the plan (FinRL §§ 41, 42).

Reorganisation plans can be approved in two ways. A plan can be confirmed if all classes of creditors accept the plan. A class is deemed to have accepted the plan if more than half in the amount and number of the creditors have voted in favour of the plan (FinRL § 52). Even the needed majorities have been attained, the court must confirm the plan only if certain conditions are met (FinRL § 53). A plan can also be approved in the absence of a majority of all creditor-classes under certain conditions. These specify that at least one class of creditors has voted in favour of the plan, and more than one-fifth of all known creditors have approved the plan. The court should then confirm the plan (FinRL § 54).

Data and sample characteristics

The study compares a sample of firms that filed for reorganisation during the first year of the Finnish reorganisation law, with a sample of firms that filed for liquidation bankruptcy before the implementation of the reorganisation law.

Debtors, or any of the firm's creditors, file for reorganisation in one of nineteen court districts. The sample consists of filings by all non-public, and non-farm cases, in ten of the nineteen districts during the period February 1993 to February 1994. The districts were chosen based on their number of cases. Filings in the studied districts made up 74% of all reorganisation filings in 1993.[1] In total, 362 reorganisation cases were identified, of these 28% (102/362) emerged with a confirmed plan. The data used were principally taken from documents at district courts, but if the cases were involved in legal proceedings and documents in higher courts, the data were retrieved from courts of appeal or from the supreme court. Complementary data, such as possible bankruptcy filings before and after the reorganisation filing and industry codes, were retrieved from Asiakastieto Oy, a Finnish credit office. Industry data on financial ratios is from the Union Bank of Finland (currently Merita Bank).

Data on liquidation bankruptcy filings cover filings during the 1982-1992 period in the province of Vasa (in the western part of the country) and the province of Nylands (in the southern part of the country). The primary source of information was the records of the taxation authorities. Complementary data were retrieved from the courts. The analyses include 83 firms of which 27% (22/83) were sold as going concerns.[2]

---

1 Taken from Justice 1994: 4, published by the Statistical Office of Finland.

2 A case was considered as a going concern sale if most of the bankrupt's operating assets were sold to one successor. The price received when the firm was sold in relation to total firm value (defined as sum of payments to creditors and direct costs) average 81%. The median of the ratio is 88.6%. Important reasons why the percentages do not always equal 100% are that: some assets have been sold to other parties than the successor, receivables have been collected by the trustee and increased the denominator of the ratio, or that operations of the bankruptcy firm have been continued between

The firms in the sub-samples are of approximately similar size. The median assets of the reorganisation cases are FIM 3,14 million (ECU 0,54 million), and the median assets of the liquidation bankruptcy cases are FIM 3,35 million (ECU 0.58 million). Because both samples include a few large cases, the average assets are higher, FIM 10,96 million for reorganisations and FIM 6,37 million for the liquidation cases.

Payoff to creditors in reorganisation and in liquidation

An implication of the thesis that markets for assets of distressed firms are thin and inefficient is that there is a reorganisation surplus that can be split between equity-holders and creditors. This section assesses terms of debt restructurings and whether creditors de facto are paid more in a reorganisation than in liquidation.

There are three general types of creditors in reorganisation: secured creditors (with a fixed charge or a floating charge), unsecured creditors, and sub-ordinated claims. Secured creditors shall, according to the reorganisation law, receive full payment, but interest rates and the maturity of credits can be changed. Note, however, that a creditor is deemed to be secured only to the extent that the value of the collateral, at the time when the reoganisation is conducted, covers the claim. The excess of the claim is considered to be unsecured. The typical firm in the sample has 68,3% of its claims classified as unsecured or subordinated.

Reorganisation plans seem to promise much more to creditors in reorganisation than in liquidation. The average repayment percentages to unsecured creditors, were 42,9%, and the median is 37%. The smallest repayment percentage is 5% and the largest 100%. Full payment was promised in 10,6% of the cases (9/85), however, frequently over a long period and at zero interest rates. The mean (median) repayment periods to unsecured creditors are 6,1 (5,5) years. Estimates of what creditors should receive in liquidation bankruptcy should accompany reorganisation plans. Since estimates are prepared by administrators, not the debtor, they are likely to be unbiased. Administrators are nominated by creditors and may destroy their possibility of further appointments if they try to mislead creditors by presenting biased estimates. Estimates were available in 66 of the 102 cases that emerged with a confirmed plan. The mean payoff in liquidation is 9,26% and the median is 4,38%. The estimated payoff was below 1,02% in 25% of the cases and below 10,54% in 75% of the cases.

Repayments in reorganisation are risky. In November 1995, when on average 525 days from the confirmation of plans had passed, 16 of the 102 reorganisations had failed to comply with the plan. Fourteen of these had filed for liquidation bankruptcy. A failure rate of 15.6% within 525 days would imply that the

---

the day of the filing and the sale of the company. The profits from this period also increase the denominator of the ratio.

annual failure percentage is 10,8%. The riskiness of claims on reorganisation firms implies that a high discount rate should be used in calculations of the value of the payments.

Estimating a correct discount rate for claims on small and medium-sized reorganising firms is tricky, however. Ideally, the expected payoffs to creditors in reorganisation should be discounted using an interest rate that reflects the market risk of claims on reorganising firms. Typically, the capital-asset-pricing model (CAPM) is used to estimate the risk and the required rate of return (see, e.g., Brealey & Myers (1991 pp. 155-174) for a presentation of CAPM). However, since claims on small and mid-sized reorganising firms are not publicly traded, the parameters needed in the CAPM can not be estimated. An alternative way to get an appropriate discount rate would be to use the same discount rate as for equally risky publicly traded debt. The most risky debt is CCC rated by Standard & Poors (S&P). According to a default study of more than 5,400 issuers, S&P found that the cumulative default rate for CCC rated bonds over a 15-year period was 45,1%. Therefore, on an annual basis, the average is 3% (Standard & Poor's (1996 p. 6)). As reported above, the annual default rate for the firms in the sample studied in this study is 10,6%, or more than three times higher. Thus, a higher discount rate than for CCC-rated bonds has to be used.[3]

Here the discount rate used is calculated as follows. Assuming risk-neutrality, and that creditors receive nothing in liquidation if the firm defaults after a reorganisation plan has been approved, the discount rate (r) can be calculated using:[4]

$$r = 1 - \frac{1}{(1-p)/(1+i)} \qquad \textbf{(1)}$$

where p is the probability for default each year and it is the required rate of return on risk-free loans. To illustrate if the risk-free rate is 8% and the annual default rate is 5% (i.e., 5% of the surviving firms are failing each year), the appropriate discount rate is 1 - 1/((1-0,05)/(1+0,08)) = 13,7%. In essence, the formula discounts the *expected* payments to creditors with the riskless interest rate. The assumption that creditors would receive nothing in a liquidation after an unsuccessful attempt to reorganise is a conservative estimate. In practice, creditors probably do receive a positive payoff also in such cases, although the payoff may be lower than if the firm would have filed for liquidation bankruptcy in an earlier phase of the financial difficulties. The *expected* payments should be discounted with a higher interest rate than the riskless rate, since creditors are risk averse and claims on risky firms do have market risks (that is, positive betas) because default is more likely to occur in recessions when all businesses are doing poorly (compare Brealey & Myers (1991 p 579)).

---

[3] Altman (1989 p. 917) found that CCC-rated securities gave a premium of 7,07% over risk-free securities.

[4] The formula is a variant of the discounting formula appearing in Gibbons (1992) on page 90.

The parameters p and i in the formula are estimated as follows. If the same percentage of the surviving cases as during the first year continued to fail each year, the correct estimate of p is 10,8%. This annual failure rate would imply that, in total, 50% of the cases would fail within 6 years (6 years approximates the average length of the payment periods to unsecured creditors).[5] The fact that a 50% failure rate corresponds with the U.S. evidence, indicates that the estimate of p is reasonable.[6]

The mean interest-rate of new bank loans to the corporate sector, during the time when firms in the sample emerged from the reorganisation, is about 8%. This rate is somewhat higher than the rate on government debt commonly used as the riskless interest rate, and thus, at least partially reflects the fact that the theoretically correct interest rate should be higher than the one suggested in formula (1). Using 8% as a proxy for i and 10,8% as the proxy for p give us the interest rate 1 - 1/((1-0,108)/(1+0,08)) = 21%. Since this is an imperfect measure of the theoretically correct discount rate, how sensitive the magnitude of the reorganisation surplus is for the choice of the discount rate is studied in some of the analyses below.

Table 6.1 displays the reorganisation surplus, defined as the value of payments to creditors less estimated liquidation proceeds, in relation to total debt. Using 21% as the discount rate, the mean (median) surplus is 12,7% (9,9%). It can be seen

Table 6.1 The reorganisation surplus to unsecured creditors in reorganisation using various discount rates

Discount rate:	r=14%	r=21%	r=27%	r=35%	r=44%	r=54%
Mean value of surplus to unsecured debt	17,1%	12,7%	10,0%	7,3%	5,0%	3,0%
Median value of surplus to unsecured debt	14,0%	9,9%	7,6%	6,3%	4,4%	3,5%
Percentage of cases with value of payments < liquidation value	7,6%	10,6%	13,6%	22,7%	24,2%	30,3%
N	66	66	66	66	66	66

[a] The reorganisation surplus is calculated as the value of payments with the chosen discount rate less estimated payments to creditors, and is divided by total unsecured claims.

[5] That only 50% of all cases would pay according to the plan if the annual failure rate is 10,8%, is calculated as $(1-0,108)^6 = 0,5$ or 50%.

[6] A failure rate of 50% corresponds with that reported by Jensen-Conklin (1992) for U.S. reorganisations. She found that 26 of 45 firms in the sample paid in accordance with the reorganisation plan. However, when the part of the reorganisation plans that prescribed a liquidation of the firm is excluded, in total 18 of 36 firms paid according to the plan.

from the table that the finding that creditors are paid more in reorganisation than in liquidation is not very sensitive to the choice of interest rate: the average surplus is 10% when the interest rate is 27% (implying that the annual default rate, p, is 15%), the surplus is 7,3% when the interest rate is 35% (p = 25%) and 5% when the interest rate is 44% (p = 25%). The median internal rate of return, assuming that estimated liquidation proceeds were invested in the firm and promised payments received as in the reorganisation plan, is 122,74%!

Thus, the results suggest that creditors receive more in reorganisation than what they would receive in liquidation. However, as indicated by the last row in the table, creditors do not receive more in every single case. Using 21% as the discount rate, it can be seen that the payments in liquidation would have exceeded the present value of the payments in reorganisation in 10,6% of the cases. Furthermore, the table illustrates that the proportion rises considerably with higher interest rates. For instance, with 35% as the discount rate, payments in liquidation exceed the present value of payments in liquidation in 22,7% of the cases.

Let us consider next a comparison of payments in reorganisation with actual payments to creditors in liquidation bankruptcy. These analyses are based on the sample of firms that filed for liquidation bankruptcy before the reorganisation law came into effect, not on the administrator's estimates of liquidation values. Since the priority rules were changed simultaneously as the reorganisation law came into effect, results on payments to all creditors, not just to unsecured ones, are reported. Following the argument above, unsecured claims in reorganisation were discounted by 21%. Secured claims were discounted by 8% if the promised interest was below 8%, and otherwise by the interest rate according to the plan. Thus, calculations reflect that secured creditors sometimes accept concessions, such as lower than prevailing interest rates. Payments in liquidation bankruptcy are reported at their nominal value. The present value of the payments may be somewhat lower, since liquidation bankruptcies are frequently lengthy. Discounting the payments in liquidation bankruptcy would increase, not reduce, the possible net gain to creditors in reorganisation.

The mean (median) value of payments to all creditors in reorganisation was 42,8% (39,4%), which is significantly more than the payments to creditors in liquidation bankruptcy. The mean (median) payments in liquidation are 32,1% (30,9%) for cases sold as a going concern and 34,6% (33,0%) for cases liquidated in a piecemeal way. A regression is needed to further verify differences in payments, since payments may be due to systematic differences in solvency upon filing, industry-effects and size effects. Since a going concern sale would have been the likely fate for a firm reorganised under the current Finnish code, the comparison focuses on payments in reorganisation and in a going concern sale. However, results were basically similar when all liquidation bankruptcy cases were included in the sample. Regression results reported in Table 6.2 confirm that creditors are paid more in reorganisation. The coefficient of the code variable is 0,11 indicating that the difference in payments is 11%.

Table 6.2 Payoff to creditors in reorganisation and going concern sales

Independent variables	Coefficients	T-value
New code dummy variable (takes the value 1 for reorganisations and zero for liquidation bankruptcies)	0,110	(2,78)***
Total assets to debts	0,194	(3,91)***
Ln assets	-0,019	(1,39)
Construction dummy	0,052	(0,85)
Manufacturing dummy	0,036	(0,76)
Other industries (dummy)	0,026	(0,45)
Constant	0,315	(2,64)**
R-squared	19,37%	
N	105	

* p-value<0.1

** p-value<0.05

*** p-value<0.01

[a] The dependent variable in regressions is payments to creditors in relation to debts, defined as actual payments to debts in going concern sales and value of payments to debts in reorganisations.

[b] T-statistics are based on robust standard errors (White, 1980).

Direct costs of reorganisation and liquidation bankruptcy

A possible reason why creditors are paid more in a reorganisation is that the direct, or administrative, costs are lower. In the comparative analysis, direct costs are defined as the administrator's fees and expenditures in reorganisation, and the trustee's fees and expenditures in liquidation bankruptcy.[7] These figures represent a low estimate, since fees to lawyers and accountants other than the administrators' (trustees') fees, were not included in amounts.[8] The court shall confirm the administrators' fees and expenditures only if a creditor's committee has not been appointed (FinRL § 87). Thus, fees were typically not available for cases when a creditors' committee had been appointed. As a consequence, data was available only for 43 reorganisation cases. Three measures are used to assess the magnitude of the costs: a) book value of assets; b) book value of debt; and c) payments, defined as actual payments in liquidation bankruptcy and value of payments in reorganisation.

7 The expenditures include costs of auctions, advertisement, meeting of creditors, trustees' travelling-expenses, allowances and other similar costs.

8 Sundgren (1995 p. 90) reports that fees to accountants and lawyers average 1,39% of available assets in liquidation bankruptcy. This would suggest that the total direct costs are about 1,4% higher than what is reported in the table.

Results show that costs of a reorganisation are indeed lower. Using assets as the size measure, the mean (median) costs of a reorganisation are 5,3% (3,3%) and 6,8% (6,2%) for a going concern sale. Costs in relation to debt are 2,9% (2,3%) for reorganisations and 4,0% (3,3%) for liquidation bankruptcy, and when payments are used as the size measure, the mean (median) values are 4,8% (6,3%) for reorganisations and 15,4% (14,5%) for going concern sales.

It has been found in several studies that there is a scale effect in bankruptcy costs, i.e., that relative costs decrease with firm size (Warner, 1977; Ang, Chua & McConnell, 1982). Furthermore, it was found that the reorganisation cases, for which data on costs were available, were significantly smaller than the omitted ones, and also smaller than the firms sold as a going concern. If there is a scale effect in bankruptcy costs, this would imply that the magnitude of the difference could be even larger than what is reported in Table 6.2. To control for size and other factors, a regression was specified. The dependent variable in regression one is costs divided by assets, and in regression two, costs divided by debts. Independent variables are: size, measured with the logarithm of total assets, solvency, industry variables and a code dummy variable taking the value one for reorganisations and zero for going concern sales.

Table 6.3 Direct costs of a reorganisation and a going concern sale

	Regression 1 [a]		**Regression 2** [b]	
	Coefficient	**T-value** [c]	**Coefficient**	**T-value** [c]
Newcode dummy variable	-0,035	(3,15)***	-0,025	(5,03)***
Ln assets	-0,038	(3,34)***	-0,014	(6,74)***
Total assets to debts	-0,023	(1,94)*	0,034	(7,10)***
Construction dummy	-0,0005	(0,02)	-0,009	(0,81)
Manufacturing dummy	0,022	(1,55)	-0,007	(1,52)
Other industries (dummy)	-0,0005	(0,03)	-0,011	(1,92)*
Constant	0,390	(4,39)***	0,139	(8,22)***
R-squared	53,35%		56,66%	
N	65		65	

* p-value<0.1

** p-value<0.05

*** p-value<0.01

[a] The dependent variable is costs in relation to assets.

[b] The dependent variable is costs in relation to debts.

[c] T-statistics are based on robust standard errors (White, 1980).

The results, reported in Table 6.3, confirm that the costs of a reorganisation are lower. The coefficients of the code dummy variable in regression 2 is 0,025 indicating that the costs in relation to debts are about 2,5% lower in a reorganisation.

Summary

A question that has been continually debated during recent years is whether a reorganisation law increases or reduces the efficiency of the insolvency procedure. This paper provides some evidence on the issue by analysing samples of 362 firms that filed for reorganisation and 83 firms that filed for liquidation bankruptcy. In general, the evidence suggests that a reorganisation law does increase efficiency. Particularly, the data strongly indicates that creditors receive a better payoff in reorganisations than in liquidation bankruptcy. The finding that creditors receive more in a reorganisation corresponds with the Japanese evidence for small firms reported by Eisenberg & Tagashira (1994), and evidence for large U.S. firms reported by Alderson & Betker (1995). A reason why creditors receive more is that the direct costs are lower. However, differences in direct costs do not explain the entire surplus: the difference in costs in relation to debt is only about 2-3%, while the surplus to creditors in a reorganisation over a going concern sale is about 11%. Thus, other factors, such as the under-pricing of assets, also explain the creditor surplus.

Acknowledgements

The paper has benefited from discussions with Ted Eisenberg and comments from Tom Berglund, Jocelyn Martel, Stefan Krasa, Petri Mäntysaari and an anonymous referee. I alone am responsible for any remaining errors. I would like to thank NODFOR and the Academy of Finland for their support, Tom Hellström and Peter Nynäs for their excellent research assistance, and the court officials who helped provide access to the data. Much of the work was completed while I was a John M. Olin Fellow at Cornell Law School.

This paper is an edited version of the article that originally appeared in European Journal of Law and Economics, vol 6, issue 3, 1998. The permission to publish exerts in this book is gratefully acknowledged.

6.3 Should we abolish chapter 11: Evidence from Canada

by Timothy C.G. Fisher
Professor, Wilfird Laurier University
and
Jocelyn Martel
Professor, Université de Cerge-Pontoise, THEMA and ESSEC

Over the last decade, Chapter 11 has been severely criticised. Attacks on Chapter 11 are supported by a number of stylised facts: a) the probability of confirmation in Chapter 11 and the probability of a business emerging as an ongoing enterprise are very low ; b) small businesses filing for Chapter 11 typically end up in liquidation; and c) Chapter 11 is time-consuming, litigious, and costly. Some American jurists arguing in favour of revising Chapter 11 have raised the possibility that the Canadian reorganisation system might be a good alternative. This article examines data on firms undergoing reorganisation under the Canadian bankruptcy system and argues that there are fruitful lessons to be learned from the Canadian experience with court-supervised reorganisation. The comparative analysis is based on two criteria: a) whether reorganisation is in the best interests of creditors, and b) the administrative costs of reorganisation.

Data

The data are collected directly from plans filed by individual firms with the Montreal and Toronto bankruptcy offices. The final sample has 393 firms, of which 273 originated in Montreal and 120 originated in Toronto. Firms attempting reorganisation under the Bankruptcy Act ('BA') are quite small, with average assets of $2.5 million and average debts of $3.0 million. (All dollar figures are December 1993 Canadian dollars, deflated by the GDP deflator. To convert these figures to U.S. dollars, the average noon spot exchange rate in December 1993 was US $1.00 = C$1.33.) About 72% of firms in the sample have assets less than $1 million. The vast majority of firms in the sample are privately owned; only 10 have publicly traded shares. The mean asset/debt ratio is 58% and secured debt represents around 55% of the assets of reorganising firms, indicating that there is some room for these firms to negotiate new secured loans. Secured debt represents about one-third of total debt, indicating that the firms rely heavily on secured debt. There are, on average, 110 creditors affected by a reorganisation proposal, the vast majority of which are ordinary creditors.

According to the data, at least half the plans have been voted on by unsecured creditors within 25 days of filing. The complete reorganisation process (the time from filing to the discharge of the debtor from bankruptcy by the court) takes, on average, just over three years. Four plans in 10 are amended before creditors vote, so clearly negotiation takes place between the debtor and its creditors. Around only one-third of the creditors that are eligible to vote on the plan show up for the creditors meeting. The administration costs in reorganisation have a mean value of $46,300. Trustees' fees account for around 70% of administration costs.

Analysis

From the point of view of efficiency, an ideal bankruptcy system promotes the reorganisation of viable firms and the elimination of non-viable firms. Two events must happen in sequence for a firm to emerge successfully from financial reorganisation. First, the bankruptcy court must confirm the plan. Second, the plan must be carried out to the satisfaction of the court, or be 'consummated'.

The Canadian data indicate that 75% of proposals are accepted by unsecured creditors. Among accepted proposals, 93% are confirmed by the bankruptcy court, implying a confirmation rate of 70%. These figures support earlier findings in Fisher and Martel (1994, 1995). These results contrast with those in the U.S. Flynn (1989) finds a confirmation rate of about 17% for Chapter 11 cases filed between 1979 and 1986 and Jensen-Conklin (1992) finds a confirmation rate of 13% for cases filed in the Southern District of New York for the period 1980-89. According to one view, the confirmation rate is low because Chapter 11 attracts too many small businesses. Eisenberg (1995) reports that Chapter 11 confirmation rates decrease monotonically with firm size. This view is not supported by Canadian data, which show no correlation between either acceptance or confirmation rates and firm size. The Canadian data also clearly show that the majority of reorganising firms are small. To the extent that there are problems with the Canadian reorganisation system, they do not appear to be caused by the presence of small firms with low acceptance and confirmation rates.

According to Jensen-Conklin's data (1992), 47% of confirmed Chapter 11 plans are 'definitely' consummated. Once again, the Canadian data provide a different picture: 72% of the proposals accepted by unsecured creditors are consummated. Again, this confirms previous findings in Fisher & Martel. In addition, there is no correlation between the consummation rate and the size of the firm.

The probability of emerging from reorganisation as an ongoing entity is equal to the confirmation rate times the consummation rate. Jensen-Conklin concludes that a Chapter 11 firm has a 6.5% chance of surviving as a going concern. Baird (1993) finds that fewer than 10% of small to medium size firms group emerge from Chapter 11 as going concerns, concluding: "Chapter 11 is simply a station to eventual liquidation". Again, the Canadian data contrast significantly with the U.S. findings. The likelihood of a Canadian firm surviving reorganisation under the BA is around 53%, confirming previous results by Fisher & Martel. This means that Canadian firms are almost eight times more likely to survive reorganisation than their U.S. counterparts.

A second desirable aspect of an efficient reorganisation system is to ensure that creditors receive more in reorganisation than in liquidation. This is referred to the *best-interests test* or the *creditor' reorganisation participation constraint.* The analysis looks at two aspects of this problem. The first aspect is how quickly creditors are reimbursed. Canadian data show that the duration of payments in reorganisation ranges from immediately to 10 years after confirmation. The average time for the repayment of creditors is 14 months and 62% of the proposals complete repayment within 12 months. In addition, the average grace period for the sample is 3.7 months. These results compare with those found by Jensen-Conklin (1992) who reports that 54% of proposals complete repayment within one year of confirmation.

The second aspect is referred to as the *best-interests test*, and is conducted in the following way. First, the value of reorganisation payments is measured by the sum of the periodic payments specified in the proposal, discounted using a monthly discount rate consistent with a 10% annual rate. Second, a predicted probability of success for each proposal in the sample is estimated using a logit model proposed in Martel (1997). Third, the expected discounted payment in reorganisation is calculated by multiplying the discounted payment by the predicted probability of success of the proposal. Lastly, an expected discounted liquidation payment is calculated by dividing net liquidation value by ordinary claims and discounting the result at a 10% annual rate over 2.24 years, the average time firms spend in liquidation proceedings. According to the analysis, the expected payment on unsecured claims in reorganisation is equal to 24.3 cents for each dollar of unsecured claims. Given that creditors expect to receive 2.6 cents per dollar of claims in liquidation, they receive a surplus in reorganisation of 21.7 cents per dollar of claims. Only 4% of the proposals in the sample fail the best-interests test, which is very close to the figure reported by Eisenberg & Tagashira (1994). Note also that the surplus to unsecured creditors is larger for accepted than for rejected proposals. Also, compliance with the best-interests test is larger for accepted proposals. Overall, the data show that there is substantial compliance with the best-interests test for proposals under the Canadian BA and that there are gains for unsecured creditors from reorganisation.

Another important element measuring the performance of the bankruptcy system is the cost and time in reorganisation. In Canada, at the time of filing, administrative costs amount to 4.8% of the book value of debt, 23% of the book value of assets, and 13% of the total payment to creditors under the proposal. These values are higher than those reported for the U.S. Two factors can help explain the difference in administrative costs between Canada and the U.S. A first possible explanation is the presence of a trustee in all reorganisation proceedings in Canada while they are seldom present in U.S. proceedings. Another explanation lies in the fact that our study is based on smaller firms than the typical U.S. study and that there are fixed minimum costs of reorganisation. Regression analysis shows that the fixed costs component of reorganisation is significantly higher in Canada than in the U.S.

With respect to the time in reorganisation, Canadian data show that the average time between filing and voting is 50 days. In addition, 60% of the proposals are voted on within 30 days of filing and 90% within 90 days. Assuming that it takes about 30 days to receive the court's confirmation, the average time between filing and confirmation is just over two-and-a-half months. This contrasts with the U.S. where average time in reorganisation narrows to between 20 and 25 months. For example, Flynn and Jensen-Conklin report a mean time in reorganisation of 25 and 22 months, respectively. Thus, firms in Canada complete reorganisation between seven and ten times more quickly than their counterparts in Chapter 11.

Lessons for chapter 11

The lessons we learn from Canadian experience can be summarised as follows:

1. Contrary to common belief in the U.S., reorganisation is not simply a station to eventual liquidation. Between 50% and 60% of firms emerge from reorganisation in Canada as ongoing entities, which is about eight times higher than Chapter 11.

2. There is no support for the claim that the problem with bankruptcy law is that too many small firms try to reorganise when they should be liquidated. Canadian data show no correlation between firm size and acceptance, confirmation, or consummation. Thus we find little support for a system with two distinct reorganisation procedures, one for small to medium size firms and one for large firms. A single procedure with enough flexibility to accommodate all types of firms seems preferable to a dual system, which could give rise to strategic behaviour.

3. It is possible to have a reorganisation system that resolves quickly financial distress and ensures a net gain to creditors. This can be done by :

    a) giving the right incentives to negotiate early in reorganisation along with abolishing the exclusivity period given to debtors. The pre-1992 Bankruptcy Act did not specify any time limits for debtors to file a proposal but the system converged to an equilibrium of about 50 days. Econometric analysis shows that the probability of acceptance of a proposal decreases with the time between filing and voting. In addition, creditors should be allowed to propose amendments to the original proposal early in the process.

    b) naming a trustee in every reorganisation case. The trustee discloses information to all parties and oversees the process of reorganisation. This stimulates negotiation between the debtor and its creditors and renders the system more transparent, thereby reducing the amount of time to reach a settlement. Arguably, a more rapid solution to financial distress and a better separation of firms compensates for the increased bankruptcy costs associated with the presence of a trustee.

c) leaving more powers in the hands of creditors and less in the hands of the bankruptcy court. While we favour court intervention to dismiss inadmissible cases, we believe that, in most cases, the final decisions should be in the hands of creditors.

6.4 Cash auction bankruptcy: Summary of the Swedish evidence

by Karin S. Thorburn
Assistant Professor of Finance, Amos Tuck School of Business Administration, Dartmouth College

Different bankruptcy procedures allocate different sets of control rights to incumbent managers and the firm's security holders, thus affecting both the timing and form of management's choice of bankruptcy venue. For example, Chapter 11 of the U.S. bankruptcy code allows managers to retain a certain degree of control over the firm's assets and operations during the bankruptcy proceeding. Managers are thus encouraged to select a court-supervised debt reorganisation under Chapter 11 rather than file for liquidation in Chapter 7. In contrast, the Swedish bankruptcy code, which constitutes the empirical laboratory underlying this summary, has no reorganisation provisions and requires all bankruptcy filings to be resolved through a cash auction. This auction results either in a going concern sale of the firm or in a piecemeal sale of the assets. Importantly, an independent, court-appointed trustee runs the auction, and neither incumbent management nor the firm's security holders retain any control rights.

Proponents of the bankruptcy auction system point to the fact that it exploits the market's valuation of the firm's assets. The question of the optimal disposition of the distressed firm's assets is left to the highest-valuation bidder rather than to management or to a disinterested court. This reduces the scope for disagreement among existing claimholders, which ultimately lowers bankruptcy costs. Moreover, the cash proceeds from the auction allow settlement of debt claims strictly according to absolute priority rules. On the other hand, proponents of a Chapter 11 type of reorganisation code argue that auctions risk destroying value by forcing asset 'fire-sales' below true market value. Moreover, fearing loss of corporate control in the bankruptcy auction, managers may delay filing and substitute assets in order to increase risk, all at the detriment of the firm's going concern value.

The relative merits of court-supervised reorganisations vs. mandatory bankruptcy auctions are a largely unexplored empirical issue. While numerous studies document evidence on Chapter 11 cases, systematic evidence on the effects of mandatory bankruptcy auctions is sparse. Nevertheless, the stylised facts on Chapter 11 cases indicate that the proceedings are relatively time consuming and costly. Furthermore, a significant proportion of firms emerging from Chapter 11 require a second debt restructuring, and the average post-bankruptcy performance is below industry norms.

This paper summarises some first evidence on the efficiency of bankruptcy auctions developed in Thorburn (1997, 1998) and which is based on a sample of 263 Swedish small-firm bankruptcies. Moreover, the results are contrasted with extant empirical results on Chapter 11 cases. The analysis focuses on six major issues. The first set of issues concerns the outcome of the auctions and whether negotiations over the terms of going concern sales occur prior to bankruptcy or after filing for bankruptcy. Thorburn (1997) documents that a significant proportion (over 25%) of the going concern sales are in the form of agreements executed just prior to filing or immediately upon filing for bankruptcy. She labels these 'auction prepacks', and they have an interesting counterpart in Chapter 11 prepacks. Firms with a relatively high proportion of intangible assets, facing high-expected auction costs, are more likely to undertake prepacks.

The alternative to auction prepacks and other in-bankruptcy going concern sales is piecemeal liquidation. In Sweden, 30% of the bankruptcy filings result in piecemeal liquidation, which compares to the 30% of small firms in Chapter 11 that fail to reorganise as a going concern. (See, e.g., White 1984). This evidence is inconsistent with speculations of excessive management aversion to file for cash auction bankruptcy, since a 'late' filing should increase the chance of piecemeal liquidation (due to loss of going concern value). Moreover, there is no evidence that firms filing for auction bankruptcy are in a worse financial condition in the year prior to filing than firms filing for Chapter 11, which again fails to support the proposition of 'late' filing.

The second set of issues concerns the magnitude and determinants of direct bankruptcy costs, which are important for judging the economic efficiency of the bankruptcy regime. In the case of the one-third largest firms in the sample, the percentage direct costs of cash auctions are similar to those reported for much larger publicly held U.S. firms reorganising in Chapter 11 (average 3.7% vs. 3.6%). [9] In light of the fixed components in bankruptcy costs, cash auctions appear to provide a relatively low-cost bankruptcy procedure. Prepacks incur the lowest costs in both bankruptcy regimes, and are lowest under the cash auction system. Interestingly, direct bankruptcy costs are also found to be increasing in industry distress factors, suggesting that the bankruptcy trustee increase her auction marketing efforts when industry financial distress tends to reduce auction demand. Moreover, cash auction proceedings have substantially lower indirect costs, reflecting their speed of execution: median 1.5 *months* compared to the 1-2 *years* it typically takes to resolve small-firm restructurings under Chapter 11.

---

[9] The U.S. figure is a sample-size weighted average of the estimates in Weiss (1990) and Betker (1997).

Third, Thorburn (1997) examines debt recovery rates. Recovery rates presented for Swedish auction bankruptcy represent actual cash distributions paid out a few months after filing, while recovery rates reported in the literature for Chapter 11 cases are market and book values of claims received 2-3 years later. Debt recovery in Sweden tends to be higher for firms sold as going concerns and lower for firms filing for bankruptcy during the economy-wide downturn in 1991. Firms that filed prior to 1991 and were sold as going concerns have a median overall recovery rate that is similar to that reported by Franks and Torous (1994) for a sample of publicly traded firms completing their reorganisation under Chapter 11 (40% vs. 41%). Banks and secured creditors tend to recover approximately the same in both bankruptcy regimes (in excess of 80%). While junior debt and equity are promised a disproportionate share in Chapter 11 proceedings, reflecting deviations from absolute priority, junior claimants receive typically nothing in the Swedish auctions.

The fourth set of issues concerns whether the auction *premium* (defined as the ratio of the realised auction price to the trustee's value estimate) depends on industry wide financial distress and asset uniqueness. The econometric analysis explores switching regression models with endogenous switching and self-selection models in order to account for the possible dual role of the filing firm's bank when it decides to finance the buyer in the auction. As expected, the auction premium decreases with the fraction of the firm's assets that are unique to the industry. Surprisingly, industry distress factors tend to *increase* auction premiums, which contradicts popular asset fire-sales arguments. It is possible that the auction trustee, when facing a liquidity constrained distressed industry, increases general sales efforts to offset low expected demand in the cash auction.

Fifth, the evidence in Thorburn (1998) indicates that mandatory auctions act as a substantial managerial disciplinary force: The median loss of CEO total compensation is 40% over the two years following bankruptcy filing, an income loss that is significantly larger than what is observed for a control sample of non-bankrupt Swedish firms. Moreover, the CEO turnover rate in Swedish auctions is substantially higher than what has been reported for U.S. Chapter 11 cases (64% vs. 33%). [10] The probability of CEO turnover increases as the firm's pre-filing operating profitability increases, suggesting that auctions tend to sort out high from low quality managers and, if anything, the average CEO has an incentive to file 'early' rather than 'late'.

Sixth, the operating performance of firms auctioned as going concerns is statistically indistinguishable from the firms' industry competitors over the five-year period following the auction. In comparison, Hotchkiss' (1995) evidence on the U.S. indicates significantly poorer operating performance relative to the industry by firms emerging from Chapter 11. Whether or not the CEO remains with the

---

[10] See, e.g., Gilson (1989) and Hotchkiss (1995) for CEO turnover rates in Chapter 11.

firm has no statistically discernible effect on the probability for a second debt restructuring in Sweden, which seems contrary to U.S. evidence. Thus, bankruptcy auctions appear to successfully use the market for corporate control to eliminate the lowest quality CEOs.

Overall, the evidence presented in Thorburn (1997, 1998) on firm survival rates, costs, debt recovery rates, auction premiums, CEO compensation and turnover, and post-bankruptcy firm performance indicates that the mandatory cash auctions in Sweden provide a relatively efficient bankruptcy procedure.

Acknowledgement

This paper is a brief summary of evidence in Thorburn (1997, 1998). I would like to thank B. Espen Eckbo for comments.

6.5 Methodological issues in bankruptcy prediction

by Clas Bergström, Theodore Eisenberg, Stefan Sundgren, and Martin T. Wells[*]

This paper discusses some methodological issues related to the composition of samples and statistical techniques in bankruptcy prediction. Most bankruptcy prediction studies use ratio analysis. Accounting data are analysed to determine whether differences in financial ratios across firms relate to differences in outcomes. Early papers by Beaver (1968) and Altman (1968) show that these ratios provide information that is useful in distinguishing between bankrupt and healthy firms. Beaver used a series of univariate analyses and found that certain ratios could discriminate with about a 90% classification rate. Altman (1993) reviews related subsequent work.

Sampling issues

A major problem with this methodology is the non-random manner in which the healthy and bankrupt samples are chosen. The bankruptcy prediction studies are examples of case-control studies. A case-control study investigates the extent to which firms selected because they have a specific outcome (for example, bankruptcy) (the cases) and comparable firms that do not have the specific outcome (the control) have been exposed to possible risk factors. A major limitation of case-control studies is that they are susceptible to bias, especially selection bias, which creates non-comparability between cases and controls. In planning a

---

[11] Professors at Stockholm School of Economics, Cornell Law School, Swedish School of Economics and Business Administration, Cornell University Department of Social Statistics. An earlier version of this paper was prepared for The Second International Stockholm Seminar on Risk Behaviour and Risk Management, June 9-12, 1997.

case-control study it must be decided how to match the controls to the cases, that is, with respect to what factors and how closely. For example, many bankruptcy prediction studies have paired the cases and controls in their samples on size and industry (e.g., Beaver 1968, Altman 1968).

The matching warrants careful consideration because the decision has implications for virtually every aspect of the study. Matching attempts to mimic blocking in an experiment, that is, randomising firms within categories of a factor known (or suspected) to influence the outcome under evaluation. The concept of blocking in controlled experiments goes far back in the history of experimental design. It was noticed that it is possible to increase the sensitivity of an experiment by first grouping the experimental units so that the units within a group or block were nearly homogeneous and then applying the treatment of interest randomly to the units within the block. This concept led to the block design, which is capable of eliminating inherent heterogeneity of the experimental units via randomisation.

Laboratory works with animals such as mice or rats can illustrate blocking. Suppose that there are three treatments under comparison: different diets, different amounts of a drug, and different types of lighting. The final observations of interest might be of the amount of a certain substance in an organ of the animal at the end of the experimental period. To use randomised blocks, one begins by grouping the animals into sets of three in such a way that the final observation that would be obtained under uniform treatment is expected to be as nearly as possible constant within each set. To apply the blocking principle, three suitable animals are taken from a number of litters of three or more animals, numbering the animals in each litter 1, 2, 3. The order of treatments is then randomised within each block. To use a quantitative property, such as body weight, to form blocks, the animals are numbered in order of increasing body weight, say, 1 through 3 form the first block, 4 through 6 the second block, and so on. The order of treatments again being randomised independently within each block. The effect of this is that the animals within any one block have approximately the same body weight and the effect of weight is effectively controlled for through blocking.

Mimicking such blocking in a matched case study would mean matching by weight a subject with a known treatment effect with a subject without the treatment effect. The analogy between blocking and matching is false in one crucial respect. In experimental work, no matter how extensive the blocking, the investigator manipulates exposure to the factor under study (usually by randomisation). This guarantees that the blocking factors will not be correlated with the exposure of interest. For example, weight will not be correlated with exposure to diet treatment. But exposure to, for example, diet treatment, would not be manipulated in a case-control study. So a matching factor, unlike a blocking factor, will be associated with any exposure that differs between cases and controls. Weight in a control may be associated with diet. And firm size in a matched-case study may be associated with non-bankrupt status.

Hence any mode of analysis that fails to account for the fact that the matching process forces the controls to be more like the cases than they otherwise would be, with respect to the exposure of interest, will lead to an overestimate of any effects detected. The weakness of case control studies is that, in the end, the investigator must appeal to subjective or only semi-quantitative arguments to the effect that the information that she has from the cases and controls is equivalent in source and quality. Thus, to a great extent the problem of doing a persuasive case-control study is that of avoiding bias.

Most bankruptcy prediction studies provide little assurance that bias has been avoided. The matched samples are not representative of the actual population of firms. This issue was addressed by Ohlson (1980), who examined a sample of 105 bankrupt and 2,048 active firms (essentially the entire universe of firms for which he could obtain data). Ohlson used conditional logit analysis, which avoids some of the statistical problems associated with discriminant analysis, and found an over 80% correct classification rate. Most other bankruptcy prediction studies involve much smaller matched samples and are limited to public firms. Jones (1993) notes leading studies that include 33, 32, 53, 23, and 44 bankrupt firms. Zmijewski (1984) notes the need for weighting in matched sample studies but his study could not replicate the true proportion of healthy and bankrupt firms.

Modelling issues

Bankruptcy prediction studies also encounter modelling issues. Studies have progressed beyond the early use of discriminant analysis to use of logistic or probit models. Shumway (1996) recently argued for using proportional hazard models in bankruptcy modelling. Shumway points out that one of the problems with discriminant analysis and classical cross-sectional logit-type models is their inability to incorporate time varying covariates. He argues that a hazard rate model is more appropriate.

This may be the case if the length of the panel observations is long enough to assure that the observations are recorded in continuous time. This is not the case with the data we have, which comprise yearly data covering 1990-1994. Therefore we use a panel data logit model with varying structure on the within-panel random effects. The parameter estimates in this model represent the change in the log-odds of bankruptcy for a unit increase in an independent variable. These estimates have a clearer interpretation than the change in the log hazard ratio for a unit increase in an independent variable that one obtains from a hazard rate regression model. An additional possible problem for hazard rate regression models in this context is that the censoring rate is very heavy and is possibly dependent on the survival time, which may lead to invalid inferences (see Kalbfleish & Prentice, 1980).

This paper explores both model estimation issues and sample size issues. As noted, samples in existing studies almost always underrepresent the mass of healthy, active firms. Data kindly made available by UpplysningsCentralen AB

(UC) on all Swedish firms with 20 or more employees (N ~= 16,000) enable us to analyse a less-biased sample of firms. The UC data comprise a near comprehensive set of all large firms that file for bankruptcy in Sweden (Strömberg & Thorburn 1996) and a near complete set of active firms.

We find that a proportional hazard model is fairly consistent with logistic models but that some important differences exist. With respect to sample size, we find that logistic regression models using small samples of active firms can lead to noticeably different coefficients and to dramatic prediction differences unless corrected for sample size. Even after correction, predictive power depends on sample size.

Data description

The data consist of repeated measures over time of accounting data on all Swedish firms with 20 or more employees. The first year with substantial data is 1989 and the last is 1994. Many firms exit the sample during the years covered due to bankruptcy, merger, or liquidation. Other firms enter the sample during the period.

We use bankruptcy, a dummy variable, as the dependent variable. We use four accounting ratios as explanatory variables. 'Return on assets' is a measure of profitability. 'Leverage' is a debt-to-asset ratio. 'Cash position' is the ratio of cash to total assets (Pinches et al. 1975). 'Wage ratio' is the ratio of wages to total debt. Return on assets, leverage, and cash position are obviously relevant to bankruptcy prediction and they, or similar financial ratios, are used in prior bankruptcy studies. To these we add the wage ratio because Sweden's guarantee of wages for employees of bankrupt firms may attract firms to bankruptcy (Eisenberg 1995). The subsidy is not available outside bankruptcy.

We use one-year lags of the accounting financial ratios to model bankruptcy in the subsequent year. Therefore, the study covers the years 1990 to 1994 since one-year-earlier data are not available to us for 1989. The accounting data contained in UC's files come from annual financial statements that Swedish law requires corporations to file. UC supplements these data with information about whether a firm has granted its creditors a floating charge, a form of security interest in a firm's assets. The floating charges dummy is one if the firm reports an amount of floating charge and zero otherwise.

We compute industry relative financial ratios (return on assets, leverage, cash position, and wage ratio) by subtracting the industry-wide median value of the ratio, calculated each year, from the firm's ratio for the year. At the individual firm level, low and high extreme values of the financial ratio variables are truncated to equal the 0.25 and 99.75%iles, respectively. Shumway's (1996) bankruptcy study truncated financial ratios at the first and 99th percentiles.

The financial ratios and other variables used are summarised in Table 6.4.

Table 6.4 Variable definitions

Variable	Definition
Return on assets	Earnings after depreciation + financial costs / total assets
Leverage	Long term debt + short term debt / total assets
Cash position	Cash / total assets
Wage ratio	Wages / total debt
Sales	Sales
Age of firm	Days since founding
Floating charge	Dummy variable = 1 if floating charge as security exists
Public firm dummy	Dummy variable
Member of corporate group	Dummy variable

Table 6.5 reports summary statistics for the industry relative versions of Table 6.4's accounting ratios, for the other variables in Table 6.4, and for locale dummy variables used in the study. The descriptive statistics cover 55,492 observations of 15,828 Swedish corporations, 1990 to 1994. Active firms comprise 52,601 observations of 14,880 firms. The last column in Table 6.5 reports the significance of the differences of each variable by active versus bankrupt status.

For the variables described in Table 6.5, the number of active firms' ranges from 14,741 to 14,880. The number of bankrupt firms ranges from 1,728 to 1,770. We include in the models estimated below, but do not report here, a series of 12 dummy variables for industries. Manufacturers of metals, machinery, or equipment comprise the single largest industry group and account for 14.4% of the firms in the sample.

Not surprisingly, bankrupt firms have lower returns on assets, higher leverage, and weaker cash positions than active firms do. Table 6.5 also suggests that firms with floating charges tend to go bankrupt, that larger firms (as measured both by sales and assets) tend not to go bankrupt, and that older firms tend not to go bankrupt. Public firm status and membership in a corporate group are negatively correlated with bankruptcy. There are also significant local effects and industry effects (not reported here), suggesting the need to control for these factors in multivariate models.

Table 6.5. Descriptive statistics by firm status, Swedish firms, 1990-1994

	active firms		*bankrupt firms*		*significance*
Variable	*mean*	*median*	*mean*	*median*	*of difference*
Industry relative ratios lagged one year					
return on assets	-0.009	0.000	-0.057	-0.029	0.000
leverage	-0.022	0.006	0.079	0.101	0.000
cash position	0.067	0.014	0.025	-0.009	0.000
wage ratio	0.237	0.016	0.214	0.007	0.377
Other firm characteristics					
floating charge dummy (one-year lag)	0.671	1.000	0.767	1.000	0.000
sales (log) (one-year lag)	10.597	10.553	10.229	10.244	0.000
assets (log) (one-year lag)	10.070	9.904	9.688	9.629	0.000
age of firm (thousands of days)	8.378	7.022	6.985	6.012	0.000
public firm dummy	0.133	0.000	0.001	0.000	0.000
member of corporate group dummy	0.296	0.000	0.275	0.000	0.000
Locale dummies					
Malmö	0.041	0.000	0.029	0.000	0.010
Stockholm	0.199	0.000	0.151	0.000	0.000
Göteborg	0.077	0.000	0.072	0.000	0.408
all other locations	0.682	1.000	0.749	1.000	0.000

Model and sample comparisons

Shumway suggests the possibility of using proportional hazard models to model bankruptcy. He shows the superiority of hazard models to discriminant analysis. We report a comparison between a hazard model and generalised estimating equations using a logit link function.

Maddala (1983) and Hosmer and Lemeshow (1989: 182) show that logistic models using separate sample case data give satisfactory estimates of equation coefficients but that the prediction values generated by such models are incorrect because the constant is incorrect. The UC data enable us to compare the results of full sample estimates with those of a much smaller subset of active firms. We do so both for the full set of panel data and for one year of observations.

Sensitivity to model estimation method and sample size

Model 1 in Table 6.6 presents a Cox proportional hazard model. Model 2 and model 3 report generalised estimating equation logit panel data estimates with random effects. They differ only in the within panel correlation structure. Since the panels consist of the different time periods, the within panel correlations assess the relations among firms' status at different times. Model 2 imposes an exchangeable within panel correlation structure. That is, it assumes equal correlation among firms' status over time. For example, a firm's status in 1993 would be assumed to have the same correlation with its status in 1992 as it has with its status in 1990. Model 3 imposes no structure on the inter-panel correlations. The data are left free to estimate a more intricate correlation structure. Model 4 is the same as Model 3 except that the data are limited to a 4% sample of the healthy firms to more closely replicate the relative proportions of active and bankrupt firms in most bankruptcy studies. Robust t-statistics are in parentheses.

Table 6.6 Multivariate models of bankruptcy

	Model 1	*Model 2*	*Model 3*	*Model 4*
	Cox model	*generalised estimating equation models*		
		exchangeable correlation structure	*unstructured correlation structure*	*4% sample*
return on assets	-0.184	-0.395	-0.396	-0.570
	(-1.955)	(-3.316)	(-3.318)	(-2.088)
leverage	1.268	1.862	1.866	3.025
	(11.983)	(13.132)	(13.167)	(11.303)
cash position	-2.527	-2.566	-2.574	-2.334
	(-9.253)	(-8.557)	(-8.583)	(-6.476)
wage ratio	0.075	0.079	0.079	0.158
	(3.757)	(2.959)	(2.968)	(3.248)
floating charge dummy (one year lag)	0.380	0.214	0.213	0.110
	(6.228)	(3.064)	(3.065)	(1.177)
sales (log-one year lag)	0.002	-0.090	-0.091	-0.254
	(0.135)	(-5.833)	(-5.884)	(-7.355)
age of firm (thousands of days)	-0.009	-0.023	-0.023	-0.011
	(-2.398)	(-4.934)	(-4.910)	(-1.765)
public firm dummy	-4.913	-5.138	-5.163	-5.092
	(-6.945)	(-7.224)	(-7.259)	(-6.746)
member of corporate group dummy	0.025	0.058	0.058	0.183
	(0.451)	(0.957)	(0.966)	(2.080)
Locale dummies, industry dummies not reported				
constant	0.889	0.956	0.955	1.044
	(-0.097)	(0.107)	(0.107)	(0.153)
total time at risk or n	30,631,673	52,935	52,935	3,788

For nearly all variables the proportional hazard model coefficients are not dramatically different from those in the generalised estimating equation logit models.

The notable exception is the coefficient on sales, which is negative and significant in all three logistic models, but positive and insignificant in the Cox model. Both Table 6.5's descriptive statistics and prior studies report a firm size effect. Based on the theoretical considerations described above, we prefer the logit models.

For the full sample logistic models, the difference in correlation structure between Models 2 and 3 leads to minimal differences in the estimated model. All of the coefficients and t-statistics are substantially the same. Although an exchangeable correlation structure seems unrealistic, parameter estimates are quite consistent with the unstructured model. For this data set, the allowed correlation structure has little impact on the estimated model.

A comparison of the full-sample logistic Model 3 with Model 4, which includes only a 4% random sample of healthy firms, shows differences in coefficients. Most of the coefficients in the smaller sample model are within the 95% confidence intervals of the coefficients reported for the full sample reported in Model (3). But the small sample model estimates noticeably larger coefficients for industry relative return on assets, for industry relative leverage, for industry relative wage ratio, for firm size, and for the corporate group dummy variable. For three of these variables – return on assets, leverage, and firm size – the small sample estimates are not within the 95% confidence intervals of the large sample estimates.

For logit models, we conclude that a small sample of healthy firms does not radically distort the direction and significance level of explanatory variables. But, in this analysis, it has led to overestimation of the size of the coefficient on several important variables.

Sample size and predictive accuracy

To explore the role of sample size on bankruptcy prediction, we varied the sample of healthy firms and ran logistic regressions limited to one year of data. For logistic regression models, a probability level, or cut-off point, should be used to classify the observations. A case is classified as failing if its probability exceeds the cut-off probability. The classification results depend on the cut-off point used. If a lower cut-off is used, it will increase the number of failing firms that are identified but also increase the number of healthy firms that are wrongly classified as failing firms. The choice of cut-off ultimately depends on the cost of misclassification.

If the costs of errors are equivalent, the user might classify any company with a probability of bankruptcy that exceeds .5 as a failing one. In bankruptcy prediction, however, the costs of error are probably not equivalent. The cost of misclassifying failing firms is likely much higher than the cost of misclassifying healthy firms. Altman (1993: 256-63) analyses the cut-offs that might be used by banks in their credit decisions. He notes that the cost of classifying a failing firm as healthy approximates the credit losses in bankruptcy, and that the cost of classifying a healthy firm as failing approximates the foregone rate of return on the rejected loan. His empirical data suggest that the cost of the former error is 31 times larger than the latter error. This suggests that an appropriate cut-off probability for banks predicting bankruptcy is approximately 1/(1 + 31) or .031.

Table 6.7 explores the effect of both sample size and cut-off probability on classification performance. It first shows the percent of bankrupt firms correctly classified at a .5 cut off for various sample sizes of active firms. It then shows the percent correctly classified at a .5 cut off using an intercept corrected to reflect sample size. It reports the same data for a cut-off probability of .031.

Table 6.7 Logistic regression results by sample size

Full sample of active firms=9,713; number of bankrupt firms = 619					
Year = 1990 only; dependent variable = bankrupt	*% of active firms included in sample*				
	5%	**10%**	**20%**	**50%**	**100%**
% correctly classified, .5 cut-off					
% bankrupt firms	75.2	52.3	21.7	7.3	1.3
% bankrupt firms, corrected intercept	4.3	3.8	3.5	3.3	-
% correctly classified, .031 cut-off, after					
% bankrupt firms	86.10	87.5	88.9	89.5	88.9
% active firms	22.0	25.5	36.3	35.4	41.0

Table 6.7 contains two notable results. First, the results illustrate the importance of adjusting the intercept in logistic regression models where failing firms have been oversampled. In a sample that includes 5% of the healthy firms, 75.2% of the bankrupt firms are correctly classified if the intercept is not corrected. But only about 3% to 4% of failing firms are correctly classified after correction of the intercept. It is difficult to model rare events. As Maddala and Hosmer and Lemeshow suggest, prediction from such samples is inaccurate unless one properly adjusts the intercept.

Second, the percent of correctly classified bankrupt firms varies greatly depending on the cut-off point used. In the full sample, only 1.3% of bankrupt firms is correctly classified at a .5 cut-off probability. At a .031 cut-off, 88.9% of the bankrupt firms in the full sample are correctly classified. And the correct classification rate materially differs by sample size for active firms, even after correction.

Conclusions

We show that, in modelling bankruptcy, a proportional hazard model leads to similar but not identical results to generalised estimating equation logit models. Within the family of generalised estimating logit models, the correlation structure makes little difference for these data. Sample size influences both the size of coefficients and the predictive characteristics of logit models.

6.6 Are mandatory bankruptcy auctions more efficient?

by B. Espen Eckbo
Tuck Centennial Professor of Finance
and
Karin S. Thorburn
Assistant Professor of Finance
Amos Tuck School of Business Administration, Dartmouth College

The central role of agency costs

A firm that is unable to serve its debt must choose to either renegotiate with its debtholders out-of-court or file for bankruptcy. In a *perfect* world, where there are no costly conflicts of interest between managers and the firm's securityholders, this choice is always made efficiently. That is, the firm selects the alternative that minimises overall financial distress costs and maximises firm value. This implication also carries over to the firm's choice between available bankruptcy procedures. For example, firms selecting court-supervised renegotiation over sale of the firm in a formal bankruptcy auction do so because the choice provides the most efficient, lowest-cost solution. In this setting, the *option* to select court-supervised renegotiation over outright auction is always valuable, and a bankruptcy code, which contains this option, is necessarily superior to a code that does not.

The world is not perfect (alas!): Managerial labour contracts are costly to write and therefore leave open the possibility that managers effectuate uncompensated wealth transfers from the firm's securityholders in the process of running the firm. Financial economists refer to this as an *agency conflict* between the firm's owners and managers (the agents). Moreover, imperfect contracting leaves shareholders, being residual claimants on the firm's cash flow, with an incentive to use the firm's investment policy to transfer wealth from bondholders (*the asset substitution problem*). In the context of bankruptcy and financial distress, agency conflicts and asset substitution problems manifest themselves in terms of inefficient choices and, therefore, higher bankruptcy costs. Managers of firms in financial distress may chose to file for bankruptcy at a suboptimal time (e.g., 'too late'), and use a suboptimal bankruptcy venue (e.g., court-supervised renegotiation over auction), in order to preserve their private benefits from running the firm. To stay out of court, they may also decide to 'go for the extreme' by overinvesting in risky projects that benefit shareholders at the expense of bondholders. In this world, the design of the bankruptcy code directly affects the allocation of corporate resources and is therefore economically important. A code that provides relatively greater protection of managerial control rights risks exacerbating agency conflicts.

What, in principle, characterises an optimal bankruptcy code? Should one allow maximum managerial discretion, or should one restrict the options available to managers in bankruptcy? Should one allow debtor-in-possession financing? Should one make use of *market* valuations in allocating new claims on the restructured firm, or should one simply derive such valuations from corporate balance sheets and accounting statements? Should one adhere strictly to absolute priority rules, or should the court be allowed to deviate from absolute priority? Should creditors be forced to accept a proposed reorganisation plan (cram down)? Should a confirmed reorganisation plan be settled in cash only or should creditors be forced to accept new debt claims on the firm? The answer to these questions depends fundamentally on the magnitude of the agency conflicts and asset substitution problems referred to above. Since agency costs are difficult to quantify, the optimality of a particular bankruptcy code remains an empirically controversial issue, as witnessed by the diverse opinions expressed throughout this volume.

Renegotiation vs. mandatory bankruptcy auctions

The bulk of the debate to date has been directed towards the merits of the U.S. bankruptcy code. This code is, from a European perspective, relatively 'manager oriented'. Chapter 7 of the code allows for liquidation through an auction. However, by filing under Chapter 11 instead, managers continue to run the firm during the proceedings, they can rise new outside senior debt, and they are given bargaining power vis-à-vis existing creditors.

The bargaining power arises from managerial rights to propose a reorganisation plan backed up by a threat by the court to force creditor acceptance (cram down). Moreover, U.S. Bankruptcy courts are known to shift wealth from senior to junior claimants by deviating from absolute priority rules. In contrast, the Swedish bankruptcy code contains no such renegotiation option. Immediately upon filing, the firm is put up for sale in a public (first price) auction, either as a going concern or in a piecemeal liquidation. Debtholders are paid off using the cash proceeds from the auction and strictly according to absolute priority. In this system, managers retain no control rights unless they are hired by the new owners of the firm. The new owners determine the firm's new financing and investment policy and thus its market value in the auction. The crux of the controversy concerns whether such a mandatory auction system is more or less efficient than the manager-oriented renegotiation code found in the U.S. since the introduction of Chapter 11 in 1978.

The empirical debate

The debate reflects the fact that the bulk of the empirical evidence concerns bankruptcies in the U.S. This presents a problem since one cannot, of course, judge the relative merits of a mandatory auction system from evidence on U.S. bankruptcies alone. As pointed out above, within a given system, firms always self-select into the bankruptcy venue that managers find optimal. This implies that, in the presence of agency conflicts, one cannot infer from a sample of Chapter 7 cases (auctions) what would have happened to firms in Chapter 11 (renegotiations) had these firms instead selected the auction venue. The self-selection process ensures that firms in the two chapters most likely differ along the agency-cost dimension. This is supported by the fact that the largest firms overwhelmingly tend to select Chapter 11 and that agency problems generally tend to increase with firm size. This selection bias is alleviated in studies of bankruptcies in countries with mandatory auction systems, since the samples used necessarily capture *all* firms regardless of their inherent agency conflicts.

Ideally, if the average level of agency costs is the same in two samples of Chapter 11 cases and mandatory auction cases, then it follows that differences in case outcomes across the two legal systems, e.g., in terms of direct and indirect bankruptcy costs, recovery rates, corporate survival etc., reflect the relative efficiency of the two bankruptcy codes *per se*. This is in the spirit of the empirical analyses of Ravid and Sundgren (1997) and Thorburn (1997, 1998) who study auction bankruptcy in Finland (pre-1993) and Sweden, respectively. Moreover, Eisenberg and Tagashira (1994), Eisenberg and Sundgren (1997), and Fisher and Martel (1997) provide evidence on cases under non-U.S. reorganisation codes (Japan, Finland post-1993 and Canada, respectively). Also, Bradley and Rosenzweig (1992) and Sundgren (1998) provide longitudinal analyses where they compare the outcomes of bankruptcy cases within the U.S. and Finland, respectively, before and after the two bankruptcy codes were altered to include a stronger reorganisation provision.

The empirical literature provides evidence on bankruptcy costs, recovery rates, preservation of going concern value through the bankruptcy process, post-bankruptcy firm performance, and managerial wealth effect and turnover. In the following, we comment on each of these factors separately before making an overall evaluation of the question posed in the title of this paper.

Bankruptcy Costs

It is common to divide total bankruptcy costs in two parts; *direct* costs reflecting lawyer's fees, administrative costs, fees to trustees, etc., and possibly much greater *indirect* costs reflecting diversion of managerial effort from productive activities, loss of key employees, lower demand for the company's output, etc.. While empirical evidence on direct costs is readily obtainable, indirect costs are basically unobservable and therefore not reported. However, it is common to argue that indirect costs are increasing in the time the firm spends in bankruptcy. The evidence indicates that large, publicly traded firms spend on average two years in Chapter 11, while the duration is slightly shorter for smaller, non-listed firms. In contrast, as documented by Thorburn (1997), the average duration of a Swedish auction bankruptcy case is only two months. In sum, indirect costs of bankruptcy are most likely substantially lower under the auction system.

While indirect costs may constitute a substantial portion of firm value, direct costs are limited by the costs of an outright take-over of the bankrupt firm. A large number of studies of publicly traded U.S. firms, from Warner (1977) to Betker (1997), report average direct costs of 3-4% of pre-filing assets. Not surprisingly, most studies document a substantial size effect in direct costs, with smaller firms having higher costs. In comparison, in her sample of 263 small-firm auction bankruptcy cases in Sweden, Thorburn (1997) estimate direct costs which average 6% of pre-filing assets and 19% of the auction proceeds. Moreover, adjusting for firm size, she concludes that the auction system tend to produce lower direct costs than what is observed for Chapter 11.

Sundgren (1998) examines a sample of 22 Finnish auction bankruptcy cases and reports direct costs which average 7% of assets and 15% of auction proceeds. Moreover, this compares to 5% of promised payments for a sample of 43 Finnish reorganisation cases that took place after 1993 when the Finnish code was amended to include provisions for a Chapter 11-style renegotiation option. He concludes from this that direct costs are lower after 1993. However, the difference in costs in the two samples before and after 1993 is significant only when scaling with the value of promised payments (which must be estimated in the sample after 1993). When scaling with either total assets or total debt, both of which are measured identically across the two time periods, the cost difference is not statistically different from zero.

Sundgren (1998) also reports the results of cross-sectional regressions with direct costs (in proportion of total assets or total debt) as dependent variable. These regression contain a binary variable indicating that the average direct costs, conditional on the cross-sectional model, is significantly higher after the code-amendment in 1993. Unfortunately, his sample period before 1993 coincides with a severe recession in Finland, which the regression model does not account for. Particularly in light of the evidence in Thorburn (1997) that direct costs increase with industry distress, Sundgren's time-dummy may very well reflect the effect of recession on asset values (the denominator in the dependent variable) rather than lower costs of a reorganisation code (the numerator).

Recovery rates

Franks and Torous (1994) estimate recovery rates for a sample of 38 large, publicly traded firms successfully reorganised in Chapter 11. They report that the median value (market or face) of claims distributed in the reorganisation is 51% of total liabilities at the time of filing. In a subsample of 12 cases with market value data for all new claims, the median recovery rate is lower, 41%. They also report that junior debt receives a substantial recovery (30%) which implies a deviation from absolute priority rules. Interestingly, when using market values, the overall recovery rate in Chapter 11 appears to be similar to the recovery in Swedish bankruptcy auctions: Thorburn (1997), in her subsample of going concern auction sales (which compare to successful reorganisations under Chapter 11) report a median (and mean) recovery rate of 40%. Adding the fact that recovery rates tend to increase with firm size, this evidence suggests that mandatory auctions produce recovery rates that are at least as high as in Chapter 11.

Bradley and Rosenzweig (1992) estimate abnormal bond and stock returns surrounding Chapter 11 filing dates in subsamples before and after 1978, the time of the introduction of Chapter 11 in the U.S.. They conclude that security-holders (both debt and equity) suffer greater losses associated with filings after 1978, and attribute this loss to higher agency costs under Chapter 11. Their evidence is consistent with the hypothesis that higher agency costs lead to lower recovery rates following the adoption of Chapter 11. Sundgren (1998), however, reaches the opposite conclusion for his sample of Finnish bankruptcies: He finds some evidence of higher recovery rates after 1993, following the adoption of the renegotiation option, suggesting instead that this option is valuable.

How does one reconcile the opposing conclusions concerning the value of a renegotiation option made by Bradley and Rosenzweig (1992) and Sundgren (1998)? On the one hand, agency costs in the Finnish sample of typically small owner-managed firms may be lower than in the U.S. sample of large publicly traded companies studied by Bradley-Rosenzweig. Thus, the option to select reorganisation may very well be valuable in Finland while costly in the U.S.. On the other hand, Sundgren's estimate of the difference in recovery rates between his two reorganisation and auction samples is probably too high. As indicated above, recovery rates in the auction sample are estimated over a sample period, which includes a deep recession, while the recovery rates for the reorganisation sample reflect a period with a general economic upswing of the Finnish economy. Thorburn (1997), in her sample of small-firm Swedish bankruptcy auctions cases, finds that recovery rates tend to be lower at the trough of the business cycle. Moreover, recovery rates in going concern auctions during normal periods are at par with the recovery rates reported by Sundgren for confirmed reorganisations; median 39%.

There is a second and more subtle reason for the difference in recovery rates observed by Sundgren: Concomitant with the introduction of the renegotiation option was a reduction in the priority granted debt collateralized with floating charge (which is typically held by banks). As a result, following 1993, these senior creditors have had a greater incentive to push the firm to file for bankruptcy at an earlier point in time, i.e., when the firm is relatively healthier. This in turn tend to increase total recovery rates in the later sample period regardless of the agency cost implications of the option to renegotiate under court supervision. In sum, the evidence favours the hypothesis that auction bankruptcy leads to recovery rates that are no lower than under court-supervised reorganisations.

Preservation of Going Concern Value
Total firm value consists of the sum of the value of the assets if liquidated piecemeal (*the liquidation value*) and the value created by organising the assets under the umbrella of one firm (*the going concern value*). A financially distressed firm attempts to reorganise its debt precisely to avoid loss of going concern value. Thus, the efficiency of a bankruptcy code is measured not only in terms of costs and overall recovery rates, but also in terms of the preservation of the synergies from maintaining the firm as a going concern.

Obviously, in order to have preserved going concern value, the firm must emerge from bankruptcy as a financially healthy going concern. This suggests that one should look at: a) the frequency of going concern solutions; b) changes in the difference between total firm and liquidation values upon exit from bankruptcy; c) the financial structure of emerging firms; as well as d) post-bankruptcy firm performance. The Total number of going concern solutions is the sum of the number of auction 'prepacks' (i.e., prearranged reorganisations or auction sales which are subjected to court approval) and the number of going concern reorganisations and going concern sales in bankruptcy. Thorburn (1997) concludes that this number is similar across Chapter 11 and Swedish bankruptcy; approximately 70% under either system (of which appr. 25% are prepacks). Moreover, Ravid and Sundgren (1997) draw a qualitatively similar conclusion based on their sample of Finnish bankruptcy auctions.

Fisher and Martel (1997) compare confirmation rates (i.e., the fraction of reorganisation plans that are approved by creditors) in Canadian and U.S. small-firm reorganisations. Canada has a reorganisation code which differs somewhat from the U.S. Chapter 11 in that managers retain fewer rights during the renegotiation process and that there is no possibility for cram down. They report that confirmation rates are higher in Canada than in the U.S., which they take to indicate that the Canadian code leads to a higher survival rate. While this conclusion is consistent with the view that Chapter 11 tends to exacerbate agency problems, it also presumes a strong correlation between confirmation rates and going concern solutions which is not present for Chapter 11 cases. That is, confirmations may be plans to liquidate, and lack of confirmation does not mean that the firm is in fact liquidated. Indeed, Flynn (1989) reports that one quarter of his small-firm Chapter 11 confirmations are liquidation plans, while White (1984) finds that about half of the non-confirmed small-firm reorganisation plans represent firms that are sold as going concerns.

As to changes in the difference between total firm and liquidation values upon exit from bankruptcy, Sundgren (1998) and Fisher and Martel (1997), as well as Eisenberg and Tagashira (1994) using reorganisations in Japan, report evidence on the so called 'reorganisation surplus'. This surplus is computed as the (discounted) face value of new debt claims as a percent of an estimate of the firm's liquidation value. All three papers report evidence that this reorganisation surplus is positive, indicating that the reorganisation process leaves intact some going concern value. Similarly, Thorburn (1997) reports that the median price received in going concern bankruptcy auctions in Sweden exceeds the estimated liquidation value by 25%. Thus, there is evidence that *both* going concern auctions and court-supervised renegotiations tend to preserve at least part of the firm's going concern value. It remains to be examined in which system loss of going concern value (if any) is the greatest.

The financial structure of emerging firms and their post-bankruptcy firm performance, Gilson (1997) and Thorburn (1998) both report that 70% of firms emerging from bankruptcy (in Chapter 11 and in Sweden, respectively) have higher leverage than the median industry competitor. Moreover, comparing the results in Hotchkiss (1995) and Thorburn (1998), this leverage ratio produces a similar frequency of second debt restructuring/bankruptcy refilings within five years. Moreover, both Hotchkiss (1995) and Thorburn (1998) provide a comparison of the post-bankruptcy performance of emerging firms relative to their respective domestic non-bankrupt industry competitors. Interestingly, while Thorburn (1998) finds that post-bankruptcy performance of auctioned firms is at par with industry competitors, Hotchkiss' (1995) evidence indicates significant below-industry performance following Chapter 11 proceedings. This represents perhaps the strongest evidence that mandatory auctions are more effective than Chapter 11 in restoring the distressed firm to a normal operating health.

Managerial Wealth Loss and Turnover

Gilson (1989), Hotchkiss (1995), Gilson and Vetsuypens (1993), and Thorburn (1998) present evidence on managerial turnover rates and wage changes associated with bankruptcy. Overall, the evidence indicates that managerial turnover is higher in auction bankruptcy than under Chapter 11. Moreover, Thorburn (1998) reports that auction bankruptcy results in a substantial managerial wage loss (there is no comparable evidence on Chapter 11).

Interestingly, the post-bankruptcy performance of auctioned firms appears to be independent of whether or not the incumbent CEO remains with the firm. In contrast, post-bankruptcy performance of Chapter 11 firms tends to be lower if the incumbent CEO remains with the firm (Hotchkiss (1995)). Coupled with the finding that CEOs have a higher chance of staying with the firm following Chapter 11 than following mandatory auctions, this is consistent with the proposition that mandatory auctions represent a stronger disciplinary force than does Chapter 11. This evidence supports the hypothesis that a mandatory auction system is more effective than court-supervised reorganisation in reducing the overall level of agency costs.

Development of Market Alternatives to Chapter 11

Easterbrook (1990) suggests that, if auctions are more efficient than court-supervised debt reorganisations, then one should observe attempts to acquire firms in Chapter 11. Consistent with this view, the 1980s saw the emergence of an active market for claims of Chapter 11 firms in terms of mergers and of acquisitions of distressed debt by so-called 'vulture funds'. These and other out-of-court solutions such as prepacks, public debt exchanges, and leveraged buyouts are in part a response to the current U.S. bankruptcy code. Thus, there is growing evidence that market transactions (including auctions) may very well dominate court-supervised reorganisations also in the U.S. large-firm environment.

Are mandatory bankruptcy auctions more efficient?

As summarised above, the evidence indicates that the auction procedure is relatively inexpensive, it exploits market valuations of corporate assets, it provides relatively strong managerial discipline, and it produces reorganised firms that perform at par with industry competitors. Thus, judging in particular from the large-sample Swedish evidence, there is little doubt that auctions represent an economically efficient mechanism for restructuring bankrupt firms.

Is the auction system *more* efficient than a Chapter 11-style reorganisation code? The Swedish evidence suggests, *ceteris paribus*, that it is. As discussed above, however, this conclusion presumes that the evidence of superior performance of the Swedish auction system is driven by the efficiency of the bankruptcy system *per se* and not more fundamentally by lower total agency costs in the Swedish small-firm environment. Of course, shareownership concentration reduces only *one* of the two components of total agency costs: the manager-shareholder conflict. Equityholders' incentives to asset substitute remain strong also in a concentrated ownership environment. Furthermore, if one truly believes that total agency costs are higher in the U.S. than in Sweden, then the evidence implies that one should consider abolishing Chapter 11 which exacerbates conflicts of interest between managers and all of the firm's securityholders.

Acknowledgement

We thank Professor Theodore Eisenberg for comments on an earlier draft. Partial financial support from the Norwegian Research Council (Norges Forskningsråd), grant no. 125105/510, is also gratefully acknowledged.

6.7 Crisis and recovery: Post-Recessional changes in UK bank lending practice

by Barry Howcroft
Professor of Retail Banking and Director of Loughborough University Banking Centre

The recent economic recession in the United Kingdom was almost certainly exacerbated by the banking industry's failure to read the danger signals and take appropriate remedial action. This failure stemmed from a number of sources. For example, the previous recession of the late seventies and early eighties was regarded as being essentially manufacturing and provincial, i.e. a 'smokestack industry' phenomenon. As such it was considered a 'one-off', not applicable to the service and high-tech sectors which had emerged in the eighties. Moreover, many bank and business executives were too young to have experienced the previous recession and therefore lacked the experience of diagnosing warning signals indicative of business failure. The situation was further aggravated by the view, prevalent at the beginning of the recession, that it was simply a temporary phenomenon. Business lending, therefore, continued to increase well into the late eighties. Any lingering doubts that the recession might be long term were alleviated by the equally misplaced view that rising property prices and hence increased security values would more than adequately compensate the banks for business failures. Intense competition between lending banks also resulted in a sales orientated culture with a consequential emphasis on quotas and volumetric targeting. As a result quality lending was made the sacrificial lamb of quantity and a preoccupation with market share (Morgan, 1994).

These sorts of considerations prompted Loughborough University Banking Centre to instigate research into assessing the lessons, which could be learned from this experience, and to determine how these lessons might be transposed into best practice in corporate lending. It was, therefore, decided to conduct a series of interviews with lending bankers, key personnel in SMEs and intermediaries, i.e. accountants and solicitors. The main findings of the research were subsequently 'tested' by follow-up telephone interviews with representatives of the manufacturing, retailing and service industries. This paper provides a brief insight into the results of this research and focuses specifically on four main aspects of bank lending: the banker-customer relationship; the mix of funding; customer propensity to shop around; and the restructuring of the corporate lending function within banks.

The banker-customer relationship

The intermediaries provided some interesting and fairly objective generalisations regarding the banker-customer relationship. In particular, they suggested that lending banks should change their basic approach to counter the residual impression that they are 'watching their own positions'. Accordingly, they emphasised the importance of banks and businesses working in partnership together, especially when producing and interpreting cash flow projections and business plans (Keasey and Watson, 1993). They also suggested that there is no room for optimism either on the part of the banks or their business customers and indicated that the essence of the banker-customer relationship must be realism and pragmatism and that ambiguity, in whatever form, must be avoided (Perrein et al, 1994).

The in-depth interviews revealed a definite willingness on the part of banks and businesses to create closer relationships with each other. This impression was reinforced by the telephone interviews, which showed that 88% of business respondents welcomed such a move and would also include intermediaries, such as solicitors and accountants in the relationship. The essential constituent parts of this tripartite relationship emerged as being: mutual understanding, mutual trust, good communication, and professionalism.

Rather surprising was the fact that cost was seen by many businesses as being of less relative importance than this relationship: 51% of the telephone respondents expressed this view compared with only 16% who believed that the cost of finance was more important than the relationship. This would suggest that competition for business is moving towards a relatively fair and uniform pricing policy in this sector. However, this must not be allowed to detract from the fact that if, for whatever reason, pricing was perceived as to high or unfair, it would undoubtedly emerge as <u>the</u> single most important consideration and far outweigh anything else, including the relationship factor.

The precise nature of this relationship will clearly have an impact on bank costs and it will be interesting to see if business customers will be prepared to pay for the additional benefits associated with closer relationships with their banks. This problem may be resolved in part by introducing a differentiated service for business customers, but the key to successful implementation will be determined by the ability of the banks in demonstrating both a need for and the benefits of these services to customers. Out of these two considerations, i.e. the 'need' and the 'benefit', the research demonstrated that there is a recognised need amongst business customers for a closer relationship. Lending banks, therefore, should focus their attention on strategies, which promote differential pricing on the basis of the additional benefits to customers.

A differentiated service for business customers could be introduced according to the size of business or length of relationship with the bank, etc, but an alternative approach would be to differentiate according to the type and nature of service being provided. In this respect, it must be recognised that business services are not homogenous, but rather vary quite radically in terms of complexity and the after sales service which each require. Business services can, accordingly, be regarded as being on a continuum, ranging from basic services such as money transmission and safe custody through to more complex services (so-called 'high credence' products), such as venture capital and equity finance which require a more in-depth understanding of the customer, ideally borne out of a close banker-customer relationship (Howcroft and Beckett, 1996).

Relatively few financial services associated with business customers can be regarded as 'basic' because the majority are not readily understood and typically require a relationship involving a regular review and periodic reassessment of needs. Moreover, service complexity is inversely related to customer confidence, therefore business customers generally become less capable of identifying and choosing appropriate financial services the more complicated they become. Under these circumstances, conventional search-buy criteria, based on a comparison of prices, quality, availability, etc, become less appropriate and customers place proportionately greater emphasis on the bank's corporate image and advertising. In making an eventual choice, however, 'trust' in a bank based on an established relationship emerged as a very important consideration and may even outweigh cost of finance, provided the value added in both the bank product and the relationship is fully understood by the customer.

Mix of funding

The idea that the majority of business services are complicated and can perhaps best be described as "high credence" products might also explain why there is still an over reliance on the overdraft and term loan facilities (Morsman, 1991). Although there is a perceptible move away from exclusive reliance on the bank overdraft by business customers, it still remains the most common method of bank borrowing: 89% of telephone respondents had overdrafts and a further 6% would readily consider them. Conversely, 69% of respondents currently had term loans and a further 20% would consider them in the future.

Although tariffs can be complicated, the overdraft and term loan is generally understood by banks and customers alike. In fact, it could be argued that the banks and their customers are too familiar with these facilities and that this partly explains why the traditional regular review of business customers has, in many instances, given way to an annual roll-over of the overdraft facility. As already stated, this attitude may well have been compounded by the supposed complexity of other forms of business finance, but in many instances there are strong reasons to believe that it has been perpetuated by non-familiarity with these alternatives. For example, borrowing against receivables, i.e. factoring and invoice discounting, was typically perceived as expensive and a last resort by the respondents who had not used it (Hart, 1991). Further enquiry revealed a certain degree of ignorance and prejudice amongst non-users who had clearly not examined these facilities in detail. This 'ignorance factor' was apparently compounded by the bank's low key promotion of these services. In fact, the research revealed some positive resistance by the banks to promoting bank group products such as factoring and invoice discounting. This may be a legacy of the hard-sell approach of the eighties and perhaps also reflects the lack of 'reward' to the referring bank source.

Equity funding did attract interest in the form of venture capital (Sapienza et al, 1994): some 21% of the telephone respondents had used venture capital and a further 36% would be willing to consider it in the future. However, some respondents did express the view that venture capital was expensive and that the emphasis on exit routes reflected a short-term attitude. A market listing or flotation, however, was far less attractive then venture capital. Only 17% of the telephone respondents had used this method of finance and only a further 9% would consider it in the future. This was partly explained by a stubborn resistance to the notion of outside intervention or loss of managerial control. This was especially the case with established family concerns and entrepreneurial businesses in the early stages of bank funding.

Customer propensity to shop around

No less than 42% of business respondents already had more than one bank or would use loans from another bank and a further 31% would consider shopping around. The questionnaire did not differentiate between UK clearers, UK non-clearing banks and foreign banks, but 'post-recession' there does appear to be latent demand for bank loans and a willingness to shop around for the best deals (Chemmanur and Fulghieri, 1994).

An important consideration in determining a business customer's propensity to shop around was the personal qualities of bank staff and this consideration was especially important when companies saw little difference between competing banks. It became apparent, however, that by the term 'quality of staff' the majority of interviewees were referring to technical quality, i.e. the quality of the advice provided rather than the basic hygiene factors of quality which typically relate to being polite and well mannered, etc (Swan and Combs, 1976).

There was only limited evidence to suggest that this propensity to shop around may have been caused by overcharging. Isolated incidents of overcharging existed, but most were explained by failure to communicate the bases for charging or an absence (in the past) of formal tariffs. Businesses do not object to being charged per se and appreciate the fact that banks, like any other businesses, need to cover costs, however mishandling of the charging process can seriously damage the banker-customer relationship.

Speed of decision making was another factor, which had a direct bearing on the business customer's willingness to shop around. When managers referred lending propositions to head offices, the delays, which sometimes ensued, were identified as important sources of dissatisfaction, especially when the proposal was turned down. Speed of decision making might also partly explain why some business interviewees expressed dissatisfaction with bank organisational structures, which effectively divorced actual decision making from the staff who managed their relationship. There is a clear and natural distinction between the 'control' of business customers as opposed to the 'relationship' and 'selling' functions, but organisational changes in banks, which make these distinctions less obvious to the customer and simultaneously improve efficiency, are to be welcomed (Richtor, 1995).

The research also revealed a greater predisposition of businesses to seek professional advice in relation to financing. This raises two important questions: who to go to when seeking professional advice and how to determine an appropriate fee? At present, these questions are not easily resolved, but as suggested earlier a step forward might be to differentiate the market into two broad categories based on the type of advice required: low cost for routine advice and premium cost for advice on difficult or major decisions. At the moment the two are poorly (if at all) differentiated in the market and perceptions of what constitutes quality advice vary quite considerably. This is certainly an area, which deserves further attention from banks, accountants and other professional advisors.

Restructuring of the corporate lending function

In the 'post recession' period the clearing banks have made significant efforts to simultaneously improve efficiency and reduce costs (Richtor, 1995). This has involved radically reorganising and restructuring the way in which business clients are handled. In general, the lending function has increasingly been stripped out of branches and business centres increasingly serve the needs of mid-corporate customers with 'relationship managers' acting as the primary contacts. The specifics vary from bank to bank, but the research revealed that business customers broadly welcome these changes and associate them with improvements in service levels. The interviews also revealed a sort of empathy between the business customers and banks inasmuch as the customers regarded the bank's radical reorganisational changes as comparable with the sort of changes which they too have had to make.

The adoption of computer-based technology to improve the bank's analysis and increase the speed of credit decision making is also regarded as both desirable and inevitable. The resultant reduction in bank staffing levels is regarded with equanimity provided service levels and continuity are maintained. There was, however, some criticism of the disruption experienced during periods of rapid change and, in particular, the excessive turnover of bank personnel. In general, however, the changes do appear to have been largely accepted and any short-term inconvenience has been tolerated.

Conclusions

The research did reveal evidence of changing practices and attitudes amongst lending banks, business customers and intermediaries. In addition to the findings presented in this paper, the interviews also provided evidence of a greater willingness to rescue businesses rather than place them in liquidation. The emergence of this 'rescue culture' is very much in evidence in the way banks and accountants are making concerted efforts to forge closer links with businesses and their management. There is also evidence to suggest that the banks are beginning to place greater emphasis on portfolio management in an attempt to facilitate better credit control and more efficient differential pricing strategies. At the individual customer level expert decision systems have also facilitated better 'quality control' and greater uniformity in the credit granting process. Having regard for the mistakes of the recent recession, this development and the others reported in this paper will be especially important in the future.

6.8 Reflections on how the bankruptcy system as a whole functions

by Bo Green
Programme Director, Stockholm University

Business insolvency has been at the forefront of many nations' policy agendas. Australia, Canada, Finland, France, Germany, Sweden, the United Kingdom, the United States and other countries have revised their insolvency laws or are considering doing so. A natural question to pose is whether the many developments in business insolvency and related laws, especially reorganisations, have changed or can change the degree or nature of insolvency risks facing lenders, suppliers, employees, governments and others dealing with debtors.

There is no doubt that laws, rules and norms for business transactions determine the actions of different interested parties and the manner in which the *bankruptcy system as a whole functions*. It is, for example, obvious that treatment of secured creditors changes risk behaviour and the risks to other parties dealing with debtors.

To some extent law is an instrument to implement political will and in my view it is essential to point out to politicians the importance of ensuring that the laws are based on a careful consideration of relevant circumstances.

It is not easy to investigate a system that has multiple participants and interested parties with different perspectives and different opinions. To illuminate and comprehend all of the influences that exist in the complex bankruptcy system is almost 'impossible' for politicians, researchers, investigators and those involved.

It is furthermore quite natural that the interested parties assert their own self-interest. That is the reason why the Swedish government found it difficult to change the rules in the bankruptcy system. These difficulties also explain why we in Sweden during the last twenty-two years have used wage guarantees as 'security' for bank loans to small companies (the fact that the bank's claim over the company's assets has priority over wages reduces the bank's risks).

Since 1976 it has been efficient and profitable for banks to use bankruptcy as a tool for reorganisation. The fact that in bankruptcy the company's assets have priority over wages is a reason why the new reorganisation law in Sweden has not been uses by companies with secured creditors.

In 1985 I was chairman of the 'bankruptcy investigation' in Sweden. In my report to the government I argued that in order to reach a balance in the bankruptcy system it is necessary to give wages some degree of priority over creditors secured by company assets. My report to the government argued that a change in the order of priorities would stimulate the banks to follow up loans to small companies and create *incentives* for bank management to educate their loan officers in risk assessment. I also argued that the banks would be more prone to co-operate in a crisis situation if they were on the same footing as other creditors.

In the debate at the bankruptcy seminars organised in Sweden during 1986 I strongly pointed out that the aim of a new reorganisation law in Sweden must be to avoid bankruptcy in cases where there is a reasonable chance of the company surviving. I also stressed that reorganisation of a company is difficult and that it requires a thorough analysis and expertise in order to formulate a reorganisation plan.

In December 1992 the 'insolvency investigation' presented a new *reorganisation law* which to a large extent was based on the suggestion that I presented to the Swedish government in November 1985. The investigator used the concept of productive wages in arguing for a change in the present order of priorities in bankruptcy proceedings.

In the debate about the legislation, representatives from the banks have stressed that if a change in the present order of priorities was made, so that the floating charge becomes less important, measures would probably be taken to replace such security by other arrangements such as leasing and factoring. Bank management strongly lobbied the Swedish government not to change the present order of priorities in accordance with the investigators' suggestions. They argued that, if the government changes the priority order, it would be more expensive and more difficult for small companies to get bank financing.

In my opinion it is obvious that the present disharmony in this area of the law is unsatisfactory. But whether bankruptcy auctions are more efficient than chapter 11 or any other reorganisation law depends on how the *bankruptcy system as a whole* is constructed in the individual country. In order to reach a balance in the bankruptcy system, as a whole there is a need for the society to define the role of different participants in a well functioning business world.

INSURABLE RISKS IN BUSINESS

7.1 Introduction

by Robert W Vivian
IISA Professor of Insurance and Risk Management
Head of Department of Business Economics
University of the Witwatersrand

Kenneth J Arrow, Nobel laureate in *Insurance, Risk and Resource Allocation* (1965), pointed out that risk is pervasive and that one of the most established methods of dealing with risk is insurance. However, not every kind of risk is insurable. Traditionally, risks involving losses on damage to property, injury to people, legal liability claims arising out of damage to property or injury to people and consequential losses arising from damage to property are insurable against a wide range of perils. Generally, business risks are not insurable. A characteristic of business risks is that the loss or damage is in nature a 'pure financial loss'. This may be defined as a loss for which it does not involve damage to physical property but only results in financial losses. Insolvency is an example.

Credit insurance

One exception to the rule that pure financial losses are not insurable is credit insurance, and its use as part of the risk management strategy of a firm is examined by Wolf-Ingo Darius. He draws attention to the positive correlation which exists between well managed firms and firms which have well managed insurance programmes. Well managed companies pay attention to the management of risks and he points out that virtually all companies purchase some insurance. The economy is becoming increasingly unpredictable, reflecting an increasing number of insolvencies. Under these circumstances it is surprising that most companies do not purchase credit insurance. Alternatives to the purchase of credit insurance such as the retention of title (ownership) are not very effective, especially where goods, as part of a manufacturing process, have been merged into other goods or the goods have left the country.

Newly formed small and medium enterprises (SMEs) are particularly susceptible to failure and credit insurance can be a powerful tool to minimise this risk. Credit insurance can protect the SME from failure of its customers and reduce its transactions and information acquisition costs. Credit insurers can do this because of their extensive experience and information databases made accessible by tried and tested, customised software. It is well-known that where a company can obtain insurance this is a signal to various players in the market place. The granting of credit insurance signals to the SME's bank that the firm is well managed and has a higher credit rating. Under these circumstances banks are often more prepared to grant assistance to the SME.

Legislative framework for risk-taking

Mr Björn Palmgren approaches the issue of risk-taking from a legislative framework point of view. Legislation is primarily concerned with ensuring the stability of the insurance market and Palmgren correctly points out that "much of insurance legislation is in a natural way focused on managing and reducing risks that arise from the insurance business, which by its very nature is centred around insurance risks and investment risks".

The first foundation of financial stability is that the initial and current capital of an insurer should be adequate, where adequacy is generally defined by legislation. Legislation also deals with the internal controls and management methods, which must be adopted to manage risks. These include underwriting, reserving and reinsurance matters. Fit and proper requirements are specified. Of particular importance is the management of the investment portfolio. Insurance companies generally prepare accounts in accordance with established accounting principles, but because of their nature detailed requirements are also specified by legislation. Legislation specifies the need for regular reporting to the supervisory authorities. However, in practice it has been found that statutory returns are not enough and other lines of communication between the insurance market and authorities are sought. Industry consultative committees are an example.

Insurability of risks and insuring business risks

Insurance is a common method used to deal with risks. It is however seldom used to manage business risks. Björn Palmgren correctly points out that the set of risks against which protection is desirable is, of course, much larger than the set of insurable risks. Robert Vivian examines the reason for this situation and asks: What is it that sets the limits to insurability? While attempts are made on a daily basis to expand the horizons of insurability, no clear theoretical answer exists to the question of whether or not a specific risk falls within the limits of insurability. If the historical development of insurance is examined to determine the criteria for insurability then it is clear that the vast bulk of insurance contracts cover loss or damage to property, consequential losses arising out of damage to property, injury to people and liability claims. In these cases the losses are caused by a specific determinable event and external peril, in such a manner that damages are not (perfectly) positively correlated. Additionally, the market has developed specific measures to counter problems of moral hazard and adverse selection. Moral hazard arises where the insured brings about the insured event. The owner, for example of a company which is in financial difficulties may start a fire in order to claim on his insurance policy. Adverse selection arises when an uninsured person specifically seeks insurance, knowing that he has a high risk. Thus for example a company may grant credit to a high risk debtors and then insure that risk while at the same time declining to insure low risk debtors.

It becomes clear from the above discussion that business risks fall outside of the general criteria for insurability and it is therefore not surprising that as a rule business risks are not insured. An exception to this is credit insurance, which insures pure financial losses. But, as pointed out by Wolf-Ingo Darius, even credit insurance is not widespread. It is unlikely that this position will change in the immediate future.

7.2 Losses of receivables – a threat to small businesses. The role of a credit insurance company in providing risk coverage for growth companies

by Mr. Wolf-Ingo Darius
Chief Executive Officer, Hermes Kreditversicherungs-AG

Risk and Insurance Management

Let me start by defining Risk and Insurance Management. Risk Management in its current definition is an overall approach to safeguard the accomplishment of an enterprise's targets. This encompasses not only the prevention of financial losses, but also the reaching of planned targets. Insurance Management – as a major part of risk management – is the selection of insurance necessary for the respective company and their perpetual control. Efficient insurance management needs as its base a successful risk management programme.

Recent research by the German University of Kaiserslautern conducted by Prof. Dr. Reinhold Hölscher found that one half of small to medium-sized enterprises (SMEs) did not have any risk management at all. SMEs in this study are defined as companies with 50 to 1.000 employees. Latest available figures for Germany show that in 1994 there were approx. 68.000 companies in the industry and construction registered with more than 20 employees.

Let me mention at this point that there is no generally agreed upon definition of SMEs. Usually – at least in Germany – they are defined as companies with no more than 500 employees and a turnover of less than DM 100 m. We are talking here about a fairly heterogeneous group. Clearly, there are major differences between a company of say 50 employees and a turnover of DM 20 m and a company with 500 employees and a turnover of e.g. DM 100 m.

Professor Hölscher's study also showed that there is a positive correlation between the quality of risk and insurance management: if companies have good risk management their insurance management is of equal quality – and vice versa. Although this study was conducted in Germany, the results in other European countries would have been much the same.

Other results of the research that I would like to mention are:

- Investments in insurance – like other investments – are judged by their cost-benefit-ratio. In other words, premiums are only a point of discussion, if the performance of the insurance is questioned.
- Risks that cannot be covered by insurance are to be found, especially in the realm of environmental risks.
- Large industrial insurers generally are very efficient in consulting companies about their risk management. However, only approx. 30% of companies suited for this service actually use it.

Major risk increasing trends

Risk and insurance management today is faced with a changing economic situation. Six major structural trends can be identified, which make it ever more difficult to foresee the course the economy is taking:

Liberalisation of markets
Privatisation of former state companies is taking place in many countries. Think e.g. of airlines, telecommunication and energy producing companies. The effects of these privatisations on the economy are very difficult to assess.

Globalisation of the economy
One important consequence of globalisation is the increase of competition, because you can buy the same or largely comparable products at similar prices in all major markets.

Competition from Central and Eastern Europe
With the end of the former Eastern Block new market economies are emerging in Central and Eastern Europe. As they can produce at lower costs, there is a strong competition for market shares.

Competition from East Asia
The same is true for competition from the so-called 'tiger' states in East Asia. In addition, they have a large innovation potential.

Modern technology
Micro-electronics, more efficient software and continually faster product cycles pose threats to all companies.

Exchange rate changes
The volatility of exchange rates is forcing more and more companies to revise their economic plans. Insecurities about the planned introduction of the Euro in 1999 add a further unpredictability to the equation.

Importance of credit insurance in Europe

In this environment, virtually all companies insure themselves, taking out extensive insurance cover for their merchandise and production facilities. It is considered quite normal – sometimes it is even obligatory – to have fire, business interruption and transport insurance. But after the goods are delivered this insurance cover ends. Protection of receivables, however, should be a logical extension of insurance cover. After all, what use are impressive sales, if the money never comes?

Under these circumstances I find it quite surprising that most companies in Europe do not yet have a credit insurance. There are no exact figures available concerning the use of credit insurance in selected countries. However, let me take as an indicator the premium income of credit insurers as a portion of gross domestic product.

For the members of the EU we then come to the following results: The share as stated in a thousandth part is highest in Belgium and the Netherlands with 0.93% and 0.68% respectively and lowest in Finland, Norway, Sweden and Greece with 0.11%, 0.08%, 0.07% and 0.02%. France, Spain, Portugal and Great Britain have approximately the same importance of credit insurance with around 0.4%. This is being followed by Germany at a little more than 0.3%. The remaining countries Denmark, Austria, Italy and Switzerland vary between just below 0.3% and 0.17%.

Insolvency situation in Europe

The relatively low use of credit insurance is all the more astonishing, in view of the insolvency situation in Europe: the very risk that credit insurance covers. In the last ten years the number of company failures in Western Europe has almost doubled from about 100.000 in 1988 to just under 200.000 in 1997 (see Table 7.1). Virtually all countries are affected by this increase. Only in Denmark and Finland are the numbers of bankruptcies slightly reduced in this ten-year comparison. Their insolvency peaks to date were at the beginning of the 1990s.

Table 7.1 Insolvencies in Western Europe 1988 and 1997

Country	**1988**	**1997**	**change**	**in %**
Belgium	3.715	7.900	4.185	113
Germany	10.562	29.000	18.438	175
Denmark	2.562	2.000	-562	-22
Finland	2.435	4.000	1.565	64
France	35.052	65.500	30.448	87
Great Britain	16.700	40.400	23.700	142
Italy	12.400	15.800	3.400	27
Netherlands	3.847	5.400	1.553	40
Norway	3.894	3.300	- 594	-15
Austria	3.104	5.100	1.996	64
Sweden	5.563	10.200	4.637	83
Switzerland	1.072	4.300	3.228	301
Spain	232	1.000	768	331
Total	**101.138**	**193.900**	**95.762**	**92**

Source: National statistics, prognoses by Hermes Kreditversicherungs-AG

Bleak as this scenario already is – such a doubling of company failures in Western Europe, there is little comfort to offer for the future. We believe that insolvency figures will continue to rise for at least the next two to three years, and doubt that the number of company failures will ever go back to the relatively low levels of the eighties.

In addition, there are three important insolvency trends, which do not make things any easier for companies:

- Insolvencies increasingly come over-night, i.e. there is much less chance to react in time to cut losses
- More and more fraud is connected with insolvencies, making it extremely difficult to predict them
- The increasing – domestic and world-wide – competition will aggravate the economic selection process.

All of this clearly shows that risks to the existence of a company due to losses of receivables are and remain definitely higher than they used to be.

Credit insurance as a part of insurance management

Credit insurance covers the losses of receivables due to the bankruptcy of a company. In some countries so-called protracted default can also be insured. This is generally defined as non-payment six months after due date.

Some companies – instead of credit insuring themselves – rely on retention of title. Very often though that does not help – especially abroad. Even if it can contractually be agreed upon they are often not worth much in real life – mostly because the merchandise has already been further processed, or because the retention of title in the end cannot be legally protected.

In addition, there is no doubt that international trade offers more potential dangers than domestic trade. Differing trade customs, payment habits, languages and different legal systems offer extra challenges.

Most companies may not be aware of how severe a setback a single loss can be to their business. Clearly, profit margins will be curtailed and cash difficulties may result. The worst case scenario is the bankruptcy of the company suffering a non-payment – the so-called domino effect.

To illustrate my point let us look at Table 7.2. It shows the additional sales required to offset a bad debt loss. In order to offset e.g. a loss of only 20,000 DM a company with a pre-tax profit of 2% must make additional sales of DM 1 million.

Table 7.2 Necessary additional turnover in the case of losses of receivables

Loss of receivables in DM	Necessary additional turnover in DM		
	2%	**4%**	**6%**
10,000	500,000	250,000	166,700
20,000	1,000,000	500,000	333,300
50,000	2,500,000	1,250,000	833,300
100,000	5,000,000	2,500,000	1,667,000

Source: Hermes Kreditversicherungs-AG

The role of credit insurance for SMEs

There are obviously severe dangers posed by insurance management that overlooks or neglects the losses arising from the insolvency of a client. The example just cited should be especially alarming for a certain part of the SMEs, especially young firms, which have only recently been founded and more often than not are short of capital. It goes without saying that the consequences of a loss of receivables like those shown affects them more severely than larger companies. Receivables are for most of them their largest assets, and their cash flow is easily strained.

This statement can be established by looking at the German insolvency statistics. Again, matters will be much the same in other West European countries. About 80% of companies that go bankrupt are less than seven years old. About 60% of failed firms were founded as a limited company, which in Germany means that you need a minimum capital of 50,000 DM or roughly 250,000 SEK. In a case of crisis this does not take you very far.

What are, however, the deeper reasons for SMEs to fail? What do they do wrong that the survivors do right? According to our experience most of those that have to go out of business made management mistakes. This includes i.e. a wrong assessment of the market and false financing strategies.

For SMEs with a turnover of up to DM 4 million Hermes developed in the mid-1980s a policy that deals with their needs. We now offer it also in Sweden to companies with an annual turnover up to SEK 20 million. According to our experience this type of company is exporting more and more to markets in Europe. Therefore we see an increased need and demand for this kind of insurance cover. In addition, by using this policy these companies become accustomed to handling the more complex commercial risks that arise as companies grow. At the same time, it is a natural introduction to taking out traditional credit insurance.

Credit insurance and risk awareness

It is virtually impossible in today's highly competitive economic world not to grant a credit period for payment. As a matter of fact it is used by many companies as an important tool to promote their sales. In this respect, questions of creditworthiness are very often given lower priority, the main aim being a higher turnover. If the economic situation of a client cannot be easily assessed domestically, then this danger increases many fold internationally.

This is where credit insurance again comes in. Because it has much more to offer than just payment in the case of an insolvency – important as this is. Another major part of credit insurance is the thorough checking of the creditworthiness of the clients of the insured company. This helps to sort out the bad buyers and to find new ones with a better performance and, thus, payment perspective.

In the medium-term and long run this tends to influence the risk awareness of the insured and thus their own credit management. As a matter of fact many of our clients testify to this change in their company policy and their process of selecting buyers. Many of them see the altered credit management as enhanced by credit insurance as the most important contribution it has to offer them.

The philosophy of a credit insurer

This leads me to elaborate a little more on the philosophy of a credit insurer. The credit insurer will tend to be cautious, wanting to avoid losses – both for itself and for its clients. Thus, it finds itself in a natural conflict of interest with clients. Much as the insured wants to minimise his/her losses – he/she also wants to boost sales. That involves a generous opening of credit lines to buyers. Therefore, as a rule an entrepreneur will be ready to risk more than the credit insurer. This is especially true for fast growing companies, expanding in ever new markets – markets in which they do not have any experience at the beginning.

A private credit insurer has to take into consideration the risks it is insuring on its own account. In doing so it has to think both of its clients and shareholders. Private credit insurance, thus, is different from state export guarantee schemes, which have national export interests as a major guideline for taking up coverage.

From the viewpoint of private credit insurers, credit insurance is not in a position to single-handedly protect its clients from the effects of structural problems in the economy. Those structural problems are currently the major reason for the increasing insolvency figures in Germany and most other European countries affected by this trend. A credit insurer has to adapt its policy to these circumstances.

Part of this policy is to minimise the credit risks for the client and the credit. An isolated look at the different instruments at hand cannot help in this situation. On the contrary, all of these instruments must be seen as a combined tool to find tailor-made solutions for the client.

Credit decisions, premiums and self retention

An important question is whether the risk insurer can fulfil a broader mission than just taking away the risk by how it uses credit decisions, premiums and self retention. I will shortly answer the question.

Please note that credit decisions play a major part in structuring and limiting the risks covered. Our clients will judge us through our credit decisions. They are a vital part of the service we offer. Not only will the acceptance of our clients be based on them, just as importantly, our premium income relies on them. In addition, domestic and European competition as well as the market position of a credit insurer in the respective markets place boundaries us to how actively it can use credit decisions in helping its clients to structure their customer base.

The premiums taken for credit insurance are determined by the actual risk and claims development. However, the overall idea behind insurance – the group of insureds is carrying the risk together than one alone cannot bear – and the demands from the market are two sides of one coin. Clients with a continually good risk structure will only up to a certain rate and for a limited time be willing to accept higher premiums in the best interests of all insured. This point is determined by their individual risks. At the end of the day, credit insurance is a voluntary insurance and an additional cost in every company. Here we also have to take into account that the economic situation has put liquidity restraints on many companies. For the credit insurer, on the other hand, declining turnover of its clients means less premium income.

The retention of claims that the client has to bear is no doubt an essential part of every credit insurer's policy. It is an ideal tool for structuring tailor-made contracts. Apart from keeping the client interested in his own risk, we see in this instrument a suitable measure to adapt the credit policy to current risk situations. This is the case when instituting individual first losses in a contract which helps the credit insurer to have less minor claims to pay, thus reducing its administrative costs. At the same time, minor individual first losses can be paid for by the client without major damage to his business performance. The aggregate first loss can be used both as a substitute for high premium demands and a risk buffer.

These differing points of view can only be reconciled through mutual confidence. A prerequisite for this to happen is that the credit insurer has a profound knowledge about the markets of its clients. In addition, it has to have detailed, state-of-the-art information about the companies with which the clients are trading.

The need for on-line databases

Hermes has on-line access to databases comprising more than 20 million companies' world-wide, enabling the best credit decision to be made in every situation. Our international network, contacts and partner organisations are vital in achieving this result. I believe it is safe to say that no individual company possesses this kind of information. Based on it we take 4,000 to 5,000 credit decisions for our clients every day.

Most of these are being taken with the software programme for electronic analysis of credit worthiness. Hermes developed the EBONA-programme, which stands for "Elektronische Bonitäts-Analyse", in co-operation with the University of Kiel starting in 1979. After extensive tests it finally started working in 1989. This long planning and implementation period demonstrate how difficult was the task. But I believe it also shows that we now have a first-rate tool for the safety of our clients.

Considering to the conflict of interest, in order to minimise it further, the supplier should keep a healthy interest in the solvency of his customers – even after he is insured. Therefore, he must himself retain a share of the risk, albeit a smaller one. This also enables the credit insurer to keep premiums down. In addition the insured has – as part of the contract – certain obligations to fulfil, e.g. he has to inform the credit insurer about late payments of his clients. These are very often the first indicator of more severe problems.

Credit insurance and bank ratings

There is one other advantage to being credit insured which can be of special importance to SMEs and growing companies. I am referring to the credit rating that banks give these companies. Many of them are in need of extended credit lines by banks – which are not always easy to obtain.

In our experience it helps in negotiations with banks if the company is credit insured. Accounts receivable – if insured – are safe. They are therefore a valuable asset of the company. It can assign the benefit of the policy to the bank, thus increasing its own creditworthiness - and getting larger credit lines. In fact, credit insurers in Germany closely co-operate with banks to inform them about the advantages of their services. Thus, many bankers today recommend their clients to be credit insured.

Credit insurers and reinsurance

To end, let me briefly tackle one final aspect of credit insurance. At first sight it might not be in line with my topic. But let us look a bit closer and I am sure I can convince you that it is very much in the interest of our clients – and, thus, a part of the agenda. The catchword is: *reinsurance.*

Traditionally, credit insurers have always been highly reinsured – due to the special risks and volatility of their business. Therefore, credit insurers do not only have the factors of market risks and customer wishes to consider. Their need for a broad basis of reinsurance capacity to do business can only be maintained in the long term if their business produces an adequate level of return on equity.

The risk situation described earlier on does not only have major consequences for the clients, but also for the credit insurers. In Germany especially, the 1990s have been for credit insurers a period of unprecedented challenges. Never before have we had to pay so many claims. Never before did the individual claims reach such high levels. Needless to say the reinsurers were not unaffected by this situation.

This shows that even insurers cannot make the world a perfect place. And in this second-best world, losses of receivables cannot always be prevented – even given the best skills and information. Therefore, at the end of the day, when everything else has failed – this is when we pay.

7.3 A legislative framework for risk-taking built on insurance experience

by Björn Palmgren
Chief Actuary of Finansinspektionen, Sweden

The aim of this paper is to discuss some general questions of risk management against the background of the role that legislation has in insurance business. Examples of such questions are:

- the amount of risk capital needed initially
- the amount of risk capital needed under current operations
- the approach to what constitutes insurable risk
- internal control and risk management
- accounting and reporting

- hedging for fluctuations
- limits for fluctuations

It should be stated from the outset that the role of legislation in the field of insurance to some extent is special in character and scope, due to the role of insurance in the economy of a society like ours. There are nevertheless aspects which have found acceptance outside insurance proper, and there may be additional aspects which may serve as ideas for solutions, if adjusted properly to the realities of non-insurance activities dealing with financial risk.

Much of insurance legislation is in a natural way focused on managing and reducing the risks that arise from the insurance business, which by its very nature is centred around insurance risks and investment risks. For other activities, the legal framework is less likely to cover so many aspects of risk management. Indeed, the relative freedom from detailed regulation in most other commercial activities (excluding banking and securities firms) can in several ways be motivated in a market economy. Even the financial sector has been moving away from detail legislation to a framework approach.

The ideas of this paper are not unknown and the aim has just to present them in a comprehensive way and to focus the interest on some important aspects, which may be worth developing further.

A short review of the legislative framework of insurance

Initial and current capital requirements
According to the EU Insurance Directives, the initial capital must reach a certain level expressed in a fixed amount of ECU's, varying to some extent by insurance class. It has in addition become usual in several Member Countries to require that the initial capital should be sufficient with regard to the volume of business, as proposed in the business plan, usually for a period of at least three years.

In Sweden, the EU solvency requirements are guiding in fixing the required initial capital, and are defining a signal level (target level) for current activities. These requirements do not, for the moment, reflect the nature of business risk or the asset-liability matching conditions, but such considerations may be natural. The fundamental idea is, that there should be a reasonable amount of loss-covering resources, as a protection for adverse events and developments.

Internal control and management of risk
Areas that only recently, at least in Sweden, are becoming the subject of a more detailed regulation, are internal control and the management of risks in an insurance company. As regards the management of risks, much emphasis is laid on diversified risk, which traditionally stands in focus of insurance activities but

also is an important aspect of the management of investment portfolios. Management of insurance risks is of course more or less the core activity of an insurer, and regulation in this area has been limited to guidelines on:

- internal control and risk management
- underwriting and reinsurance risk
- reserving (valuation of debts to policyholders) risk

In addition, there are general requirements as to fit and proper owners and managers.

Management of investment risk is given an EU framework consisting of a list of admissible assets, limits on certain types of assets and a diversification requirement expressed as limits to concentrating investment to a single counterpart, piece of property etc.

Accounting and reporting

The annual accounts of insurance companies are in many respects based on general accounting principles, but it is usual to introduce certain specific regulation, by modifying the accounting or by having a statutory reporting which differs from the annual accounts. The underlying reason is the long-term character of commitments, as well as the need of policyholder protection in some cases. Two items could be mentioned in particular: technical provisions and the handling of profits.

Technical provisions measure the debt to policyholders and pose a valuation problem, since the future benefits or claims payments are not known exactly as to amount and time. Interestingly enough, the use of reinsurance cover allows insurance companies to use a similar approach to the asset, which is represented by the reinsurers' share of technical provisions. As a rule, the evaluation of technical provisions is made on a 'reasonably prudent' basis in non-life insurance and on a prudent basis in life insurance.

The handling of profits is also in focus. With long-term commitments which are difficult to evaluate, there may seem to be a need for slowing down the process of paying dividends to shareholders and keep part of the profits as a buffer for claim fluctuations and similar loss situations. Fluctuation reserving may be considered part of technical provisions or as additional will be discussed below.

Special reporting to the supervisory authorities on an annual or quarterly basis is common and provides a complement to the annual accounts. The focus is or should be on various risks and the extent of reporting should be a balance between the desire for information, the capacity to handle it and the cost of producing it. The rationale for such reporting is to receive early signals of adverse developments or increased vulnerability or exposure to risks. Experience shows, however, that reporting alone does not suffice, but must have as its complement contacts with the industry and knowledge about the market.

Reserving for fluctuations
Additional reserving may be mandatory, as is the case with so-called equalisation reserves used in some countries. Within the EU there is the requirement of accumulating profits into an equalisation reserve for credit insurance, with a certain choice of models for the accumulation. Sweden has a tradition of allowing a voluntary fluctuation reserve, into which non-taxed profits can be set aside within certain limits. The reserve can be used for covering 'technical losses', i.e., losses due to the insurance operations but not to the investment activities of an insurance company. The limits are based on the observed volatility in the ratio of claim costs to premiums in different lines of business and are set to be sufficient for covering two consecutive 'bad years', within the framework of a rather simple risk model.

Limits to risk-taking and sensitivity testing
It is common practice to reduce the probability of failure by reinsuring or by sharing the risks in co-insurance. In Sweden, it is required to have a more or less explicit rule in the articles of organisation of a non-life insurer, from which the limits to risk-taking and the need to reinsure can be deduced.

Given the risks taken, in the insurance portfolio as well as in the investment portfolio, it is of interest to measure the sensitivity and exposure to adverse developments, such as:

- higher claims than expected
- a rise in interest rates
- a drop in share or property prices
- higher administrative costs than expected

Such sensitivity testing is, of course, a natural part of risk management procedures.

Insurability
The traditional approach to insurability emphasises such aspects as claim frequency and independence in a collective of risks. A large number of independent risks having relatively small consequences (claims) is the easiest case: risks are possible to pool and can be priced in fair manner, with a premium close to the expected claim cost (including zero claims) and with a premium that is small with respect to the average claim size (excluding zero claims).

The risks from which protection is desirable are of course, much larger than the set of insurable risks. In addition, premiums paid for insurance are often accepted as a tax deductible cost, whereas other measures of risk protection may not have this advantage. Both these observations explain why there is a desire to widen the area of insurability, even if this means that the protection will change its nature, and include more of ordinary financial relations, such as lending and borrowing.

A legislative framework for risk-taking built on insurance experience

The following is focused on other enterprises than financial firms, and thus does not include banks and insurers. Let us play with the idea that a legislative framework for such enterprises could in fact include more of risk management thinking. If this idea is unrealistic, it may at least serve as a framework for the managers of the enterprise or for its creditors.

A brief list would perhaps include the following items:

- Requirements for initial and current own capital, reflecting the size of the business and its riskiness, based on failure experience.
- Internal control and management of risk, as a responsibility of the Board of Directors and the managers.
- Accounting for risks along the principles of insurance and reinsurance, when applicable.
- Reporting, in particular the risk sensitivity, to interested parties.
- Allowing, within reasonable limits, some reserving with tax effects for adverse fluctuations, on the liability and perhaps on the asset side.
- Limits to risk-taking, fixed with respect to loss-covering resources and insurance cover.

7.4 The limits of insurability and its application to business risks

by Robert W Vivian
IISA Professor of Insurance and Risk Management,
University of the Witwatersrand

It is commonly accepted that the beginning of the modern economic analysis of the insurance activity was ushered in by a number of papers published by Arrow (1963), Arrow (1965) and Borch.(1960) In one of these Arrow (1965) touched on most of the issues which over the years have been investigated in greater detail and as a consequence in these matters a degree of progress has been made in gaining a clearer understanding. One of the central issues, which Arrow (1965) recognised, was that in practice there was a restriction on the insurability of risks. It is not clear, in theory, why this limitation exists. There is a limit in practice to the insurability of risks. A number of attempts have been made to establish a theory, which can be applied to determine the limits of insurability. (Berliner, 1982). Arrow suggested moral hazard and adverse selection as factors which limit. These attempts have not been completely successful. This essay is a further attempt to set-out a theory to define the factors which determine these limits and then to discuss the application of the theory to business risks.

It is suggested that two fundamental considerations determine the limits of insurability: first, the law of contract and, second, insurance must be economically viable (the insurance mechanism). It is important not to confuse these two considerations even although they are not necessarily independent of each other. That which is economically viable is translated into a contract, which survives in the market place. The contract thus describes that which is known to be economically viable. A study of the insurance contract may also reveal the conditions of economic viability. It will not explain why the contract can be traded in an economically viable manner, but will describe that which has been demonstrated to be viable. The contract does not provide a theory but a description. The insurance contract is known to be viable since it has existed for several centuries and is fairly standardised and is traded several millions of times each year. The contract is thus a description of a transaction, which is well known, tried and tested, and economically viable. I have not lost sight of the financial troubles of Lloyd's, when I say that the insurance contract can be traded in an economically viable manner. The Lloyd's problems are usually ascribed to the American legal system that produced the asbestos and environmental impairment debacles. In these cases the American courts have deviated from the historical principles of insurance, which have received some attention with the tort reform measures. The fact that insurance could be traded in the past, in an economically viable manner, is of course no guarantee that it can in the future still be so traded if the historical rules are not obeyed.

The insurance contract

The first consideration, which imposes a limitation on what can be insured, is the law of contract. Insurance is usually arranged in terms of a contract, and cannot exist unless it is possible to form an enforceable contract. There are circumstances where use can be made of the insurance mechanism but no contract exists. For example, a company may have a very large motor fleet and during its operation it receives a number of fines. It may wish to insure itself against the cost of the fines but cannot do so since in general it is against public policy to insure fines (Carter, 1986). Under these circumstances it is not possible to enter into an enforceable contract. If a company wishes to do so it can establish an internal or even mutual fund using the insurance mechanism to operate a viable fund (Faure and Heine, 1991).

In history what was insured?

The historical development of the insurance market and contract will assist in answering the question; what can be insured? The first class of insurance was the marine contract. In England the first recorded marine policy was on the 20th September 1547. This contract provided indemnity against loss or damage of ships and or cargo against the perils of the sea. The subject matter was loss or damage to physical property, and had to be caused by the operation of an external peril, the most obvious of which is a storm. The marine contract developed into a sophisticated contract. Specific perils are not named and in a sense it is an all perils policy. It should also be noted that it is the loss or damage of the property, which is the matter of concern. The loss is not financial, it is physical, but the evaluation and then indemnification of the loss is expressed in monetary terms.

The next class of insurance is fire insurance, which came into its own as a consequence of the Great Fire of London in 1666. Fire insurance gave rise to a large number of the great fire insurers of the previous centuries. Lloyd's of London (1691) taking the date when Edward Lloyd moved to Lombard Street, The Phoenix (1705), The Sun Fire Office (1710), Royal Exchange Assurance Corporation (1720); London Assurance Corporation (1720), The Royal (1845), The London & Liverpool & Globe (1836), The London and Lancashire (1861), Commercial Union, Guardian etc. The object of the insurance was again property, the destruction of which was caused by the peril of fire. After fire insurance, came life insurance. (The date taken for purposes of this article is 1706, after the Great Fire of London, being the date that the Royal Charter was granted to form the Amicable Society. The earliest known life policy, in England is dated 18 June 1583). The object in this case was the death of the insured; upon the death of the insured a sum of money became payable. The issue of indemnity did not arise. No attempt is made is to limit the payment to the loss caused by the death of the insured. When it became clear that the indemnification granted under fire policies did not extend to the consequential losses, which can arise from a fire, the market responded with the consequential loss policy. This policy needed an underlying property policy. It is thus a form of property damage insurance.

The introduction of worker's compensation and the development of the railways gave rise to the accident market, which was well developed by the time the automobile arrived (The Railways Passengers Assurance Company was formed in 1845). The accident market gave rise to the personal accident policy. This is a non-indemnity policy the object of which is accidental death or injury to the insured and a sum of money became payable as a consequence of the accidental death or injury. The accident market also provided indemnity for loss or damage to other forms of property from perils other than fire. Liability contracts developed as part of the accident market, and indemnify the insured against all amounts which the insured becomes legally liable to pay as a consequence of loss or damage to property or death or injury to people. The term *legally liable to pay* is not defined but in terms of the common-law liability was restricted, initially at least, to damage to physical property or injury to people. The common law did not recognise liability for pure economic losses.

The above describes historically what was covered by insurance contracts. This does not mean contracts do not exist which cover some other object. Some markets such as Lloyd's of London has always been innovative and there is very little doubt that cover is offered for many other risks. It is not clear, however, that every contract which purported to cover some risk or other is in fact a contract of insurance. A number of examples of other types of insurance can be cited. Thus insurers offer hole-in-one cover. There is a tradition that a golfer achieving a hole-in-one buys the drinks. This could well be an expensive exercise and insurers will provide insurance against this contingency. This type of contract involves a very small portion of the market.

In general the vast number of insurance contracts involve indemnification against loss or damage to physical property or death or injury of people caused by an external peril. Generally insurance relates to:

- loss or damage to property of one kind or another
- death of injury to people
- legal liability claims, restricted initially at least to claims arising out of damage to property or injury to people
- caused by an external peril

Because property by nature cannot be all be concentrated at one place and perils cannot operate at all places simultaneously, the damage suffered by one insured item is generally not correlated to damage caused to other insured items. A degree of correlation may well exist. Thus a number of people may be injured in the same traffic accident, or a regional catastrophe may take place. In these cases, a degree of correlation exists. If the correlation is great doubts exist over the insurability of these losses. Damage due to war, for example, is highly correlated and is uninsurable.

If the above historical criteria for insurability are examined then it is clear that a loss which appears only as a pure economic loss does not fall within the criteria. It becomes clear that in history this was not the terrain of insurance. It could be possible to extend the historical practice, through conceptualisation, to include pure economic losses. Money as an asset should not be regarded as a pure economic loss. If a thief steals a car or a sum of money in both cases a physical asset had been stolen.

Moral Hazard

The problem of moral hazard is one of the most important reasons for the limitation of insurability. The nature of insurance, the payment of a small premium for a large amount lends itself so easily to the desire to obtain the large amount for the small premium. The insurance contract has a number of mechanisms to deal with the issue of moral hazard.

Insurable interest
Moral hazard is dealt with in many parts of the world, particularly in the case of life insurance by the concept of insurable interest. This was imposed as a result of public policy considerations. A person may not enter into an enforceable contact of insurance unless that person has an interest in the insured life or object. Under these circumstances the insured has less of an incentive to orchestrate the insured event.

Insurable interest is not a complete deterrent. An insured who is in financial difficulties may well decide to destroy his own property and claim on the insurance policy. A spouse who has an insurable interest in the life of the other spouse may nevertheless decide to murder that spouse to benefit from the insurance.

Less than complete insurance coverage: co-insurance
Moral hazard is also dealt with by ensuring that the insured cannot claim the full amount of his loss. By ensuring that the insured bears some of the loss, the incentive to cause or permit the loss to occur is reduced, since the insured is still faced with a loss.

Indemnity
Closely allied, at least in indemnity insurance, to insurable interest is the requirement of indemnity. Indemnity requires that the insured is never placed in a better position after the loss than before the loss. This again reduces the moral hazard problem.

Payment of the premium in return for the benefit
The payment of a premium related to the level of the benefits received in terms of a policy also has an effect on reducing moral hazard. If only those who pay the premium benefit from insurance, then the property rights link is maintained. People receive that for which they pay. The problems are largely the product of breaking this link. In liability insurance the beneficiary does not pay, at a first glance, the premium.

Contractual provisions – requirements to take reasonable precautions
There are a number of terms in the standard insurance contract, which limit moral hazard. One of these terms is that the insured should take reasonable precautions to ensure that the insured event does not take place. This term is not very effective in practice because of the considerable difficulties that the courts have faced in interpreting the meaning of the term.

Contractual provisions – Fraud provisions
Society has measures to combat fraud. To deliberately bring about the insured event with the intention of claiming the insurance proceeds is usually an act of fraud and measures exist to combat fraud. Insurance contracts also have specific conditions dealing with fraud.

Adverse selection

Another limitation to insurability is the problem of adverse selection. People who have knowledge that the insured event will take place may seek insurance. This is usually dealt with in terms of the doctrine of disclosure (utmost good faith) and doctrines prohibiting fraud. Adverse selection does not only occur when someone knows that the insured event will take place but knows that she/he is a higher risk but seeks insurance at a lower premium than dictated by the risk. This problem is usually dealt with by the doctrine of disclosure and through the mechanism of a competitive market. The theory is described is described in the well-known Rothschild and Stiglitz (1976). A particular problem facing the insurance industry is the desire to impose adverse selection upon the industry as happened with AIDS. In this case attempts are made to prevent the insurer from discovering if the insurance seeker has a higher exposure to AIDS with a view to forcing cross-subsidisation.

Public policy

One of the limitations to insurability specifically imposed by the doctrine of contract is that contracts may not be contrary to public policy. Public policy consideration is usually translated into specific insurance requirements. Thus it is against public policy to enter into contracts where no insurable interest exists, to commit fraud for example by deliberately bringing about the insured event.

The business of insurance must be economically viable

The second consideration is that the business of insurance must be economically viable. This requirement in essence describes the mechanism of insurance. The point of departure is Adam Smith's statement of economic viability adjusted to make provision for investment income. Smith pointed out that in order to be viable the premium income (P) of an insurance company has to be adequate to cover the claims (C), the expenses (E) and the return on investment (R) to the shareholder. To this can be added the investment income (I_I) and underwriting income I_u. Thus:

$$P = C + E + R$$

or the premium per homogeneous insured, if N such insured exists is:

$$p = \frac{P}{N} = \frac{C}{N} + \frac{E}{N} + \frac{I_u}{N} + \frac{I_i}{N}$$

where I_u is the underwriting income (which may of course be negative) and I_i is the investment income.

If the losses C are arranged in class intervals with n_i losses in the ith interval then the premium paid by each insured is :

$$p = \frac{P}{N} = \sum \frac{n_i}{N} \times C_i + \frac{E}{N} + \frac{I_u}{N} + \frac{I_i}{N}$$

Where C_i is the mid-point of the class interval.

The premium which the insured thus pays is thus equal to the insured's own expected loss plus the insured's contribution to the expenses in dealing with his involvement with the insurance company plus the insured's contribution to the shareholder's profit taking into consideration the income earned from investments.

This equation throws a different light to that gained from the law of the insurance contract. The law of contract indicates that the insured pays a premium for the right to indemnification. The above equation indicates something different. The insured's premium pays for his own losses and costs. Seen in this light, the contact of insurance is the exchange of premium for the expected annual loss. The insured has an expected annual loss equal to

$$\sum \frac{n_i}{N} C_i$$

This expected loss is of no value to the insured, since he is not diversified. He pays a premium to the insurer who is able to pool all losses and hence derives the benefit of the expected annual losses. For this service the insurer enjoys its existence and hence a return on shareholders' investment. Insurance in essence is a mechanism, which allows the insured to spread his own future losses over a period of time. It is not a mechanism for spreading losses across insureds. In a sense it is not dissimilar to banking. If loans were used instead of insurance, the debtor makes periodical payments to the bank for loans advanced by the bank to fund losses incurred by the debtor. In the case of insurance the funding is, however, off-balance sheet funding.

There is one particular problem that needs consideration and that is the funding of past losses as must happen in the case of asbestos, environmental impairment type of losses and also possibility to other forms of product liability claims. The equation above was developed on the basis of future losses. In a competitive market it is difficult to see how past losses can be funded out of future premiums. The asbestos type of loss, which confronted Lloyd's, can be used to illustrate the problem. Insurers base their calculations of the correct premium on loss histories using the loss ratio as a guide. If there are no past claims, the premium does not contain any provision for future claims. It is only once claims start materialising that current premium includes a provision for the particular risk. This is the way the short-term market works. Historically insurers accepted asbestos risks without charging any premium, since there were not claims.

This may sound somewhat extraordinary to the layman; an insurance company will accept a horrendous risk without charging any premium whatsoever. This is however not extraordinary at all. The liability policy indemnifies the insured against all amount which the insured become legally liable to pay as a consequence of loss or damage to property or death or injury to people. The policy does not at all specify the individual perils, which can cause the injury. It does not say for example that the insured is indemnified for all amount which the insured becomes legally liable arising out of asbestos, repetitive strain injuries, back injuries etc. To take this approach would make the policy document an impossible document. The common law which defined the basis of legally liable to pay n a narrow manner protected the insured and insurer against the avalanche of claims. It is the courts by expanding the basis of liability having no concept of the consequences of their action, which caused the problem.

Once the first claims began to arise, insurers would consider if this type of risk can be insured. Since in the case of asbestos the event had occurred in the past, insurers would consider the type of loss to be uninsurable and exclude it from the policies but possibly invent a new type of policy. Since the event is excluded, insurers again did not charge a premium but defended the actions. Once the courts began to hold the insurer liable, the insurer was faced with enormous costs for which no premium had ever been charged. Under these circumstances all that the insurer can do is attempt to charge a future premium for losses incurred in the past. In a competitive market the premium is a determined by the market. If an insurer attempts to recover past losses through future premiums a competitor who does not have the past losses can offer to accept the risk at a premium which does not include the past losses. His premium would be much lower and hence it will not be possible for the insurer with the past liability to recover the past losses out of future premiums. The past losses will have to be absorbed by the shareholders. Hence the problem that Lloyd's found itself in – the Names and not insureds must pay. The insurance mechanism is not suited to dealing with past losses; this is a limit of Insurability. (Chief Executive of Export Credits Guarantee, London).

A tentative application of the theory to business risks

Having developed limitations of insurability, the issue of insuring business risks can be considered.

Insuring property interests and death or injury to people

A business faces a multitude of risks. From the historical principles it clear that any risk which involved the loss or destruction of property or death or injury from a specific event which occurs in the future and does not cause damage with is significantly correlated is insurable. Where damage is highly correlated as in the case of catastrophe losses, this may not be insurable but this a involves a well known and discussed possible limit to insurability.

Insuring pure financial losses-credit insurance

Losses which do not involve loss or damage to property or injury to people but are of a pure financial nature, outside of the historical property damage-non correlated peril paradigm. Insuring these risks need to be treated with some caution and require special expertise to manage.

One of the earliest classes of insurance involving a pure economic loss is credit insurance. The first British insurer to write this class of business was the Excess Insurance Company in 1893. In 1920 the British government established the Export Credit Guarantee Scheme to cover credit given to foreign customers. The Export Credit Guarantee Department was established which in 1991 the short-term arm of ECGD was privatised and sold to the a Dutch credit insurer. It is not surprising that credit insurance was first underwritten by the government, since as Gill correctly pointed out:

> "This was a form of insurance [i.e. credit insurance] which the commercial market had not traditionally provided on any scale and the Government saw itself filling the gap in the market place. Early losses were suffered and, after a succession of reviews, it was decided to try to apply the same commercial principles to this form of insurance as to others by seeking the maximum spread..."

It is not surprising that the conventional insurers avoided this class of business since being purely financial in nature it falls outside the historical grounds of insurability. It is thus a class of insurance with special difficulties and requires considerable expertise to manage. Credit risks also are exposed to adverse selection. Why, for example, should a company, which seeks insurance and has customers with a good track record insure against non-payment by these customers? It would rather seek insurance for customers it itself has doubts about. Credit insurance is exposed to moral hazard problems as can be deduced from the comments of Gill (1986, 268):

> "As with many other fields of activity, there are potential benefits and dangers in the process of guaranteeing and organising export credit. The main danger is the removal of normal market disciplines on risk assessment and in the settling of the cost and terms of capital. There is an obvious danger that in removing the normal discipline, unsound business may be encouraged on excessive terms thus encouraging buyers to over extend themselves and indeed support uneconomical business".

The greatest problem facing the credit insurer is the correlation of losses. This could be caused by macro-economic considerations and render the risk uninsurable as noted by Hoobroeckxm (1986, 292), President of the Berne Union, President of Netherlands Credit Insurance Company Amsterdam:

> "The number of countries are limited and as regards the risk of an entire country being unable to pay its debts it is clear that the spread of risk so necessary to the insurer is quite a problem. It has long been assumed generally that the problem is too great for private undertakings...".

At this stage of the development of the insurance market and theory it can be accepted that as a general rule business risks remain uninsurable.

THE ROLE OF THE SUPERVISORY AUTHORITIES IN THE FINANCIAL SYSTEM

8.1 Introduction

by Dirk Schoenmaker
Economist, Bank of England [1]

After a relative long period of stability, several countries have recently been faced with banking crises with varying degrees of seriousness. During the 1980s, the US merged or closed many small savings & loans institutions and experienced problems with some larger commercial banks as well. In the late 1980s and early 1990s, the Scandinavian countries experienced serious banking crises. Since 1992, Japan has faced grave problems with its banks as well as non-bank financial institutions. Some Latin-American countries faced a banking crisis following the economic collapse of Mexico in 1995. Finally, several East Asian countries are faced with upheaval in their economies at the time of writing. Weaknesses in the financial system appear to be a major contributing factor to the macro-economic crisis in East Asia.

The financial system plays a vital role in the effective functioning of every economy, providing essential services to depositors and investors on the one hand and to personal, corporate and public sector borrowers on the other hand. It is difficult to overestimate the extent of the economic and social damage that would be caused if this vital process of financial intermediation were to be seriously interrupted as highlighted by the banking crises mentioned above.

An important research question is the appropriate role of the authorities in maintaining the stability of the financial system. The first paper, written by me, explores the role of the central bank as lender of last resort, while the next four papers by Charlotte Möller, Peter Wendt, Björn Palmgren and Liisa Halme discuss the role of the supervisory authority. The final paper by Bo Green analyses the role of banks in the financial system. Peter Wendt and Bo Green stress the

---

[1] The views are those of the author and do not necessarily reflect the views either of the Bank of England or the Financial Services Authority.

contribution that authorities should make to let the financial system fulfil its role in economic development. They argue that while financial stability is important, we should not lose sight of the ultimate objective of generating economic growth. That is very true. As a central banker, I would argue that a stable monetary and financial climate is a necessary, but not sufficient, condition for a flourishing economy.

Taking the papers in turn, the first paper on 'The Role of the Central Bank' discusses the need for a lender of last resort during times of crisis. This is a controversial issue in the academic literature. Should problem banks be assisted to prevent a potential deepening of the crisis, or should problem banks be closed to reinforce market discipline? I argue that assistance may be justified in some cases, but that the possibility of individual failures should not be excluded as an important market discipline.

The second paper by Charlotte Möller on 'The Role of the Supervisory Authority' also explores the balance between market discipline and government involvement. As a matter of fact, the degree of regulation and supervision to achieve a proper balance varies between countries. At one end of the spectrum, we can find New Zealand, which relies heavily on market forces and on the other end, we can find countries, which have a history of frequent intervention in their financial system. Charlotte Möller argues that financial institutions differ from other types of enterprise in that the consequences for the customers of a failure of a bank or another financial institution are much more severe. Governments must therefore contribute to a sound financial system through regulation and supervision.

In the third paper on 'The Regulator's Attitude to Risk-taking in the Financial System', Peter Wendt discusses the negative side of regulation and supervision. What are the direct, and more importantly, the indirect cost of the restrictions placed on the financial system by the supervisor? High capital requirements, for example, may reduce the risk of banking problems, but may also hamper the role of banks in financing business. The net effect is not clear. Peter Wendt stresses that both bank management and financial supervisors have more to learn to let the financial system fulfil its role in economic development.

In the fourth paper on 'The Need for Venture Capital', Björn Palmgren starts with the premise that new enterprises and entrepreneurs are crucial for economic development. It is well known that these innovative enterprises have difficulties in funding themselves. The need for venture capital has to be balanced against the need for protecting certain functions and interests (e.g. depositors) through regulation and supervision. As a way forward, Björn Palmgren suggests that venture capital provision should be concentrated in financial institutions whose activities are less subject to government protection and supervision.

The fifth paper by Liisa Halme on 'Banking Crisis and the Challenge for Regulation' takes a law-and-economics approach to evaluate the need for changes in banking regulation in the light of the Finnish banking crisis. In particular, this paper sketches a useful framework to examine moral hazard problems, which played an important role in the Finnish banking crisis as well as in banking crises in many other countries. Liisa Halme explores the extent to which moral hazard arise from the structure of regulation ('legislation'), the behaviour of supervisors, and the behaviour of banks.

In the final paper on 'The Role of Banks', Bo Green argues that the supervisory rules for the financial system should not only focus on minimising risks for banks. Rather banks should be encouraged to manage risks. This emphasis on risk management is very much in line with recent developments in the adoption of Value-at-Risk models for the measurement and management of market risks. Before the role of banks is defined in supervisory rules, it must be decided which risks banks are allowed to take. In addition, Bo Green argues that the role of banks should be defined in the light of normal market circumstances and not the crisis situation of the early 1990s in Scandinavia.

8.2 The role of the central bank

by Dirk Schoenmaker
Economist, Bank of England [2]

The debate on the need for supervision of financial institutions depends partially on the question whether there is systemic risk, or not. And if there is systemic risk, what should be the role of the supervisory authority and the central bank – potentially acting as lender of last resort – in maintaining financial stability? In the early 19th century, central banks started to intervene during banking panics in order to preserve systemic stability. Only much later – principally in the 20th century – was banking regulation and supervision introduced to attempt to prevent such banking crises occurring. While the original objective of banking supervision is thus to promote systemic stability, more recently the protection of depositors has been added as a second objective. This paper will focus on financial stability issues.

The introduction of this chapter highlights the negative impact that banking crises can have on the real economy. But the possibility of individual bank failure is an essential discipline of a market-oriented banking system. The central concern of authorities is therefore not with the failure of individual banks, but

---

[2] The views are those of the author and do not necessarily reflect the views either of the Bank of England or the Financial Services Authority.

rather with the possibility that the failure of an individual bank or financial institution will spread, affecting other financial institutions.

This paper will explore the different theories on the role of the central bank as lender of last resort in maintaining the stability of the financial system. There are basically three views in the literature on the use of the lender of last resort, the *Monetarist view*, the *Free banking view*, and the *Modern-pragmatic view*.

The monetarist school argues that open market operations are sufficient to stem a liquidity crisis (Goodfriend and King, 1988). The central bank should provide liquidity to the banking system as a whole during a crisis, but not to individual banks. The monetarists attribute banking crises, and more generally recessions, to reductions in the monetary base rather than spillover effects from individual bank failures. If only the central bank would prevent a decline in the monetary base, a banking crisis would be prevented. While such a policy can effectively stem a general liquidity crisis by maintaining the level of reserves, open market operations (i.e. a form of providing reserves by the central bank to the market as a whole) cannot influence the distribution of reserves among banks. This raises the question of how well the interbank market for reserves operates in times of crisis.

In a world of perfect information, solvent banks can always obtain reserves at the going rate, while insolvent banks are cut-off from the interbank market. But once information asymmetries are introduced it may be more difficult to distinguish between solvent and insolvent banks. The monetarist school argues that there is no reason to believe that a central bank is better able to deal with these information problems than the private sector. They recommend that the central bank should confine itself to open market operations during times of crisis and avoid lending to individual banks, as the latter give rise to moral hazard problems (the following papers in this chapter discuss moral hazard in more detail).

More radically, the free banking school promotes the abolition of central banks (White, 1984). They consider state interference in the monetary system as the main cause of instability. Competitive forces will create a stable banking system, and there is thus no need for a lender of last resort. The monetarist and free banking views are based on the assumption that the contagious effects, if any, of bank failures are not serious enough to justify lender of last resort lending to individual banks.

The modern-pragmatic school, however, argues that assistance for illiquid but potentially insolvent banks may be justified in some cases (Goodhart, 1987). They claim that the development of non-competitive central banks give these central banks an advantage over the market players. While a bank in difficulties may be reluctant to reveal information to competitors, it may be prepared to inform the central bank. Furthermore, the proponents of the modern-pragmatic school argue that the social cost of a bank failure may exceed the private cost in some cases. This in turn may justify lender of last resort lending by the central bank – acting for the public good rather than driven by profit motives – to individual banks.

The modern-pragmatic school recognises the information problem in lender of last resort lending. The root of the problem lies in the uncertainty about the true value of a bank's loan book, as the creditworthiness of a bank's borrowers is private information. Consequently, most bank loans are illiquid and can only be sold at fire sale prices. Confronted with adverse news, or just rumours, about their bank, depositors can withdraw their claims at demand prompting a bank run. A run on one bank may precipitate runs on other banks with a similar asset structure. The role of the central bank as lender of last resort is then to stop such a chain reaction in its earliest stages.

To shed light on the dispute between the monetarist and free banking schools on the one hand and the modern-pragmatic school on the other hand, we need to test for systemic risk in banking. Systemic risk – which is also referred to as contagion risk – can be defined as the risk that financial difficulties at one or more bank(s) spill over to a large number of other banks or the financial system as a whole. There has been little attempt so far to measure systemic risk. Reviewing the limited empirical evidence of bank contagion, Kaufman (1994) comes to the conclusion that concerns about systemic stability have been greatly exaggerated. However, other researchers (Grossman, 1993; and Schoenmaker, 1996) suggest the existence of systemic risk.

The existence of systemic risk is thus a controversial issue in the literature and further empirical research on systemic risk is therefore much needed. Research on systemic risk will help to determine the appropriate role of the central bank during times of crisis. The recent banking crises highlight the importance of such research for society. I would like to encourage doctoral students to do work in this area.

The following papers in this chapter discuss the appropriate role of the supervisory authority to attempt preventing such crises in the financial system occurring. Prevention is better than cure! The structure and conduct of banking supervision are also fertile areas for research.

8.3 The role of the supervisory authority in the financial system

by Charlotte Møller Wedel-Heinen
The Danish Financial Supervisory Authority [3]

[3] Views expressed are those of the author and do not necessarily reflect the views of the Danish Financial Supervisory Authority. The author is also responsible for any errors and omissions.

The Nordic countries all experienced banking crises in the late 1980s – early 1990s. The problems in Denmark were of a smaller magnitude than in Norway, Sweden and Finland. Nevertheless the problems of the Danish banks were scrutinised subsequently by several Danish government commissions with a view to determine the causes of banking problems, how best to deal with banks in distress and how best to regulate the financial system in order to avoid future problems arising.

The paper lists lessons to be learned from the problems in the Nordic banking sector compared with experiences in other EU countries. One lesson is that both depositors and debtors tend to be seriously hit by banking failures, which consequently may have repercussions on the entire economy. Banks are the most complex financial institutions. Nevertheless the finding is also true for other kinds of financial institutions such as investments companies, albeit that the effects in most such cases are likely to be smaller due to the simpler structure of those institutions.

Taking this complexity as a starting point, the paper gives a summary of the reasons for prudential supervision and regulation of the financial institutions. The question is viewed mainly from the practical and political angle. However, more theoretical aspects are also raised.

It is argued that prudential supervision and regulation of the financial sector along with deposit insurance schemes and lender of last resort facilities may be seen as means to keep an acceptable balance between the discipline of market forces and the moral hazard problems of government involvement. The degree of regulation and supervision deemed necessary in order to achieve a proper balance varies substantially between countries and also between the different kinds of financial institutions. New Zealand, for example, relies heavily on market forces to discipline the institutions. The paper points out that prudential supervision and regulation of the financial sector can only lessen the likelihood and limit the consequences of problems in financial institutions. However, problems cannot altogether be avoided.

The Danish (Nordic) experience

Banks incorporated in the respective countries dominate the banking systems in the Nordic countries. The banks are universal but have no stakes in commerce and industry as in the case in Germany. The number of banks varies from around 200 in Denmark to around 10 in Sweden. The five largest banks in each country account for the major part of total bank balances.

There are many similarities between the banking crisis in the different Nordic countries and they are often viewed as one. A banking crisis hit Denmark and Norway around 1988 and later on Finland and Sweden both were affected in the beginning of the 1990s.

However, the crises differed in proportion. In Norway, Sweden and Finland the problems were systemic, while the Danish problems were of a smaller magnitude. In Denmark only one large bank (the eight largest bank, Varde Bank) got into severe problems. This happened in 1992. The solution chosen in this case was to sell off the good parts of the bank to one of the other larger Danish banks, isolating the remainder of the loans i.e. the bad loans and the share capital in a so called "bad bank" to be eventually liquidated. To finance the bad bank the government guaranteed a credit extended by the Danmarks Nationalbank (the Danish central bank).

A number of lessons may be learned from the Danish (and Nordic) experiences.

The cause of the banking problems in all of the Nordic countries was substantial losses on loans due to a downturn of the economic business cycle. The developments in the banks' loan loss and provision accounts mirror the general economic developments as illustrated in figure 8.1 showing the Danish case. During the mid-1980s economic growth were high and the Danish banks' lending to businesses and private households increased rapidly – in some years more than 20%. Faced with the economic downturn a large part of the debtors had difficulty in servicing their debt and this led to substantial losses.

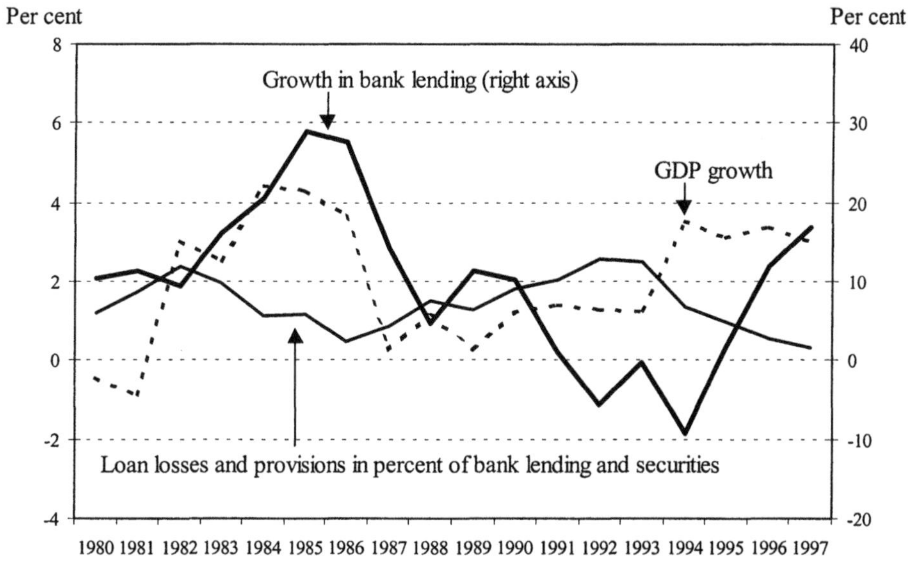

Figure 8.1 Loan Losses, Bank Lending and the Business Cycle 1980-1997

Losses and provisions on Danish banks' credits and loans accumulated for 1991-1993 amounted to 9,1% of loans outstanding, c.f. table 8.1, and the losses were even higher in Sweden and Finland.

Table 8.1 Loan losses and provisions and government support for Nordic banks

Country	Loan losses and provisions 1991-1993 (% of loans outstanding)	Government support 1991-1993 (% of GDP)
Denmark	9,1	0,4
Sweden	17,9	4,1
Norway	8,4	3,6
Finland	13,1	8,1

The finding is in line with the results of a survey of the causes of bank problems in the EU-countries. This showed that in most cases (around 75%), failures of banks were due to losses on the loan portfolio. Losses due to market risks contributed to failure in 11% of the cases. Other factors identified to lead to problems in banks were mismanagement (in 20% of the cases) and ill-liquidity (in 7% of the cases). As the factors are interrelated and as more than one may have played a role, these percentages do not add to 100. Banks may get into trouble due to excessive risk-taking in financial instruments, which is not discovered due to failure or fraud in a bank's reporting system. So far this has been the exception rather than the rule. It should also be mentioned that positions in financial instruments may be closed relatively easily albeit with a loss, whereas bank loans cannot easily be sold off in the market.

Proper valuation of assets the core subject for the supervisory authority

It follows from the above that it is important that the risks of the banks' business activities are properly reflected in the valuation of the assets on the banks' balance sheet in the financial statements. First of all, the value of the assets determines whether the bank's own capital is adequate both with respect to the legal minimum requirements and overall to cover the risks imposed by the bank's business activities. Furthermore the content of banks' financial statements makes no sense when the valuation of the assets does not reflect the market value properly. Neither the supervisory authority nor the public can rely on analysis of the statements in such a case.

Banks' financial statements could perhaps serve as an early warning of future problems. A close examination of 20 key figures based on the financial statements of the last three years of each Danish bank, which had to close or merge due to substantial problems in the period 1983-1993 (around 40 banks), however, showed no systematic deviations from the healthy banks' financial statements.

Only two of the key figures could serve as early warning signals. One of them was a strong increase in lending. This could indicate that the expansion had taken place at the expense of the quality of the banks' credit evaluation. The other was a relatively high loan portfolio/own capital ratio. The banks were consequently more sensitive to adverse economic developments, especially if the credit expansion took place without proper credit evaluation.

The financial supervisory authority discovered the problems of the banks. The banks' own certified accountants were not aware of the difficulties. This may lead to the conclusion that the accountants lack knowledge of loan evaluation.

In addition to the analysis of the financial statements of banks in distress, the line supervisors of the respective banks answered a questionnaire in order to identify the causes of the difficulties. The answers confirmed that the prime cause of the problems was losses on credits. In this respect management failure played a large role as the reasons mentioned for the losses were unrealistic evaluation of credit risks, lack of management of the large customers, lack of a broad view of the risks and lack of interest in controlling credit risks. Concentration of credits in one or a few sectors of the economy and misjudgement of the business cycle developments also played a role.

The fact that the Danish problems were far less than in the other Nordic countries may be partly answered by the Danish tradition that the supervisory authority from time to time goes through the banks' loan portfolio by on-site inspections to see whether the banks value the loan portfolio in correspondence with what may be viewed as the market value. Thus for many years Danish banks have accumulated provisions for future losses.

High capital requirements may limit problems

A simple way of reducing both the risk of banking problems arising and the cost of solving the problems should they arise, is the existence of high solvency requirements. Ample capital larger than the legal minimum enables banks to absorb losses in times of adverse economic trends without becoming insolvent. Should a bank lose a substantial share of its capital and no longer be able to meet the capital standards, it should be merged with a sound bank while there is still sufficient equity to pay for the merger. High capital requirements contribute to the success of such a policy.

As shown in table 8.1 the Danish banks experienced losses of the same magnitude as the Norwegian banks at the beginning of the 1990s but the losses did not lead to a systemic banking crisis in Denmark. This can in part be attributed to the fact that the implementation of the EU solvency directive in Denmark represented a reduction in the Danish capital requirements for banks, cf. figure 8.2, which shows the banks' overall solvency ratio. Please note that own capital in % of total balance. Thus the Danish banks in general were able to sustain losses without their solvency ratio falling below the legally required minimum.

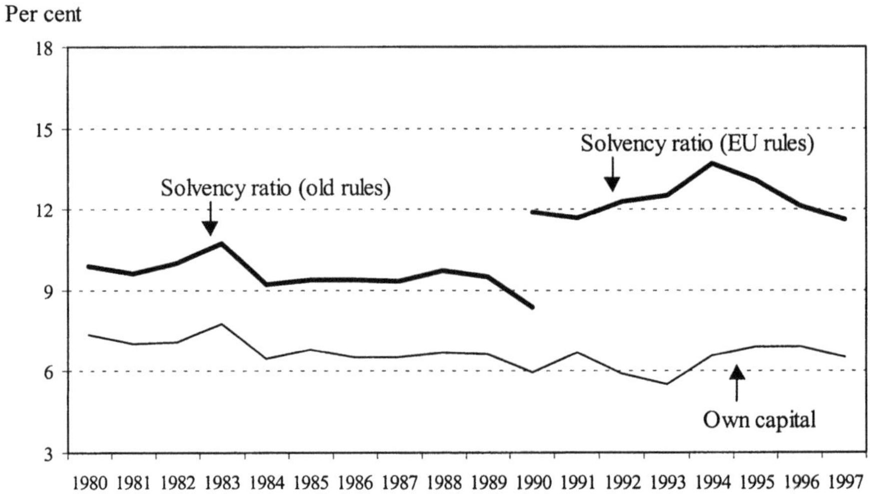

Figure 8.2 Capital of the Danish Banks 1980-1997

In this respect the 'hands on' approach of the Danish financial supervisory authority also contributed by keeping the focus on the importance of banks having to set aside sufficient provisions for future losses. Furthermore, the Danish authorities have pursued a policy of early mergers by encouraging banks with signs of problems to merge at an early stage, i.e. while some of the equity capital was still intact.

In the mid 1990s banks in several countries seemed to aim at keeping their solvency ratios well above the legal minimum. There was a trend towards relying more heavily on own 'core' capital and less on so-called tier II capital. However, as the general economic climate improved the banks appear to have reduced their focus on these goals.

Banking problems entail large costs to the General Public

Most politicians in the industrialised countries will agree with the general textbook argument that banks, like other kinds of enterprises, should be allowed to go bankrupt. In a market economy it seems logical that banks (and other financial institutions) should be disciplined by the market forces. However, financial institutions differ from other kinds of enterprises such as greengrocers in that the consequences for the customers of failure of a bank (or a pension fund) are much more severe. Therefore, most governments contribute to a sound banking (financial) sector and thus secure depositors' money by specific legislation for the financial institutions and supervision of the industry by the financial supervisory authority. In addition, deposit insurance schemes can indemnify depositors up to a certain limit in case of bankruptcy.

However, when a bank gets into trouble politicians will always find it very difficult to act according to the textbook rule. For large banks this may be explained by systemic reasons such as the domino effects on other banks. For smaller banks this argument is not valid. One reason the even small banks are not allowed to go bankrupt could be that losses to depositors are simply unacceptable politically even when the deposit insurance schemes are fairly generous.

The reason for this political concern is more likely to be due to the banks' role in the payments system. The core of banking is the financing of loans with a long maturity funded by deposits, which may be withdrawn from the bank on call or at short notice. Banks constitute a key link in the modern payment system and payments are made by transferring deposits or using credits. If a bank closes, this implies locking in deposits and credits and means that payments cannot be made for some time. This lack of liquidity is the primary problem of closing even a small bank. For a small bank with a large market share in a limited geographic area the regional impact can be quite severe.

One solution to this dilemma would be to transfer the loans and deposits to another bank. That was the solution chosen for the Danish bank, Varde Bank, where the good parts were sold off and the remaining parts were being liquidated. However, this transfer required government intervention as the government had to guarantee a loan from the Danish central bank to finance the 'bad' bank. The bad bank is still on the government's books.

General support schemes entail moral hazard/free rider problems

Government support should as far as possible only be available on a case-by-case basis. In view of the magnitude of the problems, the systemic crisis in Norway, Sweden and Finland all led to the establishment of government aid funds. This quickly led to almost all banks lining up for support because in order to ensure a level playing field they could not afford to let their competitors benefit from a free capital injection. Later, some reports have suggested that the loan losses and provisions driving the need for capital support may have been exaggerated. Another problem is that the banks are likely to stay on the government's books for some years.

EU-regulation limits government intervention

The European Commission has reviewed the French government's support to Credit Lyonnais several times and deemed part of it to be not in accordance with the EU rules on government aid to troubled industries. The French government is the majority owner of Credit Lyonnais and the European Commission has demanded that a part of the bank's business must be sold off as a condition for approving the government support. The European Commission has also previously reviewed a Spanish case and a Danish case, both of which were deemed to be in accordance with the EU-rules.

The European Commission applies the general EU rules on government aid to troubled industries to bank rescue operations. If the support is not justified on a strict commercial basis, the support is classified as government aid. Government aid is only consistent with the EU rules if it is not more extensive than absolutely necessary, if it is a once and for all operation and if the competitive advantages for the receiver are kept at a minimum.

Furthermore, rescue operations have to be approved by the European Commission in advance. As rescue operations normally have to be implemented with short notice such a procedure will not be feasible in practice.

The basic idea of referring to the general EU rules in case of banking problems is in line with the market economic framework. However, it is not possible to draw any clear conclusions regarding the European Commission's exact interpretation of the rules. The cases reviewed so far are to few and the Commission has yet to review a case of general support to a member country's banks such as the Nordic ones.

The most recent ruling of the European Commission regarding Credit Lyonnais could imply that the scope for government aid to troubled banks is quite large. The explanation in the particular case, however, may be that Credit Lyonnais is government owned. It is difficult to set up stringent rules in case the banking sector is partly government owned and partly privately owned.

Risk differentiated deposit insurance premiums

Most deposit insurance schemes cover deposits up to a certain amount. Such deposit insurance schemes can protect most depositors while at the same time exposing the banks to market forces. The deposit insurance schemes may also be viewed as an addition to the legal capital requirements, as the banks contribute to the schemes typically in relation to their share of the insured deposits.

The deposit insurance scheme of the private German banks is a special case as in practice it extends full coverage for all deposits, and it requires thorough inspections of the insured banks in order to secure its means. In effect, the scheme acts as a sort of shadow financial supervisory authority.

The reasoning behind a deposit insurance scheme is that small depositors cannot differentiate between sound banks and risky banks. Market forces must be exercised via the larger more professional depositors, who are or should at least be able to form their own opinion of the different banks. However, the existence of a deposit insurance guarantee scheme inevitably implies possibilities of free riding i.e. banks attract deposits by promising unrealistically high interest rate returns. The deposits may then be used to fund high-risk investments, as the bank knows that in case of trouble the depositors will be bailed out by the deposit insurance scheme, the cost of which is carried by all banks. One way of reducing this effect would be to differentiate the premiums banks have to pay by their risk profile, so that riskier banks pay a higher premium.

In the United States the FDIC introduced risk differentiated premiums in 1994 in order to reduce the free rider/moral hazard problems of deposit insurance. Each bank's premium is determined on the basis of the degree of capitalisation (well capitalised, sufficiently capitalised and insufficiently capitalised) and the CAMEL-rating (Capital Assets Management Earnings Liquidity-rating). The CAMEL rating partly expresses the line supervisor's subjective judgement of the bank's management. The solvency ratio and the ratios of equity capital and tier II capital measure the degree of capitalisation. In practice, however, the variation in the premiums was relatively small, ranging from 23 cents per 100 USD to 31 cents per 100 USD.

Market Discipline

In New Zealand the supervision of banks was changed radically with effect from 1996, when a new public disclosure regime was introduced. The new regime relies heavily on market forces to discipline the banks. Banks are required to publish quarterly financial statements, so-called disclosure statements, which must include a number of key figures. On the basis of this statement the customers and the investors must judge whether the bank is fit to operate and can be trusted to take good care of their funds thereby acting as financial supervisors in a market-oriented way. The responsibility for banks' risk management and supervision lies solely with the managements.

The banking legislation was also deregulated and a number of prudential regulations such as the limits on banks' large exposures were abolished. The aim of the New Zealand banking supervision is not (and has never been) to protect the depositors as such, but to encourage a sound and efficient financial system. There is no deposit insurance scheme and the government has never provided any aid to failing banks.

Some argue that the organisation of the financial legislation and the financial supervision can be explained by the fact that most banks operating in New Zealand are foreign and that New Zealand is merely free riding on the financial supervisory authorities of the respective home countries.

It is premature to state whether the general public will be able to act as effective supervisors. In Denmark, the development of the price of bank equity and tier II capital raised in the market suggest that the general public was unable to identify the problematic institutions. Internationally the professional rating agencies have only reacted very slowly and their ratings did not indicate in advance where problems might emerge.

The role of the financial supervisory authority

In a market economy it would be desirable if all types of enterprises, insurance companies as well as butchers, were regulated by the same set of rules. However, financial institutions differ from other types of enterprises as the customers rely on them to secure their pensions, their savings etc. The consequences of failure of such institutions are thus far-reaching as the customers may lose their entire fortune. Direct government ownership of the financial institutions or an unlimited government guarantee could secure the customers' means but this implies the possibility of free riding and excessive risk taking.

Consequently in order to both impose market discipline on the institutions and limit the moral hazard problems of government involvement in most countries financial institutions are for prudential reasons regulated by a special set of rules. Insurance companies and pension funds are only allowed to place the funds entrusted with them in specific assets and they also must maintain minimum amounts of own capital. Banks are required to have a certain minimum amount of capital, there are limits to the banks' risk exposures, such as large exposures and exposure in real estate, and the banks are also required to hold a sufficient amount of liquid assets. In the EU countries most of these regulations have been harmonised by the EU directives.

The financial supervisory authority is responsible for keeping the institutions under surveillance in order to ensure that they act according to the regulations. However, within the legal framework the institutions are free to conduct their business as they find best in order to maximise their earnings. The supervisory authority can and should not interfere directly in the management of institutions.

An important task of the supervisory authority is to make the financial institutions aware of the risks in which they engage and to ensure that these risks are properly valued in the financial statements. This will reduce the likelihood of severe problems. It is furthermore a way for large investors and depositors to get a good basis for assessing the institutions' risk profiles and performance.

The supervisory authority can also provide advice and know-how to the institutions on new developments and best practices. In order to improve the management's foundation for making decisions, the Danish supervisory authority in 1995 introduced a self-assessment system for financial institutions. Twice a year the supervisory authority calculates 22 key figures from the financial statements. Each institution receives their own set of key figures along with information of the key figures for a comparable peer group of institutions, thus enabling the management of the institutions to compare the performance of their institution with others.

The existence of special regulations and prudential supervision does not rule out the possibility that a bank or another type of financial institution may fail. The supervisory authority may in some instances be able to detect problems at an early stage. In such a case the supervisory authority should advise the institution to find a solution to its problems (change of business, merger or sale), while at least some of the own capital is still intact.

Deposit insurance schemes can lessen the consequences of bank failures as can government intervention. Such arrangements are, however, not in line with a market-oriented economic system and introduce the possibility of free riding and excessive risk taking. Government intervention should be reserved for extraordinary cases.

8.4 The regulator's attitude to risk taking in the financial system

by Peter Wendt
Managing director, LRF Mortgage Bank

The line taken in Charlotte Möller's paper fairly presents the main thrust behind both professional and political attitudes to financial supervision. Basically, it is the activity on the asset side of the balance sheet, which is the focus, especially unwarranted credit losses. Without proper interference from the supervisor financial institutions will tend to follow practices, which under certain circumstances (vividly illustrated by the banking crisis in Scandinavia in the early 1990s) put the depositor at risk.

Denmark was the Nordic country, which passed through the crisis with the smallest immediate losses in the way of government bail out, even though the Danish financial system experienced larger losses. This apparent contradiction was – among other factors – explained by the policy of the Danish supervisory authority. Through its specific working method – inspection on site – it was able to pick up most of the developing problems at such an early stage that solutions could be found for most of the troubled banks through arranged mergers with stronger banks.

There is no question in my mind that the policy of the supervisor during this period was efficient, leading to minuscule losses for depositors and very limited public financial support. The losses were – directly or indirectly – borne by bank shareholders and the mutual mortgage institutions' reserves. In this way, the Danish financial system had no crisis. Those who are supposed to bear the consequences of unsuccessful business management – the owners – did so. With some prodding from the supervisor, the right solution was obtained, without the real world mechanism of systemic collapse going into action.

This success story does, however, warrant some further examination. The lesson that seems to be drawn from the experience might very well result in dynamic repercussions, which will entail future losses in the form of production foregone, due to the disciplining of the financial sector.

The activities of financial intermediaries obviously play a principal role in resource allocation in the national economy. In academia this had led to an interest in the effects of supervisory regulation on the efficiency of the financial system. In other words: what is the negative side of regulation ?

While this type of question may be anathema to supervisors, whose success is measured solely by the stability of the banking system and the number of bank foreclosures they avoid by early action, the lack of finance for new commercial ventures has been a recurrent economic-political theme in most European countries during the last decade. The concerns have been voiced by parliamentarians and government offices, and numerous examples of public policy to relieve the plight of new firms have seen the light of day in the form of guarantee schemes, special incubator capital markets etc. There seems to be a general consensus in the economic growth lobby that financial markets and banks especially, do not fulfil the financing needs of industry.

One can discern an ambivalent attitude to financial risk-taking at the official level. While the financial supervisors have never spoken out against the principle of risk-taking, they do entertain the concept of excessive risk and in practice tax the management of what they judge to be an excessive risk-taker by forcing an increase in loan loss provisions.

While this has its positive side during a general downturn in the national economy, which shifts the chance of loss to a fact of loss, it also reduces the profitability of banking. The consequence then is a less satisfactory performance of financial shares, difficulty for the financial sector in obtaining the risk capital and the application of stockholder pressure on management to concentrate on more profitable business, which usually implies safer (i.e. larger and well known) customers.

There is thus a gulf between the idea of a well functioning capital market, which is able to furnish adequate capital to the most profitable ventures, and the practical day-to-day operations of banks under the watchful eyes of supervisors. A careful investigation of the many facets of decisionmaking in the financial communities and its interplay with the content of prudent supervision is therefore of interest to all parties concerned.

In this discussion it should be remembered that high capital requirements have two sides. Own capital is a costly way of financing banking. Banks compete in the open market for capital, and the cost of capital in an economy reflects the average operational result of all quoted companies. The logic is that during periods of general prosperity, banks will have to pay out larger shares of their operating surplus in order to avoid a drop in their market valuation. Accumulation of reserves is not an easy decision. New share issues – a possible solution during a bull market – just adds to the drag on the bottom line when the economy turns less buoyant.

In the Danish case, high solvency ratios by international standards allowed the Danish society to let the loan loss bill – which to a large extent resulted from a long period of mismanaged public economic policy in the 1970s and early 1980s – remain with the bank shareholders. But the high capital was due to special circumstances, related to a period of banking restrictions, which insulated Danish banks from domestic and especially foreign competition. The same high legal capital requirements would have been a crushing burden in a situation of freer competition.

The true, long term cost to the economy is not just the measurable wealth destruction connected with bank losses – whether it falls upon the share holders, the depositors or the government through intervention as in the other Scandinavian countries. It is also the less measurable growth effect of a more negative attitude to risk-taking in the wake of the banking crisis.

The over all financial structure of an economy will play a role in this connection. If the main source of risk capital is the banking system – as is the case in Denmark – the hidden costs of too much prudent supervision and the pressure it puts on bank management will be larger than in countries with a well developed free market for risk capital, typically of the Anglo-Saxon countries and Sweden.

On a more positive note, it could be pointed out that the swings in banking profitability over the business cycle probably could be reduced with a diversified loan portfolio. There will always be limits to the efficacy of the process of credit granting. Deep analysis and constant monitoring has considerable direct costs both to the bank and the customer and can be a severe disadvantage for the new, small firms. If the economic system is to have a chance of thriving, the best way might very well be for the supervisor to insist on an overall balance of the loan portfolio. In other words, does the bank shrink from its prime function as active lender and turn inwards, acting as an investment company? Should the brake on further credits to old, stagnating customers be coupled with the advice to lend more freely to new customers in other industries in order to diversify its loan portfolio as a mean to reduce the overall risk?

In my opinion, both bank management and financial supervisors have more to learn in order to let the financial system fulfil its potential for business development in the coming century.

8.5 Risk limitations for financial institutions and the need for venture capital in new and innovative enterprises

by Björn Palmgren
Chief Actuary of Finansinspektionen, Sweden

Let us recall that one of the underlying themes of this book volume consists of the difficulties in finding risk/venture capital those new and/or innovative enterprises and entrepreneurs need. We shall accept as an axiom that new and/or innovative enterprises and entrepreneurs are needed in all economies. 'Innovative' should be understood in a broad sense, comprising both innovations in technology and services, as well as the ability to find business opportunities and niches.

My aim is to put the risk/venture issue in a wider perspective and use this perspective for discussing legal and supervisory frameworks for risk-taking.

Roots and nature of the difficulties in finding venture capital

Seen from the viewpoint of investors, lenders or contractors, the fundamental problem with engaging in ventures is the risk of failure as manifested by the non-payment of debts and loss of capital or other resources. Depending on the attitude, such potential loss can be accepted if there is an acceptable chance of success of the venture and/or a corresponding price or premium for risk-taking. Risk-averse attitudes increase the problems, as does lack of information and of confidence in the venture and the enterprise. An unsuitable legal framework and procedures in situations of winding-up and non-payment may worsen matters. The occurrence of fraud and economic crime undermines confidence in enterprises and entrepreneurs in certain areas.

Reducing the risk of failure

Irrespective of who is the investor, lender or contractor, there are measures that can be taken to promote success and reduce the risk of failure of the single enterprise or entrepreneur. An efficient legal framework and bureaucracy governing the rules for starting up and capitalising an enterprise and producing annual accounts (ignoring taxation) can certainly be of importance. Local risk management in a wide sense, including a rational approach to the innovation procedure, to production and business comes naturally. With respect to the reportedly high mortality of ideas, diversification may be desirable to a certain extent, as may be pooling of risks. In many cases it is natural to try to transfer the primary risk at an early stage by requiring security for a loan or bringing in someone to stand surety for the borrower. Concrete risk prevention measures go together with a proper insurance cover (fire, theft, etc.).

The present framework for risk-taking of financial institutions

If the enterprise does not have sufficient capital, it must turn to investors. Financial institutions can act as intermediaries between enterprises and investors or act as investors themselves, i.e. as institutional investors. There is a range of financial institutions, from banks to insurance companies and from securities firms to pension funds. These institutions perform different roles and face varying restrictions. Banks have an important role in the monetary system, executing the payment function and fulfilling the expectations of savers. Securities firms act more as intermediaries, linking investors and buyers with sellers, individual firms in need of investors, and with mutual funds. Insurers and pension funds are supposed to make investments suitable for the obligations to policyholders, retired persons and beneficiaries. Depending on the role and the interest groups to be protected, most legislators have established restrictive prudential measures, requiring complementary capital for less liquid assets (assets with high counterpart risk or assets subject to fluctuations in value difficult to predict), requiring diversification, spread and suitability of assets (matching obligations), often adding capital requirements to ensure the ability to pay claims of savers and policyholders and to ensure that obligations can be met with an acceptable probability (almost certainly).

Prudent supervision – an illustration from Sweden

Finansinspektionen is the joint supervisory authority for the insurance market, the credit market and the securities market in Sweden. It works within the framework of the different directives of the European Union as transposed into national legislation. The implementation of this framework has occurred in steps since 1994 but it has been accompanied by a number of reforms motivated by past events and by the supervisory challenges of the market. A number of factors and decisions led to the Swedish bank crisis in the early nineties, which left credit institutions and others exposed to credit risk manifested in falling property values and credit losses. The challenge to bring back stability in the financial market was successfully met by a number of measures, including the efforts to provide Sweden with a modern and efficient financial supervision.

The objectives of Finansinspektionen, as laid down by the legislator, are the promotion of stability and efficiency of the financial system and the provision of effective protection for consumers of financial services. It should be pointed out that, as regards the efficiency of financial markets, the focus is on information given, including a transparent picture of the financial position of each enterprise, and on self-discipline and self-regulation. There is no reference to any promotion of the risk capital market as such. Obviously, the legislator has left this question to the market itself, provided that the other objectives are fulfilled and the legislative framework is respected.

Another legislator may very well choose to try a more active approach, fixing as an objective the promotion of a stable and efficient risk capital market for innovative enterprises. Such an approach would probably emphasise the competence to handle credit risk as well as the market's ability to price such risk in an efficient manner.

Stability as a more general objective has led Finansinspektionen to focus on such aspects as ensuring that the financial markets and the institutions under supervision function within a reasonable level of risk and that the corresponding business activities are conducted in a prudent manner. One approach, which may be of a more general interest in this connection, is the formulation of a number of guidelines on internal control and risk management. Finansinspektionen has issued such guidelines, partly common for all supervised institutions, partly specific, e.g., for credit risks, market risks as well as underwriting and reinsurance risks. These guidelines emphasise the general responsibility of the Board of Directors and underline the need for instruments for monitoring, modelling, managing and controlling risks within the institution. It seems that these guidelines have been well accepted and they have been a recurrent theme for on-site inspections during the last years.

Thus, in a way, the Swedish example shows that the supervised institutions may very well be prepared to handle the risks which are of importance in the furthering of economic development, so long as the incentive to take such risks is left to the market and is not among the objectives laid down by the legislator.

A widened perspective for the role of financial institutions in economic development

There may be the need of a wide perspective when balancing the requirements for venture capital against the need for protecting certain functions and certain interests, which may be affected by the risk-taking of financial institutions. On a general plane this seems to require co-ordination of the relevant legislation and regulation, as well as a clarification of the framework for the actions and responsibilities of the supervisory authorities. The following is a list, by no means exhaustive, of more or less realistic measures.

1. Concentrate lending of venture capital in financial institutions which is less involved with functions and interests in need of protection. Institutional investors with a long-term investment horizon as well as those providing intermediation to less risk-averse individual investors should be the focus.

This point does not say very much more than that life insurers and savings institutions, for example, should see their risk-taking against the background of their liabilities towards individuals and that prudent regulation may be motivated by the need to protect these persons' interests.

2. Let the economy as a whole assumes part of the cost of venture capital, at least on a level comparable with the long-term benefits to the economy of the activities of the users of venture capital. This could mean offering certain guarantees to

lenders in return for part of future profits or revenues. Encouraging and simplifying the participation of investors on a voluntary basis may be an option.

One should of course be aware of the risks of intervention in an economy and it should be restricted in time and scope. Nevertheless, markets are not perfect and investment opportunities in another segment may easily crowd out the venture capital market, where costs of information seeking and profitability analysis may well be seen as prohibitive at times. It is of course desirable that such allocation of venture capital be made in an efficient manner.

3. Organise effective collection of information on the enterprises and entrepreneurs and the analysis of such information. The margin available for such data collection and analysis may depend on the volumes of venture capital in question and on alternative investment opportunities, and could be quite small. This emphasises effective procedures, offered as a service at a cost or organised inside the financial institutions. This information gathering would be enhanced with a relevant international classification of business sectors and corresponding national statistics on failure and success of enterprises.

The positive feedback to be expected from such an analysis is an increased understanding of the factors governing failure and success, which in the end could result in more effective accounting, management and organisation of the innovative and high growth enterprises.

4. Organise a proper diversification of loans to the enterprises in question; in order to reduce the risk for the lender of not receiving payments duly. This more or less must build on the efforts outlined in above recommendations. For small national markets, the opportunities of pooling the credit risks across national borders should be investigated. Conditions for pooling might be improved by common classification standards, common currency and a certain degree of independence or negative correlation between markets and business lines.

Systematic risk will, naturally, still be of importance and may be even enhanced to the extent that national economies become more interdependent. Still, it is to be believed that a consistent approach to classification and statistics will help the clarification of the structure of the innovative enterprises seen locally and internationally.

5. Learn from insurance pricing and reserving. This implies the consistent collection of statistics, conscious diversification and the use of model reasoning as a basis for pricing and an analysis of writing-downs corresponding to the analysis of reserve development in insurance. As mentioned, the systematic part of the risk must be taken into account, much like insurance treats the catastrophic and serial claims or macroeconomic factors.

6. Explore, with due care, the possibilities that the use of credit insurance, as well as of derivative instruments, may offer.

This amounts essentially to the use of financial guarantees in various forms, and is in a sense only a reformulation of the problem of estimating the credit risk of an enterprise. The fact that such credit risks range from low to high probability as well as from near independence to complex dependence, should warn us from expecting any simple solutions.

Reflections

As can perhaps be understood from what I have said, I find limited room for the supervisors of the financial institutions to act on their own in order to promote risk taking, except by insisting on a prudent and effective treatment of the risks that legislation and regulation permits. There may, however, be all the more room for co-operation and co-ordinated efforts between different government agencies and other parties involved, in order to arrive at a full view of any problems connected with the need for venture capital.

8.6 The banking crisis and the challenge for regulation

by Liisa Halme
LL M, M Sc., Head of Office, Bank of Finland

The paper is the first part of a project to evaluate the need for changes in banking regulation in light of Finland's recent banking crisis. It assesses Finnish banking legislation against economic views on the effects of regulation.

The paper looks at the rationale that economic analysis provides for regulation as well as negative effects of regulation, especially moral hazard and related excessive risk-taking. The paper takes a law-and-economics viewpoint and looks at legal rules as incentives, rational agents as lawmakers and lawtakers and the means by which the desired incentive effects of regulation can be enhanced.

Moral hazard problems are examined in three contexts:

- potential distortions in the structure of legislation, i.e. incentives to moral hazard in legislation;
- behaviour of banks (bank management and owners) as rational agents.
- behaviour of regulators as agents and as principals.

It can be assumed that moral hazard and excessive risk-taking are partly the result of legislative distortions, partly the result of the behaviour of authorities and partly the result of the behaviour of banks. The question for the researcher is then to determine the extent to which moral hazard originates from legislative distortions, distortions in the behaviour of regulators, distortions in the behaviour of banks, or the interplay of all three factors.

Finnish economic studies have indicated that unlimited deposit protection schemes and more particularly protection of creditors other than depositors have generated significant moral hazard effects. There are also findings showing that implicit protection of bank owners (the too-big-to-fail syndrome) encourages excessive risk-taking. Protection of bank owners is also related to provisions on liquidation and bankruptcy.

Economists are suspicious of any reluctance or delay on the part of competent authorities to apply relevant provisions, because inaction can diminish the credibility of provisions and increase risk-taking behaviour by owners and managers. Finnish provisions on bankruptcy and liquidation, however, were originally drafted as dire forms of recourse that would never need to be invoked. Specifically, it was felt that depositors' claims were best protected as long as potential problems could be resolved without recourse to liquidation measures and proceedings. As for the later stages of legislative drafting, there has been no need to amend the provisions, because there has been no imminent risk of bank failure owing to the existence of an implicit safety net.

Finnish banks have traditionally played an important role in the creation and application of banking legislation. In line with public choice theory and the economic theory of regulation, banks have endeavoured to influence the content of legislation right from the start. As a result, legal provisions reflect conflicting objectives or means in conflict with objectives, because the lawmaker takes into account the views of various interest groups. Of course, one can clearly justify the participation of banks in the legislative drafting process as their experience and expertise is welcome. The problems arise when the outcome is a set of legal rules that transfers the ultimate responsibility from banks to the public treasury or creates perverse incentives.

The rationale for amending existing banking legislation is based on the view of legal rules as incentives to induce the rational economic agent to act in accord with the lawmaker's objectives. The challenge for the legislator presupposes that legislative structure will provide the appropriate incentives to all concerned groups to take full responsibility for their actions, in both the positive (responsibility and power) and negative (responsibility and liability) dimensions.

Using a three-by-three matrix, it is possible to outline directions for change in the regulatory framework that would reduce the moral hazard effects of regulation. The three principal agent groups in the Figure 8.3 are *bank management*, *bank owners* and *regulators*.

In order to get these three groups to take full responsibility for their actions, the matrix does not rely solely on *control*, but sees *commitment* and *market discipline* as more important factors.

	Commitment	Market Discipline	Control
Management	*Responsibility* *Sanctions*	*Obligations for disclosure* *Code of ethics*	*Efficient internal control* *Efficient shareholder control*
Owners	*Responsibility* *Sanctions*	*Take-over threat* *Effective competition*	*Efficient legal form for ownership* *Control of abuse of legal form*
Regulators	*Responsibility* *Sanctions*	*Obligations for disclosure* *Role as a communicator*	*Supervision vs. Norm-setting* *Control by legislator*

Figure 8.3 Directions for change in the regulatory framework

Commitment means clear cut rules for responsibility as well as clear cut rules for sanctions in the event of non-compliance. Management commitment to responsibility can be intensified by clear and explicit rules for a separation of responsibility and functions between a bank's board and managing director. Owners' commitment to responsibility means maintaining adequate equity capital, while their commitment to sanctions means accepting the threat of losing their investment in the equity of a bank in the event of bankruptcy or take-over by the authorities. Regulators' commitment to responsibility means limitations of regulators' discretionary power by *ex ante* schemes for early interventions as well as by clear cut procedures in the event of a bank's non-compliance with regulators' instructions.

Market discipline means mostly obligations for disclosure of relevant information. Management is responsible for disclosing, above all, key financial ratios as well as key exposures. This information, together with the existence and disclosure of a bank's code of ethics make it possible for market analysts to assess the reliability and financial soundness of a bank. Market discipline in relation to owners can be achieved by the threat of take-over. As for regulators, market discipline can support them in their supervision but also discipline them to do their work effectively. This requires, however, that the regulators disclose key features and decisions – positive and negative – related to their supervisory actions. In general, regulators could work as communicators, while processing private information for disclosure.

Control is needed to support commitment and market discipline. Due to the asymmetry of information, the potential for control in reducing moral hazard in banking is quite limited. However, management internal control and owners control mechanisms such as audit committees and non-executive directors are needed to oversee management. Although debatable, it appears that it may be necessary to separate the supervision from the norm-setting function in order to safeguard the effectiveness of supervision measures for the regulators.

8.7 The role of the banks in the financial system

by Bo Green
Programme Director, Stockholm University

In recent years several international forums have addressed the regulatory and supervisory framework for institutional investors, such as banks and insurance companies. Examples are the Basle Committee (banking), IOSCO (securities), IAIS (insurance) and OECD (Financial Markets Committee and Insurance Committee). An important place has been given to investment regulations and guidelines for internal control and risk management. The regulatory framework should be clearly perceived by the institutional investors, since it is against this background that any financial risk-taking and risk assessment systems must be judged.

In the papers and discussions at the Seminar, participants have pointed out that at present the supervisory authorities cannot encourage institutions under their supervision to take financial risks; they can only provide the legal framework for such risk-taking.

There is no doubt that the aim of supervision must be to encourage a sound and efficient financial system. An important task of supervision is of course to make management in banks fully aware of the risks they undertake. In my view the role of the supervisory authorities should also include the task of ensuring that the financial system as a whole functions well. This may mean, for example, that in the legislation process the supervisory authority has to develop rules for the financial system, which not only minimise risks for banks but also stimulate the banks to *take risks*.

One of the main tasks of banks should be to manage risks. They should be able to *pool their risks* by specialists in risk management techniques, including efficient loan portfolio management.

One goal of education and training is to provide the individual bank officer with the ability to make a comprehensive assessment of the business potential of an enterprise. This necessitates good analytical skills in the search for relevant information.

At the Seminar I observed that the role of the banks in the financial system must be clarified before new guidelines are created for the supervision of banks in Europe. In order to ascertain how risk management is organised in banks, it must first be decided which risks banks are to assume in order to play the role defined by the needs of an efficient trade and industry complex.

The role of banks and other institutional investors as providers of 'capital' is of importance to society, particularly in periods of economic development. There are, however, tendencies operating in the opposite direction, as the institutions, not least the lenders or policyholders, can during certain periods show a distinct aversion to taking risks.

Thus it is essential for society must define the role of the banks in the financial system in the light of a 'normal' situation rather than a crisis situation (such as the experience of Sweden during 1990-1994). There is no doubt that many policymakers in Sweden overreacted to the exigency of protecting banks when they claimed in the debate after the bank crisis, that banks do not need to provide risk capital, only capital for business. At the same time, bank managers in their desire to avoid credit losses, similarly overreacted when they declared that *banks shall not take any risks* and would exercise greater financial stability when granting loans to small and newly started companies.

As a bankruptcy investigator for the government in 1985 I stressed the need for more *knowledge* in personal judgement and risk assessment in risk management in the banks. By this I meant that the banks in Sweden did not have enough experience for the "imminent" deregulation of the financial market.

Bank managers in Sweden were aware of the need for this sort of knowledge within their credit organisations. A comment, typical of those in key positions in banks, which was quoted in the magazine, *Dagens Industry*, prior to the deregulation of the credit market 1985 was: "We shall become much, much, much better at assessing the business potential of the individual business". This goal was not achieved during the late 1980s.

In my view it is not sufficient to rely upon self-regulation, i.e. that the banks themselves adjust to the demands necessary to establish a well-functioning business world. The policymakers must define the framework (laws, rules and norms) for the system in which banks and others compete.

As indicated in my paper 'Reflections on how the bankruptcy system as a whole functions' (Chapter 6), politicians in Sweden have not understood that the goal of promoting small businesses by providing sufficient amounts of risk capital is not compatible with the current insolvency rules. These rules stipulate that business owners can take loans themselves, using their businesses as security by means of a wage guarantee fund, which in turn raises the value of the security and, thus, decreases the need for business owners to supply capital. This is an example of how society fails to comprehend just how important it is to define the role that banks are to occupy in the financial system.

At the starting point for the 'Risk Research Project', which I managed during 1990-1994, it was assumed that the crisis in the Swedish bank system was to a considerable extent the result of insufficient knowledge of risk management and risk assessment. At six regional risk seminars organised during the spring of 1991, I argued that if deregulation had been combined with strict rules for credit granting, this would have created the opportunities for bank senior executives to assess the need for improved competence as early as the mid 1980s.

Several of the bank officers who participated in these risk seminars agreed that loan granting always involves some risk-taking, and that good assessment can in different ways limit losses on loans to small and newly started enterprises. The bank officers also agreed on the need for more knowledge of risks, as well as for insight regarding to the characteristics of entrepreneurs. One bank manager emphasised the importance of having sufficient knowledge about the behaviour of managers in small enterprises in crisis situations. This would allow the loan officer to learn more about the risk attitude of entrepreneurs, and the capacity of owners of small companies to manage a reorganisation.

In the Risk Research Project the bank officers all agreed that a close relationship with the client during the entire loan assessment process was important and that risk competence is essential in loan assessment. One bank manager pointed out the importance of being able to charge different rates in a manner that reflects risk-taking. Others recognised that banks need to acquire both knowledge and competence in order to fulfil the continuing role of banks in the financial system.

One problem is that there is little opposition to the idea that banks should avoid risks and that they should only lend risk-free business capital. This was apparent in the hesitation that the politicians responsible showed in passing a new reorganisation law in Sweden 1995. This law requires banks to obtain more knowledge of the conditions that apply to trade and industry.

One of the reasons why I emphasise that society must define the role of banks in the financial system is that Sweden has a relatively small financial market. This has meant that branch banking has been composed of a few very influential members. The risk has always been that behaviour is similar (if not identical) in this tiny banking circle, and reinforced by a lack of competition. Banks have not felt pressured to develop competencies because legislation has been favourable both in terms of their situation in Sweden and internationally. This continuing situation and the fact that research on risks has been limited is one of the main causes of the Swedish banking crisis.

During the last few years there has been a growing interest by chief bank officers in using loan portfolio techniques and actively managing risk in their respective portfolios. In my view it would be interesting and relevant to discuss both a sound framework for risk taking and initiatives from governments and legislators to pool risk when organising the raising of risk capital for various groups of companies.

In Björn Palmgren's paper 'Risk limitations for financial institutions and the need for venture capital in new and innovative enterprises' he reflects on the need for a widened perspective for the role of financial institutions in economic development. There is a definite need for co-ordination of the different government agencies in determining roles for the various parties involved in the financial system. There is also a need for comprehensive discussions between interested parties and researchers about the roles for different participants in the complex business world. Such a dialogue could be a fruitful base for actors in the financial sector with different perspectives and horizons. The dialogue could also be of great value for politicians and legislators in their work on promoting adequate supervision and control of the financial system both nationally and across Europe. The European Commission should aim to reach an understanding about changes in the different systems related to business conditions.

There is also a need for an open discussion about how to obtain a fair balance of interests in complex financial systems. The practitioners and the researchers who participate in the dialogue should do their utmost to forget the present roles, rules, laws and norms (e.g. The Supervisory Authority does not exist. Forget the classical bank loans. We do not have models for pooling risks etc.). They should use *lateral thinking* when viewing the 'problem' (De Bono, 1990). Neither practitioners nor the researchers should be selected as experts, as this dialogue will involve a steep learning curve for all participants.

References

Ackerlof, G. (1970). "The Market for Lemons: Quantitative Uncertainty and the Market Mechanism". *Quarterly Journal of Economics*, Volume 84:488-500.

AECM, (1994). *Comparative Analyses of Mutual Guarantee Societies*. Hamburg.

Aernoudt, R. (1997). "European Union Policy and Loan Guarantee Schemes". A paper presented at *the second International Stockholm Seminar on Risk behaviour and Risk management*, June 1997.

Aghion, P., Hart, O. and Moore, J. (1992). "The Economics of Bankruptcy Reform". *The Journal of Law. Economics & Organization,* 8:323-546.

Alderson, M. and Betker, B. (1995). *Liquidation vs. Continuation: Did Reorganized Firms Do the Right Thing?* Unpublished Working Paper, Ohio State University.

Altman, E.I. (1989). "Measuring Corporate Bond Mortality and Performance". *Journal of Finance*. 64:909-922.

Altman, E.I. (1968). "Financial ratios, discriminant analysis, and the predicting of corporate bankruptcy". *Journal of Finance*, 23(4):589-609.

Altman, E.I.(1993). *Corporate Financial Distress and Bankruptcy*. New York, John Wiley.

Anderson, J.R. (1983). *The Architecture of Cognitio*. Harvard University Press, Cambridge, Mass.

Anderson, J.R. (1995). *Cognitive Psychology and it Implications.* 4th Edition, W. H. Freeman and Company, New York.

Anderson, J.R., Farrel, R. and Sauers, R. (1984). "Learning to program in LISP". *Cognitive Science*, 8: 87-129.

Ang, J., Chua, J. and McConnell, J. (1982). "The Administrative Costs of Corporate Bankruptcy: A Note". *The Journal of Finance.* 37:219-226.

Argenti, J. (1986). "Spot danger sings before it's too late". *Accountancy.* 101-102.

Argote, L. (1982). "Input Uncertainty and Organizational Coordination in Hospital Emergency Units". *Administrative Science Quarterly*. 27:420-434.

Armstrong, J.S. (1985). *Long-Range Forecasting: From Crystal Ball to Computer.* 2nd Ed. John Wiley & Sons, Inc., New York.

Arnold, J., Robertson, I.T. and Cooper, C.L. (1992). *Work Psychology – Understanding Human Behaviour in the Workplace.* London: Pitman Publishing.

Arrow, K. (1963). "Uncertainty and the Welfare Economics of Medical Care". *American Economic Review.* 941-969.

Arrow, K. (1965). "Insurance, Risk and Resource Allocation". reproduced in *Foundations of Insurance Economics*. 220-229.

Artis, M.J. and Zhang, G. (1996). *Business Cycles, Exchange Rate Regimes and the ERM: is there a European Business Cycle?* EUI Working Paper RSC 96/55, Robert Schuman Centre. European University Institute.

Aston Business School (1991). *Constraints on the Growth of Small Firms*. Department of Trade and Industry, UK

Aynsley, M. (1995). "Minimising the Risk in Derivatives". *Decisions*, National Australia Bank, 7(2, June):14-16.

Baen, J.S. (1996). "Synchronicity and Indexing Theory of International Real Estate Cycles". *The Real Estate Finance Journal*, Spring:69-73.

Baird, D. (1993). "Revisiting Auctions in Chapter 11". *Journal of Law and Economics*. 633-669.

Baird, D.G. (1986). "The Uneasy Case for Corporate Reorganizations". *The Journal of Legal Studies*. 15:127-147.

Baldwin, J. and Picot, G. (1995). "Employment Generation by Small Producers in the Canadian Manufacturing Sector". *Small Business Economics*. 7:317-331.

Ball, M. (1994). "The 1980's property boom". *Environment and Planning A*. 26:671-695.

Bandura, A. (1982). "Self-efficacy mechanism in human agency". *American Psychologist.* 37: 122-147.

Barber, B. (1983). *The Logic and Limits of Trust,* Rutgers University Press, New Brunswick.

Barras, R. (1983). "A simple theoretical model of the office-development cycle". *Environment and Planning A.* 15:1381-1394.
Bass, Bernard, M. (1990). *Bass & Stogdill's Handbook of Leadership* (3rd Ed). New York: The Free Press.
Baum, A. and Schofield, A. (1991). *Property as a Global Asset.* Working Papers in European Property. University of Reading.
Baumard (1992). "Shifting Intelligence Needs". In: Sigurdson, J. & Tågerud, Y., (eds.) *The Intelligent Corporation.* London: Taylor Graham Publishing.
Beaver, W. H. (1968). "Alternative financial ratios as predictors of failure". *The Accounting Review*, 71:111.
Berger, A.N. and Udell, G.F. (1992). "Some Evidence on the Empirical Significance of Credit Rationing". *Journal of Political Economy*, 100(5, October):1046-1077.
Berliner, B. (1982). *Limits of Insurability.* Prentice-Hall. Inc, Englewood Cliffs, NJ.
Betker, B. (1997). "The administrative costs of debt restructurings: Some recent evidence". *Financial Management* 26 (winter):56-68.
Bhandari, J.S. and Weiss, L. A. (1993). "The untenable case for chapter 11: a review of the evidence". *American Bankruptcy Law Journal.* 67:131.
Binks, M. and Ennew, C.T. (1997). "The Relationship Between UK Banks and their Small Business Customers". In Cressy and Olofsson (eds), 1997.
Birch, D. (1979). *The Job Generation Process.* Final Report to Economic Development Administration. Cambridge, MA: MIT Program on Neighborhood and Regional Change.
BIS (Annual Report 1996/97). *Financial fragility in Asia.* Basle: Bank for International Settlements.
Blixt, L. (1997). *Tillväxtföretag i Sverige.* Working Paper, Stockholm: NUTEK.
Bolger, F. and Wright, G. (1992). "Reliability and Validity in Expert Judgment". In G. Wright & F. Bolger (Eds), *Expertise and Decision Support.* Plenum Press, New York.
Borch, K. (1960). "The Utility Concept applied to the Theory of Insurance". *Austin Bulletin.* 245-255.
Bradley, M. and Rosenzweig, M. (1992). "The untenable case for Chapter 11". *Yale Law Journal.* 101:1043-1095.
Brealey, R.A. and Myers, S.C. (1991). *Principles of Corporate Finance.* Fourth Edition, McGraw-Hill, Inc.
Brehmer, B. (1980). "In one word: Not from experience". *Acta Psychologica.* 45:223-241.
Brehmer, B. (1981). "Models of diagnostic judgments". In J. Rasmussen, & W. B. Rouse (Eds.), *Human detection and diagnosis of system failur.* 231-241. New York: Plenum Press.
Britton, W., Connellan, O.P. and Crofts M.K. (1991). *The Cost Approach to Valuation.* Research Report for the Royal Institute of Chartered Surveyors. The School Of Surveying at Kingston Polytechnic. Kingston upon Thames.
Brockhaus, Sr., R.H. (1980). "Risk Taking Propensity of Entrepreneurs". *Academy of Management Journal*, 23(3):509-520.
Bromwich, M. and Bhimani, A. (1989). *Management Accounting: Evolution Not revolution.* Research Studies, Chartered Institute of Management Accountants, London.
Brown, G, (1992). "Valuation accuracy: developing the economic issues". *Journal of Property Research.* 9:199-207.
Brown, G, Matysiak, G.A. and Sheperd, M (1997). "Valuation Uncertainty and the Mallinson Report". Paper presented at *the Pacific-Rim Real Estate Society, Annual Conference*, January 1997.
Brunsson, N. (1976). *Propensity to change.* Gothenburg, Sweden: BAS.
Brunsson, N. (1985). *The Irrational Organization: Irrationality as a Basis for Organizational Action' and Change.* Chichester: Wiley.
Buchanan, D.A. and Huczynski, A.A. (1985). *Organizational Behaviour. An Introductory Text.* Hemel Hempstead: Prentice Hall.
Burt, C.D.B.and Kemp, S. (1993). "Construction of activity duration and time management potential". *Applied Cognitive Psychology.* 8:155-168

Campbell, C.A. (1992). "A Decision Theory Model for Entrepreneurial Acts". *Entrepreneurship Theory and Practice*, Fall:21-27

Campbell, D.J. (1988). "Task Complexity: A Review and Analysis". *Academy of Management Review*, 13(1):40-52.

Campbell, S.S. (1990). "Circadian rythm and human temporal experience". In Block, R. A. (Ed.) *Cognitive models of psychological time*. 101-118. Lawrence Earlbum Associates

Carter, RL (1986). *Public Policy and Insurability*. The Geneva Papers on Risk and Insurance 145

Chaiken, S., Wood, W. and Eagly, A.H. (1996). "Principles of persuasion". In E.T. Higgins & A.W. Kruglanski (Eds.), *Social psychology: Handbook of basic principles*,. 702-742. New York: Guildford Press.

Chant, E.M. and Walker, D.A. (1988). "Small Business Demand for Trade Credit". *Applied Economics*. 20:861-876.

Chase, R.B. and Tansik, D.A. (1983). "The Customer Contact Model Organizational Design". *Management Science*, 29(9)1037-1050.

Chase, R.B. (1978). "Where Does the Customer Fit in the Service Operation?" *Harvard Business Review*, 56(6):137-142.

Chase, R.B. (1981). "The Customer Contact Approach to Services: Theoretical Bases and Practical Extensions". *Operations Research*, 29(4):698-706.

Chase, W.G. and Simon, H. A. (1973). "The mind's eye in chess". In: Chase, W. G. (Ed.). *Visual information processing*. Academic Press, New York.

Chemmanur, T. and Fulghieri, P. (1994). Reputation, Renegotiation and the Choice Between Banks. *The Review of Financial Studies*. 17(3):475-500.

Chi, M.T.H., Feltovich, P.J. and Glaser, R. (1981). Categorization and representation of physics problems by experts and novices. *Cognitive Science*. 5:121-152.

Cialdini, R.B. (1993). *Influence, Sience and Practice*. New York: Harper Collins.

Coase, R. (1991). *Företaget, marknaden och lagarna*. Ratio, Timbro AB

Cooper, A., Woo, C.Y. and Dunkelberg, W.C. (1988). Entrepreneurs Perceived Chances of Success. *Journal of Business Venturing*. 3:97-108.

Cooper, R.G. (1994). "Third generation new product processes". *Journal of Product Innovation Management*. 11:3-14.

Cox, T. (1997). *Organizational health & stress*. Manuscript. University of Nottingham, Department of Psychology.

Cressy and Toivanen (1997). *Is there Adverse Selection in the Credit Market?*, Working Paper, Warwick Business School, UK.

Cressy, R.C. (1997). "Finance, in the Fourth Report of the European Observatory for SMEs". *EMI Small business Research and Consulting.*

Cressy, R.C. (1996a). "Are Business Startups Debt-rationed?" *The Economic Journal* 106(438), September: 1253-1270

Cressy, R.C. (1996b). "Small business failure: failure to fund or failure to learn by doing?" In Entrepreneurship, SMEs and the Macro Economy, Acs, Z. and Carlsson, B. (eds), *Cambridge University Press*, April, 1998

Cressy, R.C. (1996d). "Finance, Chapter V" of The European Observatory for SMEs, *Fourth Report to the European Commission* (DGXXIII), EIM, Zoetermeer, Netherlands

Cressy, R.C. and Cowling, M. (1997). "The UK Loan Guarantee Scheme 1987-1995: A First Look". A paper presented *at the 2nd International Stockholm Seminar on Risk behaviour and Risk management*, Stockholm, June.

Cressy, R.C. and Olofsson. C. (1997). "European SME Financing: An Overview". *Small Business Economics* 9(2):87-96, Special Issue on European SME Financing, April 1997

Cressy, R.C. and Cowling, M. (1994). "Credit Rationing of Monetary Illusion? Evidence from Defaults under the Loan Guarantee Scheme", SME Centre Working Paper, Warwick Business School

Crosby, N., Newell, G., Matysiak, G., French, N. and Rodney, B. (1997). "Client perception of property investment valuation reports in the UK". *Journal of Property Research*. 14:27-

Crosby, N., Keough, G. and Rees, G. (1992). "Methodology and Convention in the Standardisation of Retail Rents". *Journal of Property Valuation and Investment.* 10:740-756.

Cummins, JD. "Statistical and Financial Models of Insurance Pricing and the Insurance Firm". *Journal of Risk and Insurance.* 261-301

Daily, C.M. (1994). "Bankruptcy in strategic studies: Past and promise". *Journal of Management.* 20:263-295.

Danish Financial Supervisory Authority (1995). *Report on the Self Assessment System for Banks.*

Danmarks Nationalbank (1994). *Report on the Danish Banking Sector.* Monetary Review November.

Datainspektionen (1994). *Tillämpning av inkassolagen - Allmänna råd.* Stockholm.

D'Aveni, R.A. (1989). "The aftermath of organizational decline: A Longitudinal study of the strategic and managerial characteristics of declining firms". *Academy of Management Journal.* 32:577-605.

Davidsson, P., Lindmark, L. and Olofsson, C. (1993). *Business Dynamics in the Swedish Economy: A Regional Perspective.* report submitted to the EC Commission.

Davidsson, P., Lindmark, L., and Olofsson, C. (1994). *Dynamiken i svenskt näringsliv.* Lund, Sweden: Studentlitteratur.

Davidsson, P., Lindmark, L. and Olofsson, C. (1996). *Näringslivsdynamik under 90-talet.* Stockholm: Nutek.

Davis, S.J., Haltiwanger, J and Schuh, S. (1996). *Job Creation and Destruction,* Boston, MA.: The MIT Press.

Day, D.V., and Lord, R.G. (1988). "Executive leadership and organizational performance: Suggestions for a new theory and methodology". *Journal of Management, 14,* 453-464.

De Bono, E. (1990). *The use of lateral thinking.* England Penquin Books.

De Roover, R. (1954). "New interpretations of the history of banking". *Journal of World History.* 1(4):38-76.

Delis, S. (1997). "Transnational development of SME's and the role of the bank". In *Perspectives,* n° 19.

Delmar, F. (1997a). "Measuring growth: methodological considerations and empirical results". In R. Donckels & A. Miettinen (Eds). *Entrepreneurship and SME Research: On its Way to the Next Millennium.* 199-215. Ashgate Publishing Ltd, Hants, England.

Demirag, I. (1995a). "Short-term performance pressures: is there a consensus view?" *The European Journal of Finance.* 1: 41-56.

Demirag, I. (1995b). "Assessing Short-Term Perceptions of Group Finance Directors of UK Companies". *British Accounting Review,* September. 27:247-281

Demirag, I. (1996). "The Impact of Managers' Short-term Perceptions on Technology Management and R&D in UK Companies". *Technology Analysis & Strategic Management,.* 8(1): 21-32.

Dernroth, J. (1993). *Leverantörers kredithantering – en problemanalys.* Lund: Institutionen för Industriell Organisation, Lunds Tekniska Högskola.

Deutsch, M. (1962). *Cooperation and Trust: Some Theoretical Notes* in Jones, M. R. (ed), Nebraska Symposium on Motivation, University of Nebraska Press, Lincoln.

Dionne, G and Harrington (1992). "An Introduction to Insurance Economics". *Foundations of Insurance Economics: Readings in Economics and Finance.* Kluwer Academic Publishers: Boston/Dordrecht/London.

Dougherty, D. (1992). Interpretive barriers to successful product innovation in large firms. *Organization Science.,* 3:179-202.

Dovan and Livitsky. (1997). *Credit Guarantee Schemes for Small Business Banking.* Bannock and partners, London, February.

Easterbrook, F. (1990). Is corporate bankruptcy efficient?, *Journal of Financial Economics* 27: 411-418.

Economic and Social Committee (1992). *The role of Mutual Guarantee Societies for the financing of SMEs.* Advice of the Committee, CES 492/92, 29 April.

Edwards, W. (1983). "Human Cognitive Capabilities, Representativeness, and Ground Rules for Research". In Humphreys, P., Svenson, O. and Vári, A. (Eds), *Analysing and Aiding Decision Processes*, Akadémiai Kiadó, Budapest.

Edwards, W. (1983). "Human cognitive capacities, representativeness, and ground rules for research". In P. Humphreys, O. Svenson, and A. Vari, (Eds.), *Analyzing and aiding decision processes*. Budapest: Akademiai Kiado.

Egeln, J., Licht, G. and Steil, F. (1997). "Firm Foundations and the Role of Financing Constraints". In Cressy and Olofsson(Eds) (1997)

Einhorn, J. (1974). "Expert judgment: Some necessary conditions and an example". *Journal of Applied Psycholog.*, 59:562-571.

Eisenberg T. and Tagashira, S. (1995). "Should We Abolish Chapter 11: Evidence from Japan". *Journal of Legal Studies*, (1994). 23:111-157.

Eisenberg, T. (1995) . *Creating and Effective Swedish Reconstruction Law*. A report prepared for the Center for Business and Policy Studies, Stockholm, Sweden. 1-79.

Eisenberg, T. and Sundgren, S. (1997). "Is Chapter 11 too favorable to debtors? Evidence from abroad". *Cornell Law Review*. 82:1532-1567.

Eisenberg, T. (1993). "Baseline problems in assessing chapter 11". Univ. Toronto *Law Journal*, 43:633.

Eisenberg, T. (1995). *Konkurs eller Rekonstruktion*, SNS Förlag, Stockholm.

Elliehausen, G.E, Wolken, J.D. (1993). "The Demand for Trade Credit: An Investigation of Motives for Trade credit Use by Small Businesses". *Staff Study 165*, Board of Governors of the Federal Reserve System, Washington.

Emery, G. (1984). "A Pure Financial Explanation for Trade Credit". *Journal of Financial and Quantitative Analysis*. 19:271-285.

Emory, C.W. and Cooper, D.R. (1991). *Business Research Methods*. 4th edition, Homewood, Boston, MA: Irwin.

Englander, T. and Tyszka, T. (1980). Information seeking in open decision situation. *Acta Psychologica*. 56:113-123.

ENSR (1994). *The European Observatory for SMEs, Second Annual Report*, Zoetermeer: EIM Small Business Research and Consultancy/European Network for SME Research.

ENSR, (1996). *4th Report of the European Observatory for SMEs*, presented to DGXXIII

Epstein, S. Pacini, R. Denes-Raj, V. and Heier, H. (1996). "Individual differences in intuitive-experiential and analytical-rational thinking styles". *Journal of Personality and Social Psychology*. 71:390-405

Epstein. S. (1989). "Values from the perspective of Cognitive Experiential Self-Theory". In N. Eisemberg, J. Reykowsky, and Staub, E. (Eds.), *Social and moral values*. Hillsdale, NJ: Earlbaum.

Erera-Weatherley, P. I. (1996). "Coping with stress: Public welfare supervisors doing their best". *Human Relations*. 49:157-170.

Ericsson, K.A., Krampe, R. T., Tesch-Römer, C. (1993). "The Role of Deliberate Practice in the Acquisition of Expert Performance". *Psychological Review*, 100(3):363-406.

Eriksson, K. (1991). *The Heterogeneous Technology of Retail Banking*. Working Paper 91/2, Department of Business Studies, Uppsala University, Uppsala, Sweden.

Eriksson, K. (1994). *The Interrelatedness of Environment Technology and Structure*. (Diss.) Department of Business Studies, Uppsala University, Uppsala, Sweden.

European Commission, (1991). *The role of Mutual Guarantee Schemes for the financing of SME's in the EU*, SEC(91), 1550 Final Report.

European Commission (1996). "Third Multi-annual Program for SME's". *Official Journal* 22/12/1996.

European Commission (1997). "The system of credit guarantee consortia in Emilia Romagna". In *Perspectives*, n°19, March

European Commission (1997). *Round Table of Bankers and SMEs: Final Report*, February 1997.

European Debt Collectors Association (1989). *Debt Collection Manual*.

European Investment Fund (1996). *Rules of Procedure*, Luxembourg.

Evans, D and Jovanovic, B. (1989). " An Estimated Model of Entrepreneurial Choice Under Liquidity Constraints". *Journal of Political Economy 97* (4):808-827.
Faure, M and Gunter Heine, G. (1991). "The Insurance of Fines: the Case of Oil Pollution". *The Geneva Papers on Risk and Insurance.* 39.
Ferris, S. J. (1981). "A Transactions Theory of Trade Credit Use". *The Quarterly Journal Of Economics*. 243-270.
Fiet, J.O. (1995). "Risk Avoidance Strategies in Venture Capital Market". *Journal of Management Studies*, 32(4):551-574.
Fisher, A., Chitose, A., and Gipson, P. S. (1993). "One agency's use of risk assessment and risk communication". *Risk Analysis,* 14:207 - 212.
Fisher, T., Martel, J. (1997). *Should we abolish Chapter 11? Evidence from Canada.* Working paper. University of Montreal.
Fisher, T., Martel, J. (1994). "Financial Reorganization in Canada". *Canadian Business Economics.* 54-66.
Fisher, T., Martel, J. (1995). "The Creditors' Financial Reorganization Decision: New Evidence from Canadian Data". *Journal of Law, Economics, and Organization.* 11:112-126.
Flynn, E. (1989). *Statistical Analysis of Chapter 11.* The Administrative Office of the United States Courts, Bankruptcy Division. 1-42.
Franks, J. and Torous, W. (1994). "A comparison of financial recontracting in distressed exchanges and Chapter 11 reorganizations". *Journal of Financial Economics.* 35:349-370.
Freear, J. and Wetzel, W.E. (1990). Who Bankrolls High-Tech Entrepreneurs? *Journal of Business Venturing*. 5(2):77-89.
Freeman, R.E. (1991). *Business Ethics – The State of the Art*. Oxford: Oxford University Press.
Fuglseth, A. M. (1989). *Decision Support: Method for Diagnosis of Managers' Information and Situation Perceptions.* Unpublished doctoral dissertation (in Norwegian), The Norwegian School of Economics and Business Administration, Bergen.
Gardner, H. (1985). *The mind's new science: The history of the cognitive revolution.* NY: Basic.
Gartner, W.B. (1988). "Who Is an Entrepreneur? Is the Wrong Question". *American Journal of Small Business*. Spring:11-32.
Gelvan, D.J. (1995). *Technological Entrepreneurship and the Utilization of External Resources.* Unpublished dissertation, Department of Economics and Planning, University of Roskilde, Denmark.
Gibbons, R. (1992). *Game Theory for Applied Economists*. Princeton University Press. New Jersey.
Gilad, B. (1994). *Business Blindspots*. Chicago: Probus Publishing.
Gilbert, L.R., Menon, K. and Schwartz, K. B. (1990). "Predicting bankruptcy for firms in financial distress". *Journal of Business, Finance and Accounting.* 1:161-171.
Gill, J. (1986). "Export Credit Insurance – Why Government". *The Geneva Papers on Risk and Insurance.*
Gilson, S. and Vetsuypens. M. (1993). "CEO compensation in financially distressed firms". *Journal of Finance.* 48:425-458.
Gilson, S. (1989). "Management turnover and financial distres"s. *Journal of Financial Economics.* 25:241-262.
Gilson, S. (1997). "Transactions costs and capital structure choice: Evidence from financially distressed firms". *Journal of Finance.* 52:161-196.
Goetzmann, W.N. and Wachter, S.M. (1995). *The Global Real Estate Crash: Evidence from An International Database*. Working Paper No. 48, Yale School of Management, April.
Goldberg, L.R. (1959). The effectiveness of clinicians' judgments: The diagnosis of organic brain damage from the Bender-Gestalt test. *Journal of Consulting Psychology.* 23:25-33.
Golde, R. A. (1969). *Can you be sure of your experts?* NY: Award Books.
Goodfriend, Marvin and King R. (1988). "Financial Deregulation, Monetary Policy, and Central Banking". *Federal Reserve Bank of Richmond Economic Review.* 74:3-22.
Goodhart, C. (1987). "Why Do Banks Need a Central Bank?". *Oxford Economic Papers.* 39:75-89.
Graham, J.D. (1988). *Preventing Automobile Injury*. Dover, Mass: Auburn House.

Grossman, R. (1993). "The Macroeconomic Consequences of Bank Failures under the National Banking System". *Explorations in Economic History*. 30:294-320.
Grönroos, C. (1982). "An Applied Service Marketing Theory". *European Journal of Marketing*. 16(7):30-41.
Gumerlock, R.S. (1996). "Internal Organisation of Risk Control and Management in a Bank with Large International Operations". *Risk Management in Volatile Financial Markets*, edited by Bruni, F., Fair, D.E. and O'Brien, R. for SUERF. Dordrecht: Kluwer Academic Publishers.
Hagstad, C. and Ljunggren, L. (1980). *Likviditetsplanering i medelstora företag* (Thesis in Business Administration). Stockholm: Stockholm University.
Hall, B. (1992). "Investment and Research and Development at the Firm Level: Does the Source of Financing Matter?" *National Bureau of Economic Research* Working Paper #4096, Cambridge, Massachusetts.
Harr, N.E., Starr, J. and Macmillan, I.C. (1988). "Informal Risk Capital Investors: Investment Patterns on the East Coast of the U.S.A". *Journal of Business Venturing*. 3:11-29.
Hart, D. (1991). "Factoring: A Lender's Option". *Journal of Commercial Bank Lending*. 73(12): 36-41.
Hart, O. (1995). "Corporate Governance: Some Theory and Implications". *The Economic Journa.,* 105 (May):678-689.
Hayek, F. A. (1948). *Individualism and Economic Order.* University of Chicago Press, Chicago.
Hedelin, L. and Sjöberg, L. (1995). "Credit Assessors' judgments of loan applicants in regard to new ventures". In B. Green (Ed.), *Risky Business – An anthology of findings and reflections from the Risk Research Project in Sweden*. Risk Research Group Report No 1:67-94. Stockholm: Risk Research Group, University of Stockholm.
Hedman, P. (1991). *Cash-Management*. Stockholm: Almqvist& Wiksell.
Heidbreder, E. (1933). *Seven psychologies*. NY: Appleton-Century Co.
Herring, J. (1996). "Creating the Intelligent System that Produces Analytical Intelligence". In Gilad B. & Herring, J. (eds.) *The Art and Science of Business Intelligence Analysis*: Part A; Business Intelligence Theory, Principles, Practices, and Uses. London: JAI Press.
Hershey, D.A., Walsh, D.A, Read, S.J. and Chulef A.S. (1990). "The evidence of expertise on financial problem solving: evidence for goal-directed, problem-solving scripts". *Organizational Behavior and Human Decision Processes*. 46:77-101.
Himmelberg, C.P. and Peterson, B.C. (1994). "R&D and internal finance: a panel study of small firms in high-tech industries". *Review of Economics and Statistics*. 38-51.
Hofstede, G. (1991). *Cultures and Organzations: Intercultural Cooperation and its Importance for Survival - Software of the Mind*. London: Harper Collins.
Hoobroeckx, J.W. (1986). "The Boundaries of Credit Insurance: A Comment". *Geneva Papers on Risk and Insurance.*
Hosmer, D. and Stanley, L. (1989). *Applied Logistic Regression*, New York, Wiley.
Hotchkiss, E. (1995). "Post-bankruptcy performance and management turnover". *Journal of Finance* 50, 3-21.
Howcroft, J.B. (1988). *Evolution of Retail Branch Banking in the UK.* LUBC (Loughborough University Banking Centre) Research Paper No 55.
Howcroft, J.B and Beckett, A. (1996). "Branch Networks and the Retailing of High Credence Products". *International Journal of Bank Marketing*. 14(4):3-11.
Hoyt, H. (1933). *One Hundred Years of Land Values in Chicago.* Chicago: University of Chicago Press.
Huber, O. (1997). "Beyond gambles and lotteries: naturalistic risky decisions". In Ranyard, R., Crozier, W.R. and Svenson, O. (eds) *Decision making: Cognitive models and explanations,* London: Routledge.
Huber, O., Wider, R. and Huber, O. (1997). "Active information search and complete information presentation in gambles and naturalistic decision tasks". *Acta Psychologica*. 95:15-29.
Hughes, A. (1997). "Finance For SMEs: A UK Perspective". In Cressy and Olofsson (eds) 1997.

International Monetary Fund. (1995). *International Financial Statistics*. Washington D.C.: International Monetary Fund.
Intrum Justitia (1994a). *Press Releases*. Amsterdam: Intrum Justitia International.
Intrum Justitia (1993). *Inkasso Guide*. Amsterdam: Intrum Justitia International.
Intrum Justitia (1994b). *Annual Report 1994*. Amsterdam: Intrum Justitia International.
Intrum Justitia (1995a). *Semi Annual Report 1995*. Amsterdam: Intrum Justitia International.
Intrum Justitia (1995b). *Internal Documentation*.
Jackson, T. (1986). *The Logic and Limit of Bankruptcy Law*. Harward University Press, Cambridge, Massachusetts, USA.
Janis, I. L., and Mann, L. (1977). *Decision making*. New York: The Free Press.
Janis, I.L. (1968). *Victims of Group Think: A Psychological Study of Foreign Policy Decisions and Fiascos*. Boston, Mass: Houghton Mifflin.
Jenkins, J.M. and Ward, W.C. (1965). "Judgment of contingency between responses and outcomes". *Psychological Monographs*. 79(1):1-17.
Jensen-Conklin, S. (1992). "Do Confirmed Chapter 11 Plans Consummate? The Results of a Study and Analysis of the Law". *Commercial Law Journal*. 97 1992:297-331.
Johnson, E.J. (1988). "Expertise and Decision under Uncertainty: Performance and Process". In: Chi, M. T. H., Glaser, R. and Farr, M. J. (Eds) *The Nature of Expertise*, Lawrence Erlbaum Associates, Publishers, N.J.
Johnson, H.T. and Kaplan, R.S. (1987). "Relevance Lost: The Rise and Fall of Management Accounting". Boston: *Harvard Business School Press*.
Johnson, N. (1996). *Accidents and Disaster*: Ed C Hood and D Jones: London UCL Press:
Johnson, P.E. (1983). "What kind of an expert should a system be?" *The Journal of Medicine and Philosophy*, 8:77-97.
Jungerhem, S. (1992). *Banker i fusion*. Ph.D. Dissertation, Uppsala University.
Kahneman, D. and Tversky, A. (1979). "Prospect theory: An analysis of decision under risk". *Econometric.*, 47:263-291.
Kahneman, D. and Tversky, A. (1984). "Choices, values, and frames". *American Psychologist*. 39:341-350.
Kahneman, D., Tversky, A. (1979). "Prospect Theory: An Analysis of Decision Under Risk. *Econometrica*, 47(2, March):263-291.
Kahneman, D., Slovic, P. and Tversky, A. (Eds.). (1982). *Judgment under uncertainty*. New York: Cambridge University Press.
Kalbfleisch, J.D. and Prentice, R.L. (1980). *The Statistical Analysis of Failure Time Data*. New York, Wiley.
Kaufman, G. (1994). "Bank Contagion: A Review of Theory and Evidence". *Journal of Financial Services Research*. 8:123-150.
Keasey, K. and Watson, R. (1993). "Banks and Small Firms: Is Conflict Inevitable?" *NatWest Bank Quarterly Bulletin*. May: 30-40.
Keasey, K. and Watson, R. (1991). The state of the art of small firm failure prediction: Achievements and prognosis. *International Small Business Journal*. 9:11-29.
Kelly, G.A. (1955). *The Psychology of Personal Constructs*. Vol. I & II, W. W. Norton & Company, Inc. New York.
Kemdal, A.B. and Montgomery, H. (1997). "Perspectives and emotions in personal decision making". In: Ranyard, R., Crozier, W.R. and Svenson, O. (Eds) *Decision making: Cognitive models and explanations,* London: Routledge.
Klein, G.A. et al (1989). "Critical decision method for eliciting knowledge". *IEEE Systems, Man and Cybernetics*. 19:462-472.
Koskelo, P. (1994). Yrityssaneeraus. Helsinki. Lakimiesliiton kustannus.
Kruglanski, A.W. and Webster, D.M. "Motivating closing of the mind: 'Seizing' and 'freezing'". *Psychological Review*. 103:263-283.
Kuhl, J. and Beckman, J. (Eds.), (1985). *Action Control: From cognition to behavior*. New York: Springer.
Kunreuther, H. (1979). "Why aren't they insured?". *The Journal of Insurance*. XL, 5.
Kuznets, S. (1930). *Secular Movements in Production and Prices*. Boston: Houghton Mifflin.

Landström, H. (1990). "Co-operation between venture capital companies and small firms". *Entrepreneurship & Regional Development*. 2:345-362.
Landström, H. (1992). *Informellt riskkapital i Sverige. En beskrivning med avseende på investerarnas karaktäristik, investeringsaktivitet, samarbete med företagen och resultat*. Paper, Ekonomicentrum, Högskolan i Halmstad, Sweden.
Larkin, J. (1981). "Enriching formal knowledge: A model for learning to solve textbook physics problems". *Cognitive skills and their acquisition,* Erlbaum, N.J.
Larsson, R. and Bowen, D.E. (1989). "Organization and Customer: Managing Design and Coordination of Services". *Academy of Management Review*. 14(2):213-233.
Larsson, C-G. (1988). *Cash-Management för företag*. Lund: Studentlitteratur.
Larsson, S. (1972). *Affärsföretagets kreditgivning*. Malmö: S H Larsson Konsult AB.
Larsson, S. (1973). *Kreditgivning, centralisering*. Malmö: S H Larsson Konsult AB.
Le Blanc, G. and Nguyen, N. (1988). "Customers' Perceptions of Service Quality in Financial Institutions". International Journal of Bank Marketing.6(4):7-18.
Lee, Y.W. and Stowe, J.D. (1993). "Product Risk, Asymmetric Information and Trade Credit". *Journal of Finance and Quantitative Analysis*. 28(2):285-300
Les notes bleues de Bercy, (1993). "Sofaris, un levier efficace pour le financement des PME". *Economie et Conjuncture*, October
Lewis, M.K. (ed.) (1995). *Financial Intermediaries*. Cheltenham: Edward Elgar Publishing Ld.
Lewis, M.K. and Morton, P. (1996). "Asset and Liability Management in Retail Banking". In: by Bruni, F., Fair, D.E. and O'Brien, R. (1996) (Eds). *Risk Management in Volatile Financial Markets*. For SUERF. Dordrecht: Kluwer Academic Publishers.
Lewis, M.K. (1990). "Banking as Insurance". In: E.P.M. Gardener (1990) (Ed). *The Future of Financial Systems and Services. Essays in Honour of Jack Revell.* London: Macmillan.
Lewis, M.K. (1994). "Banking on real estate". In: D.E. Fair and R. Raymond. (Edited on behalf of the Société Universitaire Européenne de Recherches Financières). *The Competitiveness of Financial Institutions and Centres in Europé*. Kluwer Academic Press, Dordrecht. 47-71.
Lewis, M.K. (1996). "Banks and the Property Cycle". *Joint International Cambridge-Wharton Conference on Commercial Real Estate Investment,* Queen's College, Cambridge. March: 20-22.
Levitt, T. (1972). "Production Line Approach to Service". *Harvard Business Review*. 50(5):41-52.
Levitt, T. (1976). "The Industrialization of Service". *Harvard Business Review*. 54:63-74.
Li, S. and Adams, A.S. (1995). "Is There Something More Important behind Framing?" *Organizational Behavior and Human Decision Processes*. 62(2, May):216-219.
Llewellyn, D.T. (1994). *The Future of Banking: Is Banking a Declining Industry?* Loughborough University Banking Centre Research Paper Series, No 84.
Lopes, L.L. (1987). "Between Hope and Fear: The Psychology of Risk". *Advances in Experimental Social Psychology*. 20:255-295.
Low, M. and MacMillan, I.C. (1988). "Entrepreneurship: Past Research and Future Challenges". *Journal of Management*. 14:139-161.
Loveman, G. and Sengenberger,W. (1991). "The Re-emergence of Small Scale Production: An International Comparison". *Small Business Economic*. 3:1-37.
Luhmann, N. (1979). *Trust and Power*. John Wiley & Sons, Avon.
MacCimmon, K.R. and Wehnung, D.A. (1986). *Taking Risk: The Management of Uncertainty*. New York: The Free Press.
MacMillan, I.C. , Siegal, R. and Narasimha, P.N.S. (1985). "Criteria Used by Venture Capitalists to Evaluate New Venture Proposals". *Journal of Business Venturing*. 1:119-128.
Maddala, G.S. (1983). *Limited-Dependent and Qualitative Variables in Econometrics*. Cambridge University Press, Cambridge.
Mahon, M.R. (1996). *Justice Report of the Royal Commission to inquire into the crash on Mount Erebus of a DC10 aircraft operated by Air New Zealand Ltd, Wellington*, by Authority P D Hasselburg: Government Printer 1981: London UCL Press.
Maister, D.H. and Lovelock, C.H. (1982). "Managing Facilitator Services". *Sloan Management Review*. 23(2):19-32.

Maksimovic, V. and Phillips, G. (1998). "Asset efficiency and reallocation decisions of bankrupt firms". *Journal of Finance*. October 1998.

Mallinson (1994). *The Mallinson Report: Commercial Property Valuations*. The Royal Institute of Chartered Surveyors. London.

March, J.G. and Simon, H.A. (1958). *Organizations*. John Wiley & Sons, Inc. New York.

March, J.G. and Shapira, Z. (1987). "Managerial Perspectives on Risk and Risk Taking". *Management Science*. 33(11, November):1404-1418.

Martel, J. (1997). *The Information Content of Financial Reorganization Contracts: Theory and Evidence*. Unpublished manuscript, Université de Cergy-Pontoise, Oct. 1997.

Mason, C.M. and Harrison, R.T. (1994). "The Informal Venture capital Market in the UK". In Hughes, A & Storey, D.J. (eds.). *Financing Small Firms*, London: Routledge. 64-111.

Mason, C.M. and Harrison, R.T. (1996). "Informal Venture Capital: a study of the investment process, the post-investment experience and investment performance". *Entrepreneurship & Regional Development*. 8:105-125.

Matysiak G.0 and Wang, P. (1995). "Commercial property market prices and valuations: analysing the correspondence". *Journal of Property Research*. 12:181-202.

Maule, A.J. (1989). "Positive and negative decision frames: A verbal protocol analysis of the Asian disease problem of Tversky and Kahneman". In Montgomery, H., & Svenson, O. (Eds.), (1989). *Process and structure in human decision making*. Chichester: Wiley.

McGough, A.J. and Tsolacos, S. (1997). "The stylised facts of the UK commercial building cycles". *Environment and Planning A*. 29:485-500.

Mead, G. H. (1959). *Mind, self and society*. Chicago: University of Chicago Press.

Mester, L. (1989). "Owners Versus Managers: Who Controls the Bank?" *Business Review*, Federal Reserve Bank of Philadelphia, May-June: 13-22.

Mitroff, I.I. (1988). "Crisis management: Cutting through the confusion". *Sloan Management Review*. Winter: 15-20.

Montgomery, H. (1984). "Towards a perspective theory of decision making and judgment". *Acta Psychologica*. 87:155-178

Montgomery, H. (1989). *From cognition to action. The search for dominance in decision making. Process and Structure in Human Decision Making*. John Wiley & Sons Ltd.

Montgomery, H. (1997). "Surrender at Perevolochna: A case study of perspective taking and action control in decisionm aking under stress". In R. Flin, E. Salas, M. Strub, & L. Martin (Eds.). *Decision making under stress: Emerging themes and applications*. 193-204. Aldershot: Ashgate.

Moore, B. (1993). *Financial Constraints to the Growth and Development of Small Hi-Technology Firms*. Working Paper No. 31, Small Business Research Centre, University of Cambridge, July

Morgan, B. (1994). "How Competitive is Banking?" *Journal of Retail Banking*. XVI(3): 13-18.

Morsman, E.M. (1991). "Commercial Loan Structuring". *Journal of Commercial Bank Lending*, 74(3):24-42.

Mowen, J.C. (1995). *Consumer behavior*. 4th ed. Englewood Cliffs, NJ: Prentice-Hall.

Møller Wedel-Heinen, C. (1994). "The Banks' Financial Statements". *Danmarks Nationalbank Monetary Reveiw*, May

National Economic Research Associates, NERA (1990). *An Evaluation of the Loan Guarantee Scheme*. Research Paper No. 74, Department of Employment.

Neufeld, R. (1988). *Boken om kreditgivning*. Stockholm: MR Consult AB.

Newell, A. (1990). *Unified Theories of Cognition*, Harvard University Press, Cambridge, Mass.

NUTEK (1996). *Småföretagen i Sverige 1996*. B1996:11. Stockholm: NUTEK.

Nytoft Rasmussen, F. and Møller, C. *Management Failure is the Major Cause of Banking Problems*. Danish Bankers Association Finans & Samfund August/September 1995 (available in Danish only).

Oakland, S. and Ostell, A. (1996). "Measuring coping: A review and critique". *Human Relations*. 49:133-155.

OECD (1992). *Risk Management in Financial Services*. Paris: OECD.

Ohlson, J.A. (1980). "Financial ratios and the probabilistic prediction of bankruptcy". *Journal of Accounting Research*. 18(1):109-131.
Perrein, J., Filiatrault, P. and Ricard, L. (1992). "Relationship Marketing and Commercial Banking". *International Journal of Bank Marketing*. 10:25-29.
Perrow, C. (1986). *Complex Organisations - A Critical Essay*. New York: Randon House.
Peterson, M.A. and Raghuram G.R. (1994). "The benefits of lending relationships: Evidence from small business data". *Journal of Finance* XLIX (1). March: 3-37.
Pettersohn, E. (1976). *Kreditgivning mellan företag*. Intrum Justitia. 1994. Stockholm: Stockholm School of Economics (EFI).
Phelps, R.H. and Shanteau, J. (1978). "Livestock judges: How much information can an expert use?". *Organizational Behavior and Human Performanc.*, 21:209-219.
Phillips, B.D. and Kirchoff, B. A. (1989). "Formation, Growth and survival; small firm dynamics in the U.S. economy". *Small Business Economics*. 1:65-74.
Picot, G. and Dupuy, R. (1998). "Job creation by company size class: The magnitude, concentration and persistence of job gains and losses in Canada". *Small Business Economics*, 10: 117-139.
Pinches G.E., Aubank, A.A., Mingo, K.A. and Caruthers, J.K. (1975). "The hierarchical classification of financial ratios". *Journal of Business,* October: 295-310.
Porter, M.E. (1980). *Competitive Strategy*. New York: The Free Press.
Pratten, C. (1993). "The Accuracy of Property Valuations". *Cambridge Discussion Papers in Accounting and Finance*. AF.7. University of Cambridge.
Pulvino, T.C. (1998). "Do asset fire sales exist? An empirical investigation of commercial aircraft transactons". *Journal of Finance*, 53:939-978.
Quinn, J.B. (1992). *Intelligent Enterprise: A Knowledge and Service Based Paradigm for Industry.* New York: MacMilllan.
Raaheim, K. (1961). "Problem Solving: A New Approach". *Acta Universitatis Bergensis – Series Humaniorum Litterarum,* Norwegian Universities Press, Bergen/Oslo.
Ranyard, R. and Craig, G. (1995). "Evaluating and budgeting with instalment credit: an interview study". *Journal of Economic Psychology.* 16:449-467.
Rasmussen, J. (1995). "Deciding and doing: Decision making in natural contexts". In G. A. Klein, J. Orasanu, R. Calderwood, & C. E. Zsambok (Eds.), *Decision making in action: Models and methods.*158-171. New Jersey: Ablex.
Ravid, A., and Sundgren, S. (1997). *The comparative efficiency of small firm bankruptcies – a study of the S and Finnish bankruptcy codes*. Working paper, Swedish School of Economics and Business Administration, Wasa, Finland.
Report of the Second Round Table of Bankers and SMEs (1997), The European Commission.
Richardson, J. (ed.) (1993). *Debt Recovery in Europe*. London: KPMG Peat Marwick.
Richtor, V. (1995). "Organisational Changes for Relationship Banks". *The Treasurer*, March, 29-31.
Riding, A.L. and Summers, B. (1995). *Networks that Learn and Credit Evaluation*. Unpublished Research Paper, Credit Management Research Group, Management Center, University of Bradford.
Riquelme, H. and Richards, T. (1992). "Hybrid Conjoint Analysis: An Estimation Probe in New Venture Decisions". *Journal of Business Venturing*. 7:505-518.
Rokeach, M. (1960). *The open and closed mind.* New York: Basic Books.
Rose-Ackerman, S. (1991). "Risk taking and ruin: Bankruptcy and investment choice". *Journal of Legal Studies*. 10:277-310.
Roth, E.M. and Woods, D.D. (1989). "Cognitive task analysis: an approach to knowledge acquisition for intelligent system design". In G. Guida and C. Tasso (eds) *Topics in expert system design.* New York: North-Holland.
Rothschild, M. and Stiglitz, J.E. (1976). "Equilibrium in Competitive Insurance Markets: An Essay on the Economics of Imperfect Information". *Quarterly Journal of Economics.* 629-650.
Rotter, J.B. (1966). "Generalized expectancies for internal vs. external control of reinforcement". *Psychology Monograph.* 609.

Rubenstein, A.H. (1989). *Managing technology in a decentralized firm.* NY: Wiley Interscience.
Russo, J.E., Johnson, E.J. and Stephens, D.L. (1989). "The validity of verbal protocols". *Memory and Cognition.* 17:759-769.
Sandford Jr., Charles S. (1994). "Financial Markets in 2020". *Federal Reserve Bank of Kansas City Economic Review,* 79(1), First Quarter:19-28. Reprinted in the *The Globalization of Financial Services*, The Globalization of the World Economy No. 10, ed. By M.K. Lewis, Cheltenham: Edward Elgar, 1998.
Sapienza, H., Amason, A. and Manigart, S. (1994). "The Level and Nature of Venture Capital Involvement". *Managerial Finance.* 20(1):3-17.
Sasser, W.E., Olsen, R.P. and Wyckoff, D.D. (1978). *Management of Service Operations: Text, Cases, and Readings.* Allyn & Bacon, Boston.
Schank, R.C. (1990). *Tell me a story: A new look at real and artificial memory.* NY: Charles Scribner's Sons.
Schemenner, R.W. (1986). "How Can Service Businesses Survive and Prosper?". *Sloan Management Review.* 3:21-32.
Schinasi, G.J. and Hargraves, M. (1993). "'Boom and Bust' in asset markets in the 1980s: causes and consequences". *Staff Studies for the World Economic Outlook,* Washington: International Monetary Fund.
Schleifer, A. and Vishny, R. (1992). "Liquidation Values and Debt Capacity: A Market Equilibrium Approach". *The Journal of Finance*, 67:1343-1366.
Schneider, B. (1980). "The Service Organization: Climate is Crucial". *Organizational Dynamics.* 9(2):52-65.
Schneider, W. and Shiffrin, R.M. (1977). "Controlled and Automatic Human Information Processing: I. Detection, Search, and Attention". *Psychological Review,* January. 84(1):1-66.
Schoenmaker, D. (1996). *Contagion Risk in Banking.* London School of economic, Financial Markets Group Discussion Paper, No 239.
Schroder, H.M., Driver, M.J. and Streufert, S. (1967). *Human Information Processing.* Holt, Rinehart and Winston, Inc., New York.
Schwartz, R.A (1974). "An Economic Model of Trade Credit". *Journal of Financial and Quantitative Analysis.* 9:643-657.
Schwartz, R.A; Whitcomb, D.K (1978). "Implicit Transfers in the Extension of Trade Credit". In *Redistribution Through The Financial System: The Grants Economics of Money and Credit*, Boulding, K E Wilson; T F (eds), Praeger Special Studies, New York, 191-208.
Sexton, D.L. and Bowman, N. (1985). "The entrepreneur: A capable executive and more". *Journal of Business Venturing.* 1:129-140.
Shanteau, J. (1992), "The Psychology of Experts – An Alternative View". In: Wright, G. and Bolger, F. (Eds) *Expertise and Decision Support,* Plenum Press, New York.
Shanteau, J. (1992). "Competence in experts: The role of task characteristics". *Organizational Behavior and Human Decision Processes.* 53:252-266.
Shanteau, J. (1992). "The psychology of experts: An alternative view". In: G. Wright & F. Bolger (Eds.), *Expertise and decision support.* NY: Plenum Press.
Shanteau, J. (1998). "Decision making by experts: The GNAHM effect". In: J. Shanteau, B. Melers, & D. Schum (Eds.), *Decision science and technology: Reflections on the contributions of Ward Edwards,* Norwell, MA: Kluwer Academic Publishers.
Shanteau, J., et al. (1991). "Teaching decision making skills to nurses". In: J. Baron & R. Brown (Eds.). *Teaching decision-making skills to adolescents.* Hillsdale, NJ: Erlbaum.
Shumway, T. (1996). *Forecasting bankruptcy more efficiently: A simple hazard model* (unpublished paper).
Silverman, D. (1993). *Interpreting Qualitative Data: Methods for analyzing Talk, Text and Interaction*, London: Sage.
Simon, H.A. (1977). *The New Science of Management Decision..* Prentice-Hall, Inc., Englewood Cliffs, N.J.
Simon, H.A. (1987). *Rationality in psychology and economics.* In R. M. Hogarth & R. W. Reder (Eds.), Rational choice. Chicago: University of Chicago Press.

SIND (Statens Industriverk). (1985:7). *Konkursutredningen*. Stockholm: Liber Allmänna Förlaget.
Singley, M. and Anderson, J.R. (1989). *The Transfer of Cognitive Skill*. Harvard Univ. Press, Cambridge, Mass.
Sitkin, S.B. and Pablo, L.A. (1992). "Reconceptualizing the Determinants of Risk Behavior". *Academy of Management Review*. 17(1):9-38.
Slovic, P. (1984). *Facts vs. Fears: Understanding perceived risks*. Washington, DC: Federation of Behavioral, Psychological and Cognitive Sciences.
Smith, J.K. (1987). "Trade Credit and Informational Asymmetry". *The Journal of Finance*. 62(4):863-872
Solomon, R.C. (1993). *Ethics and Excellence – Cooperation and Integrity in Business*. Oxford: Oxford University Press.
Stabell, C.B. (1978). "Integrative Complexity of Information Environment Perception and Information Use". *Organizational Behavior and Human Performance*. 22:116-142.
Statistics Sweden, (SCB) (1995). *Nyföretagandet i Sverige 1993 och 1994*. Statistiska Meddelanden F 15 SM 9501. Örebro: SCB, Publishing Service.
Statistics Sweden, (SCB) (1997). *Nyföretagandet i Sverige 1995 och 1996*. Statistiska Meddelanden F 15 SM 9701. Örebro: SCB, Publishing Service.
Stewart, T.R., Roebber, P.J., and Bosart, L.F. (1997). "The importance of the task in analyzing expert judgment". *Organizational Behavior and Human Decision Processes, 69*, 205-219.
Storey, C. (1996). *The Ten Percenters - Fast Growing SMEs in Great Britain*. London: Deloitte & Touch.
Storey, D.J. (1994). *Understanding the Small Business Sector*. London: Routledge.
Storey, D.J. (1994). *Understanding the Small Business Sector*. London: Routledge.
Storey, D.J. (1995). Symposium on Harrison's, Lean and mean: a job generation perspective. *Small Business Economics*. 7(5): 5-8.
Storey, D.J. and Johnson, S. (1987). *Small and Medium Sized Enterprises and Employment Creation in the EEC Countries*: Summary Report (Study No. 85/407): EC Commission, Programme of Research and Actions on the Development of the Labour Market.
Strömberg, P. and Thorburn, K. (1996). *An empirical investigation of Swedish corporations in liquidation bankruptcy* (unpublished paper).
Strömberg, P. (1997). *Conflicts of Interest and Market Illiquidity in Bankruptcy Auctions: Theory and Tests*. Unpublished Manuscript. Carneige Mellon University.
Summers, B. (1997). "Demand for Credit and Influences on Payment Behaviour". University of Bradford.
Summers, B. (1996). *The Trade Credit Game*. Unpublished manuscript, Credit Management Research Group, University of Bradford.
Sundgren, S. (1998). "Does a reorganization law improve the efficiency of the insolvency law? the Finnish Experience". *European Journal of Law and Economics*. 6.
Sundgren, S. (1995). *Bankruptcy Costs and the Bankruptcy Code - A Case Study of the Finnish Code*. Ph.D-thesis, Swedish School of Economics and Business Administration, Helsinki, Finland.
Swan, J.E. and Combs, L.J. (1976). "Product Performance and Consumer Satisfaction: A New Concept". *Journal of Marketing*. 40(April):25-33.
Sweica, R. (1989). "Stay Alert: How to Detect Warning Signals of Account Failure". *Business Credit*. 2.
Svensson, K. (1997). "Payment Behaviour, Trade Credit in Europe today". A paper presented at *the 2nd International Stockholm Seminar on Risk behaviour and Risk management*, June 1997.
Svensson, K. and Ulvenblad, P-O. (1994). *Bankmäns hantering av krediter till små företag – en studie ur ett informationshanteringsperspektiv*. Licentiate thesis, Lund University.
Svensson, K. and Ulvenblad, P-O. (1995). *Management of Bank Loans to Small Firms in a Market with Asymmetric Information*. SIRE Working Paper 1995:2.
Taylor. S.E., and Gollwitzer, P.M. (1995). "Effects of mindsets on positive illusions". *Journal of Personality and Social Psychology*. 69:213-226.

The Danish Ministry for Economic Affairs (1995). *Rescue Operations for Banks Since 1983.* Copenhagen. (available in Danish only).

The Danish Ministry of Economic Affairs (1994). *The Danish Banking Sector.* Copenhagen. (available in Danish only).

Thompson, J. (1967). *Organizations in Action.* New York: McGraw-Hill.

Thorburn, K. (1997). *Cash auction bankruptcy: Costs, recovery rates and auction premiums.* Working paper, Dartmouth College.

Thorburn, K. (1998). *Managerial compensation and corporate performance following cash auction bankruptcy.* Working paper, Dartmouth College.

Titchener, E.B (1916). *A beginner's psychology.* New York: Macmillan.

Tubia, E. (1996). *Supporting SME's with credit guarantee schemes in central and eastern Europé.* Seminar on SME financing, Budapest, October.

Tversky, A. and Kahneman, D. (1974). "Judgment under Uncertainty: Heuristics and Biases". *Science,* 185, 1124-1131.

Tversky, A. and Kahneman, K. (1981). "The framing of Decisions and the Psychology of Choice". *Science,* 211, 30, January, 453-458.

Tversky, A. and Kahneman, D. (1986). "Rational Choice and the Framing of Decisions". *The Journal of Business.* 59(2):251-278.

Twining, D. (1996). "Lessons of the recession for financiers". *Joint International Cambridge-Wharton Conference on Commercial Real Estate Investment,* Queen's College, Cambridge, March: 20-22.

Tyebjee, T.T. and Bruno, A.V. (1984). "A Model of Venture Capitalist Investment Activity". *Management Science.* 30(9):1051-1066.

Tyszka, T. (1986). "Information and evaluation processes in decision making: the role of familiarity". In B. Brehmer, H. Jungerman, P. Lourons and G. Sevon (Eds). *New Directions in Research on Decision Making,* Amsterdam, North-Holland.

VanLehn, K. (1996). "Cognitive Skill Acquisition". *Annual Review of Psychology.* 47:513-539.

Vlek, C.A.J. (1995). "Understanding, accepting and controlling risks: A multistage framework for risk communication". *European Review of Applied Psycholog.* 45:49-54.

von Schéele, F. (1996). *Just-in-case, New business logic for service companies.* Stockholm Liber Hermods.

Warner, J. (1977). "Bankruptcy Costs: Some Evidence". *The Journal of Financ.* 32:337-347.

Weick, K. E. (1995). *Sensemaking in Organizations.* Sage Publ., Thousand Oakes.

Weir, D.T.H. (1996). *Why does the Pilot sit at the Front?* Disaster Prevention and Management: MCB Publications, Bradford.

Weiss, L. (1990). "Bankruptcy resolution: direct costs and violation of priority of claims". *Journal of Financial Economics.* 27:285-314.

Weiss, L.A. and Wruck, K.H. (1998). "Information problems, conflicts of interest and asset stripping: chapter 11's failure in the case of Eastern Airlines". *Journal of Financial Economics,* 48:55-97.

White, H. (1980). "A Heteroskedasticity-consistent Covariance Matrix Estimator and a Direct Test for Heteroskedasticity". *Econometrica.* 48:817-838.

White, L. (1984). *Free Banking in Britain: Theory, Experience and Debat.* 1800-1845. Cambridge University Press, Cambridge.

White, M. (1984). "Bankruptcy liquidation and reorganization". In: Dennis Logue, (Ed.) *Handbook of Modern Finance.* Warren, Gorham & Lamont.

Wilensky, H. (1964). *Organizational Intelligence; Knowledge and Policy in Government and Industry.* New York: Basic Books.

Wilson, N. (1997). *Short term Finance and the Demand for Trade Credit: An Empirical Study of Small Businesses.*

Wilson, N. Singleton, C. and Summers, B. (1997). "Short Term Finance and the Demand for Trade Credit: An Empirical Study of Small Businesses". A paper presented at *the 2nd International Stockholm Seminar on Risk Behaviour and Risk Management*, Stockholm, June 1997.

Wilson, N., Watson, K., Singleton, C. and Summers, B. (1996). *Credit Management, Late Payment and the SME Business Environment.* Credit Management Research Group, University of Bradford Management Centre.

Wilson, N., Watson, K. and Summers, B. (1995). *Trading Relationships, Credit Management and Corporate Performance: A Survey.* Credit Management Research Group, University of Bradford Management Centre.

Woo, T. (1997). *Proceedings of the 1997 NSF design and manufacturing grantees conference.* Arlington, VA: National Science Foundation.

Woods, D.D. (1993). "Process-tracing methods for the study of cognition outside the experimental psychology laboratory". In: G. Klein et al (eds). *Decision making in action: models and methods.* Norwood, New Jersey: Ablex.

Yin, R.K. (1994). *Case Study Research: Design and Methods.* Thousand Oaks, CA: Sage.

Zeithaml, V.A., Parasuraman, A. and Berry, L.L. (1985). "Problems and Strategies in Service Marketing". *Journal of Marketing.* 49(2):33-45.

Zmijewski, M.E. (1984). "Methodological issues related to estimated of financial distress prediction models". *Journal of Accounting Research.* 22, suppl:59-82.

Zucker, L.G. (1986). "Production of Trust". *Research in Organizational Behavior.* 8:53-111.

www.ingramcontent.com/pod-product-compliance
Ingram Content Group UK Ltd.
Pitfield, Milton Keynes, MK11 3LW, UK
UKHW020134160926
475607UK00003B/39

* 9 7 8 0 7 9 2 3 5 8 6 8 8 *